Garden Plants for
Mediterranean Climates

Garden Plants for Mediterranean Climates

Graham Payne

The Crowood Press

First published in 2002 by
The Crowood Press Ltd
Ramsbury, Marlborough
Wiltshire SN8 2HR

www.crowood.com

British Library Cataloguing-in-Publication Data
A catalogue record for this book is available from the British Library.

ISBN 1 86126 548 4

Acknowledgements
A very special thanks must go to Dr David Sturge.
Without his practical help in checking the book, his unflagging
encouragement and support, I may never have finished this book.
Also a grateful thanks to all the people who kindly allowed
me to photograph their plants or gardens. Thanks must also
go to Ashley Stephenson, whose enthusiasm and sheer love
of plants fired me into starting this book.

The author can be contacted by email at: g.payne@delcam.com.

Typeset by Textype Typesetters, Cambridge

Printed and bound in Singapore by Craft Print International

Contents

Foreword

Gardeners from other climates who make the move to a Mediterranean one get a surprise, British gardeners especially. Surely mild winters and guaranteed summers are the perfect recipe? The early bulbs like jewels, the mimosa like honey, the rush of iris and cistus, the scents of herb and pine, the blaze of bougainvillea, the silver calm of olive trees, the shade of cypresses . . . late frosts forgotten, tender plants safe, all the treasures you have dreamed of glorying in the energy of the sun. Surely this is horticultural heaven.

It can be. But it can be purgatory too. The ground rules of Mediterranean gardening are so different from the norms of northern Europe that it can be like learning a new language. The job that never ends in a northern garden is weeding. In a Mediterranean one it is watering. The growing season in the north starts slowly and lasts until autumn – often right through autumn. In the south it comes in an express-speed spring, then closes down for summer and reopens in autumn. There are no refreshing rains to make summer growth possible.

Summer is gruelling: a time for long meals and siestas, for splashing water about, for dead-heading flowers, for making plans, and for explaining to visiting friends that the Mediterranean does have winters too.

Until the later years of the twentieth century the gardening cultures of the Mediterranean and northern Europe (and in particular Britain and the Netherlands, the most horticulturally-minded countries) were poles apart. A scattering of celebrated gardens in the Cote d'Azur, the Italian Lakes, in Tuscany and Lazio and on Capri, and two or three in Portugal, were the only evidence of northern horticulture in countries blessed with a Mediterranean climate. They represented the colonization of the poor south by the rich north, and hence had few indigenous imitators.

Then two things happened. Unprecedented numbers of northerners with a taste for garden pleasure set up house in Mediterranean countries, and the new leisured classes of these countries caught the gardening bug.

Italy in particular has always gardened, if at all, on a grand scale. Travellers between Florence and Pisa have seen the miles of nurseries specializing in oversize evergreens: massive magnolias, ancient olives and perfect cypresses and cedars waiting for their permanent garden homes. The peasant, of course, has his vegetables. But the gardener in between had always been poorly served – until now, when suddenly the garden centre is as much a part of an Italian, a Spanish or Provengal suburb as the garage.

Plants have now become much easier to find than information about them. In the countries where domestic gardening has a long history you have only to look around you to see what is easy, less easy and on the limits of the possible. Magazines and even TV programmes offer advice. Not so, or not often, in Mediterranean countries. You may find an elderly inhabitant to pass on the wisdom of the ages, but that wisdom is usually more concerned with nourishment than ornament.

Long trial and a high proportion of error has been the pattern for most new gardeners around the Mediterranean up to now. What has been needed is a dedicated and comprehensive reference book. The best up to now has been *The Sunset Western Garden Book*, published in California for gardeners in the western states. Southern and Central California have a range of climates often described as Mediterranean. But the culture is different, and so are many of the conditions, and the plants.

Now Graham Payne, from his Portuguese garden, has set out the ground rules for Mediterranean gardeners clearly and comprehensively. Here is the vast range of plants to consider growing, what they offer and what they demand. This is an eminently practical book. The Introduction is a succinct and masterly course on the ecology and aesthetics of Mediterranean gardening. The plant list is the stuff of dreams – not to mention decisions.

Hugh Johnson

Introduction

While writing this book I have realized how extremely fortunate we are, living in a Mediterranean climate where we can grow an immensely wide range of plants from cool temperate to tropical regions of the world. A glance through this book looking at their origin reveals that the plants that we grow in the Mediterranean region come from such diverse countries as Mexico, South Africa, Australia and Russia, as well as India, Madagascar and Malaysia. If you are lucky enough to live in a frost-free area with a good water supply, you should be able to grow all of the plants in this book that are suitable for your soil.

Whether you live in a home with a large or a small garden, there is a wide range of attractive and colourful plants to create a beautiful garden with interest throughout the year. Even in a flat or apartment it is still possible to do some gardening. A flat with a small balcony can happily accommodate a few pots or a trough.

Most of the plants described in this book can be obtained from local nurseries or by mail order. With the advent of the Internet many nurseries are now on-line, so it is possible to order plants from the comfort of your home. Do be aware of any plant health restrictions that may apply to your country, for which it is advisable to check with the relevant customs department. There may be a local gardening society that organizes various kinds of meetings and has plant exchanges. These are always a good way to find out about the local gardening scene and the types of plant that will grow. If there is not a local club or society, then why not start one? Once you know a few friends who are interested in gardening, just start to meet on a regular basis, say once a month, ask them to tell their friends, and soon it will grow into a club.

When visiting nurseries allow plenty of time to have a good look around, as there may be some interesting or unusual plants forgotten about in a far corner. I have found that small nurseries that are untidy and often muddy, where you have to clamber through the undergrowth, offer excitement for the adventurous, and the best value. The plants may not be labelled accurately or even at all, but real gems may be found at reasonable cost. By contrast, tidy, well managed nurseries and smart garden centres tend to be more expensive, but with much better information.

Those people who are faced with gardening in a 'foreign country' will want to know what plants will grow in their gardens. For most of us, we start by going around the local nurseries and garden centres to see what is on offer. If these plants are unfamiliar, then we turn to a book to guide us. In this book I have tried to describe the 400 or so plants that are in my garden, plus those that grow in the area, and those that I know will grow in a Mediterranean climate. Fortunately there has been a great increase in the number of plants that are available. Many new plants that are suitable for the area are constantly being added to those already grown in nurseries.

I hope that this book will provide some help to the many people who enjoy growing Mediterranean-type plants in their garden. Whether you live in the Mediterranean region itself, or one of the areas in the world that has a similar climate, you can enjoy these plants.

The Mediterranean Climate

In this book I have listed plants that will grow in a Mediterranean climate – but what is it? For many people their first taste of the climate is when they come here on holiday. Long, warm summers and almost guaranteed sunshine are ideal for lazing about on the beach. The Mediterranean climate is generally recognized as one with about four months of dry, hot sunny weather in summer, and cool wet winters. Temperatures may vary considerably, some areas have hard frosts in winters, while others have barely any frost at all. In some areas summers are unbearably hot and dry, in others mild and foggy.

The regions of the world with a Mediterranean climate are, of course, the area surrounding the Mediterranean Sea: the Cape region of South Africa, California's central and southern coastal region, central Chile, and southern and south-western Australia, and parts of New Zealand. Coastal southern England, Ireland and even western Scotland have a similar climate where they are affected by the warm Gulf Stream. Large cities such as London with radiated heat and shelter from buildings create their own microclimate that could count as being Mediterranean, where many tender plants can be grown. Many factors will affect the climate locally, such as closeness to the sea or altitude. Gardens that are up in the hills are likely to be several degrees cooler than those at sea level. It is often easy to spot if you are in a Mediterranean climate by the plants that grow there. These are typified by the olive, fig and almond. To these we should now add oranges, as they are being grown in the area in ever larger quantities, although they require a great deal of water.

The normal lowest winter temperature goes down to around 2°C to −6°C. If the temperature falls too low, many plants will be damaged, the leaves may be burnt and the plant set back; but most will usually recover. Others may be cut completely to the ground, but will shoot out from the base the following spring. Generally those plants that will not take any frost at all, the tender tropical plants, have been individually described as being tender.

The blue Mediterranean sky that all holiday makers enjoy gives the region the highest solar radiation and light intensities on earth. For some plants this is too much, and the leaves simply burn up. I have found that this happens in my garden with variegated plants and those with coloured, particularly yellow or white variegated leaves. For example *Catalpa bignonioides* 'Aurea' with its beautiful golden foliage becomes scorched and brown-edged by midsummer, even in dappled shade.

Another factor that is often forgotten is the low humidity of the air during the summer, and often in the winter as well. For some plants the transpiration rate is so high that although the roots are moist, the plant cannot supply enough water to the young growing tips, which then die. On a few days a year a wind that has originated from the central mass of the continent is so dry that it decimates the tips of the plants. While an established *Eucalyptus* tree will soon recover from such a scorching, a newly planted small shrub or perennial may succumb. The only defence is to provide plenty of shelter by planting trees on the windward side of the garden.

Getting Started

So, you have found that old ruin, which when modernized will make the wonderful home that you have always dreamed of owning. It comes with a lovely plot of land with fantastic views, and maybe has an old olive tree on it. If you are lucky you may have a fig and some almond trees as well. Perhaps you splashed out and had your new dream house built with all modern luxuries. After months and months, not to mention the delays – there are always delays – the building work has come to an end. No matter how much you plan there is always one important item the builders cannot finish on time. Now the cement mixer that has been churning away for what seems forever is finally

being taken away, and the builders are clearing away their mess – how do they manage to make such a mess? Now at last the heaps of sand and piles of bricks have been cleared away, and what will be the garden is now visible again.

Now is the time to give some serious thought to the garden. What sort of a garden is it going to be? Personal choice will be a great deciding factor. We all have our own ideas of what we want in a garden, but there are many other factors that have to be considered. The physical shape, size and orientation of the plot are all relevant. The contours of the land will make a difference, as will the position of the house and its entrance. Any mature trees must be looked after carefully and worked into the design. Is it on a hilltop where most of the soil has been washed away, or is it in a valley with deep, rich soil? If it is on a hilltop, then wind may be a problem, while a valley may be a frost pocket. Is it close to the sea, ideal for the beach – but what about those salt-laden winds that can decimate so many plants? What is the soil like, is it good deep rich loam, or more likely is it poor and rocky? Is it mostly chalk?

If the house is to be a holiday home, then low maintenance is an important factor. If it is to be your permanent home, then how much time can you spend in the garden? If you are working or have a lot of commitments, then you will have less time to spend in the garden than if you are retired. Cost is also an important factor. Many people take great pride in creating a wonderful garden from seeds or cuttings given to them by friends, which is an extremely economical way to make a garden. Other people feel time is more important, wanting an instant garden, and are prepared to pay for large trees and shrubs to fill it.

When planning a garden from scratch we all have certain features that we want to include, perhaps a covered archway giving summer shade, a path leading to a shady corner with a seat, or a pool with a bubbling fountain. Choosing a style is important. Some people envisage a more formal style with straight paths, tall trees and neatly clipped shrubs as architectural features along with restrained plantings, while others prefer a more natural look.

Some will go for colour, either mixed borders themed by colour, or plantings where one colour will merge into another. This will mean that all plants are carefully chosen and planted according to their colour. Perhaps guests normally arrive at a certain time of the year and the garden is planted to be at its most colourful at this time. Other people such as myself just love plants, and enjoy the thrill of finding unusual ones that will grow well in the area. We enjoy a real thrill from seeing a rare plant flower for the first time. This means that the overall design is based on the plants, their needs and how they grow.

To design a garden effectively it is important to have a knowledge of the plants that are available locally and the way what they will grow. I hope that those listed in this book will help you choose successfully. Most people never have the opportunity to design an entirely new garden. They move into a house with one already established, though one which it is usually possible to redesign and improve. Keen gardeners can always think of changes or add new plants for variety or to create a different effect.

Many books have been written about garden design, giving a mass of styles and ideas to choose from, from the formal to the completely informal, to the modern and all shades in between. The main deciding factor is that you are happy with your garden: after all, you are going to live with it, be there every day, and you must be comfortable with its feel.

When planning the garden, sketch out your ideas on squared paper to see how your ideas will work. Start with hard features such as terraces, walls, pergolas and suchlike; then go on to mark the important trees, allowing them enough room to grow, and then fill in with the beds and borders. Transfer your ideas to the ground, marking paths, walls and other hard features out with string or sand to give an idea of the structure and shape the garden will take.

If you choose to have any hard landscaping, it is far easier to construct it before the planting begins. If earth has to be moved to create a raised bed, or rocks to make a feature, it can be done with an earth-moving machine that can do a great deal of work in a short time at reasonable cost. Think about this carefully before any planting is carried out, as there may not be access for a machine later. Moreover, when you have builders working on the house, remember that while they have all their equipment there it is easy for them to build any features that you want. Broad, sweeping paths can be laid at the construction stage, as can any walls, pergolas, seats and so on. It is often difficult to get a builder back to do a small job once he is finished.

When you are ready to start planting, begin with any trees. These are the slowest growing, and will be important features of the garden. Some will eventually become large, so think of what they will look like when mature. Will they block the light to the house or obscure the view? With any planting, think of where the drains are, because roots seek out moisture and can block them. If wind is a problem, then planting a windbreak is important: *Acacia*, *Eucalyptus* and *Juniperus* are examples of windbreak plants.

A big question is 'Do you want a lawn?' If you are used to living in a cooler region, then you will probably be used to having one, but is it right for a Mediterranean garden? On the down side, to plant a lawn the ground needs a lot of preparation, constant maintenance, cutting about once a week, feeding regularly and lots of water. On the plus side, a lawn feels cool as there is no reflected heat, it is pleasant to walk on – and what is nicer on a hot, sunny day than to sit on grass in the shade of a tree?

One of the many attractions of living or holidaying in the Mediterranean is being able to eat 'al fresco' on warm summer evenings. So it is wonderful to be able to create an intimate outdoor living room. A paved area with some night scented plants around it such as *Brugmansia*, *Cestrum nocturnum* or a *Solandra* growing over a pergola will create the conditions for a memorable meal. To improve the effect, add some shade trees and perhaps some plants with lush foliage such as *Strelitzia*, *Phormiums* and *Hedechiums*, and a palm if there is room. This area can be part of a large garden, in which case choose the position carefully so that it is sheltered from the prevailing wind,

and if possible faces the evening sun. For those with a small garden you may decide to devote the whole of it to an outdoor room, where it can be intensively planted with many climbers on the walls, and shade-loving, colourful plants such as Impatiens growing low down, and plants in pots in the corners.

Many people will choose to have a swimming pool built. Developers usually site it close to the house, and terrace the area between the house and pool, but although this may be fine for a holiday home, this area can become terribly hot with the reflected heat from the walls and the terrace. If you already have a pool close to the house, you may be able to soften this hard area with some raised beds, pots and containers. If it has not yet been built, then consider moving it some distance away: certainly it is wonderful to be able to walk out of the house and jump into the water on a hot summer's day, but it doesn't look so inviting during the winter! Even a freeform pool is still a hard object that can be softened with some carefully chosen plants. When well designed it can merge into the background and become part of the garden and an attractive feature. If enough water is available, a lawn by the pool is pleasant to relax on.

Plants near pools must be safe, with smooth branches and leaves, and no thorns, spines or prickles that may injure people. They should be as litter-free as possible, with no mess to clog up the filter system. Palms associate well with pools, and you can create a tropical look with *Ficus*, *Schefflera*, *Fatsia*, *Cordylines* and some *Cannas*.

When a hole for a pool is dug, a large volume of material is removed and this can be used to good effect to create a rock garden. There will usually be some rocks brought to the surface, so with some thought, an attractive feature can be made of this material.

The one factor that will have more effect on the look of your garden and what plants you can grow will be the amount of water available. How much have you got, how is it supplied, and how do you feel about using it in the garden?

Water in the Garden

For the holidaymaker who can enjoy the almost guaranteed sunshine and

lack of rain during the summer months, the Mediterranean is a wonderful place; but water in the region is becoming scarce, and will no doubt become more so. As you drive about the countryside you can see public wells that are now disused but were working within living memory. As the region develops, more and more water is extracted from the ground, so the level keeps dropping, with the result that many old wells have been abandoned.

In some regions, orchards of almonds are being ripped out and replaced with citrus fruits. As almonds need no irrigation and oranges need a vast amount, this change must have an effect on the level of the ground water. For those people who are worried about water, the proliferation of golf courses in the Mediterranean is another bone of contention. So a crucial question to ask at the design stage is how much water should be used. In the past few years there has been a tremendous move to making gardens with drought-tolerant plants that use little or no summer water once established. This does not mean that the garden will be dull in any way: by selecting plants carefully, a really colourful garden can still be achieved (see Dry Gardens, on page 15).

What sort of supply do you have? If you have mains water, which is increasingly being laid to houses in the countryside, how reliable is it, and how much does it cost? In some areas mains water can be quite expensive. Or do you collect rainwater, and have extra supplies delivered by water tanker? Perhaps you have the luxury of your own private bore-hole with an unlimited cheap supply? Just as important, how do you feel about using water in the garden? Is it an extravagance, or a necessity? Unfortunately, all too often we see the large lawns of unoccupied holiday homes being generously watered on time clocks. While the lawn and garden will look good for the time the owners are there, it is an extravagant use of water.

Now that you have thought about the water supply, how much or how little do you want to use, and how will you apply it, and when?

Some people take great pleasure in watering their garden by hand with a hosepipe, because like this they can spend time looking at each plant as they water it. Thus if any pest or disease has appeared, or the plant needs any attention, they will spot it right away. Rather than a chore, it can be a real pleasure to go into the garden in the evening or early morning and water the plants. This does, however, take time and commitment, and is more difficult in the larger garden. For these, some form of automatic irrigation system may be better. There are numerous designs and systems on the market, and it is advisable to seek some professional help before installing an expensive system.

Probably the most efficient method of irrigation is some form of drip system, where each plant has one or more drippers which can deliver from 2–10ltr per hour. These systems literally drip onto the soil which means that no water evaporates, but just soaks down to the roots where it is needed. These drippers are fed from micro-tubes, which are in turn fed from a main. You may either leave the tubes on the surface, where they are unsightly and a nuisance when weeding, or bury them. The disadvantage of having a mass of tubes buried all over the garden is that when you dig a hole for a new plant you are bound to cut through a pipe. A problem with drippers is that if you have hard water they tend to become clogged with a deposit of calcium carbonate. There are also systems that allow water to bubble up from an underground tube, and small low-level sprays. These are the next most efficient system. The low-level fixed spray-heads emit about 30ltr per hour over an area of about 1.5m, while those with spinning heads apply the same amount of water to a circle of about 3m. These systems are good for placing around large plants, and for borders needing a lot of water.

Least efficient are the pulsating sprays that are set up high: they spew out large amounts of water over a large circle, and are often adjusted badly so that part of the spray lands on a path or road and the water runs to waste. Even worse is when they are used in the heat of the day when a lot of the water simply evaporates and does not help the plants. Indeed, water landing on the leaves of some plants in full sunshine may burn the foliage.

Any automatic watering system requires a control device. This can range from a time switch that fits on to a tap, to a computerized programmable controller. With the more elaborate controller the garden can be divided into zones, each zone receiving variable amounts of water at differing times of the day, or on different days. For those gardens with lawns, the best automatic system involves sprinklers that are underground and 'pop up' when in use. As they use large amounts of water at high pressure, these systems are normally installed by professionals.

Be sure to check and adjust your irrigation system frequently. Turn the water off on rainy or cloudy days for even more savings. As temperatures change, so should your irrigation frequencies and their duration. It is amazing how many people utilize a 'set and forget' concept with their controllers.

When to water? Early morning is the best time, before the heat of the day when the plant needs it most. This is fine for automatic systems that can be set to run in the very early morning, but it may not be popular with those who have to rise with the sun to soak their plants. Late evening is the next best time, and most popular for those who water by hand. This is fine, as little moisture is lost during the night. Try not to water during the heat of the day unless you find a plant that is suffering.

How often to water? It is far better to give large amounts less often than small amounts frequently. I know of a farmer who grows wonderful oranges with a huge crop. He has made a large basin the width of the tree by mounding up the soil. This he flood-fills once a week to ten days. While this is not possible or practical in the garden, the same principle should still be applied. Whether you water by hand or with an automatic system, the principle should be to give plenty at one time, then none for a time. If plants are given a little water regularly, say every day, their roots will stay in the shallow, damp surface and will not go down to any depth; they will not develop strong anchoring roots, and so will be more liable to blow over in strong winds. Also if you have a problem with the water supply the roots will dry out and the plant will die quickly.

How much water to give? This is a much more difficult question to answer. The amount to give a plant depends upon so many factors. Individual species will need different amounts. A plant will need more water in an exposed windy situation than if it is sheltered. The type of soil will make a difference, as a heavy clay will retain more water than a light sandy soil. The size of the plant will make a difference, so a small one needs less water than a large tree – but then as plants become established and send their roots down, they may need less water. The time of year is another important factor, in that you should gradually increase watering as the weather becomes hotter, then gradually reduce it as it cools down again after the summer. I have heard it said that you should never water during the winter – but nothing is so simple in gardening. If there is a prolonged dry spell in the winter, plants may well dry out and need some water. Experience here is the key factor: so basically, watch your plants and give them water when they require it.

If you are planning a garden from scratch, it may be possible to group plants together according to their water needs. You could make a rock garden or dry garden where all plants are those that need little or no summer water. *Aeonium*, *Agave*, and *Crassula* along with *Nerium oleander* are ideal for grouping together, as they need little water. Grouping thirstier plants together saves time and effort, and precious water.

Soil

Looking around the Mediterranean during the hot summer months and seeing the soil baked rock hard, you may find it difficult to imagine turning it into a garden. But if you come during the winter when there is a torrential downpour and see the brown muddy streams and rivers, you quickly realize that improving the soil and creating terraces to prevent soil erosion is really important. Soil erosion is a major problem throughout the region. So often the owners of hilltop houses find that the topsoil has been washed away, and only the poor subsoil is left. Thought must be given as to how to manage the soil well. Avoid steep slopes that allow the water to remove the valuable soil. Terrace a slope whenever possible – even a row of rocks will break the force of the water and prevent gullies from forming. Just as bad is a poorly drained soil. If the garden is low-lying or in a basin, the water may collect during the winter and plant roots may rot. A well aereated soil is important for a healthy root structure.

Many Mediterranean soils are short in organic matter because the dryness inhibits the formation of humus, and are almost devoid of plant foods. Incorporating organic matter into the soil improves the soil structure enormously. This can be done before planting, but it should also be a continuous process.

Once the plants are in, the best possible help you can give them is to cover the ground with a mulch. You can use almond shells, mushroom compost, straw or pine needles, or better still any manure that may be available from a local farm. Or is there a bar or cafe nearby that has large quantities of spent coffee grounds to dispose of? These are slightly acid so they will help to correct an alkaline soil. Perhaps there is a carpenter nearby who would let you have some sawdust, or a wine factory that will let you have some grape residue. Look around your area for any sources of organic material.

Once the garden becomes established, one of the best pieces of equipment to buy is a shredder. This reduces prunings into chips that are suitable for spreading over the garden. I made the mistake of buying a small one, and soon found out that it was not big enough, and succeeded in burning out the motor. A large machine with hammer mills may seem like an extravagance, but it soon pays for itself: 2 or 3m lengths of *Solandra grandiflora* stems, *Arundo donax* stems and large amounts of olive wood are reduced to a usable heap in minutes. In my garden any material that will compost such as leaves, grass clippings and kitchen waste goes on the compost heap. Anything that is too big or hard to compost goes through the shredder. Any wood that is too big for the shredder is cut up and used for logs for the fire in the house, and of course the wood ash from the fire is a good source of potash. Nothing is wasted.

In many dry regions, soils are alkaline, partly because the drought inhibits the decay of plant material but mainly because of the geological structure. This means that acid-loving plants can only be grown with great difficulty or in areas with soils that have a low pH. They may, however, be grown in pots or containers, or planted in raised beds – but remember to water them only with soft water: rainwater is best, so try to store some for this purpose.

Plants need many nutrients in the soil so that they can grow, flower and fruit. Some of these are elements that are usually in the soil naturally in sufficient quantities, but in some soils some of the elements may be unavailable, and plants may suffer and show signs of deficiency. In such cases you may add the missing nutrients by applying manure or a chemical fertilizer. If using a general chemical fertilizer, choose one with added trace elements, as these are beneficial.

Iron (Fe) Deficiency

In alkaline soil some plants will become chlorotic due to the lack of available iron. Iron is connected to chlorophyll production: it is not generally lacking in soil, but can be 'locked' in unavailable forms in soil with high pH. The symptoms of this deficiency are pale green new leaves, followed by yellowing of the areas between the veins, which remain green. As the older leaves stay green it is easy to spot this deficiency. It can be treated by applying chelated iron to the soil.

Nitrogen (N) Deficiency

Nitrogen is important for cell growth of the plant, and in the formation of chlorophyll that keeps leaves green and promotes rapid vegetative growth. Plants that are deficient become yellowish in appearance, with the older leaves quite yellow. The leaves may even become bleached with dead patches on them. The young leaves remain green. The yellowness of these plants stands out when compared to healthy green plants. Nitrogen deficiency is common in sandy soils. It is easily corrected with a high nitrogen fertilizer such as urea, nitrate of soda or sulphate of ammonia. Animal manure is usually high in nitrogen.

Magnesium (Mg) Deficiency

Magnesium is essential for chlorophyll formation and therefore helps to give plants their green colour. It activates the enzymes involved in food transport and in the manufacture of sugar, fat and oil. It is important in cell multiplication and seed production. The symptoms of deficiency usually occur on older growth first, when mottling and yellowing start at the leaf tip and progress to the centre of the leaf. Leaf veins often remain green. Treat with a solution of magnesium sulphate (Epsom salts). This will have to be repeated often as it is highly soluble and will wash out with rain. It can also be applied as a foliar spray using 15–20g per litre of water.

Potassium (K) Deficiency

Potassium maintains water regulation in cells, cell strength, transpiration, photosynthesis, carbohydrate (energy) formation and storage, and fruit quality. Adequate potassium increases a plant's resistance to disease, drought and frost. Plants take up large amounts of potassium in the early stages of developing fruit. The symptoms of deficiency appear in older leaf tissues first. Leaf burn and spotting or mottling on the lower leaves follows poor growth. Younger leaves may show red pigmentation. Apply sulphate of potash around the plant.

When and How to Plant

In the autumn after almost unbroken sunshine the clouds begin to build up and darken, and then the first rains come. If it is a gentle rain that soaks into the ground rather than a torrential downpour that runs off, then we can have a 'second spring', because this is when the plants that have been dormant all summer wake up and burst into life again. This is the ideal moment to plant out your garden: the soil is still warm, the air is more moist, and the days are still long enough for the plants to become established quickly. Spring is also good, as is any time during the winter – though do remember that if there is a dry spell, the young plants will need some water. Of course plants that are grown in pots can be planted out at any time, provided they are given enough water.

It may sound obvious that you simply dig a hole and put the plant in,

13

but in fact to get it off to a good start, some care is needed. Firstly ensure that it is well watered: a dry plant will take much longer to absorb water, and for the roots to grow out of the root ball. When digging the hole I have heard it said that you should dig a hole a metre deep and a metre wide! In an ideal world this would certainly get the plant off to the best possible start, but few of us can manage such a vast hole for each one. Ideally this is the time to remove any rocks and to loosen any compacted soil at the bottom of the hole, and to improve the subsoil with organic material. Dig the hole twice as wide as the root ball and deep enough for the root ball to sit in comfortably. When planting trees that need staking, drive the stake in before putting the plant in. After removing the container, check to see if the roots are tightly bound or matted. If so, ease out some of the roots to ensure that they spread out. When filling in the hole add some organic matter to the soil. Firm the plant in well, and give it a generous watering. Try to leave a depression around it so that the water will not run away. If you are planting during the summer when the soil is baked hard, it will help to make a shallow hole and fill it with water, then allow it to soak in for a day. This makes digging the rest of the hole much easier.

Palms

A visitor to any Mediterranean region during the winter will immediately notice that its remarkable greenness is due to the abundance of evergreen trees; these include olive, carob, citrus and palms. Although most species of palms are of tropical origin, there are many that can be cultivated in a Mediterranean climate, and even in places where the temperature can fall below −15°C: thus palms can be found in Edinburgh, London and southern Russia. As well as giving a tropical look to a garden, many species are easy to grow.

Over the last few years there has been a great revival in interest in palms, with many more species now being planted. They were popular in the nineteenth century, but by the 1920s they were being ripped out. Probably the most widely planted palms are

Phoenix canariensis, *P. dactylifera* and *Washingtonia*. Now, many more beautiful species can be seen, including *Butia capitata* and *Brahea armata*, the Mexican blue palm, which is drought-tolerant and grows well in full sun. There are now nurseries that specialize in palms suitable for planting in the garden and for the home: they come in a range of sizes, from small plants to mature trees 10m high that are delivered in a lorry.

Palms can be an outstanding feature in a garden and a special attraction in themselves if given enough space to be seen at their best. Groups of just one species can be effective, especially if trees of different sizes are planted. Good results can also be obtained by grouping different kinds of palms, so that there is a contrast of colour and shape in the foliage.

Palms make wonderful specimen plants near pools as they are litter free, evergreen and slow growing. They can also create a beautiful mirror effect in the water. When choosing a palm, take into account the height to which it will eventually grow. Small gardens need small species such as *Phoenix roebelinii*, while larger gardens need larger palms where there is space for them to grow, and be seen. The proportions, the scale and the volume of the trees must always come first when choosing a plant. They transplant easily even when mature, and need only a small amount of soil compared with other trees of a similar size. They also need very little maintenance.

Palms can grow in a great variety of soils, although on the whole they prefer well-drained soil. A rich, neutral or slightly acid soil is ideal if the palms are from moist rainforests, while those from an arid area, or places that have seasonal periods of drought, will grow in poor soil. Many palms prefer sunny positions from the start to achieve maximum growth, and some sun when they are fully grown. Those species that require shade grow in places sheltered from the sun in their native habitat, and generally do not grow very tall.

The best time to plant palm trees is in the spring, and planting can continue until midsummer. Many palms are extremely tolerant of dry conditions if they are already well established, but they will have a much better appearance

if they receive enough water during the growing season. *Chamaerops humilis*, found in the ravines and cliffs of the western Mediterranean, is among those that need the least amount of water to survive.

Some species that are suitable for growing in the Mediterranean are listed in the section 'Plants for a Purpose'.

Pots and Containers

Wherever you go in the Mediterranean you will see plants growing in pots or containers, on steps, windowsills, balconies, terraces, or anywhere that colour is wanted. The containers can range from old paint cans, plastic water bottles and car tyres, painted white of course, to the large antique oil jars that are large enough to climb inside. Only your imagination and the size of your wallet will determine what container you will use. If you go to Cordoba in Spain during May there is a festival devoted to the courtyard garden, when many people open their private gardens: then you can see the wonderful array of pots that line the walls and often cover the windows of the houses. There is a spectacular display from each garden, which is often quite small. It is easy to think that a plot is too small to do anything with, but the gardens of Cordoba are an inspiration as to what can be achieved.

Container growing in a hot, dry climate is challenging with regard to what will do well, but it is not difficult. When planting up a container it is important to remember that there will be rain during the winter and a badly drained container can soon become waterlogged, resulting in the plant dying. Good drainage is therefore essential. If the container has a flat base and is going to stand on a flat surface, check to see if the hole in the bottom will be able to let the water drain out. It may be necessary to raise the container up on a support such as some tiles, to allow it to drain freely.

Soil in containers in hot sun will heat up during the day – though the larger the pot and the thicker the sides (preferably terracotta or concrete), the less this will happen. As plants in pots have only a relatively small amount of soil, they perforce have only a small reserve of water to draw on: watering any pots is therefore crucial. Do this frequently, especially in the heat of summer. If the soil in a pot becomes too dry, then it shrinks and is difficult to make wet again. Feel the soil, if it is dry then give it a good soaking. Containers will dry out fast, be sure to have a large saucer under each pot to allow it to sit in water for a while. This will help extra moisture absorb into the pot and help thoroughly wet the soil area (water often runs through too fast to do this the first time). A slow drip system also works very well. Remember, too, that your plants will need feeding regularly: it is better to give them a weak solution of fertilizer once a week than to feed them generously less often.

Plants in pots can be used to add colour to a garden. A *Clivia minata* is a spectacular plant when in full flower, but for the rest of the year it is rather dull. When it is in flower it can be brought on to a shady terrace near the house to be seen at its best. Once flowering has finished, it can be removed to a leafy corner of the garden to be cared for until it flowers next year. Many plants can be treated this way. Another advantage of having plants in pots is that they can be moved around like furniture in the house, and can be rearranged to suit your moods. Be aware, however, that larger containers are heavy and can be difficult, if not dangerous, to move. Plant them where they are intended to be, and know that moving them will be difficult.

Plants in pots usually do best if given some shade. A pot that is standing on a sunny terrace in full sun all day can become so hot that the roots that run around the inside of the pot bake and die. Some shade will prevent this sort of overheating.

Climbing Plants and Pergolas

All gardens are greatly enhanced by climbing plants, whether they are used to clothe walls, to hide unsightly objects or to give some shade. The walls of the house cry out for climbers that are carefully sited. A *Jasminum polyanthum* on the wall near the living room is wonderful, filling the air with its scent at night. However, any plant that is against a wall must be placed with care, as a wall in full sun all day can become extremely hot, and many plants will suffer. Some wall plants are rampant and become a problem, while others, such as *Hedera* species, can damage the wall itself. Nevertheless, a well sited and well managed wall plant can add great beauty to a house. Probably the most popular one for the Mediterranean must be the *Bougainvillea*. There are many spectacular varieties that come in vibrant shades of white, pink, red, orange, lilac, cerise, copper and so on, and as it can make 2m of growth a year, it will quickly cover a large area – and it thrives in the hottest location. Often large old plants of *B. glabra* with its purple bracts can be seen covering an abandoned ruin, where it receives no water or attention, yet flowers profusely.

To add another dimension to a garden many people add a pergola. These can be simple ones made from wooden poles, to attractive stone columns. Eucalyptus poles are sometimes used, but these will rot after a few years. Do not use metal as it can become intensely hot and burn any plant that is attached to it. Pergolas can be formed to make shaded walkways or outdoor eating areas. You will find about ninety climbers listed in this book, so the choice is overwhelming. Use deciduous climbers near the house to let the winter sunshine into the house, and evergreen ones for that dark, secluded walkway. For an exotic look, a *Thunbergia grandiflora*, with its huge racemes of pendulous flowers, is spectacular. Or how about a grape vine covering a terrace pergola? This has several purposes: it will give you shade in summer, you can enjoy the fruit, and it is deciduous, thus allowing the light in during the winter.

Dry Gardens and Xeriscaping

For those with a limited water supply, or those who only spend a short time in the home, a dry garden may be the answer. A term that is often used is 'xeriscaping', a concept for garden design with efficient use of water, that originated in Colorado, USA.

So what is xeriscaping? The term 'xeriscape' comes from 'xeros', the Greek word for 'dry', combined with 'scape', which literally means a picture or a view of a type of scene: thus we have the term for a dry landscape. Many people have a negative association with this word, thinking that all xeriscapes are hot, hostile and very thorny. Some associate the term with minimal plant material and lots of rock. Actually, xeriscaping can be, and often is, very attractive, quite lush and extremely colourful. One feature that is often used is that of a 'dry river bed', in which a natural-looking river is created using rocks and careful planting, with the water represented by well worn riverbed stones carefully laid to create the illusion of a dry river. When well constructed this can look stunning.

The use of water-efficient plants does not necessarily mean drab plants with lots of thorns or just cactus, as many Mediterranean natives will look attractive with little or no water. Just look through the book to see just how many plants are marked with a single water droplet, indicating that they need little or no summer water. There is a vast array of cacti and succulents available that come in a wide range of shapes, sizes and colours that can make a most interesting year-round display. *Kalanchoe* species come in many different forms, *K. beharensis* with its huge silver leaves, *K. blossfeldiana* with its attractive red flowers, while *Aloes* have their wonderful spring flowers. Drifts of *Lampranthus* look spectacular in spring. There are so many colourful plants that you can use successfully.

If you really want a lawn, keep it small. Place modest quantities of grass in areas where it will be used for cooling the environment, or for play and recreation. There is no sense in placing large areas of grass where no one will use it. Consider using alternatives to grass: some areas can be paved, while some can be planted with drought-tolerant groundcover plants such as *Gazania*, *Vinca*, *Santolina* or *Juniper*s. Different types of gravel can be laid in large sweeps to give a pleasing effect.

One important principle is to avoid over-planting. Too many gardens are planted densely in a belief that 'more is better', and in the desire to have a mature look at the time of planting. Too often, as the plants grow, the garden takes on a cluttered appearance, with everything jamming one into the other. Even the most experienced designer needs to remember that some open space will allow for better appreciation of the plants.

Symbols for Water Requirements

In the book I have provided each plant with a symbol of one, two or three water droplets, in an attempt to give the reader an idea of its water requirements. Thus a plant marked with a single water droplet is partially or completely drought-tolerant, meaning that once established, it can survive the long hot summer with little or no water. These plants come from the drier regions of the world, and can cope with such harsh conditions. Many bulbs are summer dormant, losing their leaves in the early part of summer. Many native plants also 'shut down' for the summer by going into dormancy, *Cistus* and almond being good examples.

Succulents also belong here, though some of these may look a little sad by midsummer and a good soaking will see them through to the autumn rains. Water conservatively once the plants become established. Obviously new plantings require considerable amounts of water to survive the first and second year. Few, if any plants can survive simply on the water provided by the winter rains while in the establishment period, but once they become rooted in, start 'weaning' them by providing deep, infrequent soakings that encourage deep rooting. Remember that more plants are lost from being over-watered as opposed to being too dry.

A plant marked with two water droplets will certainly need some water during the summer, being less drought-tolerant that those marked with a single water droplet, perhaps once a week or so, according to the weather and conditions. These plants usually need a moderate amount of water to keep them healthy. *Grevillea robusta*, *Euphorbia characias*, *Hardenbergia comptoniana* are examples. Generally they will grow bigger and stronger with more water, and may even become rampant with generous water.

A plant marked with three water droplets is one that must have its roots moist at all times. These plants tend to be the more tropical plants that come from areas with constant, year-round rain. Even these plants will probably survive short periods of drought. Note that although they need generous water, most also need good drainage as their roots must not become water-logged. Exceptions include *Cyperus* the papyrus, a bog plant that needs to have its roots in shallow water, and *Zantedeschia* which loves wet boggy places.

A

Abelia
Caprifoliaceae

A genus of about thirty species of evergreen, partially evergreen, or deciduous summer-flowering shrubs native from the Himalayas to east Asia and Mexico.

A. *floribunda* MEXICAN ABELIA))

A medium-sized evergreen shrub up to 3m high spreading to 3m wide with arching, downy red branches. The 4cm long, ovate leaves are dark glossy green. The tubular, 5cm long, trumpet-shaped flowers are brilliant shocking purplish-magenta with a white throat, hanging in pendulous clusters from the ends of the branches. They are normally produced during summer but may also appear in winter. A striking shrub that may need some protection from the sun. Needs a moderate amount of summer water. Native to Mexico.

A. × *grandiflora* GLOSSY ABELIA))

This vigorous, rounded, semi-evergreen shrub is a hybrid of two Chinese species and is the most popularly grown. The dainty, arching stems may reach 2m high, spreading 2–3m wide. The 3cm, glossy, ovate leaves have a bronze tint in winter. The flowers are in loose terminal panicles, white flushed pink, bell-shaped, 2cm long. They appear over most of the summer and autumn. The shrub needs a moderate amount of summer water, growing best in a well drained, rich soil. Suitable for growing in sun or part shade. Prune Abelias by removing selected branches after flowering, not by shearing, in order to keep the graceful appearance of the shrub. The variety 'Francis Mason' has gold variegated leaves, but does not grow well in full sun.

A. *schumannii*

A deciduous slender shrub to 1.5m or more with pendulous arching branches.

Abutilon × hybridum

The small oval leaves are 3cm long with a sharp tip. The rosy-pink, 3cm-long flowers are blotched with orange and are slightly fragrant. These make a continuous display during summer and autumn. The shrub will thrive in a well drained soil enriched with leaf-mould in a sunny, protected site. Needs a moderate amount of summer water. More hardy than other Abelias. Native to western China.

Abutilon 'FLOWERING MAPLE'
Malvaceae

A large genus of about 150 species of evergreen and deciduous shrubs and perennials, with simple, three to seven lobed leaves, mainly coming from the tropical or subtropical parts of the world. Abutilons prefer partial shade and moist soil, and given these conditions they make rapid growth. They can easily be propagated by cuttings of the soft young growth. Often used as house or terrace shrubs.

A. × *hybridum* (syn. *A. globosum*)
FLOWERING MAPLE))

This is the name given to a large number of garden hybrids, probably arising as hybrids of *A. pictum*, *A. striatum* and *A. darwinii*. They are large, fast-growing, soft, woody shrubs up to 5m high and spreading to 2–5m wide. The ovate to rounded, soft

Abelia × grandiflora

velvety leaves are up to 16cm long and 10cm wide. They are usually three- or five-lobed, green or variegated. The solitary, 10cm-long flowers are drooping and bell-shaped with protruding stamens. The colour varies from white, yellow, pink or red to purple. If given plenty of summer water and full sun the flowers are produced almost continuously throughout summer. If the shrub becomes too large it can be cut back in winter. Garden origin.

A. *megapotamicum*
WEEPING CHINESE LANTERN ◡◡◡
The slender, willowy stems can grow to 3m high, spreading to 2m wide, with woody, wire-like arching branches. The lance-shaped leaves are usually three-lobed, and 4–8cm long. The small solitary flowers, 4–6cm long, resemble red and yellow lanterns hanging along its stems; they are produced from summer until autumn. The shrub also looks good in a hanging basket, but then needs ample summer water. Usually planted against a wall or fence to support its weak growth. Will flower well in full sun, but will take some shade. Native to southern Brazil. The variety 'Variegata' has yellow-mottled leaves and is more often grown.

A. *pictum* 'Thompsonii'
SPOTTED FLOWERING MAPLE ◡◡
An evergreen shrub or small tree up to 5m high and 2–5m wide. The ovate to rounded leaves are usually 3–5 lobed, 5–8cm wide and mottled with yellow. Throughout summer the pale orange bell flowers 6cm long which have deep red veining are produced. These compliment the yellow of the leaves perfectly. The variegated leaves can be scorched by the hot summer sun, so for better growth partial shade is required. The shrub needs a moderate amount of summer water. As the leaves can lose

Abutilon 'Souvenir de Bonn'

their variegation any plain green shoots should be removed. This is one of the best golden variegated Abutilons.

A. 'Souvenir de Bonn' ◡◡
A soft-stemmed shrub up to 3m high and 2–3m wide. The soft, maple-like, five-lobed leaves have a 15cm-long stalk. The leaves are greyish-green, bordered with a creamy-white edge. The bell-shaped flowers, in colour salmon to orange, veined with red, are produced along the length of the stem throughout summer. The shrub needs a moderate amount of summer water. It needs to be grown in full sun. As with any variegated shrub, the leaves can lose their variegation, so any plain green shoots should be cut out. Garden origin.

A. *vitifolium* ◡◡◡
A large, handsome, fast-growing shrub to 4m high and 3m wide, with downy shoots. The downy, grey-green, ovate leaves are up to 15cm long and as wide, usually three to five-lobed. The saucer-shaped flowers are 6–8cm wide, with long protruding stamens; they are borne singly or in clusters along the stem throughout summer. The colour varies from pale to deep mauve to white. The shrub is happiest in a sheltered, sunny site with high humidity and ample summer water. A short-lived shrub that grows quickly and readily from seed. Self-sown seedlings are frequently produced. Native to

Chile. The variety 'Album' has white flowers that generally come true from seed. 'Tennant's White' has large, pure white flowers that are produced over a longer period.

Acacia 'WATTLE, MIMOSA'
Mimosaceae

A vast genus of perhaps 1,100 species of deciduous and evergreen shrubs and trees that come from dry tropical or warm temperate regions of the world, particularly Australia and Africa. They are among the most popular and colourful trees in Mediterranean gardens. In Australia they are known as 'wattles', in Europe as 'mimosa'. Of the many species known, only a few are commonly planted in gardens – many have escaped and become naturalized.

A. *baileyana* GOLDEN MIMOSA ◡◡
A shrub or small tree that can grow to 10m high with a wide spread. The leaves are 4–6cm long, and doubly

Abutilon pictum 'Thompsonii'

Acacia baileyana

pinnate, with many small leaflets 5mm long; silvery blue-grey in colour. The small clusters of yellow fragrant flowers appear in racemes up to 8cm long; the flowers are produced profusely from winter to early spring. This is one of the most commonly planted acacias, making a wonderful multi-stemmed tree. The cultivar 'Purpurea' has purple-tinged foliage that should be cut back to encourage the new growth, as this has the best colour. Unfortunately more tender than the species. Native to Australia (New South Wales).

A. dealbata SILVER WATTLE, MIMOSA ☙

A shrub or small tree that can quickly reach 10m or more high, with an equal spread. The silver-grey leaves are bipinnate, and finely hairy; up to 12cm long. The masses of tiny, bright, yellow-scented flowers grow in clusters of small, round balls. They are produced on the ends of the branches from winter to spring. The tree is much appreciated for its flowers: it provides the florists' Mimosa, and is commonly grown for cut flower. Has become naturalized in the Mediterranean region. Native to Australia (New South Wales to Tasmania).

A. karroo KARROO THORN ☙

A shrub or small tree that grows slowly up to 12m high, with a wide spread, usually having a flat top. The trunk and older branches are armed with sharp white spines to 8cm long. The deep green, doubly pinnate leaves are 5cm long and have many tiny leaflets. The fragrant, clustered flowerheads form

Acacia longifolia

golden balls that almost cover the tree in summer. They are usually followed by seedpods up to 12cm long. The tree is extremely drought-tolerant, needing no summer water. Will grow in any well drained soil. Makes an attractive and effective hedge for the dry garden. Also useful near the coast as a sand binder. Native to southern Africa.

A. longifolia SYDNEY GOLDEN ☙

A tree or shrub that grows to 10m high with willowy, spreading habit. The bright green or greyish-green leathery leaves are 8–15cm long and willow-like. The flowerheads are in loose spikes to 6cm long, and golden yellow in colour; they appear along the branches in late winter to early spring. This fast-growing shrub tolerates different soil conditions. Often planted near the beach where it makes a good soil binder, where the wind will make it prostrate and the branches may root in the sand. Native to Australia (Tasmania).

A. paradoxa (syn. *A. armata*) KANGAROO THORN ☙

A bushy shrub that grows up to 3m high and perhaps as wide. The stems have thorns 1–2cm long. The leaves are light green and 2–3cm long. The solitary, round heads of yellow flowers, 1cm across, appear during early spring. The shrub produces its flowers when young. Because of its thorniness it can

make an impenetrable hedge, or it can be used as a sand barrier. Like all Acacias, it requires little summer water once established. Native to Australia (New South Wales).

A. retinodes SILVER WATTLE, SWAMP WATTLE ☙

A shrub or small tree growing 4–5m high and as wide, often with pendant stems, and usually having most of its foliage towards the ends of the branches. The narrow, willow-like leaves are up to 13cm long. The rich, yellow flowers are freely carried in large, loose, many-branched racemes during spring and early summer. One of the few lime-tolerant species. Wind-resistant, so it grows well near the coast. A large, rather short-lived and greedy shrub that is best planted away from more formal areas. Native to southern Australia (Victoria, Tasmania).

Acacia karroo

Acacia saligna

A. saligna BLUE LEAF WATTLE 🌙
A fast-growing tree, growing 5m or more high, spreading to 3–5m in perhaps three or four years, with a somewhat weeping habit. The leaves are narrow, blue-green, and 15–30cm long. The rich yellow flowers are freely carried in large, loose, many-branched racemes during early spring. The tree grows well in most soils. The stems are brittle, and large limbs can be damaged by wind, so prune to keep an open centre. Do not over-water as this encourages excess growth. Native to western Australia.

Acalypha
Euphorbiaceae

A genus containing about 430 species of evergreen shrubs, trees or annuals, coming from the tropical and subtropical regions of the world. They are mainly grown for their attractive leaves, and are often used as foliage pot plants in cooler climates.

A. wilkesiana COPPERLEAF 🌙🌙🌙
A bushy shrub up to 2m high and 1–2m wide. Grown for its attractive leaves that can be up to 20cm long and almost as wide; they are brilliantly marked with red and purple, or red, crimson and bronze, or green edged with yellow. There are many cultivars available. The flowers are fairly insignificant, appearing on spikes 20cm long.

Acalypha wilkesiana

The shrub grows best in a warm, sheltered spot as the leaves may be damaged by wind. It needs plenty of water during summer. Only grow in areas that have mild winters, as it can easily be killed by frost. In favoured locations it can make a spectacular hedge. It can also be used as a pot plant on sheltered terraces or balconies, where it should be kept on the dry side during winter. Native to Polynesia.

Acanthus 'BEAR'S BREECHES'
Acanthaceae

A genus of about thirty species of large-leaved herbaceous perennials or sub-shrubs. Native to the Mediterranean region. The bold leaves have inspired decorative features in Western art and architecture. They are ideal for planting in key positions where their striking features will be seen.

A. mollis GREEK ACANTHUS 🌙
A fast-growing, spreading, herbaceous perennial. The large basal leaves are a rich deep green, deeply lobed, and may be up to 60cm long. The stout spikes of white or lilac-pink, tubular flowers grow 60–90cm high; each flower has a spiny bract underneath, appearing from spring to early summer. The plant grows well under trees where little else will grow, as it tolerates light shade. Grows best in a rich, well drained soil but will also grow in dry, sunny areas.

Cut back stems after flowering, and remove the leaves when they become old or messy. Established clumps can be divided in the early spring. Native to south-west Europe, north-west Africa.

A. spinosus 🌙
This species is similar to *A. mollis* except that the leaves are more deeply cut, and each division is spined. The flowers are white and purple with shiny green bracts, and are produced from late spring to summer. This plant is more tolerant of drought. Use with caution as it can easily become invasive: the seed grows easily and the plant will regrow from any part of the root.

Acanthus spinosus

Acca
Myrtaceae

A small genus containing two to three species of evergreen shrubs or small trees from South America. One species is planted in warm countries for its edible fruit and ornamental flowers.

A. sellowiana (syn. *Feijoa sellowiana*)
PINEAPPLE GUAVA 🌙 or 🌙🌙
A large shrub or small tree up to 2m high with an equal spread, normally having many stems; these are often picturesquely twisted with a reddish-brown trunk. The oval, leathery leaves are 5–8cm long, grey-green above with a white felt underneath. In the late spring, flowers 4cm wide appear in the leaf axils, with fleshy crimson and white petals and a central bunch of long, crimson stamens. The petals are edible, making an unusual addition to a fruit salad. They are followed by 5–8cm, egg-shaped, greyish-green fruit: these are filled with soft, sweet, pineapple-like pulp that makes a good jelly. After flowering, the shrub can be pruned hard to keep it in shape. Can be

trained to form an espalier, screen, hedge or small tree. Drought-tolerant, but also grows well with plenty of summer water, including lawn-watering. Also withstands some frost. Can be propagated by seed, but selected, named varieties fruit best. Native to southern Brazil and Argentina.

Acer 'MAPLES'
Aceraceae

A genus of around 200 species of deciduous trees native to northern temperate regions of the world that flower in late winter or spring. Most Maples show leaf burn in summer heat and are therefore unsuitable for the Mediterranean region.

A. negundo
ASH-LEAVED MAPLE, BOX ELDER ☽

A fast-growing, hardy tree that quickly reaches 15m high and 10m wide, with bright green stems. The bright green, pinnate, toothed leaves are 5–10cm long, and divided into three to five lobes. The flowers appear before the leaves in spring; they are yellowish-green in pendulous bunches. Grow the tree in full sun; it requires little summer water once established. An

Acoelorrhaphe wrightii

Acca sellowiana

open tree that casts light shade and makes a good specimen. There are a number of brightly variegated and coloured forms that are susceptible to the burning heat of summer. Native to North America.

Acoelorrhaphe
Arecaceae

A genus containing a single species of clumping palm native to south Florida, the West Indies and Central America. Often used in Florida as a street tree, and for park decoration.

A. wrightii (syn. *Paurotis wrightii*)
SILVER SAW PALMETTO, EVERGLADES PALM, SAW CABBAGE PALM ☽☽☽

A clustering palm that can spread from 2–6m wide, with stems up to 6m high. The slender stems are covered with brown fibres and old leaf bases. The rounded, fan-shaped leaves, up to 1m wide, are deeply cut, bright green above with a silver back, and borne on long leaf stalks armed with teeth. This palm grows well in full sun or partial shade. Fairly drought-tolerant, but it grows better with generous watering, and will even tolerate occasional boggy conditions. Grows well in a fertile soil, but it can take poor soil. Surprisingly hardy, it will generally resprout even if the stems are killed by severe frost. A mature clump of this palm makes an attractive specimen.

Actinidia
Actinidiaceae

A genus of about forty species of twining, climbing shrubs that are native to eastern Asia. Several make excellent climbers for the garden as they have handsome foliage, flowers or fruit.

A. deliciosa (syn. *A. chinensis*)
KIWI, CHINESE GOOSEBERRY ☽☽

A vigorous, deciduous, twining climber that can reach a height of 9m. The new growth has reddish, hairy shoots that have a habit of twining back upon themselves, so the stems can tangle easily. The large, bold, heart-shaped leaves are 15–23cm long and up to 20cm wide. In spring, the creamy-white, cup-shaped, 4cm wide, richly fragrant flowers appear in clusters. On female plants, edible fruits will develop, egg-sized and bristly brown. These are the kiwi fruit of commerce. A male should be grown nearby to provide pollination. To obtain good fruit buy named varieties. Grow in a deep, rich soil, and give generous feeding with ample summer water. Grows best in full sun, but will 'take' in partial shade. As it becomes large and heavy, strong supports should be given. Excellent for covering old walls, fences, or a large pergola. Native to China.

Adhatoda duvernoia
See *Justicia adhatoda*.

Adhatoda vasica
See *Justicia adhatoda*.

Aeonium
Crassulaceae

A genus of about thirty-six species of beautiful evergreen perennial succulents or subshrubs that come from Madeira, the Canary Islands, and nearby north-west Africa. It includes a number of popular greenhouse plants for cooler or temperate climates.

A. arboreum (syn. *Sempervivum aboreum*) TREE HOUSELEEK ☽

An upright, growing subshrub up to 1m high, with many branched stems, each ending with 15–20cm rosettes of leaves, each one 7–8cm long, giving it an appearance of a miniature tree. The leaves are 15cm long, and a glossy light green, fleshy and lightly fringed. The flowers are produced in pyramidal heads to 30cm high, containing many yellow, star-like flowers during winter. The plant is commonly grown on the tops of banks and walls, or in rock gardens. Especially good in hot, dry, sunny situations needing little summer water once established. Native to Morocco. The cultivar 'Atropurpureum', a beautiful purple form, is more often grown. The stems and leaves are a deep copper to dark purple colour during summer. For best leaf colour, grow in full sun.

Aeonium arboreum 'Atropurpureum'

A. canariense (syn. *A. exsul.*)
VELVET ROSE ☽

A short-stemmed succulent up to 20cm high that usually branches at the base. Produces beautifully symmetrical, large, deep, cup-shaped rosettes of leaves, up to 40cm across. They are dark green and spoon-shaped, up to 25cm long, with sticky hairs. The small, bright yellow flowers are produced in a pyramidal spike in spring, which can be up to 1m high. Suckers are readily produced, giving rise to many new plants. Can be grown in full sun, but grows better if given partial shade. Grow in fertile soil that is well drained. Give it deep but infrequent summer watering. Withstands light frosts. Native to the Canary Islands.

Aesculus 'BUCKEYE, HORSE CHESTNUT' *Hippocastanaceae*

A small genus of about fifteen species of deciduous trees and shrubs native to North America, south-east Europe and east Asia. They are grown for their long, dense, showy clusters of flowers produced at the ends of the branches.

A. californica CALIFORNIA BUCKEYE ☽

A low, broad tree or shrub, often with several stems up to 8m high, spreading to 10m wide, with silvery trunk and branches. Summer deciduous in dry areas, with leaves appearing with autumn rains. The leaves have five to seven leaflets 8–10cm long. In early summer it produces a mass of fragrant, white or pink-tinged flowers, with long, protruding stamens in dense, erect panicles up to 20cm long. They are followed by rough-skinned fruit 5–7cm long. Grow the tree in full sun. Easily cultivated, thriving in any soil. Only needs occasional water during summer. Native to California.

Agapanthus 'AFRICAN BLUE LILY' *Alliaceae*

A genus of about ten variable species of perennials with thick rhizomes and basal leaves native to the Cape of South Africa. The genus is much confused, with many garden varieties and hybrids being grouped under the names *A. africanus*, *A. orientalis* or *A. umbellatus*. Agapanthus should be lifted and their crowns divided every few years.

A. africanus (syn. *A. umbellatus*)
AFRICAN LILY ☽☽

A clump-forming, evergreen perennial with attractive metallic green leaves that are shorter and narrower than *A. orientalis*, to 35cm long. In early summer the stout flower stalks grow to 30–60cm high from within the leaves. Each stalk is topped with umbels of twelve to thirty deep violet-blue, trumpet-shaped flowers up to 4cm

Agapanthus praecox orientalis 'Albiflorus'

long; these may last for up to a month. The plant thrives with ample water during the spring growing season, but when established can survive without summer water. Grow in fertile, well drained soil in full sun or partial shade. This species is often confused with *A. praecox*, but is much less common in cultivation.

A. praecox subsp. *orientalis* (syn. *A. orientalis*) LILY OF THE NILE ☽☽

A clump-forming, evergreen perennial with evergreen leaves that are broad and arching, and up to 60cm in length. The 5cm or more long, trumpet-shaped flowers are borne on immense umbels with up to 200 blooms on a single head. The flower stems are 60–90cm long. Colours vary from light blue to deep violet and white. The plant is adaptable in that it can be grown in full sun or in shade. Thrives with plenty of water during spring, but can withstand

Agapanthus praecox orientalis

drought when established. If grown in containers or tubs it can make attractive displays on terraces or balconies. Free drainage especially in winter is important, as it must not become waterlogged. There are many cultivars, including 'Albiflorus' with white flowers, 'Nanus' which is dwarf and compact, and 'Variegatus' with striped leaves.

Agathaea

See *Felicia*.

Agave
Agavaceae

The genus contains about 300 species of small to giant, usually rosette-forming succulents, with stiff sword-shaped leaves. Native to Mexico or tropical America. Most species only flower when they are quite old, and then die leaving behind an offshoot for the next generation. They are ideal for coastal gardens as they withstand salt-laden sea-spray. They thrive in heat and drought.

A. americana CENTURY PLANT ☽
A stemless succulent that forms a large rosette next to the ground. The blue-green, stiff, thick, fleshy leaves are up

Agave americana

Agave americana 'Marginata'

to 30cm wide and 2m long, with hooked spines along the edge and a stout spine at the tip. The flower spike is produced in early summer on mature plants, and can grow to a gigantic 10m high before producing its masses of small, 9cm long, greenish flowers on many short branches. Once the plant has flowered it dies, but usually leaves a rosette of suckers at the base of the old stem. Not fussy about soil conditions, but requires full sun. Drought tolerant, needing no summer water. *A. americana* is often referred to as the Century Plant, which is misleading. This is because it was originally thought to flower only once a century, whereas in fact it can flower from ten years old to perhaps sixty years, depending on the soil and situation. Native to Mexico, but now naturalized over a wide area of the Mediterranean. There are many variegated forms, such as 'Marginata' with attractive, yellow-margined leaves; 'Mediopicta' with a broad, central splash of yellow; and 'Striata' with yellow or white stripes. It can make an attractive container plant when young.

A. angustifolia 'Marginata' ☽ or ☽☽
An evergreen perennial succulent that forms suckering, formal rosettes with short stems to 50cm high. The stiff, sword-shaped leaves are up to 50cm long, with white margins and short black spines. The terminal spine is usually tipped with red. The inflorescence can be 3m or more high, with

panicles of greenish-yellow flowers 5cm long. A beautiful plant that is more tender than other agaves. Grow in a warm, sheltered spot, and give occasional water during summer. Native to the West Indies.

Agave angustifolia

A. attenuata SWAN'S NECK AGAVE ☽☽
An evergreen perennial succulent that forms a trunk, which may branch, up to 2m high. When older it makes a clump of 2m across. The grey-green, fleshy leaves are 50–70cm long, and spineless on the margins. They are rather narrow at the base, wide in the centre, and taper to a soft tip. The beautiful, arching flower spike may reach to 4m high, and has dense clusters of greenish-yellow flowers, up to 6cm long, along the length of its spike. This plant is often called the Swan's Neck Agave because of the curious shape of the flower stem, which curves gracefully. Grows well in full sun or partial shade. Unlike other agaves it grows best in rich soil with ample summer water, but must have

Agave attenuata

good drainage. Makes a good container plant on a terrace near a pool. Native to central Mexico.

A. foetida
See *Furcraea foetida*.

Agonis
Myrtaceae

A small genus of about twelve species of evergreen trees and shrubs native to western Australia. They make attractive specimen trees.

A. flexuosa PEPPERMINT TREE, AUSTRALIAN WILLOW MYRTLE
A spreading, medium- to fast-growing tree, 6–12m high and 5–10m wide, with pendant, willow-like branches. The bright green, lance-shaped leaves, to 15cm long, densely cover the branches; they smell of peppermint when crushed. Many clusters of two to three, small, white, fragrant flowers, to 1cm across, are produced in summer. Grow the tree in full sun in fertile, neutral to acid soil. Requires little summer water once established. Makes an elegant specimen tree. Native to south-western Australia.

Ailanthus
Simaroubaceae

A small genus of about five species of tall, deciduous, fast-growing trees from east Asia to Australia. The male and female flowers are produced on separate trees.

A. altissima TREE OF HEAVEN
A rapid-growing tree up to 25m high, spreading to 15m wide. The pinnate leaves can be 60cm long, with up to thirty lance-shaped leaflets 8–14cm long. The young leaves open reddish-green. The small, greenish flowers are produced in terminal panicles to 30cm long in late summer. Female trees produce large bunches of reddish-winged seedpods. Only female, seed-producing trees should be grown, as male flowers produce a sweetish, unpleasant smell. An imposing tree that is often used as a street tree as it is extremely tolerant of atmospheric pollution, and keeps itself free from pests and diseases. Grows well in any soil, needs no summer water, and grows readily from seed. The tree is frost hardy. Often condemned as a weed, as it suckers freely and can soon form a thick mass of trees. Native to China.

Ajuga 'BUGLE'
Lamiaceae

A genus of about forty species of annuals or perennials native to much of Europe and Asia. Most of them have square stems. They reproduce vegetatively by means of runners, making them good groundcover.

A. reptans CARPET BUGLE
An evergreen perennial that spreads along the ground by means of runners forming a mat about 20cm high. The oblong leaves are up to 9cm long and 3cm wide. The normally blue flowers are in compact, pyramidal spikes 10–15cm high. They are produced in spring and early summer. The plain, green-leaved form is rarely grown as there are many coloured-leaved and variegated varieties with more interest. These include 'Bronze' with bronze leaves; 'Atropurpurea' with purple leaves; and 'Variegata' with grey-green leaves edged

Ailanthus altissima

Akebia quinata

with cream. All make good ground-cover in full sun, but grow better in partial shade. They need regular summer water and occasional division: they are easily increased by division. They are completely hardy. Native to Europe.

Akebia
Lardizabalaceae

A small genus of five species of vigorous, semi-evergreen, twining shrubs native to east Asia with attractive foliage and unusual fruit.

A. quinata CHOCOLATE VINE ☘☘
A semi-evergreen or deciduous hardy climbing shrub up to 10m high. The deep green leaves are divided into five oblong leaflets 5–8cm long, carried on stalks 8–10cm long. The small, vanilla-scented male and female flowers are produced separately along the same pendant raceme, to 12cm long, in spring. They are chocolate-purple and not very showy. Its main attraction is the 5–10cm long, sausage-shaped, greyish-violet fruits which, when they split open in autumn, contain numerous black seeds embedded in a white cottonwool-like pulp. They are edible but rather insipid. The climber can be grown in full sun but prefers some shade, but should not be given too rich a soil as it may become invasive. Benefits from an annual pruning to keep it a reasonable size, and will quickly recover if cut to the ground. Makes an unusual climber for covering a pergola or for climbing over other shrubs and into trees. Easily raised from seed. Native to Japan, Korea and China.

A. trifoliata THREE-LEAVED AKEBIA ☘☘
This deciduous species is similar to A. quinata, but smaller and more dainty. The wavy-edged leaves are divided into three leaflets instead of five. The dark maroon flowers appear in pendant racemes in spring. The 12cm long, sausage-shaped fruits are often in groups of three. Native to Japan and China.

Albizia
Mimosaceae

A genus of about 150 species of mostly deciduous trees or shrubs and climbers native to tropical and subtropical regions of Africa, and from Asia to Australia. They are grown as ornamentals in tropical and subtropical gardens for their light, feathery, attractive foliage.

A. julibrissin SILK TREE ☘☘ or ☘☘☘
A deciduous tree to 10m high with a spread of 6m and a domed crown. The light green, pinnate leaves are 30–45cm long, and are light sensitive so they fold at night. The beautiful flowers are pink, in terminal, fluffy clusters 7–15cm wide, and appear in summer. They are followed by thin seedpods that are 15cm long. The flowers look their best when viewed from above. This tree can be difficult to establish. Can make an excellent shade tree with its flat top, ideal for a patio or terrace. Grows best with high summer heat and ample water. Native from Iran east to Japan. The variety 'Rosea' has richer, pink flowers.

A. lophantha (syn. A. distachya, Paraserianthes lophantha)
PLUME ALBIZIA ☘
A fast-growing, semi-evergreen tree that quickly reaches up to 10m high, spreading to 3m wide. The beautiful pinnate or doubly pinnate leaves are dark velvety green, and can grow up to 30cm long. The yellow or greenish-yellow 'bottle brush' cylindrical racemes of flowers are 5cm long, and are produced in axillary spikes in the early spring. This fast-growing tree soon ages, so treat it as a temporary screening while other plants become established. Drought tolerant, and often naturalizes. Native to Australia.

Albizia julibrissin 'Rosea'

Albizia lophantha

Alcea 'HOLLYHOCK'
Malvaceae

A genus of about sixty species of biennials, or short-lived perennials, native to temperate regions of Europe and Asia. They are grown for their tall flower spikes.

A. rosea (syn. Althaea rosea) ◡
A tall, vigorous, upright, leafy-stemmed, hairy biennial, up to 3m high. The big, roundish, heart-shaped leaves are up to 4cm long. They are three- to seven-lobed and roughly hairy. The single, semi-double or double, open, funnel-shaped flowers 8–15cm wide appear in long, terminal spikes in early summer. The colours range from white, pink, rose, red and purple, to yellow, apricot and deep chocolate-maroon. An old-fashioned, favourite plant that grows well in a hot, sunny place in any light, well drained soil with added organic matter. Easily raised from seed sown in autumn or winter. Grows well with no summer water, but flowers better if given regular summer water. Native to Turkey, but naturalized around the Mediterranean region. 'Charters Double' is a fine double strain, and 'Majorette' is a dwarf strain growing to 60cm high.

Allamanda
Apocynaceae

A genus of about twelve species of evergreen shrubs and climbers native to Brazil and tropical America, usually having a milky sap. They are much grown in the tropics for covering trees and fences.

A. cathartica GOLDEN TRUMPET VINE ◡◡◡
A tall, evergreen, tropical climber that can reach up to 15m high. The leathery, dark, lance-shaped leaves, 10–15cm long, are arranged in whorls of three or four. The large, golden-yellow, showy, trumpet-shaped flowers are up to 10cm long. They are produced in small racemes at the ends of the branches. The flowers are produced almost continually from summer until autumn. The climber flourishes on baking south and west walls and over banks. Allamandas should be given plenty of summer water so they never dry out. They should also be given some protection from the wind. Easily propagated from cuttings. Native to Central and South America. 'Grandiflora' has larger and more profuse flowers; 'Hendersonii' has bronze-tinted buds, and the yellow flowers have white flecks in the throat.

Alcea rosea

Allamanda cathartica

Allium 'ONION'
Alliaceae

A vast genus of perhaps 700 species of bulbous or rhizomatous perennials that have a strong smell when bruised; native mainly to the northern hemisphere. The following are just a selection from the many that are worth growing in the garden. All alliums are easy to grow in most well drained soils, in full sun or partial shade. They are drought tolerant, but need water while in growth. They are effective in borders and rock gardens. Many make good cut flowers.

A. caeruleum (syn. A. azureum)
BLUE ALLIUM ◡
A bulbous perennial with bulbs that are nearly round. The linear, stem-clasping leaves are 7cm long. They die before the flower spike appears in early summer. The flower spike, up to 60cm high, is topped with a dense, round cluster, 5cm across, of thirty to fifty bright blue, star-shaped flowers each 2cm across. Native to north and central Asia.

A. flavum ◡
A bulbous perennial with narrow, semi-clasping leaves to 20cm long. The 1–2cm wide, yellow flowers are bell-shaped in pendant clusters of up to sixty with prominent stamens. They appear on stalks of 10–30cm in summer. An easily grown species. Native to southern Europe.

A. giganteum GIANT ALLIUM ◡◡
A bulbous perennial with strap-shaped leaves up to 45cm long and 5cm wide. They die before the flower spike appears. Spectacular, dense, ball-like clusters 12cm across may contain fifty or more lilac, star-shaped flowers with prominent stamens. They appear in summer on stout stems up to 1.5m

Alocasia macrorrhiza

high. An eye-catching species that makes good cut flowers.

A. *moly* GOLDEN GARLIC

A bulbous, clump-forming perennial with lance-shaped leaves up to 30cm long and 5cm wide. In summer the bright yellow, star-shaped flowers are borne in open clusters to 5cm across, containing up to forty flowers on stalks 25–45cm high. Spreads rapidly; ideal for naturalizing around shrubs. Native to southern Europe.

A. *sikkimense* (syn. *A. kansuense. A. tibeticum*)

A bulbous, clump-forming perennial with narrow leaves to 30cm long. The bell-shaped, bright blue or white flowers hang in clusters on stems up to 25cm high. They appear in early summer. Native to Tibet, Nepal, India (Sikkim).

Alocasia
Araceae

A genus of about seventy species of upright-growing perennials that form rhizomes, native to tropical Asia. They are grown for their bold and often variegated or marked foliage.

A. *macrorrhiza* ELEPHANT'S EAR

A massive perennial with a stout, thick stem, up to 2m high. Grown for its huge, shield-shaped leaves that can reach to 1m wide and over 1m long, and are carried on 1.5m long stalks. They are mid- to deep green, with a prominent midrib and a wavy edge. The tiny flowers on a spike are surrounded by a greenish-white spath. Give the plant plenty of summer water, and a good rich soil with lots of organic material and fertiliser. Grow in a well sheltered place with some shade, even

deep shade. It can also be used as a bog plant, standing in the edge of the water in a pond. Makes a good pot plant for a shady terrace, giving a lush, tropical effect. This is the hardiest Alocasia, as it will withstand a light frost. Native to Malaysia and Sri Lanka.

Aloe
Aloeaceae

A large genus of around 300 species of succulents, shrubs and trees native to the arid parts of Africa, Madagascar and the Arabian peninsula. Usually stemless, but sometimes with simple, branched stems. Showy, easily grown, needing little summer water.

A. *arborescens* TREE ALOE

A much-branching succulent that forms clumps up to 4m high with an equal spread. The grey-green, sword-like, fleshy, tapering leaves, to 60cm long, form rosettes: these are curved, with spikes along the edges. In winter this aloe produces 80cm-high spikes of bright red; 4cm-long flowers. Ideal for coastal planting as it withstands salt-laden sea spray. Thrives in the heat and drought, growing happily in the poorest of soils. When older it makes a most impressive and beautiful mound

Aloe arborescens

of leaves. Native to South Africa. 'Variegata' has yellow-striped leaves.

A. *ciliaris* CLIMBING ALOE

A climbing, sprawling succulent with weak, branching stems to 3m long. The 15cm long leaves with white teeth along the edge are evenly spaced along the stems in spirals. In spring to early summer the scarlet-red flowers with yellowish-green tips appear on stems 30 cm long. Each flower is about 3cm long. Like other aloes, it likes hot dry conditions, but will take some shade. Native to South Africa.

Aloe ciliaris

A. *ferox* FEROCIOUS ALOE

A succulent with a bold rosette of leaves that usually produces a single stout stem to 2m high. The fleshy, broadly lance-shaped leaves are hollow above, curved underneath and often spiny. They are grey-green to bronze-green, edged with brown-red teeth and up to 1m long. The upright terminal flower spike produced in summer is 1m or more long with many branches. This is covered with tubular scarlet or orange flowers 2–3cm long. The plant is slow-growing. Thrives in the heat and drought, although it grows better if given occasional summer water. Grow in full sun or partial shade. This large, bold plant is ideal for the dry garden. Native to South Africa.

A. *plicatilis* FAN ALOE

A many-branched shrub or tree that with age may reach to 3m or more high. The strap-shaped leaves are 30cm long, pale glaucous blue with a pale edge, and completely spineless. They are closely packed on the tips of the stems in one plane-like a fan. In spring, 50cm-high spikes of scarlet to orange,

Aloe ferox

6cm long flowers appear. The plant is slow-growing, reaching perhaps 1.5m in ten years. With age it develops an attractive, gnarled trunk; it makes a good container plant when young. Native to South Africa.

A. saponaria SOAP ALOE ⌡
A short-stemmed or stemless succulent that makes large clumps. The fleshy, broad, thick, lance-shaped leaves are 15–20cm long; they are bluish-green with yellow-green bands, and have sharp teeth along the edges. The branched flower stalk rises from the centre to 70cm high in summer. This is topped with yellow to red, 4cm-long flowers over a long time. The clumps spread rapidly so may need dividing after a few years. Thrives in the heat and drought, although grows better if given occasional summer water. Native to Zimbabwe and Botswana.

A. vera TRUE ALOE, MEDICINAL ALOE ⌡
A succulent that forms a stemless clump of vase-shaped rosettes that can spread to cover several metres. The narrow, fleshy, dagger-shaped upright leaves are up to 60cm long, and edged with whitish to reddish teeth. The 2cm long, round, yellow flowers hang on spikes up to 1m long, which appear from winter to spring. Although the plant is drought tolerant, it looks better if given some summer water. Looks impressive when planted in bold groups in a landscape. A major source of the drug aloe which is used to treat burns and skin abrasions. Native to the Mediterranean region.

Aloysia
Verbenaceae
A genus of around thirty species of aromatic, tender shrubs native to the warmer parts of North and South America. Only one species is common in cultivation, which is often sold incorrectly as *Lippia citrodora*.

A. triphylla (syn. *Lippia citrodora*)
LEMON VERBENA ⌡
A deciduous or partially evergreen shrub that makes straggly, open growth to 2m high and wide. It is mainly valued for the lemon scent of the leaves. They are narrow and lance-shaped, 8–10cm long, normally in whorls of three or four along the stems. The tiny, pale lilac, insignificant flowers are borne in spiked terminal panicles 12cm long during summer. The leaves can be used in potpourri and in cooking. The shrub can be grown in pots or containers near the house so that the lemon scent can be appreciated. For this purpose it should be kept small by frequent pinching of the shoots. Grows best in full sun, in soil with good drainage, and given little summer water. Native to Argentina and Chile.

Alpinia 'Ginger Lily'
Zingiberaceae
A large genus of over 250 evergreen rhizomatous perennials that grow in clumps. Native to moist tropical areas of India, China and south-east Asia. They are grown for their spectacularly showy flowers.

A. zerumbet SHELL FLOWER,
SHELL GINGER ⌡⌡⌡
A majestic perennial that forms a clump of leafy stems. Individual stems grow up to 2m high, with broad, strap-like leaves 60cm long and 15cm wide arranged in two rows. The terminal inflorescence is pendulous to 40cm long, containing many shell-like flowers. The individual flowers are magnificent as they are fragrant, white, tipped with a delicate pink, opening to show a yellow and red interior. They have a porcelain-like texture. The plant is commonly grown in warm regions, but will withstand slight frost. Grows best in a shady border, but will take the sun. Needs a wind-free location with frequent watering. Propagation is by division in spring, but individual stems need to be established two years

Aloysia triphylla

Alpinia zerumbet

before they flower. Remove the stems that have flowered in autumn. Native to subtropical China and southern Japan.

Alstroemeria
Alstroemeriaceae

A genus of about sixty species of herbaceous perennials native to South America, with thick, elongated fibrous roots. Nurseries differ as to what name they sell them by, so there is much confusion. Hybrids are easily raised from seed.

A. aurea (syn. *A. aurantiaca*)
PERUVIAN LILY ﻪﻪ
A tuberous, herbaceous perennial with leafy stems to perhaps 1m high. The narrow, lance-shaped leaves are 10cm long and pale green, often having a twist in the leaf which brings the

Alstroemeria hybrids

underside of the leaf uppermost. The stems are topped with many long stalked, bright orange or yellow flowers about 5cm in length. They are often spotted with chocolate-brown. There are many cultivars, such as 'Dover Orange' with orange-red flowers, and 'Lutea' with pure bright yellow flowers. They are best planted in a moist, deep, sandy soil 30cm apart. They should be planted carefully, as their roots are delicate. Leave the clumps undisturbed for many years. The tops will die down when flowering has finished. The plants need an average amount of summer water while they are flowering. They are ideal for Mediterranean gardens as the flowers are produced in great quantities during summer, making masses of colour in the border. The flowers are also long-lasting when cut. Native to Chile.

A. Ligtu hybrids ﻪﻪ
These hybrids are the most commonly available as they look most attractive. The growth is similar to the above, but the trumpet-shaped flowers come in a wide range of colours – pink, whitish, orange or yellow, and often streaked or speckled with darker colours. Cultivation is the same as the above species. They are easily raised from seed sown in autumn or early spring. Garden origin.

Althaea rosea

See *Alcea rosea*.

Alyogyne
Malvaceae

A genus of about six species of small shrubs from southern and western Australia. They were formerly included in Hibiscus.

A. huegelii (syn. *Hibiscus huegelii*) ﻪ
An evergreen shrub with upright growth to 2m high. The stems are usually covered in a fine bloom. The small, coarsely hairy leaves are deeply three- to five-lobed, dark green and up to 6cm long. The numerous single flowers are 10–12cm wide, lilac blue to deep purple with spreading petals. The flowers last two to three days each, and are produced in flushes throughout the year. The plants are easily raised from seed, but the colour will vary. Pinch out the tips to encourage bushiness. The shrub grows best in full sun. When established it requires little summer water. Native to western Australia.

Alyogyne huegeii

Amaranthus
Amaranthaceae

A genus of about fifty species of coarse annuals native to mild and tropical climates around the world. Cultivated for their coloured foliage or large spikes of flowers. Some are grown as vegetables, while others are weeds.

A. caudatus LOVE-LIES-BLEEDING ﻪﻪ
A stout, branching upright annual, to 2m high. The ovate leaves are up to 25cm long and 10cm wide. The tiny, vividly coloured, red flowers appear in long, trailing tassels that are extremely showy. The plants are easily raised each

Amaranthus paniculatus

year from seed, indeed it may self-seed. Prefers full sun, but will take partial shade. During summer it needs a moderate amount of water. Cultivated in India for food, the seeds are used as grain and the young leaves are edible. Native to the tropics.

A. paniculatus ◡◡

A widely grown, summer-flowering annual, to 2m high, with stems often splashed with red or entirely red. The large, ovate leaves can be up to 30cm long with an 18cm stalk. They are highly variable in colour, from pale green to splashed or marked with red, or reddish-green with a brilliant red or bronze underside. The minute flowers are in a large, branched inflorescence perhaps 45cm long. The colour is normally red, but can vary to purple. The plant prefers to be grown in full sun with a moderate amount of summer water. Easily raised from seed. Native to tropical America.

A. tricolor JOSEPH'S COAT ◡◡

A vigorous, erect, much-branching annual, to 1m or more high. The ovate, pointed, brilliantly coloured leaves are up to 15cm long and 10cm wide. They are blotched and marked with colours of crimson, marbled red, green and yellow. The slender flower spikes are insignificant and should be removed for better leaf colour. The plant prefers full sun, but will

take partial shade. Needs a moderate amount of summer water. Easily raised from seed. Green-leaved strains are grown in tropical Asia as a vegetable.

Amaryllis
Amaryllidaceae

A genus of just one species of deciduous South African bulb. For plants with the common name 'Amaryllis', *see* Hippeastrum.

A. belladonna BELLADONNA LILY ◡

The strap-like leaves of this deciduous bulb are 20–40cm long, appear in autumn and fade in spring. The bulb is dormant after the leaves have disappeared. In autumn the clusters of solid reddish flower stalks appear 30–60cm high. They are topped with clusters of four to twelve lovely trumpet-shaped, rosy pink, fragrant flowers, each one 10cm long. The bulb grows well in full sun in most fertile, well drained soils. When established it withstands drought, but grows better with some summer water. Naturalizes well in hot dry climates. This long-lasting bulb should not be disturbed as it flowers better if crowded, and indeed may not flower for several years if divided at the wrong time. Only divide immediately after flowering. Plant with the neck of the bulb at ground level.

Anigozanthos
Haemodoraceae

A genus of about ten species of clump-forming perennials with thick rootstocks, native to Australia. They bear curious tubular flowers that resemble kangaroos' paws.

A. flavidus KANGAROO PAW ◡◡◡

An evergreen perennial that will grow into a clump 60–80cm wide. The narrow, dark green, lance-shaped leaves are 35cm or more long. From late spring to autumn it produces stiff, branching flower spikes to 1m or more high. They carry about ten large, curious woolly flowers comprising a long bent tube that is yellowish-green, tinged red, and 4cm long with blue petals. They hybridize freely both in the wild and in cultivation, the colours of named hybrids ranging from deep red to pure yellow. The plant grows best in full sun in light sandy soil, with regular water during summer. Remove old flowerheads from the base. Divide in early spring. Native to south-west Australia.

A. manglesii
MANGLES' KANGAROO PAW ◡◡◡

An evergreen perennial, with rosettes of upright grey-green leaves up to 60cm long. From mid-spring to autumn it produces stiff flower spikes to 1m or

Amaryllis belladonna

more high, covered in red hair. They carry racemes 5–14cm long, of up to seven yellowish-green, woolly 8cm tubular flowers. They are red at the calyx with dark green lines, while the lip is reflexed and darker. Cultivation is the same as *A. flavidus*. Native to south-west Australia.

Anisodontea 'CAPE MALLOW'
Malvaceae

A genus of nineteen species of evergreen shrubs and woody perennials native to South Africa. They are grown for their masses of small red flowers. They look good in the front of a sunny border.

A. capensis (syn. *Malvastrum capensis*) ◡

A fast-growing, woody perennial up to 2m high, spreading to 1m wide, with hairy stems. Growth is open and freely branching. The triangular, hairy leaves are about 2–3cm long, with three or five deep lobes, each of which may be lobed or toothed. The 2–3cm wide flowers are purplish-pink with deeper pink veining and a dark basal spot. They are single, or in two to three flowered racemes from the leaf axils. Large quantities are produced mainly from summer until autumn, but it may continue to flower throughout the year. The plant will grow in most well drained soils in full sun, needing little or no summer water once established. Easily grown from seed.

Anisodontea capensis

Annona
Annonaceae

A genus of about a 100 species of trees and shrubs native to tropical America. They are generally grown for their fruit, but also make attractive specimen trees.

A. cherimola CHERIMOYA, CUSTARD APPLE ◡◡◡

A briefly deciduous tree up to 8m high, that grows fast in the first few years, then slows down, eventually spreading up to 6m wide. An attractive tree with a spreading, picturesque habit. The large, luxuriant, leathery leaves are 10–25cm long, dull green with pale veins, and velvety on the underside. Thick, fleshy, fragrant flowers 3cm long appear directly from the woody branches in spring. They are yellow or brown hairy outside, whitish with purple spots inside. They open as the leaves begin to drop and continue for three to four months. The flowers are followed by large, conical, green fruit, 12cm long and containing large black seeds. The skin looks like overlapping scales. The creamy-white flesh tastes like custard or bananas, and is usually eaten fresh. For best fruiting, flowers are hand-pollinated. Grow the tree in full sun in well drained soil, giving generous summer water. Native to Peru and Ecuador.

Anredera
Baselliaceae

A small genus of ten species of tuberous-rooted, twining evergreen climbers native to South America.

A. cordifolia (syn. *Boussingaultia baselloides*) MADEIRA VINE ◡◡

A rapidly growing, twining climber to 6m high and wide, with reddish-green stems. The fleshy, ovate to lance-shaped leaves are 3–8cm long, often with tubers in the axils. The tiny, sweetly fragrant white flowers appear in racemes 30cm long, in late summer. Grow the climber in full sun with moderate summer water. Useful for summer screening over a patio, or grown into a tree. Divide the tuberous roots in early spring. Native to Paraguay, to southern Brazil and to northern Argentina.

Antigonon
Polygonaceae

A small genus containing just two or three species of climbers with tendrils that are native to moist tropical Mexico and Central America. Only one species is grown, which has tuberous roots.

A. leptopus CORAL VINE, QUEEN'S WREATH ◡◡ or ◡◡◡

A strong deciduous climber that makes rapid growth to 10m high. The dark green, deeply veined leaves are heart- or arrow-shaped and 8–13cm long. The strong, hooked tendrils appear from the leaf axils. The pretty, bright rose-pink flowers are 1–2cm long, borne in long racemes ending in tendrils; they appear in profusion from summer to autumn. The climber is easily grown in full sun, loving the high summer heat. While it will tolerate some drought, it may die back with prolonged dry periods. It flowers best with ample summer water. The tubers are edible, having a nutty flavour. A wonderful climber to grow in the hottest part of the garden where it can grow over the eaves of the house, over garden walls, or climb into trees. It could also drape its flowers and foliage over pergolas, or provide shade for a terrace. As it flowers mostly on new growth, cut it back in autumn to promote strong, new growth. Native to Mexico. 'Album' has white flowers.

Antigonon leptopus

Aptenia
Aizoaceae

A genus of just two species of prostrate, shrubby, short-lived perennial succulents native to South Africa.

A. cordifolia (syn. *Mesembryanthemum cordifolium*) DEW PLANT ◡◡

A many-branched succulent with trailing stems 60cm long, but growing only 5cm high. The cylindrical, soft fleshy stems are greenish. The fleshy, ovate, bright green leaves are 2–3cm long. The small, solitary flowers, just 1cm wide, are red or purple, and are produced continuously throughout the summer. The succulent needs little summer water and is tolerant of heat and poor

Aptenia cordifolia

soil. When grown on the tops of walls or on banks in full sun it will flower profusely. Also makes good ground cover. Easily propagated from cuttings. Often misnamed *Mesembryanthemum* to which it is closely related. The variety 'Variegata' has leaves attractively edged with white.

Aralia japonica
See *Fatsia japonica*.

Aralia papyrifera
See *Tetrapanax papyrifer*.

Aralia sieboldii
See *Fatsia japonica*.

Araucaria
Araucariaceae

A genus of about eighteen species of tall coniferous trees native to South America, Australia and the Pacific Islands. They make elegant specimen trees for the larger garden and parks.

A. araucana MONKEY PUZZLE TREE
A large, coniferous tree up to 20m high spreading to 10m wide with whorled branches. The tree is conical when young, but becomes rounded with age, losing its lower branches. The greyish-brown trunk is straight, with strongly rigid, heavy, spreading branches that are closely set with dark green leaves, 3–5cm long with a sharp point. They are arranged radially on the branches, and can persist for many years. Cones are produced on the upper branches, though male and female cones are borne on separate trees. Grow the tree in full sun in any well drained soil, with regular summer water. An arboreal oddity that makes an elegant specimen tree for the larger garden. Native to Chile and Argentina.

A. bidwillii BUNYA-BUNYA
A large, coniferous tree that makes moderate growth up to 30m high, spreading to 10m wide, with whorled branches. The tree is conical when young, but develops a rounded crown with age, which gives dense shade. The tree gradually loses its lower branches revealing its blackish-brown bark. There are two kinds of leaves: juvenile ones 2–5cm long that are narrow, glossy, deep green and lance-shaped, spreading mostly in two rows; and adult ones 2–3cm long, oval to lance-shaped, thick leathery, dark glossy green and spine-tipped that are spirally arranged and overlap along the branches. The female cones are huge, up to 27cm long and spherical in shape, resembling pineapples; these weigh several kilograms, crashing to the ground when ripe. Grow the tree in full sun in any well drained soil with regular summer water. An interesting specimen tree for the larger garden. Native to Australia.

A. cunninghamii
HOOP PINE, MORETON BAY PINE
A majestic, evergreen coniferous tree that may eventually reach 50m high with a spread of 6m wide. Generally columnar or conical in shape, with a reddish-brown peeling bark. Mature

Araucaria bidwillii

Araucaria cunninghamii

trees have tufted twig clusters at the ends of naked branches. On young trees the leaves are short, 1–2cm long, needle-like, bluish-green and spirally arranged; on mature trees they are crowded, awl-shaped to lanceolate, overlapping and incurved 6–8mm long. The cylindrical male cones are 5–9cm long, while the ovoid female cones are up to 10cm long and 5cm in diameter. Grow the tree in full sun in any well drained soil with regular summer water. An interesting specimen tree for the larger garden. Native to eastern Australia where it is an important timber tree.

A. heterophylla NORFOLK ISLAND PINE
A usually conical, coniferous tree. Mature trees may reach 25–30m or more high, and spread 7–10m wide, with whorled branches. Makes moderate growth at first, then slow with age. When juvenile it makes a formal pyramid shape, with horizontal branches in tiers of bright green. The juvenile leaves are 1–2cm long, incurved with a sharp point; older leaves are triangular and overlapping. Although the tree will eventually become large, it makes an interesting pot or container plant for many years. It needs to be grown in full sun and given regular summer water. Grows well in coastal

Araucaria heterophylla

areas as it withstands salt-laden sea breezes. When older it makes a striking skyline tree, with evenly tiered branches. Native to Norfolk Island.

Arbutus 'STRAWBERRY TREE' *Ericaceae*

A genus of about fourteen species of evergreen trees and shrubs native from western North America to Mexico and Guatemala, and the Mediterranean region. They often have attractive peeling bark and showy fruit.

A. menziesii MADRONO ❯

An evergreen shrub or tree that can grow from 6m to 15m high, and spread as wide, with a distinctive reddish bark that peels in flakes. The leathery, glossy green leaves are oval to elliptic, to 15cm long, with a dull grey-green underneath. Large erect clusters, to 20cm high, of white to pinkish, bell-shaped flowers 5mm long appear at the branch ends in spring. They are followed by brilliant orange to scarlet, pebble-skinned fruit, 1cm wide, which ripen in the autumn of the following year. The shrub can be difficult to establish as its requirements are exacting. The soil must be fast draining and slightly acid. When established it withstands some drought, but it grows better with occasional deep watering. Native to western North America.

A. unedo STRAWBERRY TREE ❯

An evergreen shrubby tree up to 8m high and spreading as wide, often with basal suckers and a reddish bark that peels. The trunk tends to become twisted, giving it a gnarled appearance when old. The leathery, glossy green leaves are oval to elliptic to 10cm long. The small white or pinkish bell-like flowers open in pendant panicles to 5cm long in autumn. The 2cm round red fruit ripen the following autumn, so that the flowers and fruits are produced simultaneously. The tree grows well in a wide range of soils and climates, being unusual among ericaceous plants for its lime tolerance. It also tolerates wind, so it grows well in coastal gardens as it withstands salt-laden sea breezes. Grow in full sun or partial shade. It needs little summer water once established. The fruit are sometimes distilled into a fiery spirit called 'Medronho'. Native to southern Europe.

Arbutus unedo

Archontophoenix 'KING PALM' *Arecaceae*

A genus of just two species of single-stemmed palms native to Queensland, Australia. They make magnificent palms for warm gardens.

A. cunninghamiana
BUNGALOW PALM ❯❯❯

A slender-stemmed, fast-growing palm with a smooth green trunk that is not enlarged at the base, up to 20m high and with a spread of 2–5m. The graceful, arching, pinnate fronds are up to 3m long, with broad, lance-shaped leaflets, dark green on both sides, and 8–10cm wide. When mature it produces small lilac flowers in a pendulous inflorescence to 90cm long in summer. These are followed by small red fruit. Grow the palm in sun or shade in a deep, well drained, humus-rich soil. It looks its best

Archontophoenix cumminghamiana

with a moderate amount of summer water. When young it will tolerate the shade of tall trees, but it can be damaged by strong wind. Easily grown from seed, but difficult to transplant successfully when large. Mature palms are frost hardy, but young palms can be damaged by frost. A good palm for warm, nearly frost-free areas.

Arctotis (syn. Venidoarctotis, Venidium) *Asteraceae*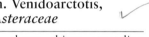

A genus of about thirty spreading annuals or perennials native to South Africa. 'African Daisy' can refer to many plants, as there is much confusion on the part of seed companies and nurseries.

A. × *hybrida* AFRICAN DAISY ❯

An evergreen, stemless perennial that grows to 30cm high, and spreads 30cm or more wide. The leaves are 15–30cm long and felted, indented or lobed, and lance-shaped; they are silvery-green, and grow from the base in rosettes. The solitary, daisy-like flowers come in many colours: cream, yellow, orange, pink, red or purple, and many have central zones of contrasting colours. They are 8–10cm across, borne on stems up to 45cm high, and are produced from spring to early summer, the best occurring in the plant's first year. The flowers tend to close in the

Arctosis × hybrida

afternoon or during dull weather. The plants need water only during the winter growing season once established. They make an excellent, quick-growing groundcover for sunny, dry areas, especially on slopes. If the conditions are right they will self-sow, but will probably revert to orange.

Areca lutescens
See *Dypsis lutescens*.

Arecastrum romanzoffianum
See *Syagrus romanzoffiana*.

Argyranthemum 'MARGUERITE'
Asteraceae

A genus of twenty-three species of evergreen subshrubs native to the Canary Islands and Madeira. They are grown for their abundant daisy-like flowers that make them popular in gardens in southern Europe.

A. foeniculaceum ⏾ or ⏾⏾

A compact, evergreen subshrub that grows to 1m round in its first year. The feathery, glaucous, blue-green leaves, 5–10cm long, are finely dissected. The single, daisy-like flowers, 3–5cm wide, consist of a central yellow disc floret with radiating white ray florets; they are produced mainly during winter, but can appear almost continuously. The plant is quick-growing, but it should be replaced every three to four years to look its best. Fairly drought tolerant, needing little summer water, but it will flower better with the occasional soaking. Excellent for the front of a sunny border; it also makes an ideal pot or container plant for a sunny terrace. Do not prune back into hard wood as it seldom shoots out. With care it can be trained into a standard, which looks wonderful in a pot.

Argyranthemum 'Jamaica Primrose'

Argyranthemum foeniculaceum

A. frutescens (syn. *Chrysanthemum frutescens*) PARIS DAISY ⏾ or ⏾⏾

A variable evergreen subshrub, to 70–120cm high, with an equal spread. The coarsely dissected, bright green to greyish leaves are 5–10cm long. The single white flowerheads have a central yellow disc floret, 2–3cm across; they are produced throughout most of the year, but mainly in spring. Like *A. foeniculaceum*, it is fairly drought-tolerant and needs little summer water, but will flower better with the occasional soaking. Grows well in any well drained soil. For continual flowering, prune lightly and frequently. Replace the plant every three to four years as it then becomes old and woody, with few flowers.

A. hybrids ⏾ or ⏾⏾

Much hybridizing has taken place, resulting in a wide range of attractive flower colours and forms. The foliage and cultural requirements are similar to the above. 'Jamaica Primrose' bears primrose yellow, single flowers. 'Mary Wootton' bears anemone-centred, light pink flowers. 'Powder Puff' is compact with pale pink, double flowers. 'Snow-flake' has semi-double, white flowers.

Aristea
Iridaceae

A genus of about fifty evergreen, clump-forming perennials, native to tropical and southern Africa. They are grown for their spikes of generally blue flowers. Once established, they resent being moved.

Ariesta ecklonii

A. ecklonii ⏾⏾

A strong-growing, evergreen, rhizomatous perennial that forms a clump to 40cm or more, with sword like basal leaves to 60cm long. The branched flower-stalk rises from among the leaves, bearing smaller stem-clasping leaves. The bright blue, six-petalled, saucer-shaped flowers, 2cm across, are borne throughout the summer. Each flower is short-lived, but new ones are being continually produced. Grow this perennial in full sun or partial shade, in well drained soil. Give moderate summer water, though it will withstand some drought once established. Easily raised from seed. Seedpods should be removed to prevent it becoming invasive. Native to central and southern Africa.

Aristolochia
Aristolochiaceae

A large genus of 300 perennial or evergreen climbers native to warm or tropical areas worldwide. They are grown for their unusual flowers that resemble a smoker's pipe, often with long tails protruding from the flowers.

A. *littoralis* (syn. *A. elegans*)
CALICO FLOWER ⌣⌣⌣

A tender, evergreen perennial that climbs by twining the stem around any support up to 5m high. The pale green, heart-shaped leaves are 8cm long. The solitary, whitish flower buds open to reveal heart-shaped, 10cm wide, purple-brown-splashed flowers; they become dark brown towards the centre, then a greenish-white, and are shaped like a Dutchman's pipe. These curious flowers are borne throughout summer. The climber needs to be grown in rich soil, and responds well to ample summer water. For best flowering, grow in partial shade. A wonderful and exotic climber for a shady wall. Native to Brazil.

A. *macrophylla* (syn. *A. durior*)
DUTCHMAN'S PIPE ⌣⌣⌣

A strong-growing, deciduous, twining climber that will extend to 6m high and wide. The large, heart-shaped to kidney-shaped, deep glossy green leaves are up to 30 cm long. The small (2cm across), solitary, yellowish-green flowers are mottled with purple and brown; they are shaped like a saxophone or curved pipe, and appear throughout the summer. The flowers are mostly hidden by the dense foliage. This climber grows best in partial shade, in a rich, well drained soil. Generous watering and feeding will produce the best growth and flowers. Can be cut back in winter if it becomes too big. Native to eastern USA.

Armeria 'SEA PINK, THRIFT'
Plumbaginaceae

A genus of perhaps eighty species of evergreen, low-growing, tufted perennials or subshrubs widely distributed in alpine regions, mountain meadows and coastal shores of Europe, Turkey and the Pacific coast of North and South America.

A. *maritima* SEA THRIFT ⌣

A cushion-forming, small perennial – to 20cm high, spreading to 30cm wide. The dense, narrow-linear, rich green basal leaves are up to 12cm long. The small flowers are in globular heads to 2cm diameter, on stiff stems to 20cm long. They are normally white to rose-pink, but selections have been made with brighter or deeper coloured flowers. The flowers are produced from spring into autumn. The plants are easily grown in full sun with little to moderate summer water, but need excellent soil drainage. They are ideal for the rock garden or for edging paths and borders. They also make good container plants. Native to mountain and coastal areas of the northern hemisphere.

Artemisia
Asteraceae

A large genus of 200 or more species of mostly aromatic annuals, biennials, perennials, evergreen and deciduous shrubs. Native mostly to dry areas of the northern hemisphere, with a few from South Africa and western South America. Some have long been grown in the herb garden.

Artemesia arborescens

A. *abrotanum*
SOUTHERNWOOD, LAD'S LOVE ⌣

A deciduous or evergreen shrub, to about 1m high and as wide. The silky-hairy, grey-green leaves, up to 5cm long, have thread-like lobes with grey hairs underneath; they are highly aromatic. The insignificant clusters of small, yellowish-white flowers appear in late summer. Grow the shrub in full sun in borders, with little summer water. Useful near paths where its lemon-scented leaves can be appreciated. Native to southern Europe.

A. *arborescens* ⌣

A woody-based, shrubby perennial or shrub, to 1m or more high and wide, with silver-grey stems. The finely divided, silver, hairy leaves are up to 10cm long. Small yellow flowerheads are borne in leafy clusters to 30cm long in summer and through to autumn. A most attractive silver shrub, though it can become untidy with age; cut back hard in spring to maintain a compact habit. Grow in full sun in borders, with little summer water. Native to the Mediterranean region.

Aristolochia littoralis

Arundo donax

A. 'Powis Castle' ☽

A beautiful small shrub that forms a silvery, dense, bushy mound, 1m high and spreading to 2m wide. The deeply cut, silver-grey leaves are up to 6cm long. The insignificant panicles of yellow flowerheads appear in late summer. The shrub makes a good background for bright flowers, and an excellent ground-cover in full sun. Prefers to be grown in a well drained soil, with little summer water once established. Garden origin.

A. schmidtiana ANGELS' HAIR ☽

A rhizomatous, tufted perennial that forms a dome 30cm high and 45cm wide. The downy, silver, semi-evergreen leaves are much divided and about 4cm long. Tiny yellow flowers appear in pyramidal panicles to 10cm long in summer. Grow in a well drained soil, giving a little summer water once established. Looks good in a large rock garden. Native to Japan.

Arum 'LORDS AND LADIES'
Araceae

A genus of twenty-six species of tuberous perennials native to southern Europe, northern Africa and western Asia. They are grown for their glossy, often shield-shaped leaves and some-times brightly coloured spathes. All parts of the plant are poisonous, and the sap may irritate the skin.

A. dioscoridis ☽

A handsome, tuberous perennial, 20–30cm high; it is summer dormant. The thin, arrow-shaped, glossy dark green leaves, 20–30cm long, appear in autumn borne on long leaf stalks. The colourful, pale yellowish-green spathe appears in spring, up to 30cm high, with large purple blotches. This encloses thin spadices of tiny flowers that are unpleasantly scented. Grow the plant in a humus-rich, well drained soil in a sheltered site in sun or partial shade. Because it is summer dormant it needs only winter rains, so water during any dry spell in winter. Native to the eastern Mediterranean.

A. italicum ITALIAN ARUM ☽

A robust, tuberous perennial, 30cm high; summer dormant. The tubers are mostly cylindrical. The arrow-shaped, glossy dark green leaves, 20cm long with whitish veining, appear in autumn; they gradually wither during the early summer. In spring and early summer the greenish-white spathe appears; 15–40cm, it is upright at first, then folds over and conceals the short yellow spadices of tiny flowers. They are followed by spikes of attractive, berry-like, fleshy fruit: this turns scarlet red as the foliage withers, and may last until the new leaves appear. Grow the plant in a humus-rich, well drained soil in a sheltered site in partial shade. Because it is summer dormant it needs only winter rains, so water during any dry spell in winter. Native to Europe, Turkey and northern Africa. 'Marmoratum' has pronounced cream-veined leaves.

A. pictum BLACK CALLA ☽

A tuberous perennial, 15–25cm high, with arrow-shaped, glossy dark green leaves, 25cm long and carried on long leaf stalks, and with fine, creamy-white veins. The spathe is dark purple, almost black, and up to 20cm long; it appears in autumn, with the dark purple spadix extending beyond it. Like other arums, it is best grown in a humus-rich, well drained soil in a sheltered site in partial shade. Summer dormant, so it needs only winter rains, so water during any dry spell in winter. Native to Corsica, Sardinia and the Balearic Islands.

Arundinaria japonica
See *Pseudosasa japonica*.

Arundinaria murieliae
See *Fargesia murieliae*.

Arundo
Poaceae

A genus of about six species of giant rhizomatous grasses or reeds, native to riversides, dunes and ditches in the warm temperate regions of the northern hemisphere.

A. donax GIANT REED ☽☽☽

A rhizomatous perennial with some-what woody stems 2–5m high that resemble bamboo. It forms large clumps that can spread almost indefi-nitely. The arching, broadly linear, flat green leaves are up to 60cm long and 8cm wide, with rough margins. The inflorescence is a slender, erect, white to green or purplish plume, to 60cm high. The plant grows best in full sun. It grows in any soil, even coastal sand dunes, as long as it is always moist. For best foliage, cut the stems to the ground annually; for best flowers, leave canes for a second year. In the right condi-tions it can become invasive. Native to the Mediterranean region, naturalized in southern USA. The variety 'Versicolor' has grey-green leaves striped creamy-white; the stems grow to about 2m high. It is less invasive, but looks most impressive with its bold, bamboo-like canes and variegated leaves.

Asarina erubescrus

See *Lophospermum erubeoceus*.

Asclepias curassavica

Asclepias 'MILKWEED, SILKWEED'
Asclepiadaceae

A large genus containing about 200 species of perennials that are widely distributed, but are mainly native to North America and Africa. Most have a milky sap.

A. curassavica BLOOD FLOWER ꙮꙮ

A showy, evergreen perennial up to 1m high, with a single or branched stem. The pairs of lance-shaped leaves are up to 15cm long. The clusters of small flowers, 5–10cm across, appear terminally and in the leaf axils. The five-parted corolla is brilliant red and reflexed, exposing the crown of five orange hoods. They are produced from summer to autumn. An easily grown plant that will self-seed readily. Prefers to be grown in full sun, but requires regular summer water to flower well. Also prone to attacks by aphids. Native to South America.

A. fruticosa
See Gomphocarpus fruticos

Asparagus
Asparagaceae

A large genus of about 300 species of evergreen and deciduous perennials, woody climbers or shrubs native to sandy coastal areas of Europe, Asia and Africa. They are grown for their attractive foliage, often being used as house plants.

A. densiflorus 'Myersii'
PLUME ASPARAGUS ꙮꙮ

An evergreen, tuberous-rooted perennial with many stiff, upright, plume-like stems to 60cm or more high. They are densely clothed with needle-like, deep green leaves up to 2cm long. Insignificant, small white flowers appear amid the foliage in summer, which may be followed by red berries. The plant can be grown in full sun, but it also grows well in partial shade. Grows best with regular summer water, but can survive for periods without water. Useful for edging shady borders.

Makes an excellent container plant. Native to South Africa.

A. densiflorus 'Sprengeri'
SPRENGERI FERN ꙮꙮ

An evergreen, tuberous-rooted perennial with many arching or drooping, many-branched stems up to 2m long. The fluffy branchlets are set with soft, fresh green needles, the true leaves being reduced to thorns. Small white flowers appear along the branches in summer, and are followed by small red berries. Popular as a container plant both indoors and outside. It will take full sun and some drought, but grows best in light shade in a moisture-rich sandy soil. Grows in ordinary, even poor soil. Can be used as an interesting groundcover. Often sold as A. Sprengeri. Native to South Africa (Natal).

A. setaceus (syn. A. plumosus)
ASPARAGUS FERN ꙮꙮ

An evergreen, tuberous-rooted perennial, bushy at first, then becomes a branching, woody, twining climber, up to 3m high with wiry, spiny stems. The fern-like, rich green, triangular fronds are arranged horizontally with tiny thread-like leaves. Small white flowers are produced solitarily in the leaf axils in summer. They are followed by purple-black berries. The plant grows best with regular summer water, though it can survive for periods without water. A popular foliage plant for floral arrangements. Useful for screening walls, fences and trellis. Native to South Africa.

Asparagus densiflorus 'Sprenger'

Asparagus setaceus

Aspidistra
Convallariaceae

A genus of about eight species of evergreen perennials that form thick roots. Native to the Himalaya, China, Taiwan and Japan. Although often thought of as a houseplant, it can be grown outside in mild areas.

A. elatior CAST-IRON PLANT ⏾⏾⏾
A rhizomatous perennial with basal leaves, rising singly from the roots; it will slowly spread to 60cm wide. The arching leaf blades are ovate to lance-shaped, dark blackish-green, shiny, and 30–75cm long. Inconspicuous, purple, bell-shaped flowers, 2–3cm across, appear on a short stem at soil level in spring or summer. The plant is tolerant of neglect and unfavourable conditions, including low light; however, it is happiest when grown in light shade in a humus-rich, sandy loam. Grows well with moderate to generous summer water. Makes a good ground-cover for a shady border. Native to China. 'Variegata' is an attractive variegated form, having creamy-white-striped leaves. These, however, are liable to burn in bright light.

Aster amelloides
See Felicia amelloides

Asteriscus
Asteraceae

A genus of about fifteen species of annuals, herbaceous perennials or shrubs native to the Mediterranean coast, the Canary Islands and north Africa. Only one species is in common cultivation.

A. maritimus (syn. Odontospermum maritimum) ⏾
An evergreen perennial that forms a tuft, to 30cm high and 1m wide. The silky, greyish-green leaves are oblong, and grow to 6cm long. The solitary, deep yellow flowers are 4cm across, with finely toothed petals, and appear almost continuously throughout summer. A tough, tolerant plant for most soils, good near the coast, but dislikes cold, wet conditions. Grows well in full sun and needs little summer water once established. Looks good in a sunny rock garden or when growing in a crevice of a stone wall. Easily raised from seed. Native to the Canary Islands.

Atriplex 'SALTBUSH'
Chenopodiaceae

A genus of 100 or more species of annuals, perennials, subshrubs and evergreen or semi-evergreen shrubs found near the coast or in salt marshes worldwide.

Aspidistra elatior

A. canescens
CALIFORNIAN SALTBUSH ⏾
An evergreen shrub, to 2m high and 2.5m wide, with much branched, spreading growth. The narrow, grey-green leaves are 1–5cm long. The small flowers grow in clustered spikes in summer. They are followed by golden fruits in clusters at the ends of the branches. As its common name suggests, the shrub is resistant to salt-laden

Atriplex canescens

sea breezes, so is good for coastal gardens. Although it tolerates dry conditions, it looks better with moderate summer water. Grow in full sun. Native to USA and Mexico.

A. halimus SHRUBBY GOOSEFOOT ⌣
A loosely branching, semi-evergreen shrub, to 2m high with an equal spread. The oval to diamond-shaped, silver-grey leaves, up to 6cm long, are sometimes toothed and leathery. The terminal panicles, up to 30cm long, of tiny, greenish-white flowers, appear in late summer. This attractive silver shrub is easy to grow in full sun, with little summer water; it will even grow in highly alkaline soils. Wind-resistant, so it makes a good screen in a coastal garden. Native to southern Europe.

A. hortensis var. **rubra** RED MOUNTAIN SPINACH, RED ORACHE ⌣⌣⌣
A fast-growing, upright annual, to 2m high, usually with a single red stem. The alternate or opposite triangular or lance-shaped leaves are deep purple, to 15cm long. They are edible, and can be used when young in salads or as a substitute for spinach. Tiny, reddish-brown flowers are borne in terminal spikes up to 20cm long in summer. The plant is easily raised from seed. Grow in moist, fertile soil in full sun, and water generously during summer. Attractive as a temporary hedge, or contrast to other plants. Native to Asia, but naturalized in Europe and north America. The variety 'Copper Plume' has deep red flower spikes, 'Gold Plume' buff yellow, while 'Green Plume' has vivid green spikes.

A. semibaccata
AUSTRALIAN SALTBUSH ⌣
A semi-herbaceous, evergreen shrub that spreads to 2m or more wide, forming a dense mat to 30cm high. The grey-green leaves are 1–4cm long. The small flowers are in spikes, and are followed by red fruit in autumn. Makes an excellent groundcover when planted 1m apart for continuous cover. Grow in full sun, and give little summer water. Ideal for coastal conditions. Native to Australia.

Aubrieta 'AUBRETIA'
Brassicaceae

A genus of about twelve species of

Aucuba japonica

hardy evergreen mat-forming perennials, native to dry, rocky places of eastern Europe to Lebanon and Iran. They are grown for their colourful spring flowers.

A. deltoidea (syn. **A. × cultorum**) ⌣
A hardy evergreen, mat-forming perennial with straggly stems 5–15cm high, spreading to 60cm or more wide. The small grey-green leaves, up to 1cm long, are oval with toothed edges. The tiny four-petalled flowers, 3cm wide, are borne in elongated clusters that cover the plant during spring. The colour varies from violet to red-purple, rose to deep red and sometimes white. The plant is ideal for the rock garden and for dry sunny walls; it also looks good when grown among gravel or between paving. Grow in any well drained soil in full sun. It needs little summer water, but does need moisture for flowering. After flowering, shear off spent flowers to keep plants looking neat. Easily raised from seed. Native to the eastern Mediterranean region. Many named varieties have been raised, including some with variegated leaves.

Aucuba
Aucubaceae

A small genus of three species of dioecious (male and female flowers on different plants) evergreen shrubs native to temperate areas from the

Himalayas to Japan. They are grown for their ornamental foliage and colourful berries. Only one species is in common cultivation.

A. japonica SPOTTED LAUREL, JAPANESE LAUREL ⌣ to ⌣⌣⌣
An evergreen rounded to spreading shrub that grows slowly up to 3m high and wide. The dark green, ovate to oblong, irregularly and finely toothed leaves grow up to 20cm long. The tiny, purplish-red flowers, in terminal panicles to 10cm long, appear in spring. Female shrubs produce bright red berries 1cm across that ripen in autumn. Male and female flowers appear on separate shrubs, so both sexes should be grown together to ensure a fruit crop. They thrive in shade or even deep shade. A tough shrub that will tolerate pollution, coastal conditions, and a wide range of soils. Drought-tolerant, but looks better with adequate moisture, indeed will grow well with generous watering. Grows well in containers in shady terraces or courtyards. Native to Japan. There are many cultivars that have brightly marked leaves that are more often grown than the type. 'Crotonifolia' (female) has leaves that are heavily marked with golden yellow. 'Goldieana' has dark green leaves with white or yellow marks. 'Variegata', the best known aucuba, has dark green leaves spotted with yellow; it is male or female.

B

Ballota
Lamiaceae

A genus containing about thirty-five species of herbaceous perennials or small evergreen subshrubs that are native to Europe, the Mediterranean region and west Asia.

B. acetabulosa ☽

An extremely woolly, bushy subshrub growing to 60cm high and spreading to 75cm wide, with cottony, erect stems. The heart-shaped, grey-green leaves up to 5cm long, with rounded, toothed margins, are wrinkled with woolly upper surfaces and dense white cotton underneath. The 1–2cm long flowers are white or pink, flushed with purple, and are produced in the leaf axils during late summer. The shrub can be grown in poor, dry, free-draining soil. To grow well it needs to be in full sun. For the best results it should be cut back hard in autumn or early spring to promote strong new growth. Native to Greece and Turkey.

B. pseudodictamnus ☽

A low, spreading subshrub that forms a dense mound to 60cm high and wide, entirely covered in greyish-white wool. The small, heart-shaped leaves, up to 3cm long, are also covered in silver hairs. The tiny, two-lipped, lilac-pink flowers 1–2cm long are produced in whorls in summer. For the best results it should be cut back hard in autumn or early spring to promote strong growth. Looks most effective when planted in groups of three or five, or as an edging to a path. Makes an attractive foliage plant. Grows well in a sunny, well drained position, with only a little water during summer. Native to Greece and Turkey.

Bartlettina sordida
See *Eupatorium sordidum*

Bauhinia
Papilionaceae

A large genus of perhaps 300 species of trees, shrubs or climbers coming from the subtropical and tropical regions of the world. The simple, but deeply notched or lobed leaves that are common to most normally grown bauhinias are the shape of camels' hoofs. Only a few species are grown in the Mediterranean climate.

B. galpinii (syn. *B. punctata*) RED BAUHINIA, PRIDE OF THE CAPE ☽☽☽

A rambling evergreen or semi-deciduous climbing shrub to 3m high and wide. The oval, two-lobed, pale green leaves are 3–8cm long. From spring to autumn it produces beautiful brick-red to orange flowers, in no more than a few flowered axillary racemes; each flower is 8cm across, with spoon-shaped petals. The tree cannot take much cold, so it should be grown against a warm, sunny wall. Water and feed generously during summer. Native to tropical and southern Africa.

B. variegata PURPLE ORCHID TREE ☽☽☽

A spectacular, spreading, semi-deciduous tree 6–10m high, spreading to 8m wide, sometimes grown as a multi-stemmed shrub. The curiously shaped, light green, 10–20cm long leaves may be up to 18cm wide, and deeply two-lobed at the tip. In spring it makes a beautiful show of fragrant flowers, produced on the previous season's wood; they are light pink or lavender to deep purple. The five-petalled flowers, each spreading 5–8cm wide, are borne in short, terminal racemes. They are followed by a large number of beans up to 30cm long. The tree requires a lot of water during summer, especially when young. Grows well in full sun. It will need some encouragement to form a tree, by tying the leading stem to a cane, otherwise it may become a shrub. When young it is

Bauhinia variegata

susceptible to damage in low temperatures, so some protection should be given. Prefers a rich, loamy soil as it may become chlorotic in strongly alkaline soil. Native to northern India and southeast China. 'Candida' is a beautiful cultivar which has pure white flowers that are slightly fragrant.

Beaucarnia
Dracaenaceae

A genus of about twenty species of evergreen succulent shrubs or treelike perennials native to dry regions of southern USA. They have tall trunks, usually swollen at the base.

B. recurvata (syn. *Nolina recurvata*)
PONYTAIL PALM, BOTTLE PALM 🌙

A tree-like perennial with a tall trunk to 10m high, greatly swollen at the base, and branches sparingly with age. The trunk is grey-coloured, which with age forms a thick, deeply grooved bark. The branches are topped by a rosette of linear, pendulous, concave, green leaves up to 2m long. Ancient trees may produce 1m long clusters of inconspicuous mauve-tinted, creamy-white flowers in summer. The plant grows best in full sun, but will grow in partial shade. Grow in well drained soil that is never soggy, giving only occasional deep summer watering. A succulent that can store a year's supply of water. An excellent house or container plant if not over-watered. Native to south-east Mexico.

Beaucarnia recurvata

Beaumontia
Apocynaceae

A small genus of about eight species of evergreen, woody climbers, native from India to Vietnam. Only one species is commonly grown.

B. grandiflora HERALD'S TRUMPET 🌙🌙🌙

A magnificent, strong-growing, rather heavy climber that can grow 4–5m high and as wide, and which climbs by its twining young stems. With age the woody trunks will stand alone, but the climber must be given support when young. The huge, oval leaves are 25cm long by 10cm wide, dark green, and glossy above and downy underneath. During summer it has wonderfully fragrant, pendant, trumpet-shaped flowers appearing in terminal clusters; they are white with pale green veins, and five twisted lobes 8–15cm long, flaring up to 10cm wide. Large, well grown plants can have many flowers at a time. The climber needs a deep, rich soil with plenty of summer water and generous feeding. A beautiful climber that is well worth growing. It will only withstand a light frost, so should be grown against a warm wall giving shelter from the wind. The flowers appear on one-year-old growth, so only prune after flowering to keep it in size. With such large leaves and heavy flowers it should be given strong support. Native to northern India and Nepal.

Beloperone
See *Justicia*

Bergenia 'ELEPHANT'S EARS'
Saxifragaceae

A genus of twelve or more species of evergreen perennials, native to central and east Asia, with thick, tough rhizomes. They are commonly seen in woodland gardens in northern Europe, but will also grow in the Mediterranean region.

Bergenia cordifolia

B. cordifolia WINTER BEGONIA 🌙🌙🌙

A perennial that forms a clump up to 45cm high and wide, with a thick, woody rootstock. The large, round to heart-shaped, fleshy leaves are dark shiny green, 20–30cm long with wavy, sparsely toothed edges. They become red-tinged in winter. The branched, reddish-green flower stems bear rose, lilac or purple flowers in clusters well above the leaves. The funnel to bell-shaped flowers, 2cm across, appear in late winter or early spring. The plant grows best in partial shade but will take full sun. Makes an excellent ground cover for shady damp places where the ornamental leaves look good all the year. It needs a generous amount of summer water. Native to Russia. There are many hybrids that come in a wide range of colours from pale pink to deep red and white, some with beautiful bronze-purple leaves.

Beschorneria
Agavaceae

A small genus of about ten species of evergreen, clump forming, perennial succulents with rhizomatous stems. They are closely related to Agave. Native to dry areas of Mexico.

B. yuccoides

A succulent that forms a clump 1.5m high, spreading to about 1m wide. The rosette of about twenty lance-shaped, grey-green leaves, 45cm long and 5cm wide, are rough on the margins and underneath. In summer the much-branched, coral-red flower stem grows to about 2m long; this carries a drooping raceme of bright green flowers 8cm long with red bracts. The plant grows well in full sun in a sharply drained rich soil. Dislikes being water-logged in winter, or shallow chalky soils. When established it withstands drought, but grows better with some summer water. Looks good as a speci-men plant, or near the front of a border.

Bignonia
Bignoniaceae

A genus that is now understood to contain just one species of evergreen climber native to the tropical regions of North America.

B. capensis
See *Tecoma capensis*

B. capreolata (syn. *Doxantha capreolata*) CROSS VINE

A vigorous, evergreen, tendril climber, up to 10m or more high, with hooks or adhesive pads at the tips of the tendrils to help it climb. The opposite leaves are up to 15cm long, and are composed of two ovate to lance-shaped, glossy leaflets with wavy margins. The tubular flowers are 4–5cm long, orange-red, and paler inside, with flared lobes; they are carried in axillary clusters in groups of two to five during summer. Grow the climber in full sun in a moist, humus-rich, well drained soil. Give moderate summer water, although it will withstand some drought once established. Train against a wall, or over a pergola or into a tree. Also useful as a screen. Can be pruned severely after flowering, as it flowers on new growth. The climber is just frost-hardy.

B. cherere
See *Distictis buccinatoria*.

B. grandiflora
See *Campsis grandiflora*.

B. jasminoides
See *Pandorea jasminoides*.

B. pandorana
See *Pandorea pandorana*.

B. radicans
See *Campsis radicans*.

B. rosea
See *Podranea ricasoliana*.

B. speciosa
See *Clytostoma callistegioides*.

B. stans
See *Tecoma stans*.

B. tweediana
See *Macfadyena unguis-cati*.

B. unguis-cati
See *Macfadyena unguis-cati*.

B. venusta
See *Pyrostegia venusta*.

B. violacea
See *Clytostoma callistegioides*.

Billardiera
Pittosporaceae

A small genus of about eight species of twining, evergreen climbers, native to Australia, that are grown for their pendant, bell-shaped flowers.

B. longiflora CLIMBING BLUEBERRY

A small, evergreen, woody climber to about 3m high. The ovate to linear, 4cm long, deep green leaves are on wiry stems that twine for support. The solitary flowers are bell-shaped with a flared mouth, yellowish-green with small black tracery, and up to 2cm long. They hang on slender stalks from the leaf axils during summer and autumn, and are followed by small, metallic, deep violet berries. Purple, red, pink or white forms are available. Grow the climber in neutral to acid soil which is well drained to prevent stem rot in winter. Give moderate summer water. Will grow in full sun or partial shade. It is not difficult to grow if given the correct conditions. Looks good against a wall or clambering over rocks in a rock garden or scrambling through a low bush.

Bismarckia nobilis

Bismarckia
Arecaceae

A genus containing a single dioecious (male and female flowers on different plants) species of solitary, moderately tall, attractive tropical palm; native to Madagascar.

B. nobilis

A spectacular palm that grows up to 8m high or more. The relatively thin trunk, usually no more than 30cm in diameter, is short, smooth and grey. The huge fan leaves are up to 3m across, heavy, thick and a beautiful waxy blue-grey colour. The leaf stalks are streaked with a scurfy white. The palm is slow-growing, especially when young. With age, the female trees produce 3cm, plum-like brown fruit in huge clusters 1m or more long. The palm is fairly drought-tolerant once established, but grows better with regular summer water. Grow in full sun in a rich, well drained soil. Difficult to transplant when young, and should not be moved bare-rooted. A beautiful palm that makes a spectacular speci-men with its attractive blue foliage.

Bocconia cordata
See *Macleaya cordata*.

Bolusanthus
Papilionaceae

A genus containing a single species of deciduous tree native to southern Africa that is grown for its clusters of highly coloured, pea-like flowers.

B. speciosus TREE WISTERIA ꙮꙮ
A slow-growing, small tree, 4–6m high, spreading to 4m wide, with a grey trunk. The glossy green leaves are up to 15cm long, and are composed of up to fifteen lance-shaped leaflets. The briefly deciduous pinnate leaves appear after the flowers open. The pea-shaped, bright purple flowers, 2cm long, appear in pendulous racemes to 25cm long in profusion during winter and spring. They are followed by 6cm long seedpods. For best flowering, the tree should be grown in full sun in a rich, well drained soil. Fairly drought tolerant once established, but grows better with regular summer water. This handsome tree in easily propagated by seed. Rarely flowers well in a container, but makes an attractive specimen.

Borago
Boraginaceae

A genus of just two to three species of hairy annuals and perennials native to the Mediterranean region. One species has long been cultivated as a herb.

B. officinalis BORAGE ꙮ
A freely branching annual, 20–60cm high and 45cm wide. The hairy, grey-

Borago officinalis

green basal leaves are 10–20cm long, egg-shaped and toothed. The lance-shaped stem leaves are up to 15cm long. The leaves and flowers are edible, with a cucumber-like flavour. The 2cm wide flowers, produced during spring, are pure blue, opening to a star with dark purple, projecting anthers. Grow the plant in full sun, although it will tolerate shade. Grows well in poor, dry soil. Although it seeds itself freely, it does not transplant well. Cultivated throughout the Mediterranean region as a culinary herb. Use tender leaves in salads and drinks, and use the attractive flowers as a garnish. Will grow without water, but grows better if given some summer water. Native to Europe. 'Alba' has white flowers.

Bougainvillea 'PAPER FLOWER'
Nyctaginaceae

A genus of about fourteen species of shrubs and climbers native to tropical and subtropical South America. They are possibly the most spectacular and widely grown climbers in warm countries. They should be grown in full sun against walls, pergolas, or trees with plenty of room. They tolerate poor soil and need little summer water, or else they can make rampant growth with little flower. Bougainvillea can also be trained to make good groundcover on dry banks. Will even withstand sea spray.

B. × buttiana ꙮ
A cross between *B. peruviana* and *B. glabra* which has produced a vigorous, woody climber easily growing 10–12m high. The ovate leaves are up to 8cm long. The clusters of wavy floral bracts are 3–5cm long, ranging from yellow to red and purple in colour. They are produced from summer, through autumn and into winter. This garden hybrid has been used to produce a large number of named varieties. 'Golden Glow' has yellow bracts, 'Mrs Butt' is pure dark crimson.

B. glabra ꙮ
A climbing shrub that will grow to almost any height, but is often seen up to 10m high with a wide spread. The vigorous, stout stems have straight spines. The bright green, oval leaves have a slender point and are 5–10cm

Bougainvillea glabra

long. The vibrant colour comes from the three large purple or white bracts that surround the small, white, insignificant flowers. These floral bracts, 4–6cm long, are produced in great profusion throughout summer and autumn, while some flowering bracts can be seen at almost any time of the year. Native to Brazil. Some of the oldest varieties have been bred from this species. 'Snow White' has pure white bracts. 'Magnifica' has bright purple bracts.

B. hybrids ꙮ
Bouganvillea has been hybridized a great deal, predominantly from *B. spectabilis*, *B. glabra* and *B. peruviana*. The true species are rarely found for sale. There are many spectacular varieties that come

Bougainvillea hybrid

Bouganvillea hybrid

in shades of white, pink, red, orange, lilac, cerise, copper and so on. There are some double varieties, and some with variegated leaves. Some varieties have more compact growth, which makes them more suitable for growing in containers, while others are rampant growers.

B. 'Raspberry Ice' (syn. 'Tropical Rainbow') ☽

A bushy, scrambling, evergreen climber to 12m or more high. The ovate, deep green leaves, 8cm long, are beautifully edged with cream. The flowering bracts, up to 3cm long, are deep pink to red. These are produced from summer through to autumn, and into winter making a spectacular sight.

B. spectabilis ☽

A vigorous and dense climber growing 7–10m high. The stems have many large curved thorns. The ovate leaves are up to 10cm long, and downy underneath. The purple, pink or reddish bracts, 5–6cm long, are produced during spring and summer. Native to Brazil. This is the main parent of the many differently coloured and free-flowering hybrids that are now grown.

Boussingaultia baselloides
See *Anredera cordifolia*.

Brachychiton 'BOTTLE TREE' *Sterculiaceae*

A genus of about thirty species of evergreen or deciduous tall shrubs or trees, often with large, swollen trunks. Native to Australia.

B. acerifolius (syn. *Sterculia acerifolia*) FLAME TREE ☽

An evergreen or briefly deciduous tree that grows up to 30m or more in the wild, but usually 6–12m in cultivation. The tree usually forms a pyramidal shape, but may spread wide. The usually green trunk is smooth, solid-looking and may be swollen at the base. The attractive, glossy bright green, palmate leaves have five to seven deep lobes, and are up to 30cm across on long stalks. In summer the tree covers itself with terminal clusters of small, bright red tubular flowers, 2cm across. This gives it the common name 'Flame Tree'. A large tree in full flower is a spectacular sight. It usually drops its leaves at the time of flowering. It needs to be grown in full sun, with a little summer water once established. Native to Queensland and New South Wales.

Brachychiton acerifolius

B. populneus (syn. *Sterculia diversifolia*) Kurrajong ☽

An evergreen tree with a heavy, often swollen trunk. It starts out quite vertical in form, maturing to a handsome, dome-shaped tree 6–15m high. The glossy, bright green, simple leaves usually have three to five pointed lobes 5–8cm long, of at least three

Bouganvillea 'Raspberry Ice'

Brachychiton populneus

different shapes (the source of its former name), which shimmer in the wind. In summer the glossy, bell-shaped flowers, 1–2cm across, appear in large clusters on the ends of the branches. They are white or greenish-yellow outside, and yellowish or red inside. They are followed by 6–8cm, boat-shaped woody pods. The tree likes warm, dry soils requiring no summer water once established. Tolerates alkaline soil. Widely used as a street tree, sometimes as a lawn or shade tree, or as a high windbreak. Native to Queensland or New South Wales.

Brachyglottis
Asteraceae

A genus of about thirty species of trees, shrubs, herbaceous perennials and climbers native to New Zealand. Many species formerly listed as *Senecio* are now listed as *Brachyglottis*. They are grown for their attractive foliage and flowers.

B. greyi (syn. *Senecio greyi*)

An evergreen shrub up to 2m high and 3m wide, with stout, spreading branches covered in white felt. The oblong, 10cm-long, leathery leaves are dark green, margined silver-grey, with white felt underneath. The young leaves are also densely white-felted. The 14cm-wide clusters of daisy-like, deep yellow, 3cm-wide flowers appear

profusely during summer. The shrub thrives in full sun with little to moderate summer water. Grows best in free-draining soil. May be pruned hard to keep a compact shape, otherwise it can become leggy. Easily propagated from cuttings. Looks most attractive in a shrub border. Thrives in coastal gardens, as it withstands salt-laden sea breezes.

Brahea 'HESPER PALM'
Arecaceae

A genus of about sixteen species of mostly low- or medium-growing, single-stemmed palms. They are all slow-growing, making attractive specimen trees. Native to Mexico and central America.

B. armata (syn. *Erythea armata*)
MEXICAN BLUE PALM, BLUE FAN PALM

An upright-growing palm that makes slow growth to 12–15m high, with the leaves spreading to 7m wide. The solitary trunk of the mature tree is usually straight, thick and grey. It may either be covered with persistent dead leaves, or be smooth and free from leaf bases. The stiff leaves, 1–1.5m across, are waxy-textured, silver-blue, and deeply divided into about fifty fan-like segments. They are borne on long stalks, armed with stout, curved teeth. The spectacular, arching or pendulous inflorescence, up to 4m long, is borne

on mature plants during summer. The showy clusters of yellow or creamy flowers are 1.5cm across. Grow the palm in full sun and give a little summer water once established. Will tolerate great heat, slight frost, wind, and poor, dry soil. A wonderful palm for the dry garden, also making a good specimen. In moonlight the beautiful blue leaves can look almost white. It can be temperamental, and difficult to transplant. Native to Mexico.

B. edulis (syn. *Erythea edulis*)
GUADELOUPE FAN PALM

A robust palm with a mature height of 12m, with a dense spread of 3m, and a stout trunk; as the spent fronds fall, they naturally clean the trunk. The rigid palmate leaves, up to 2m across, are grassy green in colour and thinly glaucous on both sides. The leaves are borne on leaf stalks 1m long that have stout curved or hooked teeth along their margins. On mature plants the flower stalk appears from among the leaves, arching out far beyond them. The flowers are in clusters of three. The fruit are dark brown to black, 2cm in diameter, hanging down in bunches; when ripe they are edible, with a sweet pulp. Grow the palm in full sun in a well drained, rich soil. It needs only a little summer water once established. It is slow-growing, and will take slight

Brahea armata

frost, beach and desert conditions. A wonderful and dramatic palm that is ideal as a specimen. Native to Guadeloupe Island off Baja California.

Brassaia
See *Schefflera*.

Brodiaea uniflora
See *Ipheion uniflorum*.

Broussonetia
Moraceae

A genus of about seven species of deciduous trees or shrubs that are dioecious (male and female flowers on different plants), with milky sap; native to eastern Asia and Polynesia. Only one species is usually cultivated for its large leaves and unusual fruit.

B. papyrifera PAPER MULBERRY, TAPA-CLOTH TREE ☽

A deciduous tree that makes moderate growth to 15m with a dense, rounded crown to 12m across, and a smooth grey bark. The ovate leaves are up to 20cm long and either unlobed or deeply lobed. They are roughly hairy above and grey velvety underneath. The flowers appear in late spring and early summer. The male flowers have creamy anthers and are borne in pendant catkins to 7cm long. The female flowers are in rounded heads 2cm

across. They develop into orange-red fruits that closely resemble mulberries, and are edible with a sweet taste. Grow the tree in full sun as it needs hot summers to ripen its wood. Needs no summer water once established. Suckering can be a problem in the garden. Its tolerance of pollution, heat, strong winds, and poor, stony or alkaline soil has made it popular as a street tree. Also valuable as a shade tree. Its bark was used to make cloth, shoes and helmets in Polynesia, the cloth fashioned as togas for the wealthy in Europe, and as loincloths for warriors on some islands. Native to China, Japan and Polynesia.

Brugmansia (syn. Datura)
'ANGELS' TRUMPETS'
Solanaceae

A genus of about five species of evergreen shrubs or small trees that are native to South America with large, simple, entire leaves. The large, trumpet-shaped or tubular, pendulous flowers are generally fragrant in the evening with flower colours of many shades of pink, yellow, white, orange, peach and gold. There are many different *Brugmansias* on the market, and many new hybrids appearing as there is a lot of hybridizing work being carried out. They tend to bloom in waves or flushes about every six to eight weeks. Note that *Brugmansias* are poisonous!

Broussonetia papyrifera

B. arborea COMMON ANGELS' TRUMPETS ☽☽

A vigorous shrub or tree up to 4m high and 2.5m wide. The oblong, bright green leaves, up to 30cm long, are entire or coarsely toothed. The large, nodding, trumpet-shaped flowers are usually white, but may be yellow. They are up to 15cm long, night-scented, and produced from early summer to autumn. Like other Brugmansias, it can be grown in full sun or partial shade, and should be generously watered during summer. For good flowering, generous fertilizer should be applied during summer. Native to Ecuador and northern Chile.

Brugmansia arborea

B. × candida (syn. *Datura × candida*) ANGELS' TRUMPETS ☽☽

An open-growing shrub or small tree that makes fast growth up to 5m high, spreading to 3m wide, with soft, pulpy stems that are easily damaged by frost. The young stems and leaves are pubescent. The broad, dull green leaves are 30–60cm long. The flowers are single or double, usually white, rarely yellow or pink, and 20cm or more long, appearing in flushes throughout summer. They are strongly fragrant, especially at night. Grow the shrub in a warm, sheltered garden and fertilize regularly to encourage strong growth. For the best flowering it should be generously watered during summer. Can be grown in full sun or partial shade. 'Grand Marnier' has beautiful peach-coloured flowers. Garden origin.

B. × insignis (syn. *B. suaveolens × versicolor*) ☽☽

A hybrid that is often sold as *B. suaveolens*. An open-growing shrub or small tree that makes fast growth up to 4m high and spread to 2m wide. The

Brugmansia arborea

dull green leaves are oval to elliptic and up to 15cm long, with toothed margins. The huge, tubular flowers are pink to almost red or white, and up to 40cm long, with a delicate fragrance. They appear in flushes from mid to late summer. The shrub can be grown in full sun or partial shade. For the best flowering it should be generously watered during summer. The variety 'Frosty Pink' with pink flowers is often seen. Garden origin.

Brugmansia insignis 'Frosty Pink'

B. sanguinea (syn. Datura rosei, D. sanguinea) RED ANGELS' TRUMPETS ⌣⌣
A fast-growing shrub or small tree up to 5m high and 2–3m wide. The 20cm long, oblong, bright green leaves are pubescent. Flowers are large, generally 20–30cm long, normally orange-red at the mouth, fading to yellowish-green at the base. They are tubular, not trumpet-shaped, and hang down from the new growth. They appear from late spring to autumn. The shrub can be grown in full sun or partial shade. For

the best flowering it should be generously watered during summer. Native from Columbia to northern Chile.

B. suaveolens (syn. Datura suaveolens) ⌣⌣
A vigorous shrub or tree up to 5m high and 3m wide. The oblong, bright green leaves are up to 20cm long, and pubescent. The large, nodding, funnel-shaped flowers are usually white, but sometimes yellow or pink. They are up to 30cm long, night-scented, and produced from early summer to autumn. A double form exists. Like other brugmansias, it can be grown in full sun or partial shade, and should be generously watered during summer. Native to south-east Brazil.

Brugmansia suaveolens 'Yellow'

Brunfelsia
Solanaceae

A genus of about forty species of evergreen shrubs or small trees native to tropical America. None are frost-hardy. All have fragrant flowers to some extent. No species are found in limey soils, as they prefer neutral to acid soils.

B. pauciflora (syn. B. calycina, B. eximia) YESTERDAY-TODAY-TOMORROW ⌣⌣⌣
A small, bushy shrub with upright branches to about 2m high or more in partial shade. The normally evergreen, leathery leaves are oblong, 8–15cm long, dark green above and pale green below. They may drop if it becomes too cold. The 5cm wide, purple to lavender, tubular flowers, with a central white eye, are produced in terminal clusters of up to ten in early spring. They cover

Brunfelsia pauciflora 'Floribunda'

the whole shrub, making a wonderful sight. The colour quickly fades, giving it the common name 'Yesterday' purple, 'Today' lavender, 'Tomorrow' white. The shrub grows best in some shade in a rich soil that is slightly acid. Give it a constant supply of summer water, with generous feeding. Native to Brazil. 'Floribunda' is a variety that flowers more freely, with flowers that open a rich violet colour; 'Macrantha' has larger flowers up to 8cm across.

Buddleja (syn. Buddleia)
Buddlejaceae

A genus of over 100 species of deciduous and evergreen shrubs or sometimes small trees or climbers, with colourful flowers of great garden value. They are native to tropical and subtropical parts of North and South America, Africa and Asia.

B. alternifolia
FOUNTAIN BUTTERFLY BUSH ⌣
A deciduous shrub or small tree up to 4m high, spreading as wide, with slender, arching, willow-like branches. The lance-shaped leaves, up to 7cm long, are dull green above with whitish down underneath. The flowers are lilac-purple in dense, rounded clusters, to 4cm long, and intensely fragrant.

Buddleja madagascariensis

The flowers are produced in spring from the previous year's growth. Grow the shrub in full sun or partial shade. Although drought-resistant, it grows better with some summer water to maintain growth. Grows well in poor, dry, even gravelly soils. Can be trained to make a fine weeping tree. Native to China.

B. asiatica ↴

A large, evergreen shrub up to 12m high, and spreading as wide when scrambling through trees in the wild. The shoots are white or grey-woolly. As it has long, lax stems it needs support and is classed as a climber. The narrowly lance-shaped leaves, up to 30cm long, are dark green with white down underneath. The flowers are in long, thin, drooping panicles to 25cm long, creamy-white with an orange eye and a rich fragrance. They are produced from winter to early spring. The shrub grows best in full sun against a wall, or trained into a tree. Easily grown in any soil. Although drought-resistant, it grows better with some summer water. Give it an annual pruning or it may climb 6m a year. Widely distributed from the Himalayas to Nepal, China and the Philippines.

B. davidii BUTTERFLY BUSH ↴ or ↴↴

A vigorous, semi-deciduous shrub that makes fast, rank growth, up to 4m high, with long, arching branches. The leaves are tapering, 20cm long, dark green above with a white down underneath. The slender terminal panicles are 30cm or more long, and densely packed with fragrant flowers. Smaller panicles appear at the ends of the side branches. The flowers vary in colour from pink, lilac, purple or violet to white. They are attractive to butterflies. The shrub should be cut back hard in early spring to produce the largest flowers. Grow in full sun or partial shade. Although drought-resistant, it grows better with some summer water. There are numerous named cultivars available. Native to China and Japan.

B. madagascariensis ↴↴

A vigorous, evergreen, straggling shrub that grows 4m or more high and wide. The young stems and shoots are covered with white felt. The lance-shaped leaves are 5–13cm long, dark green above, and covered in white felt underneath. During the late autumn and winter it produces 15–25cm long, terminal panicles of yellow or orange flowers, with a scent that some people find unpleasant. This large shrub needs room to grow. If given some summer water it will make an attractive silver-leaved shrub. Can be pruned to keep in shape, which is best carried out in spring after flowering. Native to Madagascar.

B. × pikei 'Hever' ↴↴

A deciduous, wide, spreading shrub up to 3m high and wide with slender, arching shoots. The opposite or alternate grey-green leaves are ovate to oblong to 15cm long. In summer, arching panicles, to 30cm long, of fragrant lilac-mauve flowers with orange centres, are produced. The shrub should be cut back hard in early spring to produce the largest flowers. Although drought-resistant, it grows better with some summer water. Grow in full sun or partial shade in any well drained soil. Garden origin.

Buddleja x pikei 'Hever'

Buddleja salvifolia

B. salvifolia

SOUTH AFRICAN SAGE WOOD ♩♩
An evergreen shrub up to 4m high, spreading to 3m wide, with more or less square stems, covered in felt. The lance-shaped, grey green leaves are 13cm long and also lightly covered in felt. This gives the appearance of sage. The 15cm terminal panicles of flowers are pale lilac-blue with an orange eye. The fragrant flowers are produced in autumn and winter. Although drought-resistant, the shrub grows better with some summer water. It should be cut back hard in early spring to produce the largest flowers. Native to southern and tropical Africa.

Butia
Arecaceae

A genus of eight to twelve, tropical to subtropical, single-stemmed palms, native to the drier parts of southern Brazil, Paraguay, Uruguay and northern Argentina. Several species of these relatively hardy palms are grown for their graceful, arching leaves.

B. capitata (syn. *Cocus capitata, Cocus australis*) JELLY PALM ♩
A slow-growing, very hardy palm with a stout, heavy trunk up to 6m high, with the leaves spreading to 5m wide. The grey trunk is patterned with the stubs of the old leaves. The graceful, silver-blue leaf fronds, 2m long, are strongly recurved. The leaf stalks are sometimes as long as the leaf, and are edged with 2–3cm spines. Small yellow flowers are borne in large, drooping clusters to 1.5m long in summer. They are not particularly decorative, but are followed by gigantic clusters of edible fruit. When ripe, the 3cm long, oval fruit turn bright orange to yellow; they are sweet, and good for making jelly.

Grow the palm in well drained soil in sun or light shade. A hardy palm that is excellent in a tub on a hot sunny terrace. Although drought-tolerant when established, it grows better with regular summer water. This species stands more heat, frost and drought conditions than any of the other feather palms. It stands out well against other green trees or shrubs. Native to Brazil, Uruguay and Argentina.

B. yatay (syn. *Cocus yatay*)
YATAY PALM ♩
A slow-growing palm that is similar in most respects to *B. capitata*, except the stem is up to 8m high and up to 45cm thick. It has the same beautiful blue, arching leaves. The flowers and edible fruit are also similar. Although drought tolerant when established, it grows better with regular summer water. This palm is highly recommended. Native to Argentina, Paraguay and Uruguay.

Buxus 'BOX, BOXWOOD'
Buxaceae

A genus of about seventy species of evergreen shrubs or small trees, with opposite, leathery leaves. Native to Europe, Mediterranean region, central America and Asia. They are grown for their foliage and their ability to withstand clipping, making them ideal for hedging.

Butia capitata

B. microphylla SMALL-LEAVED BOXWOOD ⌣ or ⌣⌣

A slow-growing, evergreen, densely branching shrub to 2m high with a rounded habit. The ovate, 1–2cm, leathery leaves are set closely together. They are a bright green in summer, but may become bronze in winter. The flowers are inconspicuous. The shrub is normally grown as a hedge, or clipped into a pyramid or other shapes in containers. Will grow in full sun or shade, it tolerates dry heat, and alkaline soil. Grows best if given some summer water. Probably garden origin. This species is more suited to the Mediterranean region than *B. sempervirens*, the 'Common Boxwood'. The variety 'Compacta' is a dwarf form only growing to 30cm high and wide after thirty years.

B. microphylla var. japonica ⌣ or ⌣⌣

A small to medium-sized shrub up to 60cm high, spreading to 75cm wide, with an open, spreading habit. The leaves are broadly ovate, thick and leathery. The twigs are square in section. Similar to *B. microphylla*, but will withstand more extreme conditions, from heat to frost. Native to Japan.

C

Caesalpinia
Caesalpiniaceae

A genus of about seventy species of evergreen and deciduous trees, shrubs and climbers native to tropical America and the West Indies. They are grown for their spectacular terminal racemes of flowers.

C. gilliesii
BIRD OF PARADISE BUSH ☙ or ☙☙

An upright or spreading shrub or small tree that quickly reaches 3–4m high, spreading 1–2m wide. The bipinnate, 20cm-long leaves contain many small leaflets, which may drop in a cold winter. The branches are rather open and lax. The spectacular flowers are borne in upright, terminal, pyramidal-shaped racemes containing thirty to forty flowers. Each bright yellow, cup-shaped flower, 3–4cm across, has tassels of bright red, 10cm-long stamens. The flowers are produced for most of the summer. They are usually followed by 10cm-long seedpods.

Caesalpinia gilliesii

Grow the shrub in full sun in a well drained soil. Once established, it only requires occasional watering in hot weather. It can be easily propagated by seeds that germinate readily. Native to Argentina and Uruguay.

Callistemon 'BOTTLE BRUSH'
Myrtaceae

A genus containing over twenty species of magnificent, sun-loving, evergreen shrubs or small trees native to Australia. The flowers are produced in cylindrical spikes, hence the common name 'Bottle Brush'. There is much confusion among nurseries, and many kinds are sold under names whose identification is uncertain. They are closely related to *Melaleucas* and are often confused with them.

C. citrinus LEMON BOTTLEBRUSH ☙
A vigorous, spreading shrub that will reach 4m high or can be trained into a tree when young, reaching perhaps 6–7m high. The narrow, rigid, lance-

Callistemon citrinus

shaped leaves are 8cm long, and have a slight lemon scent when crushed. The new growth is a copper colour, turning a vivid green with age. The flowers are bright crimson, 5–15cm long, and packed tightly together in cylindrical spikes at the ends of stiff stems during summer. The long stamens are the colourful part of the flower. Do not remove the old flowerheads, as the new growth and flowers are produced from the tips of the old flowers. An easily grown shrub that is tolerant of heat and drought, but grows best in a deep, sandy soil. There are many cultivars including 'Compacta', which is much smaller, and 'Splendens', a much improved form with denser and more brilliantly coloured flowers.

C. rigidus STIFF BOTTLEBRUSH ☙
A large shrub with erect, sparse stems, which can form a small tree 6m high with a 3m spread. The rigid, sharply pointed, lance-shaped leaves are up to 13cm long. The flowers are dark red, densely crowded into spikes 8–10cm long, appearing during spring and summer. The seed capsules are prominent, and remain on the shrub for at least a year. One of the most drought-tolerant species.

C. viminalis WEEPING BOTTLEBRUSH ☙☙
A bushy shrub or small tree with

C

Callistemon viminalis

spreading to weeping branches. Fast-growing up to 7m high, with a 4m spread. The narrow, lance-shaped leaves are 10cm long, bronze when young, then turning a light green. The bright red, 8cm-long flower brushes are produced two or three times a year. The shrub grows best in sheltered areas, as it is easily damaged by wind. Requires more summer water than other species. May also be damaged by the cold in some winters. Some branches may need removal to improve the shape and prevent it becoming top-heavy.

Calodendrum
Rutaceae

A small genus of just two species of evergreen trees native to tropical and southern Africa. They are grown for their ornamental flowers. The name comes from the Greek meaning 'beautiful tree'.

C. capense CAPE CHESTNUT ♦♦♦
A broad-crowned tree that grows slowly, 8–10m high with a wide spread. The bark is smooth and grey. It can be deciduous in cold winters. The dark green leaves are long-elliptic to 10–15cm long, either opposite or whorled on the stem. The flowers are produced in spectacular, large pyramidal- or dome-shaped terminal panicles up to 30cm long in spring. The 12–14cm-long rosy-lilac, fragrant flowers have long pink stamens. The tree does not usually flower until it reaches maturity. Grow in full sun for best flowering. Requires a good, well drained, slightly acidic soil. A generous and regular amount of water in summer is needed, particularly in the first few years after planting. Native to South Africa.

Calonyction aculeatum
See *Ipomea alba*.

Calodendrum capense

Campsis
'TRUMPET CREEPER', 'TRUMPET VINE' *Bignoniaceae*

A genus of just two species of deciduous woody climbers native to North America, China and Japan. They all climb by aerial roots that can damage plaster on houses if grown against the walls. All make a quick summer screen.

C. grandiflora (syn. *Bignonia grandiflora*)
CHINESE TRUMPET CREEPER ♦♦
A deciduous climber growing up to 12m high with few aerial roots. The 30cm-long, dark green leaves have nine to thirteen leaflets 8cm long; these are coarsely toothed and hairy underneath. The terminal clusters of spectacular flame-red, trumpet-shaped, deeply five-lobed flowers flare open to 8cm across and up to 10cm long. They are produced from early summer to late autumn. Not so vigorous or hardy as *C. radicans*. The climber can be grown in full sun or partial shade in well drained soil. Grows best if given moderate summer water, but will still grow and flower with little water. Particularly effective when trained through a fence, covering a large wall, or climbing into a tree. Native to China, Japan.

C. radicans (syn. *Bignonia radicans*)
TRUMPET CREEPER ♦♦
A vigorous climber that will grow 9–12m high. The dark green, pinnate leaves have nine to eleven leaflets 4–6cm long, with fine hairs underneath. The trumpet-shaped flowers are in terminal clusters of six to twelve. The long, deep orange trumpets are 8cm long, with flared lobes 5cm wide. They are produced from summer until late autumn. Grow the climber against

Calodendrum capense

Campsis grandiflora

cultivation are hybrids of mixed parentage. The modern Cannas with their large, splendid flowers are the result of hybridization and are not a true botanical species. They were taken to Europe in the mid-nineteenth century, proving so popular that a great deal of hybridizing took place.

C. × *generalis* GARDEN CANNA

This is the most commonly grown canna, that varies in height and in the colour of its foliage. It grows 1–2m high, producing brilliant terminal flowers on stems arising from the centre of the plant throughout summer and autumn. The large, fleshy leaves can be up to 90cm long and 30cm wide, and are green, bronze or purple in colour. The flowers come in a dazzling array of colours, including deep yellow, vivid orange, pink, salmon and red, and in bicolours. The plants should be grown in full sun, and during summer given ample water and plenty of feed. The fleshy rhizomes should be lifted and split into sections each spring. Remove faded flowers for best effect. Ideal in large pots or containers on a sunny terrace. They are easily raised from seed. To get a known flower or leaf colour, buy one of the large number of named varieties.

a wall, pergola or fence where the arching sprays of flowers can be seen at their best. Will grow in full sun or shade. Grows better if given some summer water. Native to eastern United States.

C. × *tagliabuana* 'MADAME GALEN'
A variable hybrid of C. *grandiflora* and C. *radicans*. A vigorous, deciduous climber 9m or more high. The pinnate, dark green leaves are up to 30cm long, with seven to eleven leaflets that are slightly downy on the veins underneath. The panicles of six to twelve, dark salmon-red, funnel-shaped flowers with spreading lobes up to 10cm wide are produced during summer.

Canna 'INDIAN SHOT PLANT'
Cannaceae

A genus of about sixty species of tall, erect, rhizomatous herbaceous perennials native to Asia and tropical North and South America. Most Cannas in

Canna generalis

Campsis radicans

C. 'Black Knight'
Bronze foliage, 60cm high, dark red flowers.

C. 'Durban'
dark red leaves variegated with yellow stripes, red flowers.

C. 'J. Anderson'
green leaves, yellow flowers spotted with brown.

C. 'Louis Gagueaux'
purple leaves, large bright red flowers.

C. 'Striata'
pale yellowish-green leaves and yellow veins up to 50cm long, spikes of orange flowers growing to 1.5m high.

Canna 'Striata'

C. indica INDIAN SHOT ☽☽☽
A rhizomatous perennial that grows to 2m high. The oblong green leaves up to 50cm long and 20cm wide often have a bronze tint. The flowers are 5–7cm wide, and bright red with the lip orange, spotted red. The plant grows best in full sun when given ample water during summer. Usually propagated by dividing the rhizomes in spring or from seed. Native to tropical America.

Capparis
Capparidaceae

A genus of about 300 species of tropical or subtropical shrubs or trees with usually large white or yellowish flowers. Only one species is generally grown.

C. spinosa CAPER BUSH ☽
A spiny, essentially glabrous shrub with a habit that varies from a prostrate spreading plant, to a dense round shrub, to 2m high and wide. The deep green leaves are nearly round, and up to 5cm across. The solitary flowers, 5–8cm wide, are white with showy brushes of lavender stamens. They appear on long stalks from every leaf base, opening in the morning and closing in the afternoon, and are produced continuously throughout summer. The unopened buds are pickled in vinegar as the pungent capers of commerce. The shrub needs to be grown in full sun. Tolerates or even prefers poor soil, but needs good drainage. Difficult to establish, but then needs little summer water. Can be grown as groundcover, or planted where it can hang down over a wall. Sometimes can be seen growing from old city walls. Native to dry rocky places in the Mediterranean region.

Caragana 'PEA TREE'
Papilionaceae

A genus of about eighty species of hardy, usually spiny shrubs and small trees native to central Asia and Europe. Grown for their showy, pea-like flowers.

C. arborescens Siberian Pea Shrub ☽
A fast-growing shrub to 6m high with a spread of 4m. The four to six pairs of even, pinnate leaves are up to 8cm long, with the terminal leaflet reduced to a spine. The yellow, pea-like, fragrant flowers are 1.5cm long. They appear in great profusion during spring in drooping clusters. A nearly indestructible shrub that will grow in the poorest of soils, will succeed in the most exposed areas, and is completely drought-tolerant. Useful as a windbreak or clipped into a hedge. The variety 'Pendula' is a weeping form, while 'Lorbergii' has narrow, almost grass-like leaves and smaller flowers. Native to Siberia.

Carica
Caricaceae

A genus of around twenty-five species of soft-wooded, small trees or (rarely) climbers native to tropical and subtropical America. Only one species is generally grown, for its fruit. They should be grown in groups, as they are dioecious (male and female flowers are produced on different plants).

C. papaya PAWPAW ☽☽☽
An evergreen, soft-stemmed tree that generally grows with a single straight stem up to 6m high, and is topped with a crown of leaves. The broad, fan-like leaves usually have five to seven deep lobes. They are up to 60cm across, and

Capparis spinosa

Carica papaya

Carissa macrocarpa

borne on a leaf stalk up to 60cm long. The flowers are cream or yellow and inconspicuous; the fruit that follows can be round, or 30cm or more long, green when young, ripening to yellowish-green or orange, and can weigh from 200g to several kilograms. The fruits take about six to eight months to ripen, with thick yellow flesh and many small black seeds. Trees should be grown in a warm, sheltered spot in a rich, well drained soil in full sun, and given plenty of water in summer. They are susceptible to the roots rotting due to cold, wet soil conditions in winter. They benefit from reflected heat in winter, so grow on the sunny side of a wall or house. Trees bear fruit within a few months after planting, but are not long-lived, and should be replaced by seedlings that are easily raised. Native to Central America.

Carissa
Apocynaceae

A genus of about thirty-five species of much-branched evergreen, often spiny shrubs or small trees. They are native to tropical and subtropical Africa, Asia and India. They are often grown for their tart, edible fruit. They generally have fragrant flowers, milky sap and spines.

C. macrocarpa (syn. C. grandiflora)
NATAL PLUM ↵↵
A dense, evergreen shrub 2m, or rarely 3m, high that can also be trained into a beautiful small tree. The dark, glossy green, oval leaves are variable in size, up to 8cm long and 5cm wide. They have stiff, mostly forked spines at the base of the leaves. The solitary, 5cm wide, bright white, star-shaped, five-petalled flowers are richly fragrant. They appear throughout most of summer scattered over the shrub. They are followed by edible, red, plum-shaped fruit that can be eaten raw or made into jam. To grow well the shrub needs full sun and some summer water, but it may tolerate some drought once established. As the shrub is so impenetrable it is often grown on boundaries as a screen or hedge. Also grows well in coastal areas. Native to South Africa. There are many cultivars: 'Horizontalis', which is exceptionally compact and prostrate; 'Green Carpet', which makes an excellent groundcover; and 'Tuttlei' which grows 1m high and 2m wide, with dense, compact foliage, and producing a heavy crop of flowers and fruit.

Carpenteria
Hydrangeaceae

A genus of only one species of evergreen shrub native to Sierra Nevada in California, USA, grown for its attractive leaves and for its beautiful cup-shaped white flowers.

C. californica TREE ANEMONE ↵↵
An evergreen shrub that makes slow growth to 2m high with many basal branches. The new branches are purplish, while the old bark is light-coloured and peeling. The leaves are oblong to 10cm long, green and shiny above, grey underneath. The large, pure white, pleasantly fragrant flowers are 4–8cm wide with five rounded petals and a mass of golden anthers. They are produced in clusters at the shoot tips from early to mid-summer. To grow well the shrub requires a well drained, light and sandy soil in full sun or partial shade. Although it needs little summer water, it must not be allowed to dry out. Excess water in winter is

Carissa macrocarpa

C

Carpenteria californica

especially harmful. Can be grown as a free-standing shrub, or planted against a wall. Easily raised from seed.

Carpobrotus
Aizoaceae

A genus of about thirty species of creeping, perennial succulents and sub-shrubs native to Africa, Australia, North and South America. These coarse-leaved plants are often used for binding and stabilizing sandy soil at the beach.

C. edulis HOTTENTOT FIG

A creeping, branching succulent, 15cm high that can spread to many metres wide. The individual stems can grow to 2m or more long, and root along the length. The leaves are 8–12cm long, three-angled, fleshy and slightly bent inwards. The large yellow, yellowish-pink or purple flowers are 8–10cm across, with narrow silky petals that open at midday. They are produced continuously from spring to early autumn. They are followed by large edible fruit. Grow the plant in full sun in sandy or well drained soil; it does not need water once established. Often planted as a sand binder along sea-shores, or covering sunny banks. Can be grown from seed, but easily raised

Carpobrotus edulis

from cuttings. Rooted cuttings planted out in spring will quickly cover a large area. Native to South Africa.

Caryopteris
Verbenaceae

A genus of about six species of shiny or hairy-leaved deciduous shrubs or perennials native to east Asia, often with blue flowers and aromatic leaves.

C. × clandonensis BLUE MIST

A small shrub growing only to about 1m high and wide. The lance-shaped leaves are to 5cm long, greyish-green, often white or grey underneath, and slightly toothed at the edges. The clusters of tiny tubular flowers, 1 cm across, appear on the tips of the current season's branches late in summer. They are followed by attractive seed-heads. The shrub thrives almost anywhere, but grows best in full sun with occasional summer water. Looks particularly good when planted in bold groups. As it flowers on new wood it should be cut back nearly to the base of the previous year's growth in spring each year. The variety 'Arthur Simmonds' is more commonly grown. 'Heavenly Blue' is more compact, and 'Kew Blue' is a deeper blue. Garden origin.

Caryota 'FISH-TAIL PALM'
Arecaceae

A small genus of about twelve species of single-stemmed or clustering palms native to tropical areas of Asia. These palms generally need frost-free conditions and enjoy humid air. They are grown for their dense foliage and unusual leaflets shaped like fishes' tails. Caryota is a genus that is in desperate taxonomic confusion, as they are often misidentified and probably hybridize in cultivation.

C. mitis
CLUSTERED FISH-TAIL PALM

A medium-sized palm with slender clustering stems to 6m high. Often treated as a shrub, but can be trained into a tree by removing the side shoots. The grey-green trunks, 10cm in diameter, are covered with fibrous leaf bases. They are topped with dense tufts of dull green leaves 2–4m long: these are bipinnate with up to sixty triangular leaflets with a ragged edge and a

distinctive fish-tail shape. The flowers are a pale cream colour, then the fruit yellowish-green turning orange or dark red as they mature. The rate of growth is from 15–40cm per year. Grow the palm in full sun in a rich, well drained soil, with plenty of humus. An abundance of summer water is appreciated. An interesting and easily cultivated palm, the best known and perhaps best looking of the genus. Tolerant of low light, making it a good interior palm. Native to south-east Asia.

Casimiroa
Rutaceae

A genus of about six species of large shrubs or trees native to Mexico and central America. Only one species is normally grown for its edible fruit.

Caryota mitis

C. edulis WHITE SAPOTE

A fast-growing, tropical fruit tree 6–15m high, with a wide spread. It also makes an attractive ornamental tree. The trunk has thick, light grey bark, and is often contorted with age. The branches are long and pendulous. The shiny, green, leathery leaves are divided into five to seven oval leaflets 8–12cm long, with a long leaf stalk. The small greenish or white flowers are produced in winter or spring on new growth in axillary panicles. They are followed by

Casuarina equisetifolia

Casuarina equisetifolia

handsome, apple-shaped fruit 8–10cm round. The yellowish-green fruit have a shiny skin and hang on long stalks; they ripen in late summer. The taste resembles peach or mango, and is sweet, with a fragrant aroma. The tree will thrive in any well drained soil in full sun with regular summer water. Withstands more cold than avocados, and will grow anywhere that lemons grow. Native to Mexico.

Cassia
See *Senna.*

Castanea 'SWEET CHESTNUT' *Fagaceae*

A genus of about twelve species of hardy, deciduous trees and shrubs

native to the temperate northern regions. They are grown as ornamental specimen trees and for their edible fruit.

C. sativa SWEET CHESTNUT, SPANISH CHESTNUT

A large, broad tree that can reach 30m high and 15m wide. Usually grows to about 12–18m, with a rounded crown. The lance-shaped leaves are 12–20cm long, tough and glossy with coarsely toothed edges. Extremely ornamental in mid-summer when laden with hanging catkins 15cm long. The male flowers are in the upper part of the catkin and the female flowers in the lower part. They are followed by spiny fruit 5–6cm in diameter. They contain three edible nuts that have a pleasant taste when freshly roasted. Although drought-resistant, the tree grows better if given occasional summer water. Thrives in a well drained, light soil. Tolerates acid soil, but may become chlorotic on shallow, chalky soil. The trees were introduced into cultivation by the Romans. Native to southern Europe, north Africa and Asia.

Casuarina 'AUSTRALIAN PINE, SHE-OAK' *Casuarinaceae*

A genus of about sixty species of evergreen trees and shrubs native to Australia and the Pacific Islands. A genus with no clear relatives. It was once thought to be primitive, but is now considered to be highly evolved.

C. equisetifolia HORSETAIL TREE

A fast-growing tree to 15m high, spreading to 8m wide. The long, green, pendulous branches, which look like pine needles, sway in the wind. The true leaves are inconspicuous, as they

are reduced to scales 1mm long, arranged in whorls of six to eight. The flowers are unisexual, with the male flowers borne in spikes and the female flowers in dense heads. The broadly oblong cones are about 2cm long. A seashore pioneer tree that is good for hedges and windbreaks. Tolerates many tough conditions where it will withstand wet or dry soil, salinity, heat and wind. Adaptable as a patio tree. Often grown as a street tree where it gives a wonderful light shade. Needs no summer water once established. Cultivated widely in the tropics where it has become naturalized.

Catalpa *Bignoniaceae*

A genus of about eleven species of deciduous or (rarely) evergreen trees native to North America and East Asia. They make good lawn and avenue trees, and are often used to line streets in both northern European and Mediterranean towns and parks. They are grown for their handsome, tropical-looking foliage as well as their attractive flowers and fruit.

C. bignonioides INDIAN BEAN TREE

A many-branched tree, 8–15m high, with a round, spreading head that makes it a splendid specimen tree for the larger garden. The 20cm broad, heart-shaped deciduous leaves have an unpleasant odour when crushed. The large upright panicles, 20–30cm high, of trumpet-shaped flowers appear in early summer. Each fragrant flower is about 5cm in diameter, white, with two yellow stripes inside and many soft brown spots. They are followed by the bean-shaped fruit that are 20–40cm

Catalpa bignonioides

Catalpa bignonioides

C

long. Grow the tree in full sun in any well drained soil. Although it will take some aridity, it prefers some summer water. The large leaves can be damaged by wind. When in flower it makes a spectacular sight, with the bonus of being covered in beans in autumn. Native to south-east USA. There is a golden-leaved variety, 'Aurea', but its leaves can be scorched by strong sun, and it is slower growing.

Catharanthus 'MADAGASCAR PERIWINKLE' *Apocynaceae*

A small genus of about five species of perennials and annuals native to Madagascar. Grown for their colourful summer flowers.

C. roseus (syn. *Vinca rosea*)
MADAGASCAR PERIWINKLE

An erect, fleshy perennial that is often grown as an annual. It makes a bushy plant up to 60cm high and wide. The oblong, glossy, dark green leaves have a white centre vein and are 2–8cm long. The showy, 4cm wide, solitary or terminal clusters of flowers cover the plant. They are normally rosy-red with a purple throat, but vary to mauve and white. This charming perennial flowers profusely for months on end, and is good for summer and autumn colour in hot climates. The plant can be grown in full sun or partial shade, and only requires a moderate amount of summer water. Easily grown from seed, it will flower the first year if sown early. There are also dwarf and trailing varieties.

Catharanthus roseus

Ceanothus 'CALIFORNIA LILAC' *Rhamnaceae*

A genus of about fifty-five species of deciduous and evergreen shrubs or small trees native to western USA, particularly California, and also to eastern USA and Mexico. They are grown for their often spectacular displays of blue, sometimes white or pink flowers. Grow the shrub in full sun. As it occurs naturally on dry, rocky slopes, it needs no summer water once established. The roots are liable to rot if kept in waterlogged soil, so ensure they are given excellent drainage. Although lime-tolerant, the shrub may become chlorotic on shallow chalk soils. Dislikes being hard pruned, and generally will not resprout from old wood. Should be pruned lightly after flowering by cutting off dead flower spikes. It is not considered long-lived, five to ten years being usual, but it does make rapid growth in early life.

C. arboreus 'Trewithen Blue'

A vigorous, evergreen shrub or tree, up to 5m high, with a wide spread to 5m or more. The broadly oval to rounded mid-green leaves, 8–10cm long, are shallowly toothed, with fine soft hairs underneath. The large, conical clusters, to 12cm long, of deep blue, fragrant flowers, cover the shrub in mid- to late spring. Garden origin.

C. impressus
SANTA BARBARA CEANOTHUS

A densely branched, broad-spreading evergreen shrub up to 2m high and wide. The alternate, broadly elliptic to round, dark green leaves are only 1cm long; they are deeply veined, with crinkled or wavy edges. The dark blue flowers are produced in rounded clusters, 2–3cm across, in great profusion during late spring. Native to California.

C. thyrsiflorus BLUEBLOSSOM

A large, broad spreading, evergreen, hardy shrub 3m high and wide, or a small tree to 8m high. The vigorous upright branches are covered with alternate, oblong, finely toothed leaves to 5 cm long which are glossy above. In spring it bears a great profusion of pale to deep blue or rarely white flowers in large terminal and lateral panicles 3-8 cm long. Native to California. The prostrate variety 'repens' is low growing to about 1m high spreading to 3m wide. Makes an excellent ground cover as it forms a dense carpet. In spring and early summer the shrub is covered with a mass of blue flowers.

Cedrela sinensis
See *Toona sinensis*.

Cedrus 'CEDAR' *Pinaceae*

A small genus of four species of large, hardy evergreen coniferous trees native to the Mediterranean region and the Himalayas. They can make majestic specimen trees if given enough room to grow, and should only be planted in large gardens or parks.

C. atlantica (syn. C. *libani* subsp. *atlantica*) ATLAS CEDAR

A conical, coniferous tree that makes slow to moderate growth to 20m high and 10m or more wide, with open angular growth when young. With age it develops fissured, silvery-grey bark. The leaves are needle-shaped, roughly four-sided, 2cm long, and arranged in whorls of thirty to forty along the short shoots of the new growth. The colour is normally a glaucous silvery-blue, but can vary. The tree is generally thirty to forty years old before it starts to flower,

Cedrus atlantica

male and female flowers being produced separately. Bluish-green female cones, which are held upright, are barrel-shaped, 6–10cm long, becoming pale brown when ripe. Grow the tree in full sun in any well drained soil. Deep rooted, so it is extremely drought tolerant once established, needing no summer water. Less spreading than other species, but still needing plenty of room to be seen at its best. Native to the Atlas Mountains in Morocco. Some cultivars are: 'Aurea', which is slower growing with golden yellow foliage; 'Fastigiata', which is narrow-conical with bluish-green leaves; 'Glauca', with vivid, glaucous blue leaves that are whitish at first; and 'Pendula' with drooping branchlets.

C. deodara DEODAR CEDAR

A large, evergreen, coniferous tree that makes fast growth to 30m high and 10m or more wide in favourable places, making it the tallest-growing species. Easily distinguished by the pendulous habit of the leading shoot of the young trees. The bark is dark brown or black. The needle-like leaves are up to 5cm long, dark green and sharply pointed. The glaucous cones, which are held upright, are barrel-shaped, up to 15cm long and 8cm wide, green at first,

Cedrus deodara

becoming pale brown when ripe. Male and female young cones usually appear on separate trees, but not always. Grow the tree in full sun in any well drained soil. Deep-rooted, so extremely drought-tolerant once established, needing no summer water. A tree for the larger garden or park. Native to the western Himalayas where it is widely distributed. Two cultivars are 'Aurea', which is slower-growing, with golden yellow foliage; and 'Pendula' ('Prostrata'), which has drooping branches that will grow flat on the ground or hang over rocks or a wall.

C. libani CEDAR OF LEBANON

A large, often majestic, evergreen coniferous tree that makes slow growth to 30m high, with wide-spreading branches to 30m or more in favourable places. The tree has a tendency to form several trunks from near the ground. The tree is conical when young, becoming flat topped when old. The slightly flattened, four-sided, needle-like leaves are up to 3cm long, dark green and sharply pointed in erect clusters. The dull green cones are barrel-shaped, and up to 10cm long. In young trees the leading shoot may droop near its tip. Extremely drought-tolerant once established, needing no summer water. This tree spreads picturesquely to become a wonderful skyline tree with its long, horizontal branches and irregular crown – definitely for the largest of gardens. Native from Lebanon to Turkey.

Celtis 'HACKBERRY'
Ulmaceae

A genus of about seventy species of deciduous and evergreen trees and shrubs native to temperate and tropical regions worldwide. Closely related to 'elms' (Ulmus sp.) and similar to them but smaller. They make attractive trees often with good autumn colour.

C. australis
MEDITERRANEAN HACKBERRY

A medium-sized deciduous tree with smooth grey bark, which grows to 20m high, spreading to 15m wide. The young branches are upright, but become less so with age. The broad, lance-shaped leaves are 5–12cm long, deep green with a rough surface, greyish-

green, hairy underneath, and sharply toothed. The small flowers are followed by small, round fruit that are edible and attractive to birds. Grow the tree in full sun or partial shade. It is deep rooting and prefers a deep, fertile, well drained soil. Fairly drought-tolerant, but grows better with some summer water. Native to the Mediterranean region and southwest Asia.

Celtis australis

C. occidentalis
HACKBERRY, SUGARBERRY

A handsome deciduous tree that can grow to 20m high, with a broad crown. The branches are spreading and sometimes pendulous. Old trees have rough, warted bark. The oval to lance-shaped leaves, to 12cm long, are bright green and finely toothed along the edges. They appear late in the year. The sweet, edible fruit are orange-red to black, 1cm across, and produced in great profusion. The tree will take wind, heat, drought and alkaline soil. Grows best in areas with long, hot summers. Native to eastern North America.

Centauria
Asteraceae

A huge genus containing 400–500 species of annuals, biennials, perennials and shrubs. They are native mostly to

C

the Mediterranean region, west and central Asia and North Africa, and contain many bright summer flowers, popular annuals and colourful perennials.

C. cineraria (syn. C. candidissima) DUSTY MILLER ⌣⌣

An erect, branching perennial that grows 80cm or more high, and will spread to 45cm wide. Grown mainly for its attractive, woolly white leaves, 10–15cm long and deeply divided into many blunt segments; they can become green on the upper surface. The solitary purple flowers, to 3cm across, with dark brown pointed bracts beneath, appear in summer. This easily grown perennial is often seen used as striking groundcover, in which case it should be kept short and bushy by cutting back in spring. Easily grown from seed. Often listed as *C. maritima*. Only occasional watering in summer is needed. Native to the Mediterranean region.

Centranthus 'Valerian'
Valerianaceae

A genus of about twelve species of annuals or perennials, native to dry, sunny areas of Europe, the Mediterranean region, Africa and south-west Asia. Only one species is in common cultivation, grown for its attractive flowers that appear over a long season.

C. ruber RED VALERIAN ⌣

A compact, bushy perennial to about 1m high and wide with glaucous stems. The oval to lance-shaped, fleshy, shiny leaves are 10cm long. The dense, terminal clusters of small deep crimson to pale pink or white, star-shaped, fragrant flowers are produced during spring and summer. A tough, rank perennial that will grow in difficult situations in full sun or in shade. Makes a wonderful sight when planted *en masse*. As it sets seed easily it can become invasive. Drought-tolerant, and thrives on poor, chalky soils. On richer soils with more water it can become softer and lax. Removing the old flowering stems will encourage a second crop of flowers and reduce seed distribution. The flowers are attractive to butterflies. Native to southern Europe, north Africa and Turkey. The variety 'Albus' has white flowers.

Cerastium
Caryophyllaceae

A genus of about a 100 species of low-growing or mat-forming annuals or perennials found throughout the world. All but a few are too weedy for use in the garden.

C. tomentosum SNOW-IN-SUMMER ⌣ or ⌣⌣

A hardy, evergreen, low creeping perennial that will spread to 1m or

Cerastium tomentosa

more. The masses of lance-shaped leaves, 2cm long, are silver-grey and woolly. During spring the plant is covered with a profusion of snow-white flowers 2cm across with five deeply notched petals. The plant will grow in full sun or partial shade. Suitable for planting in rock gardens or raised beds, but with good drainage as water-logged soil causes the roots to rot. When established it withstands drought, but grows better with some summer water. Native to Italy, but naturalized in Europe.

Ceratonia
Caesalpiniaceae

A genus of only one species of evergreen tree, with a dense crown, native to the eastern Mediterranean region. Although an attractive tree, it is generally grown for its fruit.

C. siliqua CAROB ⌣

A large, often multi-stemmed tree, 12–15m high and nearly as wide, often with branches to the ground. The stems are brittle, breaking easily in strong wind. The dark green, 15–30cm long, leathery pinnate leaves are divided into four to ten leaflets. The 15cm-long racemes of small red flowers appear directly on old wood in winter. They are followed by flattened, brown seedpods 20–30cm long. The pods are eaten by livestock, or milled into a fine powder used as a chocolate substitute. The sweet pods can also be chewed. Grow the tree in full sun in any well drained soil. Will survive well without summer water, but an occasional deep watering will improve it.

Centranthus ruber

Ceratonia siliqua

Ceratostigma 'PLUMBAGO'
Plumbaginaceae

A small genus of about eight species of small shrubs or perennials native to China and tropical East Africa. They are often called 'Hardy Plumbago' as they are closely related to *Plumbago auriculata*.

C. griffithii BURMESE PLUMBAGO

A multi-stemmed evergreen shrub, up to 80cm high and spreading to 80cm wide, with stems covered with reddish hairs. The oval leaves are up to 3cm long, often turning red in late autumn. The brilliant, deep blue flowers grow up to 2cm across in clusters. They appear from late summer until late autumn. Although drought-tolerant, the shrub will grow and flower better with regular summer water. Grow in full sun or partial shade, in any well drained soil. Can be hard pruned in spring to remove the old wood and encourage new growth. Native to the Himalayas of Tibet and Bhutan.

C. plumbaginoides
DWARF PLUMBAGO

A dwarf, multi-stemmed, deciduous shrub up to 40cm high, which spreads by underground stems that can eventually cover a large area. The bronze-green or dark green leaves are 8cm long, and may turn reddish-brown in autumn. The brilliant blue flowers are 1cm across, appearing in clusters from mid-summer until autumn. Suitable for a large rock garden or the front of a shrub border. With age the old crown may become woody, when it should be replaced with new rooted stems. The shrub will grow in full sun or partial shade in any well drained soil. Although drought-tolerant, it will grow and flower better with regular summer water. Native to Western China.

C. willmottianum
CHINESE PLUMBAGO

A low-spreading, multi-stemmed deciduous shrub that grows to 1.5m high, with angled branches. The 5cm long, oval to roundish leaves are bristly on both sides, and tinted red in autumn. The bright blue, salver-shaped flowers are 1–2cm across; they are carried terminally or in axillary heads in profusion from mid-summer until autumn. Culture is similar to C. *griffithii*. Native to Western China and Tibet.

Cercis
Caesalpiniaceae

A genus of about seven species of ornamental deciduous trees or shrubs that are native to North America, the Mediterranean and Asia. They are grown for their brightly coloured, pea-like flowers.

C. siliquastrum JUDAS TREE

A deciduous shrub or many-stemmed tree that generally grows to 10m high, with an equal spread. The leaves are roundish, 7–12cm wide, and heart-shaped at the base. Its clusters of three to six small, purplish-rose, pea-shaped flowers, 1–2cm long, appear in spring. They cover the naked branches and sometimes appear from the limbs and trunk. They are replaced by attractive clusters of reddish, flattened pods, which persist until after the leaves have fallen. The shrub withstands summer drought once established. Grows best in hot, dry, stony places. Plant when young, as it is likely to die if transplanted when mature. These shrubs are often seen growing along the sides of roads, making a wonderful sight when in full flower. Native to the eastern Mediterranean. 'Albida' has white flowers.

Cestrum
Solanaceae

A genus of around 150 species of evergreen and deciduous shrubs that are native to Mexico, South America and the West Indies. They are grown for their attractive and often powerfully fragrant flowers.

Cercis siliquastrum

C. aurantiacum
ORANGE CESTRUM

A semi-deciduous shrub to 2m or more high, spreading to 2m wide, with lax growth. Sometimes grown as a climber.

Ceratostigma willmottianum

C

Cestrum elegans

The deep green, oval leaves are up to 10cm long, and give off a strong odour when crushed. The bright orange, tubular, 3cm-long flowers are produced in terminal clusters, appearing during spring and summer, often followed by white berries. Grow the shrub in sun or partial shade in most well drained soils; may be trained against a wall or fence, or grown as a free-standing shrub. For best flowering, hard prune by cutting close to the ground annually each spring. Requires a moderate amount of summer water. Native to Venezuela and Guatemala.

C. elegans (syn. C. purpureum)
RED CESTRUM ꙮꙮꙮ
A tall, vigorous evergreen shrub that makes rapid growth to 3m or more high and wide, with stems that are slender and arching. The young stems are covered in soft red hairs. The softly hairy leaves are dark green, ovate to lance-shaped, up to 15cm long. The glowing red or reddish-purple slender tubular flowers are 2–3cm long; they appear in rather loose, pendant, terminal clusters, 10cm across, from spring and throughout summer, but a few will appear during winter. They are often followed by bright red berries. Grow the shrub in full sun or partial shade. For best flowering and growth, give it ample summer water and generous feeding. For best results it should be cut back severely after flowering. Native to Mexico.

C. 'Newellii' ꙮꙮꙮ
A fast-growing evergreen shrub to 3m high with a spread of 3m wide. The narrow, oval, dull green leaves are up to 15cm long. The shrub can cover itself in clusters of rich red, tubular flowers 2–3cm long for most of the year. Give ample water during summer, as it should not be allowed to dry out. Grow in full sun or partial shade. While it will withstand some frost, the young shoots may die back, but will quickly recover. When necessary, hard prune after flowering. Garden origin.

C. nocturnum NIGHT JESSAMINE, QUEEN OF THE NIGHT ꙮꙮꙮ
A vigorous, straggling, evergreen shrub that will grow to 3m high, spreading 2–3m wide. The shining, thin, leathery 8–15cm oblong leaves are deep green. The masses of rather open clusters of slender, tubular, creamy-white flowers are powerfully fragrant at night. Some people may find the scent too strong.

Cestrum nocturnum

They are produced from late summer into autumn. Removing the old stems that have flowered helps to encourage new flowering wood. The shrub grows best when planted in a warm, sheltered spot and given ample summer water. Native to the West Indies.

C. parqui
WILLOW-LEAVED JESSAMINE ꙮꙮꙮ
An upright-growing deciduous shrub, up to 3m high and wide, with many branches from the base. The bright green, willow-like leaves are up to 12cm long. The large, upright clusters of tubular, greenish-yellow, 2cm-long, flowers with star-shaped mouths are night scented. They are produced from summer to autumn. Grow the shrub in sun or partial shade. As with other Cestrums, cut back after flowering and give generous summer water. Not as attractive as other species, but the perfume is powerful. Native to Chile.

Cestrum parqui

Chaenomeles 'FLOWERING QUINCE, JAPONICA' Rosaceae

A small genus of three species of deciduous or semi-evergreen shrubs native to China and Japan. They are grown for their attractive flowers, which are produced in midwinter on bare stems. They are all frost-hardy.

C. speciosa ꙮꙮ
A strong-growing, bushy, deciduous shrub to 3m high and wide, with upright to spreading spiny branches. The oval, glossy, dark green leaves are up to 8cm long. In midwinter or early spring clusters of flowers 5cm across appear in profusion. The colour is normally red with attractive pale to bright yellow anthers. They are followed by fragrant, green-yellow, round to pear-shaped fruits to 6cm across. Grow in full sun or partial shade. Tolerant of most garden

Chaenomeles speciosa

soils, but may become chlorotic in highly alkaline soil. Give moderate summer water, although it will withstand some drought once established. Once buds have formed, stems can be cut for indoor decoration. A tough and practically indestructible shrub that flowers when little else is around. Many named varieties have been raised with red, pink or white flowers.

Chamaedorea
Arecaceae

A large genus of about a hundred species of medium-sized to small pinnate-leaved clustering or solitary-trunked palms native to Mexico, Central and South America. They are grown for their attractive leaves.

C. elegans (syn. Neanthe bella)
PARLOUR PALM ↝↝
A small, graceful, relatively fast-growing palm up to 3m high, spreading to 2m wide. The many slender stems have a terminal tuft of pinnate leaves loosely spirally arranged with the tips arching attractively away from the stems. The rich green leaves are up to 60cm long and comprise twenty to forty linear leaflets up to 20cm long. On older palms the branched, erect flowering inflorescence, 15–30cm long,

appears bearing many yellow flowers from spring to autumn. They may be followed by small, round fruit that are black when ripe. This is one of the most popular house palms in the world due to its ease of culture. Tolerates poor light, dry air, drought, flood and general neglect. Grows best in a shady position with a steady supply of summer water. Looks good in a shaded border or courtyard or in a pot on a shaded patio. Prefers a well drained, neutral to acid soil. Native to southern Mexico and Guatemala.

C. microspadix REED PALM ↝↝↝
A slow-growing cluster palm with slender, ringed stems to 3m high, and leaves covering most of the trunks. The alternate dark green leaves are up to 40cm long, with up to twenty widely spaced lance-shaped leaflets. The terminal pair of leaflets is usually larger than the others. In summer the pendant inflorescence, 20–60cm long, carries many small, cream-to-white flowers. They may be followed by small, spectacular, bright red fruit. This attractive palm is hardy enough to grow in a sheltered garden where it can tolerate temperatures as low as -5°C. Grows happily in full or partial shade (no sun) in a rich, well drained and peaty soil, with an abundance of water in dry weather. One of the few shade-loving hardy palms. Alternatively it is useful as a house or shaded patio plant. It can add form and colour to a difficult place. Native to east Mexico.

Chamaerops
Arecaceae

Only the one species of hardy palm native to the western Mediterranean region.

C. humilis MEDITERRANEAN FAN PALM ↝
A usually dwarf, cluster-forming palm that only in ideal conditions forms a trunk: this is rough and clothed with fibre, and it can grow to 6m high, but growth is extremely slow. The leaves are stiff and folded, 45cm long and up to 60cm wide, tough, green and fan-shaped. They are divided into many narrow segments, split nearly to the base, and are carried on flat, prickly leaf stalks up to 90cm long. Small, red-brown fruit follow the bunches of greenish-yellow flowers that are

produced in spring. One of the hardiest palms, thriving in full sun or partial shade. Completely drought-tolerant, but summer water will improve it. Not particular about soil, but grows better in deep, rich loam. A versatile palm that can be massed under trees or made into a low, informal hedge. Also a good palm for use in tubs on the patio. Easily propagated by seed, that germinates quickly with heat.

Chamaerops humilis

Chasmanthe
Iridaceae

A genus of about nine species of herbaceous perennials with corms, that are native to tropical and South Africa. They are easily cultivated and can become invasive.

C. aethiopica AFRICAN CORN FLAG ↝
An herbaceous perennial that forms clumps as the corms multiply. The bright green, sword-shaped leaves are stiffly erect, 30–60cm long and 4cm wide. They are often branched. The flowering stem that arises from the base may be up to 1m high, and is usually branched. Many orange-red, tubular flowers, 8cm long and with protruding stamens, appear along the stem. The flowering stems appear in great profusion during winter and early spring. The plant is easily grown

C

requiring no special treatment. Although it prefers full sun, it will grow in shade in most soils. Summer dormant, so it requires no water. It has often escaped into the wild. When the clumps have become too large and overcrowded, lift and divide in summer after flowering and when the leaves have turned yellow. Native to South Africa.

Chlorophytum
Anthericaceae

A genus of about 250 species of perennials, often with rhizomes, that are native to most parts of the tropical and subtropical world. They are perhaps one of the most popular and easily grown houseplants. The ubiquitous 'spider plant' is seen in vast numbers of offices and homes.

Chlorophytum comosum 'Vittatum'

Chasmanthe aethopica

C. comosum (syn. C. capense)
SPIDER PLANT مئ

An evergreen perennial that forms clumps 30–45cm high, with tufted rosettes of leaves, and long, white tuberous roots. The narrow green leaves – up to 45cm long and 2cm wide – are soft and curving. During most of the year, long racemes appear from the centre of the plant. Small (1cm long) white or yellowish flowers appear on the branches during summer. They are followed by tiny plantlets with roots,

which can easily be removed and planted. The green form is rarely grown. There is also the variety 'Variegatum', which has a white stripe on the edge of the leaves; but it is 'Vittatum', with a central white stripe, that is more popular and is usually grown; it is normally placed in partial shade, but it will take full sun, though needs generous summer watering. Although normally grown as a pot plant, it makes a good groundcover, either in shade, or in sun with adequate summer water. Native to southern and tropical Africa.

Choisya
Rutaceae

A small genus of around seven species of evergreen shrubs that are native to North America and Mexico. They are grown for their attractive leaves and for their fragrant white flowers.

C. ternata
MEXICAN ORANGE BLOSSOM مئ مئ

An easily grown, medium-sized shrub that forms a dense rounded mound up to 3m high and perhaps 4m wide. The trifoliate leaves are shiny dark green, 8cm long, and form fans, giving the shrub a dense, massive look. They have a strong, pungent odour when crushed. The clusters of white, sweetly scented flowers, 2–3cm across, cover the shrub in early spring; they are held conspicuously above the foliage. A few flowers may appear intermittently throughout summer. Although tolerant

of some shade, the best flowers are produced in full sun. Grow the shrub in a well drained soil that is not too alkaline. For good growth and flowering, water occasionally and deeply during summer. The leaves can suffer from wind damage. Makes an attractive informal hedge or screen. Native to Mexico. The variety 'Sundance' has bright golden foliage and is lower growing, but may scorch in the sun.

Chorisia
Bombacaceae

A small genus of about two species of evergreen or deciduous trees native to South America, with spiny, fleshy trunks and spectacular flowers.

C. speciosa KAPOK TREE مئ مئ

A tree with a solid, heavy trunk, enlarged at the base and covered with short, stout spines. The young trunk is green, but becomes grey with age. Makes rapid growth at first, then slows down as it becomes established,

Choisya ternata

Chorisia speciosa

Chorisia speciosa

eventually reaching 9–15m high. Mature trees are usually pyramidal or conical in shape. The palmately compound leaves have seven or more leaflets, with each leaflet up to 15cm long. The large, showy, five-petalled flowers are 8–12cm wide, resembling narrow-petalled hibiscus. They are pink to almost red, with white to yellow throats and brown or purple dots. These spectacular flowers appear in late summer or autumn when the tree may be briefly deciduous. They may be followed by pear-shaped fruits containing silky floss on the seeds, but these are rarely seen in cultivation. Grow the tree in full sun, in neutral to acid soil with good drainage. Give a

deep watering once a month when it is established. Reducing the watering of established trees in late summer is the key to successful flowering. Native to Brazil and Argentina. The variety 'Majestic Beauty' has rich, pink flowers.

Chrysalidocarpus lutescens
See *Dypsis lutescens.*

Chrysanthemum frutescens
See *Argyranthemum frutescens.*

Chrysanthemum maximum
See *Leucanthemum x superbum.*

Cinnamomum
Lauraceae

A large genus of about 250 species of evergreen aromatic trees and shrubs native to eastern and south-east Asia and Australia.

C. camphora CAMPHOR TREE

An evergreen tree growing 12m high or more, with a wide spread. The young branches are yellowish to brown. The dense crown of narrowly ovate, boldly veined, shiny dark green leaves are 5–12cm long. In winter the leaves turn a shiny yellow-green, and in spring the new leaves have a pink, red or bronze tint. When crushed the leaves have a camphor odour. Tiny, fragrant yellow flowers appear in profusion in axillary clusters during spring. They are followed by small berry-like fruit. The tree grows best in full sun when given occasional deep watering during summer. Thrives in frost-free areas with hot summers. A magnificent evergreen specimen tree for a large lawn. The twigs, leaves and wood are distilled to produce oil of camphor. Native to eastern China to southern Japan and Taiwan.

Cistus 'ROCK ROSE, SUN ROSE'
Cistaceae

A genus containing about twenty species of small or medium evergreen shrubs native to the Mediterranean region. Many hybrids have arisen in the wild and in cultivation. The leaves are normally aromatic. Being totally drought-tolerant, they are excellent for dry gardens in full sun. They thrive in

any poor, well drained soil, and can take salt spray and wind. Pinch back young plants to encourage a bushy habit, and remove a few old stems from time to time. They are excellent on a dry bank, on a large rock garden, or in rough areas along the side of paths and drives.

C. × aguilarii

An upright-growing shrub to 1m or more, spreading to 1.5m wide. The lance-shaped leaves are up to 10cm long, and shiny. The flowers are 9cm wide, and white with a yellow centre; they are borne profusely in spring. Native to Spain and Morocco.

C. albidus WHITE-LEAVED ROCKROSE

A conspicuous shrub up to 1m high. The whitish-grey, velvety, oblong leaves are 7cm long. The large, crumpled rose or magenta flowers are 4–6cm wide, and appear in heads of one to four at the ends of the branches in spring. Another flush of flowers may be produced in autumn. Native to Portugal to Italy, western North Africa.

C. algarvensis
See *Halimium ocymoides.*

C. landanifer GUM CISTUS

A compact-growing shrub to 1m or more high, with fragrant, sticky branches. The lance-shaped leaves, 10cm long, are dark green above, with white cotton hairs underneath. The flowers are 5–10cm across, appearing singly at the ends of short branches in late spring. They are white, usually with a purple blotch at the base of each petal. Native to Portugal to France, and western North Africa.

Cistus albidus

C

Cistus landanifer

C. *laurifolius* ☽

An upright-growing shrub with stiff, erect growth, to 1.5m high and wide. The 8cm long, ovate dark green leaves are sticky and aromatic with pale undersides. The white flowers with yellow centres are 5–7cm wide and borne in long, stalked clusters of three or more during early summer. Native to Portugal and Italy.

C. *populifolius* ☽

A large, aromatic shrub up to 1.5m high, with sticky, hairless branches. The heart-shaped, pointed leaves are up to 10cm long. The white flowers have a yellow centre, and are 4–6cm across. They are in few flowered heads with drooping red buds. Native from Portugal to southern France.

C. × *purpureus* ORCHID ROCKROSE ☽

A small shrub with reddish stems up to 1m high and wide. The leaves are lance-shaped, 3–5cm long, and have a wavy edge. The reddish-purple to pink flowers have a dark red spot at the base of the petal, which contrasts with the cluster of yellow stamens.

Cistus laurifolius

C. *salvifolius* SAGELEAF ROCKROSE ☽

A wide, spreading shrub that grows to 1m high and can spread to 2m wide. The small, oval, grey-green leaves are 2cm long, not sticky and hardly aromatic. The white flowers are 4cm wide and have yellow spots at the base of the petals. They are on long stalks, solitary or in few flowered heads, and are produced in great profusion in late spring. Native to southern Europe.

Citrus
Rutaceae

A small genus of about sixteen species of evergreen, usually spiny shrubs, or small to medium-sized trees native to south and south-east Asia. Several kinds are the citrus fruits of commerce, but they are also attractive throughout the year. Many are just frost hardy, but most need a minimum temperature of 5–10°C. Citrus need deep, moist, free-draining soil that is never waterlogged. To obtain the best fruit, generous summer watering is needed. The powerfully fragrant white flowers have five oblong, outward-curving petals. The scent from an orchard can be overwhelming. Citrus also make attractive tub or container shrubs, but they will be smaller.

C. *aurantiifolia* LIME ☽☽☽

A thorny tree to 5m high. The aromatic, glossy green, oval leaves are 6–8cm long. The flowers are followed by green to yellowish-green fruit 3–5cm in diameter. They are usually in clusters. The fruit is smooth-skinned with an acid, seedy pulp. Limes are the most tender of the citrus species.

C. *aurantium*
SOUR OR SEVILLE ORANGE ☽☽

A vigorous tree up to 9m high with a spread of up to 6m. The slender, pointed, oval leaves are up to 10cm long. The flowers are followed by large, orange, rough-skinned fruit 8cm in diameter. They are bitter, and often made into marmalade or into liqueur. Often grown as a street tree.

C. *limon* LEMON ☽☽☽

A small tree to 6m high, usually with short, stout spines. The glossy, oval leaves are up to 8cm long. The flowers are red-tinted in bud, and open to white

Cistus purpureus

with a purple tinge to 5cm across. The yellow fruit are 5–10cm long with a terminal nipple, and very acid. There are many varieties, with 'Eureka', 'Improved Meyer' and 'Lisbon' among the most popular. Ripe fruit are produced almost throughout the year. Lemons are more hardy than limes, but less hardy than sweet oranges.

C. × *paradisi* GRAPEFRUIT ☽☽☽

A large, spreading tree with a rounded crown up to 5m high, spreading to 3m. Usually grown on dwarfing rootstock. The dark green, oval leaves are 8cm long. The flowers are followed by large yellow fruit up to 15cm across. The smooth branches bend under the

Citrus aurantium

Citrus limon 'Lunario'

weight of the heavy fruit. 'Marsh Seedless' is the white-fleshed grapefruit with few seeds; 'Ruby' has pink flesh with a sweeter taste.

C. reticulata ♪♪♪

The Mandarin, Clementine, Satsuma and Tangerine belong here. A small tree with slender, upright branches up to 3m high, which often hang with the weight of fruit. The dark green, lance-shaped leaves are up to 8cm long. The fruit is up to 8cm across, sweet and easily peeled. They are usually ready for picking in early winter before sweet oranges are ready. They are more hardy than most citrus.

C. sinensis SWEET ORANGE ♪♪♪

A beautiful, dense tree that grows to 6m high and wide, with spiny branches. The glossy, dark green, oval leaves are up to 10cm long. The powerfully fragrant white flowers are followed by the large, orange fruit. Because of its economic importance, many varieties have been bred to suit many local conditions. They have also been bred to ripen at different stages, from autumn through to late spring. 'Valencia' and 'Washington Navel' are among the most popular varieties. A most attractive tree at all times of the year.

Clematis
Ranunculaceae

A large genus of over 200 species of perennials or mostly deciduous woody climbers native to northern temperate regions. All have attractive flowers, and some are spectacular. The choice cultivars prefer cooler conditions, cool soil and moister air. There are only a few species that grow well in warm climates.

C. armandii EVERGREEN CLEMATIS ♪♪

A fast-growing climber, to 6m high and 8m wide. The large, leathery, glossy, evergreen leaves are divided into three leaflets. They are 8–13cm long, and droop downwards. The clusters of white, fragrant flowers, 6cm wide, appear in early spring in panicles from the leaf axils. They start bell-shaped, then open out to almost flat, up to 8cm wide. Each flower has five or six widely

Citrus sinensis 'Washington Navel'

separated petals with cream anthers: they cover the climber, making a spectacular sight. It grows best with its roots in shade and the top in sun. To grow well it needs regular summer water. Slow to grow at first, but grows quickly once established. Prune after flowering to keep under control, as it can soon form a thick, tangled mat. Native to central and western China. The variety 'Apple Blossom' has blush pink flowers; 'Snowdrift' has larger, white flowers.

C. cirrhosa VIRGIN'S BOWER ♪♪

An evergreen climber eventually reaching 2m high, but which can be kept lower by pruning. The shiny, leathery, rounded leaves turn bronze in winter and may die off in the hottest part of summer. The citrus-scented, bell-shaped, creamy-white flowers are 4cm across, appearing during winter and spring. The climber will take drier soils than most clematis, but grows better with some summer water. Native to eastern Mediterranean. The variety 'Balearica' has pale yellow flowers, spotted reddish-purple; 'Freckles' is a larger, flowered form tinged pink with maroon spots; 'Wisley Cream' has large, creamy-white unspotted flowers.

Clematis armandii

Clerodendrum 'GLORYBOWER'
Verbenaceae

A large genus with about 400 species of deciduous and evergreen trees, shrubs or climbers that are native to the tropical regions of Africa and Asia. Most have attractive, or even spectacular, brightly coloured flowers.

C. bungei GLORY FLOWER ♪♪♪

An evergreen, suckering shrub that may eventually form a large clump. The mostly unbranched stems grow up to 2m high. The long leaf stalks bear

C

Clerodendrum bungei

broadly heart-shaped leaves, up to 30cm long and coarsely toothed. They are green above, reddish underneath, and have an unpleasant smell when crushed. The beautiful large clusters, up to 20cm wide, of terminal flowers are rosy-red and strongly scented. Each flower is a dark violet when in bud, and opens to five spreading lobes of pink: this gives the flowerhead two colours. They are produced during spring and summer. The shrub grows best in partial shade, but can take some sun. Give it a generous amount of summer water to grow well, as it is not drought-tolerant. The old stems that have flowered should be cut out in winter. The shrub suckers so it can become invasive. Native to southern China, Myanmar (Burma) and eastern India.

C. myricoides 'Ugandense' (syn. C.Ugandense) ♪♪♪

An evergreen shrub up to 2m or more high, with shiny stems and leaves. A shrub with lax growth that may be

Clerodendrum myricoides 'Ugandense'

trained as a climber. The dark green, elliptic or oval leaves are up to 10cm long and toothed along the edges. The most unusual, beautiful flowers are in terminal panicles 10–15cm long. Each flower is 3cm long, has four pale blue petals and one violet-blue petal. The filaments are purple and the anthers are blue, arching outwards and upwards. They make a striking effect when produced during spring. Give a generous amount of summer water. The shrub grows best in partial shade, but can take some sun. To grow well it needs a rich, well drained soil. Native to Uganda to Zimbabwe.

C. × speciosum ♪♪

A beautiful, tender, evergreen, woody climber up to 2m high with upright branches, normally grown against a wall. The glossy dark green leaves are up to 20cm long with purplish veins. The terminal clusters of flowers are 16cm wide. The flowers are 5cm long and have a pinkish calyx and deep red petals with a protruding red stamen. They are normally produced during summer, but may also appear throughout the year. The climber grows best in partial shade, but can take some sun. To grow well it needs a generous amount of summer water. A garden hybrid between *C. splendens* and *C. thomsoniae*.

Clianthus
Papilionaceae

A small genus of two species of erect or trailing tender shrubs requiring a hot, sunny position in a well drained soil. They are native to Australia and New Zealand. They are grown for their showy flowers that resemble lobsters' claws.

C. puniceus
LOBSTER CLAW, PARROT'S BEAK ♪♪♪

A vigorous evergreen, upright, shrub-like climber with growth up to 3m high and perhaps 3m wide. The glossy pinnate leaves are 8–15cm long, and are composed of many oblong pairs of leaflets. The peculiar, claw-like, brilliant red flowers have an 8cm long keel-petal swung downwards. They are borne in clusters of six to fifteen on a pendulous stalk. The flowers resemble a parrot's beak, hence the common name. They are produced for most of

summer and are followed by 8cm-long seedpods. Because of its weak growth it is best given some support, trained against a wall, or allowed to tumble down a bank. To grow well the shrub requires ample summer water. Grow in full sun in well drained soil: it can rot in winter if the soil is waterlogged. Native to New Zealand. A white form, 'Albus', is sometimes grown.

Clerodendrum × speciosum

Clivia
Amaryllidaceae

A small genus of four species of evergreen bulbous perennials native to South Africa, with fleshy roots and beautiful flowers.

C. miniata ♪♪♪

An evergreen perennial that makes bold clumps of strap-shaped leaves, 50cm long, arranged in opposition one to another in a single plane. During winter the brilliant clusters of up to twenty flowers (8cm long) appear on stems up to 60cm high. The flowers are funnel-shaped, usually orange or scarlet, with a yellow throat. They are followed by ornamental berries that will readily produce seedlings. There are many garden varieties, so the colours are

Clianthus puniceus

variable. The plants are best left undisturbed for several years: when they become too crowded they can be lifted and divided. They require a soil rich in organic matter, with plenty of water during the growing season. Clivias grow well in shade, as they flower best when given plenty of light with only a little sun. Excellent for growing in pots or containers where they flower well. Plants should be kept in the same pot for several years and given generous liquid feeding. Useful on patios and on balconies. They can also be used for edging paths or borders where there is shade from trees. This is the most widely grown clivial.

Clivia nobilis

Clivia miniata

C. nobilis 🌢🌢🌢

An evergreen perennial with clumps of strap-shaped leaves 45cm long. During spring it produces umbels of forty to sixty drooping flowers up to 40cm high. Each narrow, trumpet-shaped flower, 2–4cm long, is salmon red with green tips. Cultivation is the same as for C. miniata.

Clytostoma
Bignoniaceae

A small genus of about eight species of evergreen climbing shrubs, native to tropical South America. They are grown for their beautiful flowers that can cover the plant.

C. callistegioides (syn. Bignonia violacea, B. speciosa, Pandorea lindleyana)

ARGENTINE TRUMPET VINE 🌢🌢

A vigorous, climbing shrub, up to 10m high, that will clamber over anything by tendrils. The opposite, glossy, dark green, oval leaves, up to 10cm long, are divided into two or three leaflets. The beautiful, large, funnel-shaped lavender or violet flowers, up to 8cm wide, have spreading lobes veined with lilac; they are produced in pairs at the end of the shoots during spring or summer. The flowers appear in great abundance. The shrub requires an open position in full sun or partial shade, but dislikes the intense heat of walls. Use to clothe a pergola or climb into a tree. Prune severely during winter to prevent tangled growth. Give it a moderate amount of summer water. A beautiful shrub that is spectacular when in full flower. Native to southern Brazil and Argentina.

Clytostoma callistegioides

Cobaea
Cobaeaceae

A genus of ten or more species of evergreen, shrubby and herbaceous climbers native to Mexico and tropical South America. Only one species is generally grown for its unusual large flowers.

C. scandens CUP AND SAUCER PLANT 🌢🌢🌢

A vigorous, evergreen, climbing perennial, 10m or more high, with a wide spread that becomes woody when mature. Climbs by tendrils that cling to any rough surface without support. The rich green leaves are pinnate, composed of four to six ovate leaflets 10cm or more long; the midrib of each leaf terminates in a branched tendril. The flowers are borne on long stalks rising from the leaf axils. The calyx is bright green, lobed and wavy like a saucer. The central, bell-shaped flower, 5cm long, with prominent stamens, opens a creamy green, then ages to violet or rosy-purple. The flowers are produced mostly in spring and early summer, but may continue throughout most of the year. Grow the climber in full sun in well drained soil. Generous summer watering is needed. Use to clothe a pergola, sunny wall or grow into a tree. Perfect as a fast-growing cover or screen. Although a perennial, in warm areas it soon becomes untidy, therefore is often treated as an annual as the seeds germinate easily. Native to Mexico.

Cobaea scandens

Cocculus
Menispermaceae

A small genus of eleven species of evergreen and deciduous shrubs and small trees of wide distribution, from North America and tropical and temperate eastern Asia. Only one species is generally grown for its lush foliage.

C. laurifolius LAUREL-LEAVED
SNAILSEED, PLATTER-LEAF ꞷꞷꞷ
A slow-growing evergreen, usually multi-stemmed shrub to 5m high, with wide-spreading, wiry green branches. The shiny, leathery leaves, 12–15cm long, are a deep green, elliptic to oblong, with three prominently raised, yellow-green veins. Tiny yellow flowers are produced in spikes, followed by black berries, but it seldom flowers in cultivation. The shrub can be grown in full sun or in shade in any well drained

Cocculus laurifolius

soil. Generous summer watering is preferred. Useful as a screen or background plant: the long branches can be trained against a wall or as an espalier. The foliage is useful in flower arrangements. Native from southern Japan to the Himalayas.

Cocos plumosa
See *Syagrus romanzoffiana*.

Cocus australis
See *Butia capitata*.

Cocus capitata
See *Butia capitata*.

Cocus yatay
See *Butia yatay*.

Colchicum
'AUTUMN CROCUS, NAKED LADIES'
Colchicaceae

A genus of about fifty species of cormous perennials native to Europe, North Africa, west and central Asia, northern India and west China. They are grown for their attractive flowers that are produced during autumn.

C. autumnale AUTUMN CROCUS,
MEADOW SAFFRON ꞷ
A perennial with a corm 3-5cm long, with a blackish sheath. The upright, linear leaves are produced in spring in a group of four or more, 20–35cm long and 4–5cm wide. In autumn it produces flowers 10–25cm high, solitary or in groups of two to five, with long stalks. They are goblet shaped, and lavender-pink, rose-pink or white. Grow the plants in full sun where they are not disturbed. They may need lifting and dividing after four to five years. Give water during the spring growing season in dry spells, and none during the summer dormant period. All parts of the plant are highly poisonous. Native to Europe and North Africa.

C. cupanii ꞷ
A cormous perennial with upright, linear, glossy leaves to 15cm long, produced in spring. In autumn it produces many star-shaped, pale to deep purplish-pink flowers, 4–5cm high. Grow the plant in full sun in a sharply drained, sandy soil. Only give water during the spring growing season

in dry spells, and none during the summer dormant period. It may need lifting and dividing after four to five years. Native to southern Europe, North Africa.

Colutea
Papilionaceae

A genus of about twenty-five species of hardy deciduous shrubs or small trees native to many regions from southern Europe to northern Africa and the western Himalayas. They are grown for their pea-like flowers and inflated, bladder-like seedpods.

C. arborescens BLADDER SENNA ꞷ
A strong-growing, bushy, deciduous shrub to 3m high and wide. The pinnate leaves to 15cm long have nine to thirteen small leaflets. During summer the yellow pea-like flowers, 2cm wide, are carried in clusters of three to eight in the leaf axils. They are followed by attractive seedpods, 8cm long, green at first, then turning translucent when ripe. Grow the shrub in full sun. Ideal for hot, dry locations as it requires no summer water once established. A tough shrub that will tolerate poor soil, coastal conditions and pollution. Prune after flowering to encourage bushiness. Native to southern

Colutea arborescens

Europe, Mediterranean region.
C. × media ꞷ
A strong-growing, medium-sized, deciduous shrub to 3m high and wide. The pinnate leaves are greyish up to 15cm long, with three to six pairs of leaflets. In early summer it bears rich, bronze-yellow flowers 1–2cm long, in racemes to 10cm long. They are followed by attractive seedpods 8cm long, greenish-

brown at first, turning translucent when ripe. Cultivation is the same as *C. arborescens*. Garden origin.

Convolvulus 'BINDWEED'
Convolvulaceae

A large genus containing some 250 species of annuals, perennials that are twining or trailing, evergreen shrubs or subshrubs, the majority of which are too weedy for the garden. They are distributed around the world.

C. cneorum SILVERBUSH
A small evergreen, rounded shrub that makes rapid growth to 30–90cm high and as wide. The oblong 2–6cm leaves are covered with velvety silver hairs. The white, bell-shaped flowers 4cm across have yellow throats opening from pink buds and are produced throughout summer. A good shrub for a dry border, with good drainage and in full sun. Requires little summer water once established. Prune severely if it becomes untidy. Native to central and western Mediterranean.

C. sabatius (syn. *C. mauretanicus*)
GROUND MORNING GLORY
A low-growing evergreen perennial 15cm high that will spread to 1m or more. Although roots are produced as it spreads, it is not considered invasive. The soft, pale grey-green, pubescent, roundish leaves are 1–3cm long. The

Convolvulus sabatius

bell-shaped, lavender blue flowers 3–5cm wide are produced throughout summer and autumn. Ideal on sloping banks and for scrambling over walls and container edges. The plant grows well in full sun or partial shade in soil with good drainage, but needs a moderate amount of summer water. Native to Spain, Italy, North Africa.

Copernicia 'WAX PALM'
Arecaceae

A genus of about twenty-four species of slow-growing, fan-leaved palms native mainly to Cuba as well as South America. These attractive, but largely unknown and under-utilized species are also somewhat drought-tolerant. They make attractive specimen trees.

C. alba CARANDY PALM or
A slow-growing palm that, with great age, may reach up to 20m high with a

Convolvulus cneorum

slender trunk. It retains the leaf bases that are arranged in a spiral pattern. The stiff, fan-shaped, blue to silver-green leaves, up to 1.5m wide, are carried on a toothed leafstalk 60cm or more long. The surfaces are densely covered in wax. The undersides of the leaves are silver-grey, giving a distinctive look. They form a rounded crown at the top of the trunk. The palm grows in most well drained soils. Excellent for hot dry climates. Makes an excellent house or pool subject in sun or partial shade. Adaptable and easy to look after. For best results give generous summer water until established. Seen by the million in the wild in Argentina, but inexplicably rare in cultivation. Hardy enough to survive severe frost for a few days. Native to southern Brazil and northern Argentina.

C. macroglossa
CUBAN PETTICOAT PALM or
A small, single-stemmed palm that is slow-growing to 5m high. The short trunk is normally covered in a skirt of old leaves. The large, wedge-shaped, deep green leaves are deeply cut, and stiff with spiny outer segments, to 1.5m long. They are stalkless or have short stalks. An unmistakable palm: with its dense crown of new leaves and skirt of old leaves, it can look like a haystack. Grow in full sun or partial shade in well drained soil. When established it withstands some drought, but it grows better with some summer water. Fairly tender to the cold. Native to Cuba.

Coprosma
Rubiaceae

A genus containing about ninety species of evergreen shrubs or small trees that are native to Australia, New Zealand and the Pacific Islands. They are dioecious (male and female flowers on different plants). Many species are extremely variable and hybrids are common, so it is sometimes difficult to identify individual plants.

C. 'Beatson's Gold'
A sprawling, evergreen shrub about 1m high, spreading to 2m wide. The oval, soft leathery, bright green leaves are 6–8cm long, and variegated with yellow splashes. The small, greenish flowers in spring are followed by small

C

Coprosma repens 'Exotica'

red fruit on female plants in autumn. The shrub will take full sun, but grows better if given some shade. To grow well it requires a moderate amount of summer water, but it will tolerate some drought. A valuable shrub for difficult situations. Garden origin.

C. repens MIRROR PLANT

A large, evergreen shrub, 4–5m high with a spread of 2–3m and a dense habit. The broadly oblong leaves are 8cm long, and a very shiny, glossy dark green. This gives it the common name of mirror plant. The inconspicuous white or greenish flowers may be followed by small orange fruit. Average summer water is required. This is the commonest species in cultivation. As it withstands much clipping it makes a useful hedging plant: about two clippings a year will keep it dense and at any height required. Old, gnarled trees that have been allowed to grow can look picturesque. Native to New Zealand. There are many variegated cultivars: 'Exotica', with yellow variegated leaves; 'Marble Queen' with cream mottling; and 'Variegata', which has leaves blotched with yellowish-green. They grow better in partial shade as the strong sunlight can burn the leaves.

Coprosma repens 'Marble Queen'

Cordyline
'CABBAGE TREE, CABBAGE PALM'
Agavaceae

A genus of about twenty species of sparsely branched, evergreen, palm-like shrubs or trees that are native to southeast Asia and Australasia. They are often confused with Dracaena as they are similar in appearance, but the flowers of Cordyline are tubular. They make excellent pot or container plants when young.

Cordyline australis

C. australis (syn. Dracaena australis)
CABBAGE TREE

An upright-growing, palm-like tree that may eventually grow to 8m high, usually forming a single trunk and bearing several stout upright branches. Each branch has a large mass of narrow, sword-shaped leaves 60–90cm long and 3–6cm wide. The upper leaves are upright, while the lower leaves tend to droop: on a young plant this gives it a fountain-like appearance. The large, terminal panicles are 30–90cm long, with fragrant, creamy-white flowers that appear in late spring. A tough tree that will take any soil, will withstand frost and is drought-tolerant. Looks good when grown amongst rocks on a bank to give a tropical look. Also suited to coastal areas, as it withstands salt-laden sea breezes. Grow in full sun, as it

dislikes shade. Native to New Zealand. The form 'Atropurpurea' has purple leaves and is slower-growing, and 'Albertii' has a cream edge to the leaves. Both forms only grow up to 3–4m high.

C. indivisa (syn. Dracaena indivisa)

A small tree rarely seen more than 3m high, but which can grow to 10m high and spread to 4m wide. The normally unbranched stem has a dense head of broad, rather stiff pointed leaves. They can be 1–2m long and 10–15cm wide, with a prominent red or yellow midrib. The masses of small white or cream flowers are borne in large, drooping panicles, which may be 1m or more long. Grow the tree in full sun or partial shade. Tolerates drought and coastal conditions. A plant that looks good near swimming pools. Easily propagated from seed, sown any time of the year. Native to New Zealand. 'Purpurea' has bronze-purple leaves.

Cordyline indivisa

Corokia
Escalloniaceae

A small genus of about four species of evergreen shrubs or small trees native to New Zealand. In gardens that are subject to frost, grow in a sheltered border or against a wall. In warmer gardens they can be used for hedging or as specimen plants.

C. buddlejoides ☽ or ☽☽

A medium-sized, erect shrub up to 3m high and 2m wide, with slender stems. The oblong, lance-shaped, glossy, dark green leaves are 6cm long and leathery, with silvery-white felt underneath. The terminal racemes of small, yellow star-like, fragrant flowers that appear in spring are followed by dark red berries. The shrub can be grown in sun or partial shade, or even in dry shade. A well drained soil is essential. Grows better if given moderate summer water, but it can take some drought.

C. cotoneaster
WIRE NETTING BUSH ☽ or ☽☽

A slow-growing shrub to 3m high, and as wide. The stiff, wiry branches are nearly black; they are also contorted, and zigzag in all directions, earning it the common name. The small, oval leaves, just 2cm long, are dark green above, with white felt underneath. The tiny, yellow, star-like, fragrant flowers appear in spring, and are followed by small orange-red berries. The shrub tolerates alkaline soil and dry conditions, but grows better if given moderate summer water. A good shrub for coastal gardens as it withstands salt-laden sea breezes.

C. × virgata ☽ or ☽☽

A variable hybrid forming a medium-sized shrub, to 3m high with upright growth. The stems are normally covered in white felt. The leaves are 4cm long and normally green, but may be bronze with silvery-white felt underneath. The fragrant yellow flowers appear in spring, and are followed by small orange or red berries. The shrub grows better if given moderate summer water, but can take some drought. A well drained soil is essential. Many forms have been raised, including 'Bronze King' with bronze-tinted leaves.

Coronilla
Papilionaceae

A genus of about twenty species of deciduous and evergreen hardy shrubs and herbaceous plants that are native to Europe, the Mediterranean region, Africa, North Asia and China. They have typical pea-shaped flowers.

C. valentina ☽

A dense, evergreen, bushy shrub that grows 1–2m high, spreading 2m wide. The small, glaucous, silver or grey-green pinnate leaves are 5–8cm long, with seven to eleven rounded leaflets. In spring it produces masses of rich yellow pea-shaped flowers, just 1cm long, with the fragrance of ripe peaches. Some flowers are produced intermittently throughout summer. The shrub grows best in full sun, and once established is drought-tolerant. Native to the Mediterranean region. The subspecies 'Variegata' has leaves with cream or white edges.

C. valentina subsp. glauca ☽

A subspecies that is frequently confused with, and misnamed as the species. More compact, growing to about 80cm high and wide. The blue-green leaves have five to seven leaflets. The bright yellow flowers, 1cm long, grow in clusters of up to fourteen; they are larger and more showy than the species. The shrub grows best in full sun in well drained soil, and once established is drought-tolerant. Native to the Mediterranean region.

Correa 'AUSTRALIAN FUCHSIA'
Rutaceae

A genus of about twenty species of evergreen shrubs and small trees native to Australia. They are grown for their striking pendant tubular or bell-shaped flowers.

C. alba WHITE CORREA ☽

A prostrate to erect shrub to 2m high and wide. The leathery, oval, rich green leaves are 3cm long and grey-woolly underneath. The small (1–2cm long), creamy-white, bell-shaped flowers are split into four petals with reflexed lobes and protruding stamens. They hang down along the branches, and are produced throughout most of winter. The shrub thrives in partial shade, but will take full sun. Water until established, then give a little summer water. Grows well in poor rocky soil, though it must have good drainage: over-watering or generous feeding will kill it. Grows well in coastal conditions as it withstands salt-laden sea breezes. Attractive when grown in pots or containers. The variety 'Pinkie' has pale pink flowers.

C. blackhouseiana ☽

A medium-sized, densely branched shrub, 1m or more high and spreading as wide. The twigs are hairy and rust-red. The oval leaves are 3cm long, and greyish-green above, with brown hairs underneath. The cream to pale green tubular flowers are 2–3cm long, and hang down from the branches. They may be produced all winter. Cultural conditions are the same as C. alba.

Coronilla valentina glauca

C

C. 'Dusky Bells'

A low-growing shrub to 90cm high, with a broad spread to 2m or more. The slender stems are reddish-brown. The oval, deep green leaves are 3–4cm long. The clusters of tubular deep red to pink flowers 2–3cm long hang in clusters from the branches from autumn to spring.

C. 'Mannii' (syn. 'Harrisii')

A spreading shrub that ultimately reaches 2m high and 2–3m wide, with erect branches. The oval, deep green leaves are 2–3cm long with a paler underside. The red, tubular flowers are 4cm long and have reflexed tips, and hang in small clusters from the branches all winter.

Cortaderia
Poaceae

A genus containing about twenty-four species of large perennial grasses from South America and New Zealand. They form large clumps with leaves crowded at the base, giving them a bold and striking appearance.

C. selloana PAMPAS GRASS

A gigantic tufted grass that normally grows 2–3m high, but may reach 6m in ideal conditions. The leaves are 1–3m

Cortaderia selloana

long and 2–3cm wide, with sharp teeth along the edges. In late summer, long flower-stalks appear from the centre of the plant; these can be 3m or more high, and are topped with beautiful plumes of flowers up to 1m long, that are normally white but can be pink. A tough plant that can take the driest soils to the wettest. Normally grown in full sun. The flower plumes can be dried for indoor decoration. Native to Brazil, Argentina, Chile. 'Pink Feather' has pink plumes. 'Pumila' bears plumes on stems 1.5m high.

Corylus 'HAZEL'
Corylaceae

A genus of about ten species of deciduous small to large shrubs and some trees native to northern temperate regions. Many are cultivated for their edible nuts.

C. colurna TURKISH HAZEL TREE

A deciduous, hardy tree that grows to 15m high and 6m wide, forming a pyramidal shape on a single trunk. The striking ripples on the corky bark are an attractive feature. The oval, toothed leaves are up to 13cm long, with hairs on the veins underneath. The yellow catkins are 5–8cm long and hang from the branches in late winter. They are followed by clusters of three to six nuts, which are almost completely enclosed in the bracts. Grow the tree in full sun or partial shade. A moderate amount of summer water is needed for best growth. Native to south-east Europe and west Asia.

Corymbia citriodora
See *Eucalyptus citriodora*.

Corymbia ficifolia
See *Eucalyptus ficifolia*.

Corynocarpus
Corynocarpaceae

A small genus of about four species of evergreen shrubs or small trees native to Australasia and the south Pacific Islands. They are grown for their attractive, dense, dark green leaves.

C. laevigatus
KARAKA, NEW ZEALAND LAUREL
A handsome, slow-growing evergreen

Corylus colurna

shrub 10–15m high and 8m wide that is upright, bushy, and may eventually form a spreading tree. The beautiful, dark green, glossy, leathery, oblong leaves are 10–20cm long and 5cm wide. When mature, it may produce tiny white flowers in upright clusters 10–20cm long in summer. They are of no importance. They are followed by orange fruit 2–3cm long that are highly poisonous. A tough shrub that can withstand a wide range of conditions. Grows even in deep shade or equally well in full sun. Thrives in coastal areas as it withstands salt-laden sea breezes. A beautiful shrub that is drought-tolerant, needing little summer water. Can be used as a screen or large hedge. Good in containers, as it keeps its attractive form for many years. Native to New Zealand.

Cosmos
Asteraceae

A genus of about twenty-five species of showy, late-flowering annuals or perennials native to southern USA and central America, mostly Mexico.

C. bipinnatus

A fast-growing, much-branched annual to 1m or more high, spreading to 45cm wide. The much-divided, fern-like leaves are up to 30cm long. Produces a mass of delightful, solitary bowl or saucer-shaped flowers 8cm across, with yellow centres, from midsummer to autumn. They come in shades of crimson, rose and pink together with white. The fine, fern-like foliage makes an ideal background for the brilliance of the flowers. Although the plants look delicate they are easily grown from seed. This colourful annual will often self-seed. They are excellent on poor, well drained soil in a sunny position, needing little summer water once established. Native to Mexico.

Cotinus
Anacardiaceae

A small genus of just three species of deciduous trees and shrubs, one native to North America, one to the Mediterranean region, one to south-west China. They are among the most attractive of the larger summer-flowering shrubs that also have good autumn colour.

C. coggygria (syn. *Rhus cotinus*)
SMOKE BUSH, VENETIAN SHUMACH
A bushy shrub or tree to 6m high and usually as wide. The roundish, mid-green leaves, 4–8cm long, turn yellow to orange and red in autumn. The dramatic fawn-coloured, plume-like inflorescences, 15–20cm long, are produced in profusion during summer.

They are persistent and turn smoky-grey by late summer. The tree grows best with cold winters and dry summers. Grows well in full sun without summer watering. Gives the best effects in poor, stony soil with excellent drainage. A prime candidate for the dry garden. Native to southern Europe to Asia. *C. coggygria* '*Purpureus*' has large panicles of purplish-grey flowers that resemble puffs of pink smoke from a distance. 'Royal Purple' has deep, wine-purple leaves and reddish-purple 'smoke'.

Cotoneaster
Rosaceae

A genus of over fifty species of hardy deciduous and evergreen shrubs and trees native to the temperate regions of Europe, Asia and North Africa. The branches are covered in white or pink flowers in spring, and clusters of bright red berries in autumn and winter. All grow vigorously and thrive with little or no maintenance. Grow in full sun. They grow better in poor soil rather than rich soil. They are drought-tolerant, requiring little or no summer water once established, but an occasional deep watering will help. They are ideal in the dry garden as background planting. Also good as groundcover and in hedges, and when planted on dry slopes, they can reduce erosion.

Cotinus coggygria

C. franchetii
An evergreen shrub to 3m high, with arched branches that are hairy when young. The sage-green, ovate leaves are about 3cm long, and whitish underneath. The pinkish-white flowers appear in midsummer and are followed by a splendid display of orange red fruit. Makes a good hedge or screen. Native to China and Myanmar (Burma).

C. lacteus
A dense, evergreen shrub to 4m high and wide with arching branches. Distinct with its large, oval, 5–8cm long, leathery leaves that are grey tomentose underneath. In summer it bears flat-topped clusters of white flowers. These are followed by an abundance of long-lasting, small red fruit in 5–8cm wide clusters. Useful in difficult sites or as an informal hedge or screen. If kept clipped, the berries will be lost. Native to western China.

C. microphyllus
ROCKSPRAY COTONEASTER
A dwarf, dense, stiffly branched shrub forming a low mound. The horizontal branches trail and root to 2m wide, while other branches grow erect to 1m high. The small, dark green leaves are grey underneath. Tiny white flowers are followed by small, deep reddish-

Cotinus coggygria 'Royal Purple'

C

pink fruit. Effective on rock gardens and banks.

C. salicifolius
WILLOW LEAF COTONEASTER

An erect, spreading, evergreen or semi-evergreen shrub to 5m high and wide. The narrow, dark green leaves are 3–8cm long. The white flowers in summer are followed by a heavy crop of small, bright red fruit in autumn. A tall, graceful shrub that is useful as a screening or background plant. It is the parent of innumerable hybrids. 'Repens' is a prostrate shrub with narrow leaves and small red fruit that makes an excellent groundcover. Native to western China.

Cotyledon
Crassulaceae

A genus of about twenty species of clump-forming succulents or small shrubs native to southern Africa. They are grown for both their foliage and flowers. All make good subjects for the dry or succulent garden.

C. macrantha

A showy succulent that can grow to 1m high, with stout stems that have erect branches. The leaves are densely packed on the stems. The fleshy, green, oval leaves are concave, edged with red, up to 10cm long, and covered in a whitish bloom. In spring the stiff

Cotyledon orbiculata

flower-stalk is produced, which is topped with many tubular, nodding flowers. These are intensely red with a greenish inside. Makes a good pot or large container plant that is easily grown, best in light shade. Keep on the dry side most of the time, particularly during winter. Native to South Africa.

C. orbiculata PIG'S EAR

A shrubby succulent up to 1m high.

Cotyledon macrantha

The thick, oval leaves 6–8cm long are in opposite pairs, rounded and covered in waxy, silver-white bloom narrowly edged with red. The flower stems are up to 60cm high, carrying clusters of orange flowers. These are tubular, nodding, up to 2cm long. The plant can be grown in full sun or partial shade. A well drained soil is needed. Outstanding for the cactus or succulent garden. A showy and beautiful succulent that makes an excellent container plant. Native to Namibia and South Africa.

Crassula
Crassulaceae

A large genus of about 300 succulents or shrub-like plants native mostly to South Africa. They are grown mainly for their fleshy leaves that are always opposite, sometimes packed into basal rosettes.

C. arborescens SILVER JADE PLANT, CHINESE JADE TREE

A heavy, branching succulent, growing tree-like to 3m high and 2m wide with a thick trunk. The stems are covered with broad, oval, blue-green leaves, 4–8cm long, and covered with a greyish bloom with a red edge. The terminal clusters of small, starry, five-petalled flowers are white, turning pink, appearing during summer. The flowers are not usually produced until the plant is several years old. Grow in full sun or partial shade in a sandy, well drained soil. Needs no summer water once established. A slow-growing succulent that makes an ideal pot or container plant. Native to South Africa.

C. ovata (syn. C. argentea)
JADE PLANT, JADE TREE

A freely branching, succulent shrub with shiny stems that may eventually reach 3m high but is usually much shorter. The thick, oblong leaves are 4–6cm long, and bright jade green, usually with a red margin, turning reddish in the sun. With age it produces clusters of small, starry white or pink flowers in winter. To grow well it needs gritty soil, full sun and to be kept on the dry side most of the time, particularly during winter. Makes a good pot or large container plant. Native to Cape Province and Natal.

Crassula ovata 'Tricolor'

The variegated form 'Tricolor' is more compact, with leaves streaked with green, white and red. Outstanding for the cactus or succulent garden. They are easily propagated from stem or leaf cuttings taken in summer.

Crinum
Amaryllidaceae

A genus of about 130 species of evergreen or deciduous bulbs that are found throughout the tropical regions and southern Africa. They are grown for their large umbels of showy flowers.

C. × powellii POWELL'S SWAMP LILY ⌣⌣⌣
A deciduous perennial with a large bulb. A long, tapering neck carries about twenty strap-like evergreen leaves about 120cm long and 8–10cm wide. In spring, each plant has three to four stems 60–90cm high, bearing up to ten rose-pink, trumpet-shaped flowers that open in succession. They are scented, and flare open to 10cm across. Given ample water, the bulbs increase to form large, leafy clumps that should be left undisturbed for best flowering. When dividing, replant the bulbs 15cm or more deep. They can be grown in full sun or partial shade in humus-rich soil that is well drained. A spectacular old hybrid between two South African species raised in England in 1732. 'Album' has pure white, lily-like flowers. Garden origin.

Crocosmia 'MONTBRETIA'
Iridaceae

A small genus of only about seven species of perennials, with corms native to tropical and southern Africa. They are grown for their brightly coloured flowers produced in late spring or summer.

C. × crocosmiiflora ⌣
A cormous perennial with sword-shaped leaves 2cm wide and up to 1m long. The short, one-sided, branched spikes of orange or orange-red, curved, funnel-shaped flowers are 4–5cm long. They appear from late summer until autumn, lasting a long time. The plants grow quickly, soon forming large clumps. Divide clumps every three to four years when they become overcrowded, replanting the corms 10cm deep. Although drought-tolerant, they benefit from summer water. They will take full sun, but prefer some shade. They are widely grown in mild-climate gardens for their brilliant flowers. A popular hybrid that is much cultivated for cut flowers. Native to South Africa.

C. hybrids ⌣
There is a wide range of garden hybrids available in a range of flower colours and heights ranging from 45cm to 1.2m high. 'Canary Bird' has small yellow flowers; 'Emberglow' has dark red flowers on deep reddish-brown stems; 'Lucifer' has flame-red flowers on stems 1m high; and 'Solfatare' has orange-yellow flowers and bronze-green leaves. Cultivation is the same as C. × crocosmiiflora. Garden origin.

C. masoniorum
GOLDEN SWAN TRITONIA ⌣
A magnificent cormous perennial that forms clumps of ribbed, sword-shaped leaves 60–100cm long and 5cm wide. The branched, arching stems 60–90cm high have two-tiered spikes of bright

Crinum powellii

C

orange, upward-facing, 4cm-long flowers. The buds open slowly from the base to the tip, and are produced from mid- to late summer. They make good cut flowers that are often grown at the edge of shrub borders. Cultivation is the same as C. × *crocosmiiflora*. Native to South Africa.

Cuphea
Lythraceae

A large genus of more than 250 species of evergreen shrubby perennials and dwarf shrubs native to USA, Mexico, central and South America.

C. *hyssopifolia* FALSE HEATHER ꞁꞁꞁ
A small, much-branched subshrub 30–60cm high and wide with flexible, leafy branchlets. The densely packed, deep green, lance-shaped leaves are 1–2cm long. In summer and autumn tiny pink, purple or white flowers with six spreading petals cover the plant. It grows happily in partial shade or in full sun. A generous amount of summer water is needed. Looks good in small borders or along the edges of paths. An easily grown plant that is not long lived but can be propagated easily by cuttings. Native to Mexico, Guatemala.

C. *ignea* (syn. C. *platycentra*)
CIGAR FLOWER ꞁꞁꞁ
A compact, bushy shrub with slender stems that normally only grows 30cm high but may reach to 1m, spreading to 50cm wide. The dark green, lance-

Cuphea ignea

shaped leaves are 2–4cm long. From spring to autumn it produces solitary, axillary, tubular flowers 2cm long. They are bright red with a white mouth and a dark ring at the end, which gives it the common name. The shrub grows well in full sun or partial shade. Give a generous amount of summer water. Looks good in small borders or along the edges of paths. Also makes a good pot plant where it grows best with some shade. Pinch out tips to keep bushy. Cuttings root readily. Native to Mexico and the West Indies.

Cupressus 'CYPRESS'
Cupressaceae

A genus of about twenty-two mostly tender monoecious, coniferous, evergreen trees native to North America, Europe and Asia. They are excellent specimen trees, which tolerate dry conditions.

C. *arizonica* var. *glabra*
SMOOTH ARIZONA CYPRESS ꞁ
A coniferous tree up to 15m high

spreading to 6m wide with a conical shape and a smooth, reddish-purple bark. The seedlings are variable with the tiny, pointed, glaucous leaves 2mm long ranging from green or blue-grey to silvery. The round glaucous female cones are up to 3cm across. Grow the tree in full sun. Extremely drought-tolerant, needing no water once established. Ideal for hot, inland deserts and useful as a quick windbreak. Native to central Arizona. Selected forms include 'Blue Ice' with silvery-blue foliage, and 'Pyramidalis' with blue-grey foliage borne on dense branches. In winter the tree is covered in a profusion of yellow male flowers. (C. *arizonica* is identical to the above, except the bark is rough.)

Cupressus arizonica var. glabra

C. *macrocarpa* MONTEREY CYPRESS ꞁ
A beautiful, vigorous, coniferous tree to 15m or more high. The narrow or columnar habit when young becomes picturesque and wide-spreading with age, to 5m or more. The tiny, lemon-scented, dark or bright green leaves are borne in plume-like sprays. The round female cones are up to 6cm across. An ideal tree as a fast-growing, coastal windbreak. Grow in full sun. Very drought-tolerant, needing no water once established. Ideal for use as a hedge, but it needs regular clipping. The tree is susceptible to a fungus

Cuphea hyssopifolia

Cupressus macrocarpa 'Goldcrest'

disease for which there is no cure: destroy it if it becomes infected. Native to California, USA. The parent of many cultivars, some with golden foliage. 'Goldcrest', with its dense, rich golden-yellow leaves, is particularly popular.

C. sempervirens ITALIAN CYPRESS ♪

A coniferous tree up to 20m high, spreading to 6m wide, which can vary in shape from narrow columnar to broad and spreading. The species itself has almost horizontal branches but is highly variable in habit and texture. The tree bears upright sprays of tiny, dark green leaves. Pollen from the female flowers is produced in vast quantities in early spring, and can fill the air when the tree is shaken. The round female cones, to 4cm across, hang from the branches almost indefinitely. This is probably the best known and most typical conifer of the Mediterranean region. Very drought-tolerant, needing no water once established. A light dry soil suits it best. Useful as hedges, windbreaks and specimen trees. Grows best in full sun well away from a wall, as this will cause the leaves on that side to die. Native to southern Europe, west Asia. 'Stricta', the columnar form most typically seen in the Mediterranean region growing to 20m high and 3m

wide, is the result of a clone originally selected in Italy. Its tall, dark columns stand guard by many houses, cemeteries and villages. 'Glauca' grows in a similar way but has blue-green foliage. 'Swane's Gold' is also narrowly upright, with pale yellow or greenish-yellow foliage.

Cycas
Cycadaceae

A genus of about forty species of palm-like cycads native to tropical and subtropical regions of east Africa, Madagascar, southern Asia and Australia. They are among the most primitive of living seed plants, and are remnants of an ancient cycad flora of the Carboniferous era. All have stiff, palm-like leaves.

C. circinalis SAGO PALM, QUEEN SAGO PALM, FERN PALM ♪♪♪

A palm-like tree with a stout, upright trunk: with great age this may reach to 3.5m high or more. The trunk bears pale bands of old leaf scars. The rosette of leaves rises gracefully from the top of the trunk. Each stiff, glossy, deep green, pinnate leaf can be 2m or more long. This is a tough and attractive cycad with its graceful, arching leaves. Grow in full sun or partial shade in a well

Cupressus sempervirens

drained soil. Give it plenty of summer water, especially in dry weather. Common all over the tropics, it is arguably the most beautiful species. Native to India and south-east Asia.

Cycas circinalis

C. revoluta JAPANESE SAGO PALM ♪♪

A palm-like cycad that slowly forms an upright trunk to 3m high; great age may cause it to recline. This has a terminal crown of arching pinnate leaves 1–2m long, which are divided into many narrow glossy segments. With age it looks more like a palm or fern, but in fact it is neither: it is a cone-bearing plant related to conifers. When the young leaves unroll from the central point of the single trunk they resemble fern leaves. Plants are either male or female. The reproductive structure is borne in modified, scale-like leaves that form a cone-like structure, the female being larger than the male. The cycad is easily grown in partial shade. Although extremely slow-growing, it looks better and grows faster when given a moderate amount of summer water. Makes an excellent single specimen in a border, or as a container plant. This is the most widely cultivated cycad. Native to southern Japan.

C

Cycas revoluta

Cyclamen
Primulaceae

A genus of fifteen species of tuberous perennials native from the Mediterranean region to Iran and North Africa. The genus is enormously rewarding, as it is possible to have at least one species in flower at almost any time of year, including through the winter, and some have lovely leaves for much of the year.

C. hederifolium (syn. *C. neapolitanum*) ◡ or ◡◡

A hardy tuberous perennial. The triangular to heart-shaped leaves, 5–15cm long, are grey-green, patterned with cream and silver, and often with purple underneath. The pale to deep pink flowers, to 2cm long, are produced in late summer and autumn before the leaves, on stems 8–10cm high. The flowers are sometimes scented. A vigorous and easy plant to grow in full sun or partial shade, it thrives almost anywhere that is not baked in summer. In hot climates it may survive with a protective covering of leaf litter. Keep the soil moist during the growing season. Self-seeds with enormous generosity, often on top of the mother corm. The baby corms often

reach flowering size in as little as two years. Not fussy about soil as long as the drainage is good. Native to the Mediterranean region.

C. persicum ◡ or ◡◡

A tuberous perennial. The leaves are heart-shaped, 2–14cm long, and more or less pointed. Often beautifully marked with grey-green patches and veins. The flowers are sweet-scented, with narrow, lance-shaped petals turned upwards, often slightly twisted. They may be white, pink, mauve, purple or red. This is the wild parent of our cultivated, large winter-flowering cyclamen, commonly grown as houseplants. When grown *en masse* this beautiful miniature makes a wonderful sight. At its best when grown in light shade: it flourishes underneath deciduous trees. A spring-flowering cyclamen that is distinguished from all others by the fruiting stalks that arch downwards instead of curling up in a spring-like fashion. Native to the eastern Mediterranean region and North Africa.

C. repandum ◡ or ◡◡

A tuberous perennial. The leaves are heart-shaped, to 13cm long, marbled with silver and with lightly toothed edges. Fragrant, bright crimson flowers, to 2cm long, with long narrow petals, are borne on stems 13–16cm long in spring with the leaves. The fruit is borne on spiral stalks. Cultivation is

similar to other cyclamen species. Native to southern France, Italy and Greece.

Cydonia 'QUINCE'
Rosaceae

A small genus of just two species of thornless deciduous shrubs or small trees native to south-west Asia. The attractive pale pink flowers are followed by edible fruit and attractive autumn foliage.

C. oblonga COMMON QUINCE ◡

A tree or shrub, often with crowded branches, up to 6m high and spreading almost as wide. With age the branches can become gnarled and twisted. The ovate to oblong leaves are up to 10cm long, dark green with a grey down on the underneath. The flowers are white or pale pink, to 5cm across, and appear singly in the leaf axils at the ends of the current season's growth in late spring. The yellow pear or apple-shaped fruit, 8–10cm or more in diameter, is somewhat wrinkled and covered with light brown felt; it ripens in autumn. The fruit is inedible when raw, but is used for making jams, jellies and in cooking. Grow the shrub in full sun in fertile, well drained soil. Give it only occasional summer water. Prune only enough to stimulate new growth, and remove any suckers from the base. Native to northern Iran and eastern Turkey. Several improved varieties have

Cydonia oblonga

Cyperus alternifolius

been raised, including 'Lusitanica', which has larger dark yellow fruits, and 'Vranja' with fragrant, pale green fruit ripening to golden yellow.

Cyperus
Cyperaceae

A large genus of about 600 grass-like plants and sedges, some with fibrous roots, others with rhizomes, native to the tropics and subtropics worldwide, but mainly from Africa and Asia. Mostly grown in, or near, water.

C. alternifolius UMBRELLA PLANT ↵↵↵
A clustering perennial bog plant with woody rhizomes. The numerous tri-angular stems grow to 1m or more high, and are crowned with numerous narrow, bright green, grass-like leaves, which give it the common name. The flowers are in a greenish-brown cluster, to 12cm across, appearing from summer to autumn. This is probably the most widely grown species, often seen as a house or container plant on a patio or terrace. Tolerates full sun through to deep shade. Grow in or near shallow water. If grown in a pot, stand it in a saucer to keep wet, or grow in the edge of a pool. Native to the

swampy regions of Madagascar, Mauritius and the Reunion Islands.

C. papyrus PAPYRUS ↵↵
A perennial bog plant that forms a large clump 2m or more wide, with stout, dark green stalks 1.5–3m high. They are topped with a brush-like umbel of drooping, thread-like leaves 30cm or more long. The sedge-like flowers are inconspicuous. The plant grows best in shallow water in a rich soil with high humidity. Looks stately beside pools, and is at home in fish-ponds. This fascinating plant should be grown in full sun and protected from strong wind. The papyrus of the ancient Egyptians was made from the pith of the stems. Often found on the banks and shores of quietly flowing water. Native to swampy regions of tropical Africa.

Cyphomandra
Solanaceae

A small genus of about thirty species of erect, spineless perennials, shrubs and trees native to central and South America and the West Indies. They are normally grown for their attractive foliage and tomato-like fruit. Only one species is commonly grown.

Cyperus papyrus

C. betacea TREE TOMATO ↵↵
A tree-like shrub that makes fast growth to 4m high or more, spreading to 2m wide. The pointed, oval leaves are soft, downy, 20cm long and 10cm wide. The small, pinkish-white flowers are 2–3cm wide; they appear in spring and summer, and are followed by orange-red, plum-like fruit, 5–8cm long. These are edible only when fully ripe, and have a sharp taste. They may be eaten fresh, but are usually stewed or made into a jelly. They are produced from late summer to winter. The shrub will grow well in full sun or in partial shade. It thrives best in deep, fertile soil with average watering in summer. Easily propagated from seed, it bears fruit after one to two years. Native to Peru.

Cyphomandra betacea

C

Cyrtanthus elatus

Cyrtanthus 'FIRE LILY'
Amaryllidaceae

A genus of about fifty species of bulbous perennials native to Africa, mostly from South Africa. They are grown for their often large and showy flowers.

C. elatus (syn. C. purpureus, Vallota speciosa) SCARBOROUGH LILY ⊍⊍⊍
An evergreen perennial bulb that gradually forms a clump. The bright green, strap-shaped leaves are 30–60cm long. The slightly fragrant, scarlet, funnel-shaped flowers are 6–8cm wide, in clusters of six to nine at the top of a thick stem up to 60cm high. They appear from mid-summer to autumn. The plant grows best in light shade, but will grow in full sun. Give regular water during the summer growing season, never allowing it to dry out. There is no need to dry off the bulbs, in fact part of the bulb's charm lies in the evergreen leaves. Grows well in the dappled shade at the base of trees and shrubs. Makes an excellent pot or container plant, flowering best when the roots are crowded. Native to South Africa.

Cytisus 'BROOM'
Papilionaceae

A genus of about fifty species of deciduous and evergreen shrubs or small trees native to the Mediterranean region, west Asia and North Africa. They are grown for their showy, pea-like, often scented flowers that cover the plant.

Cytisus multiflorus

C. hirsutus
See *Genista hirsuta*

C. multiflorus (syn. C. albus) Portuguese Broom, WHITE SPANISH BROOM ⊍
A deciduous, much branched, upright to spreading shrub 3m high and 2m or more wide with erect, grooved branches. The small leaves are up to 1cm long, silvery when young, with one or three leaflets. The white flowers are 1-2cm long, and are borne in axillary clusters of one to three. They cover the shrub in spring and early summer. Grow in full sun. Tolerant of poor rocky soil, drought and pollution. An ideal shrub for the back of a dry garden. Although the flowering season is short, it is spectacular. Native to Spain and Portugal.

C. × praecox WARMINSTER BROOM ⊍
A hardy, deciduous, compact-growing shrub, up to 2m high and almost as wide, with many slender stems. The small, silky, grey-green leaves, to 2cm long, drop early in autumn. In spring the shrub is covered with a mass of pale yellow to creamy-white, pea-like flowers, 1–2cm long; they appear along the lengths of the arching stems. A tough shrub that grows in full sun and requires no summer water once established. Tolerant of wind, coastal conditions and poor, rocky, infertile soil. Can be grown as an informal screen or hedge. 'Allgold' is slightly taller, with bright yellow flowers. Garden origin.

C. scoparius COMMON BROOM ⊍
A dense, evergreen shrub, up to 3m high, with slender, bright green branches. They are sparsely covered in tiny trifoliate leaves 1–2cm long. In spring and early summer the shrub is covered in rich yellow flowers, 2cm long, either singly or in pairs. As it sets seed readily it can become invasive, which has earned the genus a bad name. More hardy and even tougher than C. × praecox. Native to west Europe.

Cytisus scoparius

Dasylirion
Agavaceae

A genus of about fifteen species of evergreen, stemless, yucca-like dioecious (male and female flowers on different plants) shrubs native to dry areas of Texas to Arizona, USA and Mexico. They make striking shrubs, and are ideal for dry cactus and succulent gardens.

D. wheeleri
BEAR GRASS, SPOON FLOWER ☽
A striking Texan form plant that makes a beautiful 'ball' 1–2m round, with leaves radiating in all directions from a central stem. The blade-shaped, grey-green leaves are up to 1m long and 3cm wide with saw-toothed edges. Older shrubs may develop multiple trunks. A flowering spike 3–4m high may appear in spring with numerous, small, bell-shaped, whitish flowers. Extremely drought-resistant once established. Withstands some frost. Tolerates most soils, including alkaline soils, but does require good drainage. Do be careful how the plants are placed, as the saw-toothed edges and sharp points on the leaves can inflict wounds if they jut out into paths. A magnificent, architectural shrub that should be placed carefully so that its form can be seen to advantage. An outstanding plant for the desert garden or succulent garden. Native to southern USA and Mexico.

Datura
Solanaceae

A small genus of about eight species of annuals or short-lived perennials native to southern USA, Mexico and southern China. Many species formerly listed under Datura are now listed as Brugmansia. There is still much taxonomic confusion over this genus. All

Dasylirion wheeleri

species are poisonous, some deadly. They are grown for their bold attractive leaves and beautiful flowers.

D. inoxia subsp. *inoxia* (syn. *D. meteloides*) ANGELS' TRUMPET ☽☽☽
A vigorous, bushy, tender annual up to 1m high spreading to 45cm wide. The broadly oval, greyish-green leaves are up to 25cm long, with a strong odour. They are covered in tiny hairs and usually have scalloped margins. The large, erect, trumpet-shaped fragrant flowers are produced from mid- to late summer. They are pink or lavender, often veined with green, up to 20cm long, and are followed by green oval fruit to 5cm long, covered in spines. Grow the plant in full sun or partial shade. Give a generous amount of water during summer. Makes an

attractive pot or container plant for the patio. Easily grown from seed sown in the early spring. Beware that all parts of the plant are poisonous, particularly the fruit. Native to southern USA and Mexico.

D. metel (syn. *D. fastuosa*) ☽☽
A glabrous, bushy annual, usually seen up to 1m high, with purple stems. The broadly oval, greyish-green leaves are up to 20cm long, with a strong odour when crushed. The erect, trumpet-shaped, fragrant flowers are large, also up to 20cm long; they are normally white, but there are yellow and purple forms both single and double. They are produced from mid- to late summer. Grow the plant in full sun or partial shade. Almost drought-tolerant, but grows better with some summer water. Makes an attractive pot or container plant for the patio. Naturalized in all warm parts of the world, but probably native to south-west China.

Delonix
Caesalpiniaceae

A small genus of about ten species of deciduous and evergreen trees native to Madagascar, Africa and India. One species is widely grown in the tropics and subtropics as a beautiful, showy, flowering tree.

D. regia (syn. *Poinciana regia*)
FLAME TREE, FLAMBOYANT TREE ☽☽
A wide, branching tree to 10m high, eventually spreading to 10m wide, with a flat or domed top. The trunk is usually short and thick, with branches that are thick and heavy. The bright green leaves are 30–50cm long and bipinnate, rather like a fern. They usually fall just before flowering time. The flowers are 8–10cm wide and a brilliant, vibrant scarlet-red or orange

with a broad cream lip marked with red. They appear from spring to summer and cover the whole tree, which in full flower is a spectacular sight. It can take brief periods of cold, but seems to prefer desert heat, and will bounce back from a brief occasional freeze. Grow in full sun in a fertile, well drained soil to flower well. Fairly drought-tolerant, but grows best if given moderate summer water. Native to Madagascar.

Delonix regia

Daubentonia

See *Sesbania.*

Delairea odorata
See *Senecio mikanioides.*

Dendromecon 'TREE POPPY'
Papaveraceae

Probably a single variable species of evergreen shrub native to dry, rocky areas of California and Mexico, grown for its glaucous foliage and brilliant yellow flowers.

D. rigida BUSH POPPY ↪
A stiff, rounded, much-branched, evergreen shrub up to 3m high and wide with shedding bark. The grey-green or bluish, leathery, lance-shaped leaves are up to 10cm long. The solitary, fragrant, clear yellow flowers to 7cm across are poppy-like. They are produced in great profusion from spring to autumn. Grow the shrub in full sun in well drained, sandy soil. As it has a brittle taproot it does not transplant well. Although drought-tolerant, some summer water is beneficial. Can also be trained against a wall. For best results, prune back after the flowers have finished. A good shrub for the dry garden or for covering banks.

Dicliptera
Acanthaceae

A genus of about 150 species of annuals, evergreen subshrubs, perennials and climbers. Native to tropical and temperate parts of the world. They are grown for their velvety leaves and tubular, brightly coloured flowers.

D. suberecta (syn. *Jacobinia suberecta, Justicia suberecta*) ↪ or ↪↪
An herbaceous perennial or evergreen subshrub, with erect or arching slender stems up to 60cm high and 50cm wide. The stems are more or less hexagonal in section. The whole plant is covered in fine, velvety grey hairs. The opposite, dull grey-green leaves are 4–8cm long. The slender, two-lipped flowers are brick-red and 4cm long, and are produced in terminal and axillary clusters throughout summer and autumn. A showy plant for the front of the border, but as the seed germinates readily in favourable locations it can become invasive. Grow in full sun or partial shade. Survives with little water, but flowers better if given moderate summer water. Useful in a hanging basket or in containers. Native to Uruguay.

Dimorphotheca barberae
See *Osteospermum jucundum.*

Dimorphotheca ecklonis
See *Osteospermum ecklonis.*

Dendromecon rigida

Dicliptera suberecta

Dimorphotheca fruticosum
See *Osteospermum fruticosum.*

Dioon
Zamiaceae

A genus of about ten species of dioecious (male and female cones on different plants) cycads which are slow-growing with stout trunks, native to dry exposed sites in Mexico. Magnificent architectural plants that should be placed carefully so that their form can be seen to advantage.

D. edule
VIRGIN'S PALM, CHESTNUT DIOON ↪↪
An extremely slow-growing cycad that eventually forms a single stout trunk to 2m high. The terminal rosette of stiff, glossy, bright green pinnate leaves 1–2m long are upright at first then incline with age. The numerous lance-shaped, sharp-tipped leaflets are a beautiful, shiny light green to bluish-green, while the lower ones are almost spine-like. Cones are rarely produced in cultivation. Grow this cycad in partial shade in a humus-rich, neutral-to-acid soil. It is fairly drought-tolerant once established, only needing moderate summer water. It needs good drainage, as it is intolerant of waterlogged soil.

Diospyros
Ebenaceae

A large genus of over 400 species of evergreen or deciduous trees and shrubs. They are widely distributed throughout most tropical and subtropical parts of the world. This genus also includes the ebony tree, but only one species is normally grown in Mediterranean gardens.

Diospyros kaki

D. kaki PERSIMMON

A deciduous tree up to 8m high, with
wide-spreading branches. The oval
leaves are 15cm long and 5–8cm wide,
a light green in spring becoming dark
green in summer, and turning a
beautiful orange-yellow to red in
autumn. The yellowish-white flowers,
2cm wide, are produced in early
summer. The edible fruit is its greatest
merit: they are rather like large
tomatoes in appearance, but a more
red-orange in colour. Female trees
whose flowers are unfertilized will
produce seedless fruit. The fruit is best
eaten when over-ripe and jellified,
when it has a delicious flavour
(especially when skinned and whipped
up with cream), or when dried. To do
this pick the fruit when hard ripe with
some stalk attached, peel, and hang up
in the sun. An easily grown tree that
thrives in rich soil with regular summer
watering. Male trees do not bear fruit,
so it is important to buy a named
female variety, of which there are
many. A handsome tree at all times of
the year, with a branch structure that
justifies a prominent spot in the garden.
Native to China.

Diplacus
See *Mimulus*.

Dipladenia
See *Mandevilla*.

Distictis
Bignoniaceae

A small genus of about nine species of
woody climbers native to the West
Indies and tropical America that climb
by tendrils. Spectacular climbers with
trumpet-shaped flowers for frost-free
gardens.

D. buccinatoria (syn. Bignonia cherere)
BLOOD RED TRUMPET VINE

A spectacular, strong-growing climber
6–9m or more high, with square stems,
that climbs by tendrils. The rough,
leathery, oval leaves, 5–10cm long,
have two leaflets with a terminal forked
tendril. The 15cm-long, trumpet-
shaped, waxy flowers start orange-red
and fade to blush-red with age. They
are produced in racemes 15–25cm long
throughout the warm weather months.
If grown in full sun it will cover itself
with spectacular flowers. Grow the
climber against a sunny wall or through

Distictis buccinatoria

a tree. A generous amount of summer
water and regular feeding is needed to
keep it growing and flowering well.
Can be cut back hard each year to keep
under control. Native to Mexico.

Dodonaea
Sapindaceae

A genus containing about fifty species
of evergreen shrubs or small trees
native to the tropics and subtropics of
both hemispheres, but mostly in
Australia. Some have medicinal
properties and most of them have
resinous, sticky excretions.

Dodonaea viscosa 'Purpurea'

D. viscosa 'Purpurea'
PURPLE HOPSEED BUSH

The purple form of D. *viscosa* is the
most popular and probably the most
beautiful. The evergreen shrub makes
fast growth to 4m high and 2m wide,
with many upright branches. The
leaves are oblong to lance-shaped,
10–13cm long, and purplish-red in
colour, turning an even deeper colour
in winter. The leaves are green in the
type. The insignificant flowers appear
in short racemes. In late summer they
are followed by showy, winged
seedpods that are also purplish-red and
long-lasting. The plants are normally
propagated by seed, so the colour tends
to vary. To retain good leaf colour,

Dombeya cayeuxii

plant in full sun. This is a tough shrub that can take a lot of rough treatment. Can be clipped to form a hedge, or left to grow into an informal screen. Not fussy about soil conditions. Can take drought once established, but it grows better with summer water. Also a good coastal shrub that will take salt-laden breezes as well as dry inland heat. Possibly introduced from New Zealand, but grown in warm regions worldwide.

Dombeya
Sterculiaceae

A large genus of around 200 or more species of evergreen or deciduous small trees and shrubs that are native mainly to southern and central Africa and Madagascar. They all have large, palmately lobed leaves, and large pendant clusters of pink or white flowers.

D. × *cayeuxii* PINK BALL ↲↲
A vigorous evergreen shrub or small tree up to 5m high spreading to 3m wide, with soft, hairy young shoots. The leaves are broad, ovate, velvety dark green with three or five points, and up to 30cm wide. They are carried on long leaf stalks. The lovely inflorescence is a pendant 8–10cm, ball-like cluster of fragrant 4cm flowers that are rose-pink with a pale centre. They appear from winter to spring.

This is a variable hybrid including many forms, but in general is similar to *D. wallichii*. Grow the shrub in full sun, although it can take partial shade. Needs a moderate amount of water during summer. Garden origin.

D. *wallichii* ↲↲
This splendid, large evergreen shrub or small tree can grow up to 10m high, forming a round, rather dense crown up to 5m wide. The soft leaves are broad, with many points, and a velvety dark green; up to 30cm long, and as wide, with dense hairs on the underneath. The flowers are formed in large, ball-shaped pink clusters 10–15cm wide, and droop from the thin stems during winter and spring. After blooming, the dry clusters remain on the plant for a long time, looking messy unless removed. This shrub responds well to being severely cut back in the late spring after flowering. Grows well in full sun, and needs a

Dombeya wallichii

moderate amount of water during summer. Native to east Africa, Madagascar.

Doxantha capreolata
See *Bignonia capreolata*.

Doxantha unguis-cati
See *Macfadyena unguis-cati*.

Dracaena
Dracaenaceae

A genus of about forty species of shrubby or tree and palm-like plants native to tropical Africa and the Canary Islands. Similar to, and often confused with, *Cordyline*. They make striking architectural plants.

D. *australis*
See *Cordyline australis*.

Dracaena draco

D. *draco* DRAGON TREE ↲
An upright evergreen tree, growing slowly to 10m or more high, eventually becoming widely branched. In its native habitat it grows to 20m high, with a huge trunk 4m in diameter. A very long-lived tree: some are said to be 1,000 years old. Makes a decorative young plant with a crowded rosette of leaves, 30–60cm long, thick, fleshy, sword-shaped and a smooth glaucous

green. With age it will eventually produce terminal clusters to 30cm long of greenish flowers during summer. Grow the tree in full sun in well drained soil. Drought-tolerant, needing little summer water once established. A good plant for coastal gardens as it withstands salt-laden sea breezes. As the plant grows, remove old dead leaves to keep it neat. Makes an ideal specimen plant for the dry garden. Native to the Canary Islands.

D. indivisa
See *Cordyline indivisa*.

D. marginata
MADAGASCAR DRAGON TREE
A tree-like plant with slender branching trunk up to 4m high, spreading 1–2m wide. Each branch is topped with a dense rosette of leaves. They are sword-shaped, up to 45cm long and 3cm wide, rigidly spreading horizontally. They are a shiny, deep olive green, with narrow red margins. Trees do not flower in cultivation until they reach maturity. The terminal panicles, 40–50cm across, are produced in summer and contain many small white flowers. The flexible stems have a tendency to branch and twist, giving an artistic appearance. Grow the plant where its beautiful form can be seen, preferably in full sun. It is easily grown, slow and durable, requiring little summer water. If it becomes too high, cut the top off and root it; the old stem will shoot out again. Native to Madagascar. The variety 'Tricolor' has leaves with creamy-white stripes with red edges, and is a most beautiful plant. 'Magenta' has attractive maroon-coloured leaves.

Drejerella
See Justicia.

Drosanthemum *floribundum*

Drosanthemum
Aizoaceae

A genus of about ninety-five species of succulent shrubs native to South Africa, mostly low to creeping, and wide-spreading.

D. floribundum DEW FLOWER
A succulent that grows less than 15cm high, but can spread 1–2m or more, with the stems rooting along the length. The leaves are tiny, cylindrical and dark green. In spring the plant is covered in pink or mauve flowers 2cm wide; they are most attractive to bees. Ideal for covering a dry slope, tumbling over rocks, or hanging down over a wall from a raised bed. Grows best in full sun, with little or no summer water once established.

D. hispidum
A succulent shrub up to 60cm high, spreading to about 1m wide. The rooting branches are covered in rough hairs. The leaves are 2cm long, cylindrical, incurved, light green to reddish and covered in glistening dots. The showy purple flowers are solitary, shiny petalled, and up to 3cm wide. They appear in late spring and early summer. The shrub grows best in full sun with little or no summer water, and endures poor soil. Ideal for the desert garden. The two species listed are often confused.

Duranta
Verbenaceae

A genus of around thirty species of evergreen shrubs, some of which have spines. They are grown for their wonderful clusters of blue flowers, which are attractive to butterflies. They are native to Mexico, the West Indies and South America.

D. erecta (syn. D. repens)
PIGEON BERRY, SKY FLOWER
A fast-growing, evergreen, strongly branching shrub 3–4m high and 2–3m wide. Tends to form a clump with many square stems that are often drooping or trailing. The stems usually have spines. The leaves are 5–8cm long, ovate, and usually toothed. The small tubular, lilac or blue flowers, which flare open to 1cm wide, are produced in

Duranta erecta 'Variegata'

pendant racemes 10–15cm long throughout most of summer. They are followed by shiny orange poisonous berries that hang in clusters. The shrub thrives in the hot sun, but needs ample summer water. Ideal for use as a tall screen, otherwise it may need constant pruning to keep it small. Useful as a hedge or windbreak. Native to USA to Brazil. 'Variegata' has beautifully variegated leaves with a bold cream or white edge; it is slower growing, and will take some shade.

Duranta erecta

Dypsis
Arecaceae

Now a genus of 160 species of palms with large pinnate leaves native to Madagascar. Most have a solitary trunk, but some are clustering. Recent taxonomic work has combined several genera of palms.

D. decaryi (syn. Neodypsis decaryi)
TRIANGLE PALM
An instantly recognizable palm to 6m high with a single trunk that is triangular in cross-section. The huge leaves grow out from the three sides with a unique triangular growth habit, giving it the common name. The fairly upright silvery-grey pinnate fronds, up

to 4.5m long, are feather-shaped, drooping at the tips. The leaves are V-shaped in cross-section. Each new spear is covered with a dark, reddish-brown velvet. Also unusual are the long, persistent threads that hang from the leaflets. Grow the palm in full sun or partial shade. Although extremely drought-tolerant, it grows best in permanently moist, fertile, loamy soil, but with the minimum of feed. Quite fast-growing, it is one of the best and easiest of these spectacular and dramatic palms. It should be given plenty of room to be seen at its best. Native to Madagascar.

D. lutescens (syn. Chrysalidocarpus lutescens, Areca lutescens)
BUTTERFLY PALM, GOLDEN CANE PALM, ARECA PALM ꙮꙮꙮ
A clump-forming bamboo palm, which when mature may grow to 6m high and

Dypsis decaryi

3m wide. The slender, graceful, yellowish stems have brown to yellow rings of leaf scars, giving it the look of a bamboo. They are sometimes branching just above ground level. Tall, arching, green pinnate leaves, up to 2m long, with yellow leaf stalks give it a look that is both graceful and colourful. Grow the palm in light shade or full sun, as in shade it will lack good leaf colour. Grows fast in good soil with plenty of summer water and generous feeding. The roots must have perpetually damp conditions, as in its native habitat it grows near riverbanks. A tropical palm that does not like the cold, the leaves are easily burnt by frost. It makes an attractive decoration for a sheltered terrace. One of the most popular palms in the world frequently seen as a houseplant. Native to Madagascar.

E

Eccremocarpus
Bignoniaceae

A small genus of about three to four species of evergreen or nearly evergreen perennial climbers native to Peru and Chile. They climb by means of coiling leaf tendrils.

E. scaber CHILEAN GLORY FLOWER

A semi-woody, fast-growing climber up to 4m high. The leaves have two lobes 3cm wide, with tendrils at the end of the main stalk. From late spring to autumn the flowers appear in terminal clusters. They are narrowly tubular, contracted at the mouth and 2–3cm long. There are several colour variations now widely available, with the old scarlet red being replaced by pale pink, lavender, mauve plus several shades in between. All have a yellow mouth to the flower. There is also a rich, almost orange-yellow form. Plants are easily raised from seed, indeed they readily seed themselves in the garden in favourable conditions. They will grow well in light shade, or full sun in cooler areas. They need moderate summer water. Grow as short-lived perennials to clothe an arch, wall or climb into a tree. A problem is their tendency to form untidy masses of stems and foliage, so it is better to raise new plants from seed each year. Native to Chile.

Echeveria
Crassulaceae

A genus of over 150 species of evergreen succulents and shrubs native to dry desert areas from Texas to Argentina, but especially in Mexico. They often have colourful leaves. Ideal for the dry garden.

E. elegans HENS AND CHICKENS

A stemless succulent that forms clusters of tight, greyish-white rosettes, each 5–10cm across, mounding up with time. The silvery-blue, waxy, spoon-shaped leaves are 3–6cm long and 2–3cm wide. They sometimes have a red or white translucent margin. The arching flower stems are a delicate pink with pink and yellow flowers 1cm long. These are striking against the pale grey-white rosettes. A good container plant. When they are grown in the ground, they tolerate regular water, but must not sit in puddles or become sodden. They rarely send roots deep into the soil, growing instead on their own leaf-litter. Depending upon the location of the planting, they may prefer some shade from hot and dry sun, which can scorch the pearly-white leaves. Easily propagated by separating any rosette from the clump. Native to Mexico.

Echium
Boraginaceae

A genus of about forty species of annuals, biennials or shrubby perennials native to Europe, especially the Mediterranean region, Africa and west Asia.

E. candicans (syn. E. fastuosum) PRIDE OF MADEIRA

A shrubby perennial with many branches that grows to 2m high, spreading to 2m wide. The 20cm long, rough, lance-shaped leaves, which form rosettes around the stem, have a coating of silver hairs. Towering above the foliage, large terminal spikes to 30cm long of 1cm, blue flowers appear during spring and summer. The plant readily sets seed, which will germinate easily. To maintain shape, remove dead flowerheads and prune lightly. Grow in full sun. When established it withstands drought, but grows and flowers better with some summer water. Makes a

Echium candicans

bold plant against a wall or on a dry slope amongst rocks. Native to Madeira and Canary Islands.

E. pininana (syn. E pinnifolium)

A biennial or short-lived perennial with a dense rosette of leaves to 90cm wide. They are lance-shaped, 8cm long, and deep green with rough silver hairs. After about two to three years, a massive flower spike appears, up to 5m high, in spring to early summer; it contains a large number of mauve or blue tubular flowers 1–2cm wide, and small leaves. The plant dies after flowering. Grow in full sun in well drained soil. Give moderate summer water. Makes a bold and dramatic plant that is not often seen. Native to the Canary Islands.

E. wildpretii

A soft, hairy, much-branched biennial

E

Echium pininana

up to 2m high, spreading to about 60cm wide. The dense, silver tufts of hairy, lance-shaped leaves are up to 20cm long. From late spring to summer it produces a single terminal spike to 90cm long of many tiny, soft, brick-red, funnel-shaped flowers. Lots of seed is produced and it self-seeds readily. After flowering the plant generally dies. Grow in a sandy, well drained soil in full sun in a sheltered position. It is known to die suddenly for no apparent reason. Native to the Canary Islands.

Elaeagnus
Elaeagnaceae

A genus of about forty-five species of evergreen or deciduous shrubs or small trees that are native to Asia, southern Europe and North America. They are primarily seashore plants, as they are excellent wind resisters. They are valuable for hedges and shelter belts in exposed areas.

E. angustifolia
OLEASTER, RUSSIAN OLIVE
A deciduous hardy shrub or small tree up to 6m high and wide, with spiny silver branches. The leaves are silver-grey, and lance-shaped up to 10cm long. The small, greenish-yellow flowers, to 1cm long, are fragrant and appear in the early summer. They are followed by berry-like fruit that are silver yellow and resemble small olives. The shrub is drought-resistant once established. It withstands salt-laden sea breezes and wind damage. Can be clipped to make a medium-sized hedge. Native to southern Europe, central Asia and China.

E. × ebbingei
This hybrid makes a large, hardy, fast-growing, dense, evergreen shrub up to 3m high with a wide spread. The dark green, leathery leaves are 5–10cm long, and silver on both sides when young. The small, fragrant white flowers are produced in autumn. They are followed by small red fruit. This is a useful shrub for dry sunny gardens. Splendid for creating shelter, even near the sea. The variegated form 'Gilt Edge' has leaves margined yellow, and 'Limelight' has leaves with a central blotch of yellow. These varieties are less strong-growing than the type. Garden origin.

Elaeagnus ebbingei 'Limelight'

E. macrophylla
An evergreen, spreading shrub up to 3m high and 5m wide. The branches are covered in white scale when young. The broad leaves are 10cm long, silvery on both surfaces, becoming dark glossy green above with age. The small, fragrant flowers appear in autumn. As the young leaves are especially pleasing, the shrub can be pruned to encourage them. The shrub is tolerant of dry soil and coastal winds. When established it needs little summer water. On shallow chalky soils it may become chlorotic. Native to Korea and Japan.

Encephalartos
Zamiaceae

A genus of about thirty species of dioecious (male and female cones on different plants) cycads that are slow-growing, sometimes tuberous or with

Elaeagnus angustifolia

stout trunks, native to central and southern Africa. Most species are clustering, many are palm-like. Magnificent architectural plants that should be placed carefully so that their form can be seen to advantage. All are frost tender.

Encephalartos lehmannii

E. altensteinii
PRICKLY CYCAD, BREAD TREE ◡◡

A variable, suckering, palm-like cycad with trunks either branched or unbranched eventually to 5m high with an equal spread. The straight to arching, pinnate, dark green leaves are up to 3m long. The stiff leaflets are about 15cm long, 2–3cm wide, and sparsely toothed at the margins. The leaflets arise at an angle, giving a trough to the leaf. In summer, mature plants produce yellowish-brown cones, mostly in clusters of two to five. The male is cylindrical, 30–40cm long, while the female is broadly oval to 45cm long. Grow in partial or light shade in well drained humus, rich neutral to slightly acid soil. Give moderate summer water. A wonderful architectural plant for a sheltered, shady situation. Native to South Africa.

E. horridus FEROCIOUS BLUE CYCAD ◡

A suckering cycad that slowly forms a stem which is underground, or to only 30cm high. The trunk is crowded with a cluster of stiff pinnate leaves that are a glaucous green and 60–90cm long. The leaves are upright at first, then arch with age. The numerous lance-shaped leaflets are 10cm long, curled, and deeply cut along the lower margin into one to three spine-tipped lobes. They open a beautiful silvery blue to almost purple, and slowly change to an icy blue or bluish green. In summer, mature plants produce reddish-brown cones. The male is cylindrical and 10cm

long, while the female is broadly oval to 35cm long. For best colour, grow in full sun. Average garden soil, but needs excellent drainage with little summer water. A spectacular and dramatic plant for a sunny border. Native to South Africa.

E. lehmannii BLUE-LEAFED CYCAD ◡

A cycad that is commonly branched from the base with a thick grey trunk to 1m or more high. The trunk is crowned with a rosette of elegant, stiff and erect pinnate leaves that are recurved at their ends. The 1m or more long leaves have numerous glaucous blue-green leaflets, to 20cm long with a spiny tip. The leaflets arise at an angle, giving a V-shape to the leaf. The solitary, bluish-green cones are produced in summer, the male up to 35cm long, the fatter female cone to 40cm long. Grow in partial or light shade in alkaline or neutral soil. The plant is drought-tolerant once established needing little summer water, but demands perfect drainage. Native to South Africa.

Epilobium californicum
See *Zauschneria californica*.

Epiphyllum 'ORCHID CACTUS'
Cactaceae

A small genus of about sixteen species of spineless, flat-stemmed, epiphytic cacti native to Mexico, Central America and South America. They often have large and fragrant flowers, which have been much hybridized.

E. hybridum ◡◡◡

These cacti have flattened, leaf-like, often deeply toothed, fleshy green stems up to 4m long. They branch freely and become two-ribbed when mature. The spines are almost non-existent. The large, spectacular funnel-shaped flowers can be up to 30cm long, appearing during summer and autumn. The flowers appear singly from the sides of the stems. A large number of hybrids have been raised among the species of this genus, and with related genera such as *Heliocereus*, *Nyctocereus*, *Hylocereus*, *Selenicereus*. This means that a wide range of colours has been developed, with large flowers of great beauty. The colours range from nearly blue through red, pink, yellow to

white, and many have blends of two or more colours. Some are night flowering, while others are sweetly scented, lasting for two or more days. All are tropical epiphytic cacti, that mostly grow on tree branches: this means that they grow best in shade with generous water. Grow in rich, well drained soil that is on the acidic side, if necessary adding sand, leaf mould, peat or other humus. They do not climb but lean against supports and can be tied to trees or walls. They can often be seen with their long branches hanging over the tops of walls. Garden origin.

Epiphyllum hybridum

Erica 'HEATH'
Ericaceae

A large genus of more than 500 species ranging from dwarf shrubs to small trees native to Europe, west and central Asia, with the largest number coming from South Africa. They are usually evergreen. Most species need acid soil.

E. arborea TREE HEATH ◡◡

A dense, upright, feathery-looking shrub generally 2–3m high, but which can occasionally grow to 6m high, spreading to 3m wide, with one or many closely upright trunks. The upper branches are soft and covered with whitish woolly hairs. The tiny, dark green leaves, just 3–4mm long, are in whorls of three to four. The tiny, fragrant, bell-shaped white flowers, 3mm long, are produced profusely in large terminal pyramidal heads in early spring. When in full flower it looks quite stunning. Grow the shrub in full sun or partial shade. It needs acid soil with excellent drainage and lots of humus to grow well. A sandy soil with added humus is ideal; heavy clay soil can be fatal. Give a moderate amount of soft water (with no lime) during summer. Native to southern Europe, north Africa.

E. australis SPANISH HEATH ♫♫

A slender, upright, open shrub to 2m high and 1m wide. The tiny, linear, dark green leaves are in whorls of four. The striking reddish-pink, bell-shaped flowers, just 1cm long, are borne in clusters at the ends of the branches in spring. One of the showiest of the tree heaths. The culture is the same as E. arborea. Native to Spain, Portugal. 'Mr Robert' is a beautiful white form.

E. lusitanica PORTUGUESE HEATH ♫♫

An upright, feathery shrub to 3m high only, spreading to 1m wide. The tiny linear leaves are light green. The pinkish white, tubular to bell-shaped, slightly fragrant flowers, 5mm long, are borne in branched racemes in early spring. When in flower it makes a spectacular sight. The culture is the

Eriobotrya japonica (fruit)

same as E. arborea. Native to Portugal.

Eriobotrya
Rosaceae

A genus of about thirty species of evergreen shrubs and small trees native to the Himalayas and east Asia. They all have large, leathery leaves with prominent veining, one bearing edible fruit.

E. japonica LOQUAT ♪

A vigorous tree or shrub to 6m high spreading nearly as wide. The leathery, heavily veined, 20–30cm long, leaves are 5–10cm wide, and toothed. They are deep green above and felted underneath where they are often rust coloured. The flowers are produced in autumn or winter in pyramidal terminal clusters up to 15cm high. Each small white single flower is sweetly scented. They are followed by clusters

of orange to yellow, small, pear-shaped fruit, 3–5cm across, with a soft downy skin, in early spring. They are edible, but contain several, often large seeds. The fruit has a pleasant, aromatic, slightly sweet taste and can be eaten fresh or used in pies or jam. The shrubs are often grown from seeds but to obtain good fruit buy a named grafted variety. It needs little or no summer water once established. It will make a good ornamental specimen tree on a patio where it casts good summer shade. Native to central China and southern Japan.

Eriocephalus
Asteraceae

A genus of about thirty species of aromatic, usually silvery or silky shrubs native to South Africa.

E. africanus WILD ROSEMARY ♪

A much-branched shrub up to 1m high and wide. The narrow, almost round, rosemary-like leaves, 2cm long, are silky white in clusters along the stem. In late autumn to spring, terminal clusters of flowers, 6–8cm long, are produced. Each white, disc-shaped flower is 1cm wide, with a cluster of dark red stamens with a slight scent. Grow the shrub in full sun with little attention. Little summer water is needed once established. A useful shrub for filling in the

Eriobotrya japonica

Eriocephalus africanus

background of a dry garden with its mass of grey foliage. Also useful for coastal gardens as it withstands salt-laden sea breezes.

Eryngium
Apiaceae

A genus of over 200 species of annuals, biennials and perennials native to Europe, the Mediterranean, central Asia and China, and north, central and south America. Those from Europe come from dry coastal areas, while those from America come from wet marshy areas. They are grown for their showy, spiny floral bracts which are usually blue or silver.

E. amethystinum
An evergreen, hardy perennial with stems to 1m high. The dark green, deeply cut, leathery, spiny-toothed basal leaves are 10–15cm long with oblong leaflets. The upper leaves are three-lobed. In late summer, striking oval, steel blue flowerheads 2cm across are surrounded by spiky darker blue bracts on branched stems. They are ideal for cutting either dried or fresh. Grow in full sun in poor to moderately fertile soil that is well drained. Drought-tolerant once established, needing little summer water. The plant is tap-rooted, making it difficult to move or divide, so it is best to grow from seed, which must be fresh. Will often self-seed. Native to Italy, Sicily and the Balkans.

E. maritimum SEA HOLLY
A tufted, short-lived, evergreen, hardy perennial to 50cm high, spreading to 50cm wide. The leathery, three-lobed, intensely glaucous-blue basal leaves are 10–15cm long, with coarse, spiny teeth. In summer the stiff-branched flower-heads, 2–3cm across, are surrounded by spiny bracts, the same intense glaucous blue as the leaves. The small flowers are pale blue. This highly ornamental plant should be grown in full sun. Thrives in poor to moderately fertile soil, which is very free draining. Drought-tolerant once established, needing little summer water. Ideal for coastal gardens as it occurs naturally in coastal sands. Attractive in a rock garden. Native to Europe.

E. × tripartitum
A clump-forming, evergreen, hardy perennial up to 1m high spreading to 50cm wide, that forms a long tap-root. The basal rosettes of three-lobed, deep grey-green leaves, 6–12cm long, are coarsely toothed. In summer the small, branched, cylindrical, violet-blue flower-heads, 1–2cm across, are surrounded by spiny grey-blue bracts. They appear on wiry stems that are ideal for cutting, either dried or fresh. Grow in full sun in poor to moderately fertile soil that is well drained. Drought-tolerant once established, needing little summer water. Of unknown origin, possibly a naturally occurring hybrid from the Mediterranean.

Erythea armata
See Brahea armata.

Erythea edulis
See Brahea edulis.

Erythrina 'CORAL TREE'
Papilionaceae

A large genus of over 100 species of semi-evergreen or deciduous trees, shrubs or perennials grown for their brilliant flowers. The stems are usually thorny, and the leaves are divided into three leaflets. Native to tropical regions worldwide.

E. caffra
CORAL TREE, LUCKY BEAN TREE
A slow-growing, multi-trunked, usually deciduous tree up to 10m high with wide-spreading, angular branches. The trunk and branches have hooked thorns. In spring the bare branches produce terminal clusters, 30–60cm long, of brilliant red, tubular, five-petalled flowers, 5cm long. After flowering, the broadly oval leaves appear, 30cm long and divided into three-pointed leaflets. This beautiful tree needs to be grown in full sun. Give it deep, infrequent summer watering. It makes an excellent shade tree. Native to South Africa.

E. crista-galli
COCKSCOMB, COMMON CORAL TREE
A deciduous tree 3–4m high, or a many-stemmed shrub with an open habit. The trunk and branches have vicious stout thorns. The trifoliate leathery leaves are up to 30cm long, each leaflet 5–8cm long, with a backward-pointing thorn. It produces masses of terminal racemes, 30–60cm or more long, of brilliant scarlet flowers, 4cm long. They appear in flushes throughout spring, giving a dazzling effect. The tree grows best in full sun in moist soil with adequate drainage, but needs protection from the wind. Remove the old flower stems to encourage new growth. During winter the stems may die back, and once the new growth has started in spring, these should be cut away. Native to southern Brazil, Uruguay and northern Argentina.

Erythrina crista-galli

E

Escallonia
Escalloniaceae

A genus of fifty to sixty species of mainly evergreen shrubs and small trees native to South America. Grown for their brilliant flowers and glossy leaves. There are many named varieties, with flowers from red to pink and white.

E. bifida (syn. *E. montevidensis*)
WHITE ESCALLONIA ⏝

A vigorous, tall and broad, evergreen shrub up to 3m high, spreading almost as wide. The dark green, glossy, narrowly oval leaves are 8–10cm long and finely toothed. The white flowers, to 2cm across, are produced in large, rounded, terminal clusters, 15cm long, from late summer to autumn. The shrub can take full sun, but in hot gardens it grows better with some shade. When established, it withstands drought, but it grows better with some summer water. Useful as a large screening shrub. Particularly good for coastal gardens as it withstands the salt-laden sea breezes. Native to Brazil and Uruguay.

E. rubra ⏝

A vigorous, upright, evergreen shrub, 2–5m high and spreading almost as wide, with peeling brown bark. The broadly ovate leaves are smooth, glossy

Escallonia bifida

dark green, and up to 6cm long. They are aromatic when bruised. The deep pink to crimson flowers, just 1cm long, grow in loose clusters up to 10cm long, and appear in abundance from summer to autumn. The shrub is much used for hedging and as a windbreak, especially near the coast where it withstands the salt-laden sea breezes. When established it withstands drought, but it grows better with some summer water. Native to Chile and Argentina. 'Macrantha' is probably the best variety of this genus for hot, dry conditions; its foliage is denser and darker, and it has tubular, bright red flowers.

Eschscholzia
Papaveraceae

A genus of eight to ten species of branching annuals or perennials native to western North America. They are grown for their showy, brightly coloured flowers.

E. californica CALIFORNIA POPPY ⏝
An annual or perennial that flowers in its first year with many branched stems to 30cm high and 15cm wide, often forming a mat. The blue-grey leaves are much dissected into fine segments. The bright, poppy-like single flowers, 5cm wide, have silky petals and are carried well above the leaves; they are produced from early summer to mid-autumn. They close at night and in shade. They are followed by long, curved seedpods. Garden seed strains are offered in a wide range of colours but mainly yellow, orange and white. An easily grown plant that flourishes in poor, dry soil as it needs little summer water. Flowering can be extended by giving it extra water. It flowers at its best in full sun. The plants commonly self-seed. As they do not transplant well, sow seeds where they are to grow. A glorious sight when naturalized on a sunny hillside or in informal areas of the garden. Native to California, Oregon.

Eucalyptus
'EUCALYPT, GUM, IRONBARK'
Myrtaceae

A huge genus of over 500 species of evergreen trees that are native mainly to Australia. They are a valuable source of timber as the wood is durable and

resistant to damp, but it splits easily. They make very fast growth, particularly in the early stages – some seedlings can grow to 2m in the first year. Most have two types of foliage: soft, juvenile leaves on young trees and new branches, and tougher adult leaves. Nearly all Eucalyptus leaves have some fragrance and are rich in oils. They are well suited to warm, dry conditions. They need to be grown in full sun, with little summer water once established. If possible grow them from seed, because containerized plants, especially when older, do not transplant well.

Some authorities now place some species of *Eucalyptus* in the new genus *Corymbia*, but as this is not generally accepted, here they remain as *Eucalyptus*. Although the term 'eucalypt' is usually regarded as applying to the genus *Eucalyptus*, it also includes the closely related *Angophora*, and the new genus (1995) *Corymbia*: the latter contains 113 species, eighty of which were formerly within *Eucalyptus*. *Angophora* consists of about thirteen species.

E. camaldulensis
RED GUM, RIVER RED GUM ⏝

A large, fast-growing, spreading tree that may reach 30–50m high, spreading 15–20m wide, usually its branches not far above the ground. The bark is smooth and whitish-blue or greyish in colour, except near the base of the

Eucalyptus camaldulensis

trunk where it is often rough. The branches may be pendulous. The leaves are lance-shaped, up to 25cm long, and blue-grey. The umbels of seven to eleven white flowers are seen mainly in late spring and summer. They are followed by small seed capsules about 6cm in diameter, with protruding valves. The flowers are unimportant, the tree being grown for its form. Probably one of the best known of all eucalyptus. A hardy tree in cultivation, but probably too large for most gardens. Adapts well to a wide range of soils, but growth is best in soils with an assured supply of water, although it will tolerate drought. A mighty tree for parks and large gardens, and often used as a street tree. Propagation is from seed, which germinates readily.

E. citriodora (syn. Corymbia citriodora) LEMON-SCENTED GUM

A graceful, slender tree that can grow to 30m high with smooth, slender, white-to-pinkish stems and weeping branches. The light green leaves are 8-15cm long, and lemon-scented when crushed. The small white flowers are inconspicuous, appearing near the top of the tree during winter. The tree makes fast growth, but the trunk is weak, so stake it securely. Older specimens make beautiful trees, becoming picturesque with age.

Eucalyptus citriodora

E. ficifolia (syn. Corymbia ficifolia) RED GUM

A slower-growing, round-headed, ornamental tree that grows 15m or more high, usually making a single trunk with deeply furrowed bark that is rough and persistent (meaning that it does not shed annually). The lance-shaped, dark, glossy green leaves are 8–15cm long, with a yellow midrib. The tree's greatest beauty lies in its spectacular flowering panicles, which

may be 30cm across and contain many flowers: these are 3–4cm long, and are normally scarlet or crimson, appearing from summer to autumn. Seedling variability means that the resulting trees may vary from the parent both in habit and in flower colour. Consequently, the flower varies from white to pink and orange as well as red. The flowers and foliage are useful for flower arranging. The tree does not grow well in alkaline soil. One of the most widely cultivated of all garden eucalyptus.

Eucalyptus ficifolia

E. globulus TASMANIAN BLUE GUM

A spreading, moderately dense, eventually tall tree, 40–50m high, with a 10–25m spread. The bark is attractive, as it peels away in long strips or sheets, leaving the trunk a smooth bluish-white. Makes an attractive tree when young with its blue, juvenile leaves to 15cm long on square-sectioned stems. Adult trees have lance-shaped, deep green leaves 10–30cm long. Often used as a pot plant or summer bedding plant in northern climates. The fresh leaves are the source of Oil of Eucalyptus. The white flowers are either solitary or two to three together, about 4cm across, appearing from spring to summer. They are followed by blue-grey seed capsules. This is a greedy, messy tree that should only be grown in large gardens. Extensively grown as a timber tree. As the tree sets seed that germinates readily, it can become invasive, and is considered a noxious weed in many countries.

E. leucoxylon WHITE IRONBARK

A fast-growing, small tree with pendulous branches 6–15m high, spreading to 20m wide. From the

ground it has a furrowed trunk, known as ironbark. The bark is shed in late summer to reveal a white to mottled trunk. The juvenile blue-green, lance-shaped leaves are high in the essential oil cineal. The adult grey-green, lance-shaped, pendulous leaves are 8–15cm long. The flowers are pink, white or crimson, 3cm across in clusters of three or more, appearing in great profusion. They are produced mainly in summer, but may appear through autumn and winter. Tolerant of adverse conditions such as heavy or rocky soil, heat and wind.

E. nicholii NARROW-LEAVED PEPPERMINT

This particularly beautiful, small tree grows fast, but rarely reaches more than 10–15m high. The reddish-brown bark is deeply furrowed. The tree has fine, weeping branches, and pendulous foliage on an upright main trunk. The juvenile leaves are blue-green, narrow and willow-like, 7–13cm long. When the leaves are crushed they smell of peppermint. Young trees retain their foliage to ground level. The small, white, inconspicuous flowers are produced mainly in summer. A good garden or street tree. The billowing, fine-textured foliage gives it a willow-like form.

Eucalyptus globulus

E. perriniana SPINNING GUM 🌙

A small, straggly tree up to 10m high and wide, with smooth, flaking, whitish bark. The stems grow through the blue-grey or green circular juvenile leaves. When the leaves loosen their hold, they spin round on the stem in the wind. The silver foliage is useful for flower arranging. The lance-shaped adult leaves are pendant and up to 12cm long. The creamy flowers are in small clusters of three, and appear during summer. Usually treated as a shrub by cutting it back to produce its attractive new leaves. Makes an attractive, grey-leaved plant for the border.

E. polyanthemos SILVER DOLLAR GUM 🌙

A fairly fast-growing, broadly conical tree 6–25m high and up to 12m wide, which may have a single trunk or be multi-stemmed. The fibrous bark is reddish-brown. The juvenile leaves are grey-green, oval or round, and 5–8cm long. The mature leaves are lance-shaped, 9cm long and grey-green. The creamy-white flowers appear in small clusters in spring and summer. Makes a popular landscaping and street tree. The foliage is useful for flower arranging. Will grow almost anywhere, but dislikes wet conditions.

E. torquata CORAL GUM 🌙

A small, slender, upright, aromatic tree to 6m high. The willowy, light-brown stems often droop with the weight of the flowers. The lance-shaped bluish-green leaves are up to 10cm long. Its spectacular, flowering panicles contain many scarlet or crimson flowers, 3–4cm long. The flower buds are like small Japanese lanterns: they appear mainly from summer to autumn, but may be produced at any time of the year. The flowers are produced at an early age. A spectacular flowering tree that makes a good specimen tree in a small area. The foliage is useful for flower arranging.

E. viminalis MANNA GUM 🌙

A picturesque, tall, spreading tree, to 50m high and 15m wide in its native habitat. The beautiful, smooth, whitish trunk has a rough cover that peels in ribbons during summer. The branches are drooping and willow-like. The light green, juvenile leaves are lance-shaped and up to 6cm long, while the adult leaves grow to 20cm long. Small white flowers in long, thin, open clusters appear for most of the year. The bark yields manna, which is eaten by Australian aboriginals, while the leaves are the principal food of Koala bears.

Eucharis
Amaryllidaceae

A genus of about seventeen species of evergreen, bulbous perennials native to central and South America. They are grown for their striking, fragrant white flowers.

E. × grandiflora (syn. E. amazonica) AMAZON LILY 🌙🌙🌙

A bulbous perennial with broad, basal, deep green leaves. The wavy leaf blade is about 30cm long, 15cm wide, and narrows to a stalk 4cm long. In early summer it produces umbels of pure white flowers individually up to 13cm across, the corona tinged with green, but the rest of the flower a pure white with long, protruding stamens. The leafless stems grow to about 60cm high. The bulbs need plenty of water while growing, but should be completely dried off after flowering. Grow in a humus-rich, well drained soil in light, dappled shade. Ideal for a sheltered courtyard. Native to the Andes of Colombia and Peru.

Eugenia
Myrtaceae

This vast genus once contained about 1,000 species of evergreen trees or shrubs, many with edible fruit, that are native mainly to tropical America. Recent workers, however, now segregate many species from south-east Asia into the large genus Syzygium, and some into other smaller genera. Most species grow best in neutral to slightly acid soil.

E. australis
See *Syzygium paniculatum*.

E. myrtifolia
See *Syzygium paniculatum*.

E. paniculata
See *Syzygium paniculatum*.

E. uniflora
SURINAM CHERRY, BRAZIL CHERRY 🌙🌙🌙

An evergreen shrub or small tree that will grow slowly to 6m high, but is usually seen around 2m high, and wide, with open growth. The oval leaves, 5cm long, are deep, glossy green and aromatic. The solitary, fragrant white flowers are about 1cm across, with many protruding stamens. The distinctive grooved, round, fleshy fruit, 3cm across, change colour from green to orange to red, when they are edible. They are sweet to slightly acid in taste,

Eucharis × grandiflora

Euonymous fortunei 'Emerald 'n' Gold'

and are used in jellies, jams and sherbets. The shrub is widely cultivated in tropical regions of the world as an ornamental. Grows best when given generous summer water, a moist atmosphere and a sheltered spot. Can be grown in full sun or partial shade. Native to eastern Brazil.

Euonymus 'SPINDLE TREE'
Celastraceae

A genus of about 175 species of deciduous and evergreen dwarf shrubs, climbers and small trees native mainly to Asia but also found in Europe, North America, Africa and Australia. They are grown for their attractive leaves, some turning a beautiful autumn colour.

E. fortunei

An evergreen shrub that will trail, form a mound or climb by rootlets. Will grow to 60cm high as a mound, or to 5m as a climber, spreading almost indefinitely. The long stems will root at intervals. The leaves are elliptic, up to 6cm long, veined underneath, and often variegated with white or gold. The flowers are small, pale green, and produced in loose clusters in summer. Small, round, white fruit appear in autumn. Grow the shrub in full sun or partial shade. Although frost hardy, it also takes the heat well. Grows well even in dry areas, with little summer water. Native to central and western China. The coloured, leafed forms are normally grown.

E. fortunei 'Coloratus'

A trailing or climbing form up to 8m high with dark green leaves. The leaves turn purple-red in late autumn.

E. fortunei 'Emerald 'n' Gold'

A dense, dwarf bush to 90cm high. The leaves are deep green with a broad, bright gold margin that becomes cream, flushed with pink in winter.

E. fortunei 'Silver Queen'

A compact shrub 2–3m high, or up to 6m as a climber. The young leaves in spring are a rich creamy-yellow, becoming green with a broad white margin.

E. japonicus JAPANESE SPINDLE

A large, densely branched evergreen shrub or small tree up to 4m high with a 2m spread. The dark, glossy green, oval, toothed, leathery leaves are up to 6cm long. The flowers are inconspicuous. The more interesting variegated forms are normally grown. A valuable shrub where heat tolerance is important and where soil conditions are poor. Fairly resistant to frost. A good windbreak shrub for coastal gardens vulnerable to salt spray, or for planting as a hedge. Grows well in full sun or partial shade. Native to China, Japan and Korea. Many varieties have been raised with beautiful foliage and upright bushy habit, which makes them suitable for planting as a hedge.

E. japonicus 'Albomarginatus'

A shrub with oval grey-green leaves 3–5cm long, with conspicuous creamy-white edges.

Euonymous japonicus 'Aureus'

E. japonicus 'Aureus'
(syn. E. j. 'Aureopictus', E. j. 'Luna')

The deep green leaf edges make a striking contrast with the golden centres. This shrub has a tendency to revert to all green leaves, so care should be taken to remove all green shoots as they are vigorous, quickly taking over. Grows to 1.5m high and about 1m wide.

E. japonicus 'Ovatus Aureus' (syn. E. j. 'Aureovariegatus')

A dense, compact shrub up to 2m high and 1.5m wide. Striking in appearance, with two types of oval leaves: yellow tinged with green, and green with yellow margins. Makes a beautiful golden mound with little tendency to revert to green.

Euonymus japonicus 'Ovatus Aureus'

Eupatorium
Asteraceae

Once a vast genus containing 1,200 species, most of which have been transferred to other genera. Now a genus of forty species of mostly herbaceous perennials, annuals, and a few evergreen shrubs native to Europe, Africa, Asia, North and South America. Some of the shrubs have striking flowers.

E. adenophorum WHITE EUPATORIUM

A perennial herbaceous plant that grows to 1m high, with many thin stems. The dark green, coarsely toothed, lance-shaped leaves are 6–10cm long. The large terminal clusters of small white or cream flowers are produced throughout most of summer. The plant grows well in full sun or partial shade. Drought-resistant once established, but it grows better with some summer water. Easily propagated by seed, and indeed readily seeds itself around the garden, so it can become invasive. Native to Europe and north Africa.

Epatorium sordidum

Eupatorium adenophorum

E. sordidum (syn. **Bartlettina sordida**)

A beautiful, bushy shrub that grows to 2m high with a spread almost as wide. The young stems are densely covered in reddish, woolly hairs. The large, ovate, toothed, deep green leaves are up to 10cm long. They are covered with reddish hairs on the underneath. The terminal, many-flowered heads of fragrant blue, violet or purple flowers to 12cm across, appear in late spring. The shrub grows in full sun but prefers some shade and shelter. The large leaves can be damaged by wind. Requires average summer water. Looks effective when grown near a lawn. Native to Mexico.

Euphorbia 'MILKWEED, SPURGE'
Euphorbiaceae

A vast genus of around 2,000 species containing a wide range of plants, including annuals, herbaceous perennials, subshrubs, shrubs, trees and cactus-like plants. Most have an acrid milky sap that can be poisonous. They come from most temperate regions of the world.

E. characias

A shrubby evergreen perennial with many upright stems to 1m high, spreading to over 1m wide. The stems are biennial, with the flowers produced on the previous season's growth. The narrow, blue-grey leaves are in close spirals, each one being about 13cm long. The greenish-yellow flowers are contained in dense masses of greenish, paper-like bracts 10–20cm long. They are borne in large, terminal heads in spring and early summer. After flowering the stems should be removed. The plant grows well in fairly poor soil conditions, in sun or partial shade. When established it withstands drought, but grows better with some summer water. Native to Portugal and the western Mediterranean. The subspecies 'Wulfenii' is the form most often seen, with yellow-green flowers.

Euphorbia characias subsp 'Wulfenii'

E. ingens

GIANT SPURGE, CANDELABRA TREE

A massive, candelabra-like, freely branching, treelike succulent up to 4m high and 3m wide. The four- or five-angled, yellowish-green to dark green branches form a broad, rounded crown. The stems are constricted into oblong segments that are wavy toothed and set with spines. A strong architectural plant for the dry garden. Grow the succulent in well drained soil in full sun. Native to tropical southern Africa.

Euphorbia ingens

E. marginata
SNOW ON THE MOUNTAIN ◡◡

This easily grown, single-stemmed, summer annual grows to 60cm high, spreading to 30cm wide. The oblong leaves, 3–8cm long, become striped and margined with white on the upper part of the plant, which gives it a dazzling effect. The stems are often used in floral arrangements. From late summer to autumn it bears terminal inflorescence in umbels with showy bract-leaves, 6–8cm long. They have a striking white border, and small, long-lasting white flowers. One of the few variegated plants that grows well in full sun. Sow seeds direct in the flowering position in spring. Grow in full sun. Looks better if given moderate summer water, but will survive on little. The sap is very corrosive to the skin and can cause dermatitis or burns. Native to North America.

Euphorbia marginata

E. milii CROWN OF THORNS ◡

A woody, slow-growing, evergreen succulent shrub with stems that are irregularly branched to 1m or more long and are covered in long spines. The leaves are oval, light green, 4–5cm long, and usually only appear near the tips of the stems. Clusters of brilliant, scarlet flowering bracts appear nearly all the year, containing tiny, fleshy, yellowish-green flowers. The shrub thrives best on dry rocky soil in full sun. When established it withstands drought, but grows better with some summer water. Ideal for coastal planting especially in hedge form. Native to Madagascar. Many varieties and hybrids have been raised, which vary in the form, size and colour of the bracts, including a purple-leaved form. 'Splendens' is semi-prostrate to scrambling, and looks most effective when grown on the tops of walls or banks and allowed to tumble down.

Euphorbia milii

E. pulcherrima POINSETTIA ◡◡

An evergreen, branching shrub up to 3m high, and spreading as wide, with a woody trunk and milky sap. The dark green, coarse, ovate to lance-shaped leaves are 10–15cm long. They are sometimes lobed or toothed. In winter the terminal, petal-like bracts, to 30cm wide, appear. The true flowers appear on the tips of the stems: they are greenish-yellow and inconspicuous, and are surrounded by brilliant red, petal-like bracts, which hold their colour for several weeks. Grow the shrub outdoors in a well drained, slightly acid soil with average water during summer. Will take full sun, but prefers some shade. Prune occasionally to prevent it becoming too leggy. Native to central America and tropical Mexico. There are many cultivars, with white, cream, pink or mottled bracts. The dwarf form 'Paul Mikkelsen' is often used as a pot plant, as the bracts are extra large. A popular pot plant seen in many homes in midwinter.

Euryops
Asteraceae

A genus of 50–100 species of evergreen shrubs, herbaceous perennials and annuals native to southern Africa. They are grown for their bright, daisy-like flowerheads.

E. acraeus ◡

A much-branched, rounded shrub to 60cm high and wide. The stems are covered with oblong, leathery, silver-grey leaves 2–3cm long. From autumn to early summer, numerous yellow flowerheads 2–3cm across are borne singly or in clusters of two to three on strong stems. They cover the shrub, making a brilliant display. Grows well in full sun in any soil, but needs excellent drainage. It needs little summer water once established. Hardier than other species, it will withstand frost. Makes an attractive shrub for the rock garden. Thrives in coastal gardens as it withstands salt-laden sea breezes. Native to South Africa.

E. chrysanthemoides ◡

A very free-flowering, frost-hardy,

Euphorbia pulcherrima

Euryops pectinatus

small evergreen shrub, to 1m high and wide, rapidly forming a low mound early in life. The deeply divided, thin, glossy green leaves are up to 10cm long. A wealth of brilliant yellow, single, narrow-petalled daisies, each up to 8cm across, are borne on very thin yet stiff stems, some distance above the foliage. They appear mostly in autumn to early summer, but can cover the plant for most of the year. The shrub grows best in full sun in any soil, but needs excellent drainage. When established it withstands drought, but grows better with some summer water. This astonishingly free-flowering shrub is ideal for the dry garden in the front of a border, or even in the larger rock garden where it will enjoy nestling between boulders. It looks most impressive in pots on a sunny terrace. Native to South Africa.

E. pectinatus

A vigorous shrub 1–2m high and wide, with strongly upright branches. All parts of the shrub are covered in soft, whitish hairs. The deeply divided, grey-green, hairy leaves are up to 10cm long. Bright yellow flowerheads, 5–6cm wide, are borne singly or in small clusters on stems 15cm long. They appear mostly in autumn to early summer, but can cover the plant for most of the year. The shrub will grow in any soil but needs excellent drainage. For best flowering, grow in full sun. Needs little summer water once established. An easily maintained shrub that is a good filler and useful for the dry garden. It makes a most attractive pot plant for the sunny terrace. Native to South Africa.

F

Farfugium
Asteraceae

A genus of just two species of rhizomatous, evergreen perennials native to eastern Asia. They are grown for their attractive bold leaves and yellow, daisy-like flowers.

F. japonicum (syn. Ligularia tussilaginea) ↵↵↵

A clump-forming perennial up to 60cm high, which spreads as wide with all leaves rising directly from the rootstock. The bold, kidney-shaped, shiny dark green leaves are 15–30cm across, and carried on stalks 30cm or more long. The flower stalk is produced during autumn and winter, is 30–60cm high, and bears yellow flowerheads 4–6 cm wide. The plant grows best in shade in a rich soil. Although it will survive periods of drought, it grows well with

Farfugium japonicum

regular summer water. A good plant to brighten up a shady spot. Native to China, Korea, Japan and Taiwan. 'Argenteum' has variegated leaves with creamy-white margins. 'Aureomaculatum' has leaves speckled and blotched with cream or yellow.

Fargesia
Poaceae

Now a genus of about four species of woody, evergreen bamboo that form rhizomes, native to North America, east and south Asia. There is much confusion over the name of these plants, as many species that were formerly grouped under the name *Arundinaria* have now been reclassified.

F. murieliae (syn. Arundinaria murieliae, Thamnocalamus spathaceus) ↵↵

A vigorous-growing bamboo that forms large clumps, with arching, evergreen stems 2.5–3.5m high. The canes are green when young, maturing to a yellowish-green. The stems have many slender branches growing from the nodes. The bright green leaves are tapered, reaching 6–10cm in length, and 1–2cm wide. Grow the bamboo in full sun or partial shade. Give it some water in spring when in growth, but it needs less during summer. The canes, correctly known as culms, make very fast growth in spring. Individual culms live for many years, but should be removed when they die. Excellent as an isolated specimen plant, or to give shade to a pathway. Native to China.

× Fatshedera
Araliaceae

An intergeneric hybrid from *Fatsia japonica* and *Hedera helix* that forms a

Fargesia murieliae

loose, spreading shrub grown for its striking evergreen leaves.

F. lizei TREE IVY ↵↵↵

A loosely branched shrub, 2m or more high and 3m wide, with rusty-coloured hairs on young stems. The stems are weak, so they grow upright at first, then tend to flop. The glossy, leathery, deep green, deeply five- or seven-lobed leaves are up to 15cm across. Round heads of white, sterile flowers are borne in terminal clusters to 20cm long in late summer and autumn. This splendid shrub is best grown in the shade. Tolerates atmospheric pollution, coastal conditions and all types of soil. Generous summer watering is needed. Widely grown as a groundcover, or it can be trained against a wall. Protect it from hot, drying winds. Good near swimming pools. There are several varieties with colourful leaves. 'Variegata' has grey-green leaves with an irregular, creamy-white margin. They make good pot or container plants for a shady terrace. Garden origin.

Fatsia
Araliaceae

A genus of only one species of evergreen shrub or small tree native to South Korea and Japan, with large-lobed leaves and terminal panicles of white flowers.

F. japonica (syn. *Aralia japonica, A. sieboldii*) JAPANESE ARALIA ♨♨♨
An evergreen, rounded shrub that makes slow growth up to 3m high, with a spread of 3m wide. Established shrubs sucker freely. The large, palmate, glossy green leaves, up to 30cm wide, have five to nine pointed, toothed lobes. They are carried on long stalks. Many roundish clusters, 2–4cm across, of tiny, creamy-white flowers are produced at the ends of the branches in autumn. They are followed by small, round black fruit. The shrub grows best in deep shade, as the leaves tend to turn a sick yellow in sunshine. Generous watering during summer is needed. An excellent container plant for a shaded terrace or courtyard. The bold leaves give it a tropical look, which makes it a popular foliage plant. Good near swimming pools. Rejuvenate old shrubs by cutting back hard in early spring. 'Variegata' has white tips to the points of the lobes and is smaller growing.

F. papyrifera
See *Tetrapanax papyrifer*.

Feijoa sellowiana
See *Acca sellowiana*.

Fatsia japonica

Felicia (syn. Agathaea) 'BLUE DAISY'
Asteraceae

A genus of about eighty species of annuals, shrubby perennials or sub-shrubs that are native to tropical and southern Africa. They are grown for their daisy-like, generally blue flowers.

Felicia amelloides

F. amelloides (syn. *Aster amelloides*) Blue Marguerite ♨♨
A shrubby perennial that rarely grows more than 50cm high, forming a dense mound up to 60cm wide. The roughish, slightly aromatic, oval green leaves are 3cm long. During summer it is covered in daisy-like flowers, 3–4cm wide, pale blue with a yellow centre. Some flowers may be produced at any time of the year. The plant is at its best when grown in full sun. A moderate amount of water during summer is required to keep it flowering. Looks good when grown in pots or containers, and when planted on the top of a wall or raised bed, from where it can tumble down. This is a vigorous plant that can become untidy after a few years, but it can be trimmed at any time of the year to encourage more flowers, or cut back hard in autumn to give it a good shape. Native to South Africa. There are many named forms, including 'Reads Blue', which is more compact with blue flowers; 'Reads White', with white flowers; 'Santa Anita' with large, rich blue flowers; and a lovely variegated form with cream-splashed leaves.

Ferula
Apiaceae

A genus of over 150 species of herbaceous perennials, with large taproots and aromatic foliage, native from the Mediterranean region to central Asia.

F. communis GIANT FENNEL ♨
A robust perennial with stems that are thick, often branched and hollow, up to 3m high and about 60cm wide. A mass of bright green foliage arises from the base of the stems. The soft leaves are up to 45cm long, and are many times divided into narrow, linear segments. The leaves die down in summer and reappear in autumn. In early summer the stems have a large, terminal, many-branched umbel of small yellow flowers. In late summer the seedheads appear, containing a mass of small brown seeds. As the roots have one or more long taproots, this plant is impossible to transplant once established. Grow in full sun, in any well drained soil. When established it withstands drought. Makes an effective foliage plant for the dry garden. The bronze- and purple-leaved forms are particularly attractive. Native to the Mediterranean region. The giant fennel should not be confused with the culinary herb called fennel, which is Foeniculum.

Festuca 'FESCUE'
Poaceae

A genus of around 300 species of deciduous and evergreen tufted grasses, widely distributed throughout the temperate regions of the world. Some species are used for lawns, others as ornamental grasses.

F. glauca BLUE FESCUE ♨
A low, densely tufted evergreen ornamental grass. The threadlike, linear leaves are rolled inwards or in a circle, and are 15–20cm long; they are erect or arching, smooth and silver-blue in colour. In early summer this fescue produces short, branched panicles of violet flushed blue-green flowers, up to 30cm high. A useful groundcover for sunny or partially shady areas. Ideal for the dry garden, as it requires little summer water once established. Divide and replant every three to four years to maintain foliage colour. Not a grass that can be walked on. Native to northern and southern temperate regions. There are many named varieties, which vary in the intensity of the blue colour in the leaves, and in height from 15–40cm.

Festuca glauca

Ficus 'FIG'
Moraceae

A huge genus of around 800 species of mainly evergreen or deciduous large trees, shrubs and woody root-clinging climbers. Most have a milky sap and insignificant flowers. Native to tropical and subtropical countries worldwide. One important member is grown for its fruit (*F. carica*), while others are grown for shade or ornament, some as pot plants.

F. benjamina OVAL-LEAVED FIG TREE, WEEPING FIG ❧❧

An evergreen tree or shrub that can reach up to 30m high and 15m wide in its native habitat; however, it is rarely seen that high in the garden. The tree becomes broad-headed with slender, drooping branches that may reach the ground. The oval, shining, light green leaves are 5–12cm long, wavy-edged and slender-pointed; in habit they droop. The tree will grow in sun or shade. Give some protection, as the leaves can be damaged by wind. Grows best in a moist, well drained soil. Frequently grown as a pot plant in the home, or as a small tree on a patio. Native to India, Asia, northern

Ficus benjamina

Australia and the South Pacific Islands. 'Variegata' has beautiful, white-splashed leaves which can be damaged by burning sunshine, so is best grown in partial shade.

F. carica COMMON FIG ❧

A much-branched deciduous tree, growing about 5–6m high, and 5m wide. The heavy, thick branches appear from near the ground forming a dense mass. Young shoots also appear from under ground. The leaves are thick, they have three to five lobes, and are 10–20cm long and nearly as wide. They are dark green in colour and rough to touch. This important ficus is grown for its edible fruit that can be eaten fresh, cooked or dried. The figs are 5cm long, pear-shaped, and green when young, ripening to yellow-green or purple depending on the variety. The fruit appears singly in the leaf axils in early summer, and ripens from midsummer onwards. The dried fruit is often seen in shops and markets. The tree needs to be grown in full sun in free-draining soil. Drought-tolerant once established, but produces better fruit with some summer water. Native to the eastern Mediterranean and west Asia. There are many named varieties raised to suit local conditions, some with green-skinned fruit, others with purple- or black-skinned fruit.

Ficus carica

F. elastica RUBBER PLANT ❧❧ or ❧❧❧

A huge evergreen, many-branched tree to 30–50m or more high, spreading to 20–50m in its native habitat; however, it is rarely seen this big in the garden. It eventually forms a huge, buttressed trunk with aerial roots hanging from the large branches. Mainly grown for its thick, deep glossy green leaves, 20–30cm long and 10–15cm wide, that are often flushed with red. The new

leaves emerge from a red or pink sheath, which adds beauty to the plant until it withers and drops off. Once established, this makes a good shade tree. Can be grown in sun or light shade, and requires some shelter from the wind. If given ample summer water in its early years it can make rapid growth, but it only needs average water once established. This is the familiar 'Rubber Plant' found in most florists' shops. Native to India and Malaysia. There are many named and variegated cultivars, including 'Decora' which has wider, thicker and very glossy leaves; and 'Doescheri', with leaves mottled grey-green, creamy-yellow and white, with pink stalks and midribs. These cultivars are more suited to the house or terrace than the garden.

Ficus elastica

F. macrophylla AUSTRALIAN BANYAN, MORETON BAT FIG ❧❧

A large, evergreen tree, to 15m high in cultivation but up to 60m in the wild. With great age it can spread to 40m or more wide, with aerial roots that become props and a massive buttressed trunk. The oblong, leathery leaves, to 25cm long and 10cm wide, are glossy green above and brownish underneath. The figs are produced in the leaf axils. They are 2cm long, ripening to dark reddish-brown with paler spots. They are only produced on mature trees. Grow in full sun. Given ample summer

Ficus macrophylla

F

Ficus macrophylla

water in its early years, it can make rapid growth, but it only needs average to little water once established. A beautiful tree that needs plenty of room to grow. Native to Australia (New South Wales).

Ficus microcarpa 'Hawaii'

F. microcarpa (syn. F. retusa)
CURTAIN FIG, INDIAN LAUREL FIG 🌢🌢
A moderate- to slow-growing evergreen tree, to 6–9m high, and which can become wide-spreading with age. The oblong, leathery leaves, to 8cm long, are dark glossy green. The round, purple figs, just 1cm long, are produced on mature trees. Grow in full sun. Given ample summer water in its early years it can make rapid growth, but it only needs average water once established. When young it makes a most attractive tree. Native to southern Asia, Australia. The variegated form

'Hawaii' has grey-green leaves splashed with white, and is slower growing.

F. pumila CREEPING RUBBER PLANT 🌢🌢
A vigorous, root-clinging evergreen climber that will grow to 10m or more and branches freely. When young it is sometimes slow to begin climbing. The bright green juvenile leaves, 4cm long and heart-shaped at first, are restricted to a thin mat covering the surface, onto which the stems cling. In maturity the leaves develop into something large and leathery, 10cm long. This is one of the finest clinging climbers, that will climb any wall in sun or shade: given the right conditions, there is no limit to its size. Give it generous water until established, then little summer water. Native to China, Vietnam and Japan.

F. rubiginosa (syn. F. australis)
RUSTYLEAF FIG 🌢🌢
An evergreen tree that can grow 12m or more high with a broad crown to 12m wide. The tree may have single or multiple trunks. The deep green, oval leaves are 12cm or more long, with rusty pubescent hairs on the undersides. They are borne on short leaf stalks. With age the tree can send

Ficus rubiginosa 'Variegata'

down aerial roots that can form trunks, but this is rarely seen in gardens. This is typical, however, of many evergreen tropical ficus. Grows well in light, sandy soil. Unusually for Ficus, it is drought-tolerant, and only requires a modest amount of summer water once established. An extremely ornamental tree that makes a wonderful specimen or shade tree. Native to Australia.

Foeniculum 'FENNEL'
Apiaceae

A small genus of just two or three species of aromatic perennials native to

Foeniculum vulgare

coastal areas of the Mediterranean region. One species is grown for the leaves and aromatic seeds, used in flavouring food.

F. vulgare COMMON FENNEL 🌢
A robust, deep-rooting, herbaceous perennial. The stems are thick, often branched and hollow, usually growing to 3m high. The leaves are soft, many times divided into narrow linear segments, to 30cm long. The leaves die down in summer and reappear in autumn. In mid- to late summer the plant produces central, flat terminal umbels, 10cm wide, of tiny yellow flowers. They are followed by aromatic seeds. The young leaves and seeds have a liquorice taste. The plant grows well in full sun. Ideal for the dry garden as it needs no summer water. Easily raised from seed, indeed it can become invasive, and is often seen growing on roadsides. Native to southern Europe. The form 'Purpureum' is much more attractive with its bronze-purple foliage.

Fortunella 'KUMQUAT'
Rutaceae

A small genus of about four to five species of evergreen shrubs or small trees that are sometimes spiny, grown for their edible fruit. Native to southern China and Malaysia.

Freesia × hybrida

F. margarita 'Nagami' KUMQUAT ♪♪♪
A shrub or small tree to 3–4m high, but less if grown on dwarfing rootstock. The slender, erect, angled branches are nearly thornless. The lance-shaped, dark green leaves are 10cm long. Axillary clusters of waxy, five-petalled flowers have a rich orange-blossom scent. They are followed by small, oblong, golden-yellow fruit, 2–3cm in diameter. The fruit are produced in autumn and ripen in spring, but will stay on the plant for most of the year. The edible rind is sweet, but the flesh is acid. The fruit can be preserved whole, or used in marmalade or jelly. The tree grows well in moist, well drained soil in full sun. Kumquats are the hardiest of the citrus, but may not fruit in cold winters. They are fine ornamentals either in the garden or in pots or tubs on a sunny patio. Known only in cultivation, but probably native to south-east China.

Freesia *Iridaceae*

A genus of about nineteen species of cormous perennials native to South Africa. They have been much hybridized to produce the florist's types that are normally grown.

F. × hybrida ♪♪
A cormous perennial with sword-shaped linear leaves up to 30cm long.

The slender, usually branched and bent wiry stems grow to 30cm or more long, and unless supported will lie on the ground. The tubular 5cm flowers, produced in early spring, are irregularly spaced along the stem. They come in a wide range of colours, including pink, red, yellow, orange and white, and bicolours. They are powerfully scented, making wonderful cut flowers. They will seed themselves if old flowers are not removed. Plant the corms 8cm deep in autumn in a sunny position in well drained soil. They look wonderful in

pots or containers. Water during the growing and flowering period, then allow to rest and bake in summer by reducing the water. Garden origin.

Fremontia

See *Fremontodendron.*

Fremontodendron (syn. Fremontia)
'FLANNEL BUSH'
Sterculiaceae

A genus of just two species of evergreen or semi-evergreen large shrubs native to southern USA and northern Mexico.

F. californicum ♪
A fast-growing, upright semi-evergreen shrub, up to 5m high and 3m wide. The leathery, dark green leaves have three, five or seven lobes up to 10cm long. They are crinkled, and the underneath is covered with dense, pale brown hairs. In early summer the shrub is covered with lemon-yellow saucer-shaped flowers up to 6cm wide. They are followed by conical seed capsules that are covered with rust-coloured hairs. Grow in full sun in soil with excellent drainage. When established it withstands drought, but it grows better with some summer water. As it makes shallow roots do not disturb the soil around the plant, and stake carefully when young. It is usually a short-lived shrub. Native to California.

Fremontodendron californicum

F

Furcraea foetida

Furcraea
Agavaceae

A genus of about twenty species of succulents native to tropical America. They are similar to, and often mistaken for, Agaves.

F. foetida (syn. F. gigantea, Agave foetida)
GIANT FALSE AGAVE

A stemless succulent that forms a large rosette of up to fifty sword-shaped leaves next to the ground. The stiff, fleshy leaves, a shining mid-green, are up to 30cm wide and 1m or more long, with hooked spines along the edge, and a spine at the tip. The flower spike, produced in autumn on mature plants, can grow up to 12m high before producing its mass of small, yellowish flowers, 4cm long, on many branches. Bulblets are commonly borne in the flower clusters. Once the plant has flowered, it dies, but usually leaves a rosette of suckers at the base of the old stem. The plant is not fussy about soil conditions, but requires full sun and good drainage. When established it withstands drought, but grows better with some summer water. Native to Brazil, now naturalized over a wide area of the Mediterranean.

F. selloa 'Marginata'
VARIEGATED FALSE AGAVE

A variable succulent that forms a large rosette of leaves, usually with a trunk 1m or more high. Shaped like a lance or sword, the leaves are 1m or more long, thin and flexible, and glossy green with broad cream margins. They are armed with vicious, brown-hooked spines. The branched inflorescence, produced in summer, grows up to 5m high and bears many white, faintly scented flowers 6–7cm wide. As the plant is more tropical, the flower spike is rarely produced in a Mediterranean climate. The plant grows well in full sun or partial shade. It is not drought-tolerant, needing moderate to generous summer watering. An excellent variegated plant for a warm, sheltered location. Native to Mexico, Guatemala, Colombia.

Gaillardia 'BLANKET FLOWER'
Asteraceae

A genus of about thirty species of annuals, biennials and perennials native to the USA and South America. They are grown for their brightly coloured flowerheads, and their long flowering period.

G. × *grandiflora* ☽
A bushy perennial, to 90cm high and 45cm wide. The grey-green, lance-shaped leaves, to 30cm long, are entire or lobed with a roughish texture. The flowerheads are 8–10cm across, and are single or double. There is much variation in the colour, mostly in warm shades of red, yellow and orange, with blood-red towards the blackish centre cushion. The flowers are produced throughout most of summer. The plants grow and flower best in full sun, thriving in heat in any well drained soil. They need only occasional watering during the hottest months. Effective in sunny borders, also making good cut flowers. The plants are not long-lived, but are easily raised from seed. If sown early, the plants will flower the first year. Garden origin. Seed companies list many varieties, including 'Dazzler', with bright orange-red flowers tipped with yellow, and 'Kobold' (syn. 'Goblin'), a compact variety with large, deep red flowers tipped with yellow.

Gardenia
Rubiaceae

A genus of about 200 species of evergreen shrubs and trees native to tropical regions of Asia and Africa. They are grown for their attractive foliage and usually powerfully fragrant flowers.

G. augusta (syn. *G. jasminoides*)
CAPE JASMINE ☽☽☽
A medium to large, bushy shrub up to 6m high and 3m wide, but usually seen much smaller. The broadly lance-shaped leaves are up to 10cm long. They are shining dark green, leathery and quilted. The strongly fragrant, creamy-white, usually semi-double or double flowers are up to 8cm across. They are produced in flushes during autumn or winter. A temperamental shrub that needs exacting conditions: it should be grown in a sheltered place with little or no frost. Grow in a moist, fertile, humus-rich, acid soil that has good drainage. If it becomes chlorotic, iron chelates will help. To grow well, it should have partial or light dappled shade and morning dew or misting to provide humidity. Often grown in a large pot or container that can be brought indoors when the plant is in flower. The fragrance is unforgettable and can fill a room. Native to eastern China and southern Japan. There are many named varieties. 'Mystery', the best known, is more compact, growing to about 1m high with semi-double flowers.

Gardenia augusta

Gazania
Asteraceae

A genus of about sixteen species of low-growing perennials or annuals, with dazzling daisy-like flowers native to southern Africa. There are basically two types: those that form clumps, and those that trail.

Gazania × hybrida

G. × *hybrida* TREASURE FLOWER ☽
A spreading evergreen perennial that may grow to 30cm high, spreading 30cm wide. The narrow, dark green leaves are 15cm long and may be lance-shaped or lobed, usually with silver undersides. The flowers, 8–10cm wide, are borne on stems 15–20cm long. They come in a wide range of colours: white, yellow, orange, pink or red, either single colours or with dark centres. They are produced continuously throughout summer, only flowering at their best in full sun. The plants need little summer water, but an occasional deep soaking will help. Excellent for planting on dry banks where they will help to prevent erosion, or for edging along sunny paths. These plants can serve as temporary fillers in between young shrubs, or as ground-cover. Seed companies list many named varieties. Garden origin.

G. rigens TRAILING GAZANIA ☽
An evergreen perennial that will grow 15cm high, spreading rapidly to 40cm or more wide. The lance-shaped leaves are silver grey, and 15cm long. There are many large-flowered hybrids in colours of white, orange and yellow, mostly with a black eye. This is a sun lover, with the flowers only opening up in full sun. The plant is fairly drought-tolerant, but does require some summer water. Grows well in most soils, but

needs good drainage. Useful for planting on banks or on the tops of walls where their stems can trail down creating a dazzling effect over a long period. Also attractive in hanging baskets if given enough summer water. Native to South Africa.

Gelsemium
Loganiaceae

A small genus of three species of twining shrubs, producing attractive fragrant flowers; native to Asia and north America.

G. sempervirens CAROLINA JASMINE, EVENING TRUMPET FLOWER

A vigorous, evergreen, twining perennial with stems up to 6m long. The oblong, glossy green leaves are 3–5cm long, and grow in pairs along the stems. The bright yellow, funnel-shaped flowers are sweetly fragrant; they are 3cm long. They appear in clusters from late winter to spring. Grow the plant in full sun. During summer it needs to be well watered, and fed generously; it may become chlorotic if the soil is too alkaline. Ideal as a cover for sunny porches, on banks, or against a wall. Prune severely if it becomes too top heavy. All parts of the plant are poisonous. Native to south-east USA and Mexico.

Genista 'BROOM'
Papilionaceae

A genus of about ninety species of mainly deciduous or evergreen shrubs or trees that are sometimes spiny. Many species are similar to, and often confused with, Cytisus. Native to Europe, the Mediterranean region and west Asia. They are grown for their masses of small yellow flowers.

G. aetnensis MOUNT ETNA BROOM

A small tree or large shrub up to 6m high and wide, with weeping branches and slender, bright green shoots. The tiny narrow leaves are almost absent and soon fall. From mid- to late summer the branches are covered in fragrant, golden-yellow flowers 1–2cm long. They are followed by pods containing two to three seeds. With its graceful habit it makes a good specimen. Ideal for a sunny, dry garden

as it requires no summer water once established. When pruning do not cut into old wood. Native to Italy.

G. hirsuta (syn. *Cytisus hirsutus*)

A dwarf, densely branched, spiny shrub to 60cm high and wide. The young branches are covered with dense, soft hairs. Many of the small lateral branches end in fine, sharp spines. The tiny, lance-shaped leaves, just 1cm long, are softly hairy underneath. The dense, silvery pyramidal spikes contain two to four yellow flowers, 2–3cm long, with a long keel. The spikes are clustered together at the ends of the branches during spring and early summer. Ideal for massing in the dry garden, as it requires no summer water once established. Grow in full sun. The shrub grows best in sandy, well drained soil. Native to the western Mediterranean, Spain and Morocco.

G. hispanica SPANISH BROOM

A dense, spiny deciduous shrub growing 60cm high and spreading to 1m wide. The 1–2cm, oblong leaves are silky underneath and only present on flowering branches. In early summer the small, golden yellow flowers appear profusely on terminal racemes up to 4cm long. Very tolerant of dry, sunny sites with poor soil, but needs good drainage. Good for rock gardens and for planting on sunny banks. Native to south-west Europe.

G. monosperma
See Retama monosperma.

Geranium 'CRANESBILL'
Geraniaceae

A genus of over 300 species of annuals, herbaceous perennials, or rarely shrubs, found throughout most temperate regions. True Geraniums should not be confused with the genus Pelargonium, which has the common name Geranium.

G. maderense
MADEIRA STORK'S BILL

A much-branched, evergreen perennial, growing 1m or more high, spreading to 1.5m wide, with many upright stems. The shiny green leaves, up to 60cm long, have five to seven lobes that are deeply divided, giving a fern-like appearance; they are carried on long, brownish-red stalks. Throughout spring and summer, massive flowerheads appear. Each flower is purple to pink, 4cm across with a dark crimson centre, paler pink veins and red anthers. The upper parts of the flower stalks are thickly covered with sticky, purple hairs. The plant is short-lived, sometimes only biennial. To grow well, it prefers a rich, moist soil in partial shade. A plant in full flower makes a wonderful sight. Ideal for the front of a shrub border or under trees. Native to Madeira.

Genista hirsuta

GLEDITSIA

Geranium maderense

Gerbera
Asteraceae

A genus of over forty species of hairy perennials native to Africa, Madagascar, Asia and Indonesia, with a rosette of basal leaves. They are grown for their striking flowerheads, often used in the florist trade.

G. jamesonii TRANSVAAL DAISY
An herbaceous, tufted perennial that forms a clump 60cm wide, growing to 45cm high. The deeply lobed leaves are 25cm or more long, and dark green above with a paler underneath, which is densely woolly. The solitary, daisy-like flowerheads, 10cm wide, rise directly from the crowns on stalks 45cm long. They appear mainly from late spring to late summer, but may appear at any time. The colour is normally orange-red, but it is also available in cream, yellow, to orange, red and pink. Double forms are also available. Grow the plants in full sun, but give partial shade in the hottest areas. They need a fertile soil with excellent drainage. As the plants are deep rooted they need to be watered deeply, then allow the soil to become nearly dry before watering again. Never allow the soil to wash over the crowns. Feed frequently. Let the plants

grow into large clumps before dividing during winter, as they resent transplanting. Good for growing in pots or containers on a sunny terrace. Fresh seed germinates readily. The flowers are excellent for arrangements. Native to South Africa.

Gladiolus
Iridaceae

A genus of 250–300 species of cormous perennials native chiefly to South Africa but also to the Mediterranean region, Africa, Madagascar and west Asia. Gladioli have been much hybridized, resulting in thousands of hybrids and cultivars being raised for garden cultivation.

G. communis subsp. byzantinus
CORN GLAG
A cormous perennial with sword-shaped leaves up to 90cm long. In spring it produces dense spikes of up to twenty purple-red, funnel-shaped flowers, 4–5cm across, marked with cream flashes on the lower segment. A tough plant that is frost-hardy and needs no summer water. The cormlets spread quickly, soon forming a colony. Ideal for the dry garden as they will give a bold splash of colour in spring. Native to the Mediterranean region.

G. garden hybrids
A strong, showy cormous perennial that is a descendant of numerous South African species. The corms are 5cm or more wide with a flattened base. The upright, sword-shaped leaves are borne in basal fans, are mid- to dark green, and 24–60cm long. The showy, wide open, funnel-shaped flowers are 10–18cm or more across, and borne on stiff, fleshy spikes 60–90cm long. The flowers open from the bottom of the spike upwards, with many open at a time. They appear from mid-summer to early autumn, making excellent, long-lasting cut flowers. A wide range of colours have been bred, including white, cream, yellow, orange, salmon-red, rose, purple and many bicolours. Plant gladioli in clumps 10–15cm deep in a border in full sun in rich soil. The large hybrids may need staking. Give regular summer water. Garden origin.

G. italicus
MEDITERRANEAN FIELD GLADIOLUS
A cormous perennial with sword-shaped leaves 5–50cm long. In spring it produces loose spikes of five to fifteen, pink to magenta, funnel-shaped flowers, 4cm across, with paler marks on the lower segment. A tough plant that needs no summer water, flowering best with a dry summer dormancy. The cormlets spread quickly, soon forming a colony. Ideal for the dry garden, they will give a bold splash of colour in spring. Native to southern Europe.

Gladiolus garden hybrid

Gleditsia
Caesalpiniaceae

A genus of about twelve species of deciduous spiny trees native to North America, Asia and tropical Africa, grown for their beautiful foliage.

G. triacanthos HONEY LOCUST
An elegant, spreading tree up to 18m high, with a spiny trunk and shoots. The spines are branched, and can be 8–15cm long. The 20cm-long pinnate leaves are divided into many oval leaflets, 2–4cm long, which turn yellow in autumn. Inconspicuous flowers are followed by shining brown seedpods, 45cm long. This resilient tree is hardy to the cold, tolerates acid or alkaline

soil, drought or generous watering, great heat or wind, and atmospheric pollution. Its feathery foliage casts light shade, which makes it a good specimen in a lawn. Native to central and eastern USA.

Gomphocarpus
Asclepiadaceae

A genus of fifty species of deciduous perennials and shrubs native to southern Africa. They usually have milky sap and large, inflated seedpods.

G. fruticosus (syn. *Asclepias fruticosa*)
WILD COTTON, MILK BUSH ◡◡

A dense, bushy, shrubby perennial 1–2m high and 1m wide. The narrow, linear, opposite leaves are up to 12cm long. The axillary clusters, 5cm across, of small, white flowers are not showy. The shrub is grown for its fat, inflated, pale green seedpods that are up to 8cm long. When the stems are cut and dried they are good for flower arrangements. The plant will self-seed readily, often becoming invasive. Requires regular summer water, and will find itself a home where the conditions are right. Also prone to attacks by aphids. Native to southern Africa, but naturalized in waste places from Jamaica to South America.

Gomphocarpus fruticosus

Graptopetalum paraguayense

Graptopetalum
Crassulaceae

A genus of about twelve species of rosette-forming, perennial succulents native to Mexico and southern USA, often with attractive leaves.

G. paraguayense (syn. *Sedum weinbergii*) GHOST PLANT, MOTHER OF PEARL PLANT ◡

A prostrate, much-branching succulent with thick fleshy stems that forms rosettes up to 20cm high. The thick fleshy leaves are a broad lance-shape 5–8cm long, a pink-tinged grey-green with a silver bloom. The foliage has a subtle opalescent blending of colours. The leaves are brittle and break easily when handled. The 1–2cm white flowers appear on stems up to 15cm long in summer. Grow the plant in well drained soil in full sun or partial shade. Makes an ideal pot or container plant.

Gomphocarpus fruticosus

Grevillea robusta

Prefers occasional summer watering, but can survive with none. A succulent that can easily be divided – even a leaf will quickly root. Native to Mexico.

Grevillea
Proteaceae

A large genus containing some 250 species of evergreen trees and shrubs that are native to Australasia. Some are grown as street trees, while others are used as pot plants when young. Most have beautiful flowers, and many new hybrids are appearing with red, pink or yellow flowers. They are well suited to dry climates.

G. robusta SILKY OAK ◡ or ◡◡

A fast-growing tree 15–30m high spreading to 10m wide, which forms a pyramidal shape when young but becomes more broad-topped when old.

Grevillea rosmarinifolia

The delicate, pinnate, fern-like leaves are 15–30cm long, pale green above and silvery underneath. There is usually a heavy fall of leaves in spring. The orange or yellow flowers appear in densely packed, horizontal, one-sided clusters 10–15cm long in late spring. The tree grows in most soil – even poor, compacted soil – if not over-watered. The branches are brittle, so they can be damaged by the wind. Young plants should be staked securely. Thrives in the heat, but when young can be damaged by frost. Easily raised from seed, growing to 30cm high in less than a year. Often used as a decorative pot and florists' plant when young. Native to Australia.

G. rosmarinifolia
ROSEMARY GREVILLEA ꙮ
A many-branched, compact shrub up to 2m high and 1–5m wide, with silky-hairy young growth. The deep green, needle-like leaves are 1–4cm long and silky underneath, similar to rosemary. The rosy-red, white or pink flowers are produced in spider-like terminal racemes, 4–8cm long, from late autumn to summer. The shrub tolerates heat and drought, but needs an acid or neutral soil that is well drained. Can be used as an informal hedge in dryish places. Native to Australia. 'Canberra Gem', with pinkish-red flowers from late winter to late summer, is outstanding and undemanding.

Griselinia
Griseliniaceae
A small genus of about six species of evergreen shrubs or trees native to New Zealand and Chile. They are grown for their attractive leathery leaves.

G. littoralis ꙮꙮ
An attractive, bulky, evergreen shrub normally seen up to 8m high, spreading to 5m wide, but in its native habitat it may become a 15m-high tree. The roundish, glossy, leathery, bright green leaves are up to 10cm wide. The flowers and fruit are insignificant. The shrub makes a good, dense, compact screen, or it can be clipped as a hedge. Grow in full sun or partial shade. Good for coastal gardens as it tolerates salt-laden sea breezes. For it to grow well, give it moderate water during summer. Native to New Zealand. 'Dixons Cream' has leaves boldly marked with cream, and 'Variegata' has leaves margined with cream and white on grey-green leaves.

G

Haemanthus 'BLOOD LILY'
Amaryllidaceae

Now a genus of twenty-one species of tender evergreen or deciduous bulbous plants that are native to South Africa. They are closely related to amaryllis, and tend to have striking flowers. Many species formerly included here have been moved to the genus Scadoxus.

H. coccineus SHAVING BRUSH PLANT ☽☽
A large bulb producing pairs of thick, fleshy leaves that can be up to 60cm in length and 15cm wide. The leaves are produced in spring and tend to lie flat on the ground. The flowers are produced in autumn after the leaves have died off. The short green flower stem is spotted with red. At the top is a cluster of bright red stamens with yellow anthers packed into a 5–8cm wide flower which is enclosed by red bracts. Give the plant ample water during summer to keep the leaves green and healthy so they can produce food for the bulb. Do not remove the leaves until they naturally turn yellow. Like most bulbs, it needs a rest after flowering by drying off. Grow in a lightly shaded spot in well drained soil.

H. katherinae
See *Scadoxus multiflorus* 'Katherinae'.

Hakea
Proteaceae

A genus of over 130 species of evergreen trees and shrubs native to Australia with small tubular flowers. All need to be grown in acid soil.

H. laurina PINCUSHION TREE ☽
A dense, rounded tree or shrub up to 9m high. The narrow, shiny, grey-green leaves are up to 15cm long, often with a red margin. The unusual, showy flower clusters are produced along the branches in winter. The tiny flowers are crimson red with protruding white or yellow styles, giving it a round, pincushion effect. Grow the tree preferably in full sun, although it will tolerate partial shade. Ideal for the dry garden as it needs no summer water once established. Easily grown from seed. When young the stem is weak, so may need staking. A tough plant, as it tolerates drought, salt winds and poor soil, but it does need good drainage.

Halimiocistus
Cistaceae

A hybrid genus between Cistus and Halimium, occurring in cultivation and in the wild. Evergreen shrubs showing characters intermediate between the two parent genera. They are found in Portugal and France where the parent genera overlap.

H. sahucii ☽
A naturally occurring hybrid that combines the best characteristics of both parents. A compact, bushy shrub 45cm high, spreading to 90cm wide and densely covered with leaves. The linear-lanceolate dark green leaves are 3–4cm long. The clusters of two to five white, saucer-shaped flowers, 4–5cm wide with a centre tuft of yellow stamens, are borne in summer. When in full flower they almost hide the foliage. The shrub needs to be grown in full sun to flower well. Grows best in poor to moderately fertile, sandy soil that is well drained. It will not live in wet soil. Ideal for a large, sunny rock garden or on a dry bank. It can look stunning when seen cascading over a retaining wall. Native to southern France.

H. wintonensis ☽
An attractive, dwarf, spreading shrub, to 60cm high and 90cm wide, covered

Haemanthus coccineus

in greyish hairs. The lance-shaped, grey-green leaves can be up to 5cm long, and are covered in hairs. The flowers, 5cm wide, are beautiful, pure white with zones of crimson-maroon and contrasting yellow stamens. Growing conditions are the same as *H. sahucii*. Garden origin. 'Merrist Wood Cream', an attractive form, has yellow flowers with a deep red band at the base of the petals and yellow stamens.

Halimium
Cistaceae

A small genus of about seven species of evergreen shrubs native to the Mediterranean region. They are grown for their showy flowers, but need long, hot summers to flower well. They are closely related to Helianthemum and are sometimes sold under that name. They are good plants for coastal gardens as they withstand salt-laden sea breezes.

H. atriplicifolium ❧

A beautiful, small, bushy silver shrub, 1–1.5m high and wide. The broad, silver-grey leaves are up to 5cm long. The golden-yellow flowers, up to 4cm across, may be unmarked or have a brown spot at the base of each petal. They are borne on long, sticky, hairy, branched inflorescences that cover the shrub in late spring and early summer. The shrub needs to be grown in full sun to flower well. Grows best in poor to moderately fertile, sandy soil that is well drained. It will not live in wet soil. Ideal for a large, sunny rock garden or on a dry bank. Good for containers on a patio or in a sunny courtyard. Native to central and southern Spain, Morocco.

H. lasianthum ❧

A low, spreading shrub 0.5–1m high and 1.5m wide. The oblong, grey-green leaves are up to 4cm long. The axillary clusters of bright, golden-yellow flowers, 3cm wide with a brownish blotch at the base of each petal, open in late spring. They are borne on flower stalks with long, silvery hairs. Cultivation is the same as *H. atriplicifolium*. Native to southern Portugal and southern Spain.

H. ocymoides (syn. *Cistus algarvensis*) ❧
A charming, much-branched, usually

upright shrub to 1m high and wide. It is easily recognized by having two types of leaves. Those on sterile shoots are 1–2cm long, obovate, with a stalk and silvery white. Those on flowering shoots are 3–4cm long, lance-shaped, green and stalkless. The flowers are brilliant yellow, usually dark spotted, and 3cm across; they are borne in terminal, lax, long-stalked clusters in early summer. Cultivation is the same as *H. atriplicifolium*. Native to Portugal and Spain.

Hardenbergia 'CORAL PEA'
Papilionaceae

A small genus containing three species of strikingly attractive twining climbers or creeping groundcovers that are native to Australia. They are grown for their colourful pea-like flowers that are produced in great profusion.

H. comptoniana LILAC VINE ❧❧

An evergreen twining climber that makes moderate growth to 3m high or more, with an equal spread. It has a light delicate leaf pattern. The dark green, narrow, lance-shaped leaves are divided into three or five leaflets, each one up to 15cm long. The brilliant violet-blue, pea-shaped flowers, 1–2cm long, appear on pendant racemes, 15cm long, in spring. A reliable and attractive climber that can be grown in full sun or partial shade. Grows best in

a light, well drained soil with an average amount of summer water. Cut back after flowering to prevent tangling. 'Rosea' has pink flowers.

H. violacea PURPLE CORAL PEA ❧❧
An evergreen, twining, strong-growing climber that grows to 3m high or more with an equal spread. The leaves are simple, lance-shaped, usually undivided, and 5–10cm long. The axillary clusters of small flowers, often in pairs, are purple to violet, sometimes white, pink or lilac, with a yellow basal spot. They are borne in pendant racemes 10–13cm long during winter and spring. Grow the climber in full sun or partial shade with an average amount of summer water. Cut back after flowering to prevent tangling. Use it to cover a pergola or wall, or grow it through a small tree. It can also be pegged down as a groundcover. 'Pink Cascade' has pink flowers; 'White Crystals' has pure white flowers in winter.

Hedera 'IVY'
Araliaceae

A genus of about ten species of evergreen woody climbers that are usually self-clinging, native to north Africa and from Europe to west Asia. They have juvenile and adult leaves. Ivies are trouble-free plants that have many uses. Ideal for covering eyesores,

Hardenbergia violacea

climbing on walls, fences, or arches. Useful as soil binders to discourage soil erosion. Especially good in shady places. There are many cultivars, with leaves boldly marked with yellow, cream or white.

H. canariensis ALGERIAN IVY

A vigorous climber that quickly reaches 4m or more high, with a wide spread. The shiny, rich green, triangular leaves are 12–20cm wide with three to five shallow lobes. The leaves become more heart-shaped as they mature. They are carried on wine-red stalks and often have reddish hairs on the underneath of the leaf. The climber grows well in full sun or even deep shade. Give a moderate amount of summer water, although it will survive with little. An attractive, strong-growing climber that needs to be sited with care. Native to the Azores, Canary Islands and north Africa. 'Glorie de Marengo', now known as 'Variegata', has long been cultivated in Europe; it has silvery green leaves variegated with yellow and cream. 'Ravensholst' is vigorous, with dark glossy green leaves. Often used for groundcover.

Hedera canariensis 'Variegata'

H. colchica PERSIAN IVY

A bold, vigorous, woody climber, easily growing to 10m or more high, with a huge spread. The largest of the ivies. The entire, leathery, dark green, somewhat heart-shaped leaves are up to 15cm across and 25cm long. The climber grows well in full sun or deep shade. When established it withstands drought, but grows better with some summer water. Ideal for groundcover or against large walls. Native from the Caucasus to Iran. 'Dentata Variegata' is a striking plant with bright green

leaves splashed with grey and broadly margined with creamy yellow that ages to white. 'Sulphur Heart' has leaves boldly splashed with yellow and pale green; some leaves are entirely yellow.

H. helix ENGLISH IVY, COMMON IVY

A vigorous and variable climber that quickly reaches 10m or more high with an almost indefinite spread. The dark to mid-green leaves with paler veins are three- to five-lobed and up to 15cm long. The aerial roots will attach themselves firmly to a wall, fence or tree – which can become a problem if it is not kept in check, as it will climb into anything that is available. Also makes an almost impenetrable groundcover. To grow well it needs regular and adequate summer water. Native to Europe. The species is seldom grown, because there are many variegated varieties that are much more attractive. Some varieties have attractively twisted or distorted leaves, some have large or tiny leaves, others are non-clinging and upright growing, while yet others are grown for their orange-yellow fruit.

Hedychium 'GINGER LILY, GARLAND LILY'
Zingiberaceae

A genus of about fifty species of tender perennials native to tropical Asia, the Himalayas and Madagascar, with leafy stems that rise from stout rhizomes. They are prized for their showy flowers and fragrance.

H. coccineum RED GINGER LILY

A robust perennial with suckering rootstock and leafy stems up to 2m high, spreading to 1m wide. The stiff, lance-shaped leaves are up to 50cm long, a smooth green above, and bluish underneath. The scarlet-red flowers have a long corolla tube and pink filaments; they are about 5cm long. They are borne in dense, stout spikes, 25cm long, which appear in late summer or autumn. This creates a spectacular floral display. Like other Hedychiums they should be grown in deep, rich, moist, leafy soils, and will even thrive in boggy conditions. They are not too happy on alkaline soil, preferring it slightly acidic. They can take the heat, but need ample summer water to compensate for the blistering

sunlight; they are probably better given light shade for at least part of the day. Remove old stems that have flowered in winter or early spring to encourage new growth. Native to the Himalayas.

H. coronarium WHITE GINGER LILY, GARLAND FLOWER

A fleshy-rooted perennial with smooth, leafy stems up to 3m high. They have lance-shaped leaves 40cm long and 12cm wide, often downy underneath. The erect, many-flowered terminal spikes, up to 30cm long, have many pure white, tubular flowers, 8cm long, produced in late summer. They are extremely fragrant with a gardenia-like scent. Grow the plant in light shade in a rich soil, which must be moist at all times. They can also be grown in large pots or containers. Like other Hedychiums, they grow better if fed generously. The plant will produce many offsets. This species is grown much less frequently than others because the leaves tend to burn with the heat, so provide shelter and some shade. Native to India and south-east China.

H. gardnerianum
KAHILI GINGER LILY

A similar species to the above, with stems reaching up to 2m high. The

Hedychium gardnerianum

Helichrysum italicum

lance-shaped leaves are 20–40cm long and 12cm wide. The large, terminal, flowering spikes are 25–40cm long. The deliciously fragrant flowers, 5cm long, are yellow to orange, with numerous long red stamens; they make large, showy clumps producing beautiful flowers all summer. The plants must be kept moist all summer. They may be grown in the sun, but prefer some shade, and need a humus-rich soil. When grown in large pots or containers they make an impressive sight. The old flowering stems should be cut down in winter or early spring to encourage new stems. Large clumps may be divided after a few years, an operation that should be carried out in spring. Native to northern India, the Himalayas.

H. greenei ⌣⌣⌣

A fleshy-rooted perennial with stems up to 2m high. The oblong, sharp-pointed leaves, 20cm or more long and 8cm wide, are light green above, bronze-red underneath. The dense, terminal spikes, 12cm long, which appear during summer, contain many bright red flowers, each 4cm long. Small bulblets sometimes develop from the spent flowers like miniature plants, from which it can be propagated. A more tender species that requires ample summer water and some shade. Native to India.

Helianthemum
'ROCK ROSE, SUN ROSE'
Cistaceae

A large genus containing about 110 species of evergreen shrubs or subshrubs native to North and South America, Europe, Asia and North Africa. They are ideal for rock gardens or raised beds. Many colourful, named hybrids between several species have been raised, with red, orange, pink and yellow flowers.

H. nummularium
COMMON ROCK ROSE ⌣

A dwarf subshrub that spreads out to about 1m wide, but only growing to 20cm high, usually forming a mat. The grey-green lance-shaped leaves are up to 5cm long. The one-sided clusters of single or double saucer-shaped flowers are 2cm across and come in a wide range of colours including red, pink, yellow, white and many pastel shades. They cover the plant in spring, with each flower lasting only a day. Grow the plant in full sun in a rock garden with poor dry soil, or in the front of a border. Good drainage is essential, as over-watering will kill it. After flowering, trim off all the dead flower-heads and lanky growth to keep it bushy. Looks good in a container on a sunny patio. Native to Europe.

Helichrysum
Asteraceae

A large genus of between 300–500 species of annuals, herbaceous perennials, evergreen subshrubs or shrubs native to Europe, Asia, Australasia, and particularly to South Africa. The shrubby plants are usually low growing, often with attractive, aromatic foliage. They are commonly found in dry, sunny sites.

H. italicum (syn. H. angustifolium)
CURRY PLANT ⌣

A hardy, variable, bushy subshrub that grows up to 1m high, spreading to 60cm wide, with silvery-grey, woolly stems, and a mass of narrow, grey, aromatic leaves, 3cm long. The terminal, long-stalked clusters, 8cm wide, carry many tiny, bright yellow flowers that appear during summer. Grow the plant in full sun in well drained soil. When established it withstands drought, but it grows better with some summer water. Probably one of the best silver plants for the Mediterranean region. It looks best when grown in groups. Native to southern Europe.

H. microphyllum
See Plecostachys serpyllifolia.

H. petiolare (syn. H. petiolatum)
⌣ or ⌣⌣

An evergreen subshrub with white woolly, trailing, branching stems, to 3m or more long, that will eventually form a huge mound 3m or more round. The grey, densely woolly, oval leaves are 4cm across. The terminal clusters of creamy-white to yellow flowers, 5cm across, appear in late summer. The plant grows well in full sun when given a moderate amount of summer water, but will survive with none. It is grown

Helichrysum petiolare

mainly for its silver foliage effect. The trailing branches can hang down over the edges of beds and borders, or climb through trees and engulf shrubs. It is strong growing and needs to be controlled by constant clipping. It can make an unusual hedge. Where moist soil is available it will readily seed itself. Native to South Africa. The variety 'Limelight' has lime-green leaves, and 'Variegatum' has cream-edged leaves. Both varieties are less strong growing and need some shade to keep the colour in the leaves.

Heliotropium 'HELIOTROPE'
Boraginaceae

A genus of about 250 species of tender annuals, evergreen subshrubs and shrubs that are native to North and South America, the Pacific Islands and the Canary Islands. Most have hairy leaves, while some have shiny leaves. They are cultivated for their small, sweetly scented flowers.

H. arborescens (syn. *H. peruvianum*)
HELIOTROPE, CHERRY PIE ꙮꙮ

A bushy, evergreen, shrubby perennial to 1m high, spreading to 45cm wide, that is often grown as an annual. The whole plant is covered in fine hairs. The oval to lance-shaped, greenish-purple leaves are up to 10cm long and 5cm wide, with prominent veins. The dense clusters, 8–10cm across, of tiny tubular flowers are from darkest violet through to silvery mauve. They are sweetly scented and are produced mostly in spring, though some appear in summer. Grow the plant in a rich soil in partial shade and give a moderate amount of summer water. Often grown as a pot plant, where it looks good on a patio or terrace. Native to Peru. Many named varieties with strong scent have been raised: 'Gatton Park' has sweetly scented, pale blue flowers and crinkled leaves, growing to 60cm high. 'Marine' is richly fragrant, with flowerheads to 15cm across, and very compact, growing to only 45cm high; it is easily raised from seed.

Hemerocallis 'DAY LILY'
Hemerocallidaceae

A genus of about fifteen clump-forming perennials native from central Europe to China and especially Japan. The species are rarely grown, most garden plants being hybrids. It has been estimated that there are well over 30,000 named hybrids in cultivation. They are grown for their brilliantly coloured, exotic flowers that come in a wide range of colours from white to darkest red, with many bicolours. Each flower only lasts one day, but they are continually replaced throughout the summer.

H. hybrids ꙮꙮꙮ

An evergreen, semi-evergreen or herbaceous perennial, growing from 30cm up to 1m high and wide, with somewhat fleshy or tuberous roots. The yellowish or bluish-green, arching, sword-shaped leaves are from 20cm to over 1m long. The flowers, 8–10cm wide, appear in open or branched clusters at the ends of generally leafless stems, to 1m or more high. The flowers are shallowly to deeply trumpet-shaped in a variety of forms, from star- or spider-shaped to circular or triangular; they can be single, semi- or fully double, and appear throughout the summer once the plants are established. Some hybrids open their flowers in the early morning, others open in late afternoon and remain open all night. Grow in full sun or partial shade in any well drained garden soil. Give generous water throughout the summer. Plants tolerate windy sites and coastal gardens. Divide crowded plants every two to three years in early spring to maintain vigour. Garden origin.

Heptapleurum arboricolum
See *Schefflera arboricola* 'Variegata'.

Hibbertia
Dilleniaceae

A genus of more than 100 species of evergreen trees, shrubs and climbers native mostly to Australia and Tasmania. The climbers are grown for their attractive, usually yellow flowers.

H. scandens (syn. *H. volubilis*)
GUINEA GOLD FLOWER ꙮꙮ or ꙮꙮꙮ

A fast-growing shrub that will climb by twining stems, 3–6m high spreading to 3m wide. The young stems are a reddish-brown with silky-hairy shoots. The lance-shaped, leathery, usually glossy leaves, 8cm long, are smooth above and silky-hairy underneath. The solitary, terminal, five-petalled flowers, 5cm wide, are produced throughout the year, but mostly during summer. They are bright golden yellow like single roses. Although unpleasantly scented, it makes a spectacular sight when in full bloom. The shrub grows best in light shade, but will also grow in full sun, though here it will not be so rampant. A good plant for training on a trellis or over a low wall. As it is native to sand dunes, good drainage is important, as is

Hemerocallis hybrid

Hibbertia scandens

regular summer water. Often used as a groundcover. Grows well in containers on a shaded patio or terrace. Native to eastern Australia.

Hibiscus
Malvaceae

A large genus that has perhaps 250 species of deciduous and evergreen trees, shrubs, annuals and herbaceous perennials from tropical and warm-temperate regions. They are grown mainly for their spectacular flowers, which are produced over a long season. One species is often used as pot plants in cooler climates.

H. huegelii
See *Alyogyne huegelii*.

H. mutabilis CONFEDERATE ROSE
A fast-growing upright to spreading evergreen shrub or small tree, to 3m or more high, and 2m or more wide. The soft green stems are covered with hairs and become woody with age. The large, three to seven-lobed leaves are 10–20cm long and wide, a dull green and covered with hairs. The flowers are produced in leaf axils near the end of the branches. They are 10–12cm wide,

Hibiscus mutabilis

opening white or rose with a crimson centre, then becoming deep red by the evening. This gives the shrub a dramatic effect with many shades of colour at the same time. The flowers are produced continuously throughout summer. This dramatic shrub is easily grown, requiring little attention with only a moderate amount of summer water. Often seen in municipal gardens trained into standards. Native to southern China.

Hibiscus rosa-sinensis

Hibiscus rosa-sinensis 'Archeri'

H. rosa-sinensis ROSE OF CHINA
An evergreen shrub that can become large, or even tree-like with age, reaching up to 4m and spreading to 3m. The broad, ovate leaves are glossy dark green, 8–12cm long. This showy plant produces large, solitary flowers from the leaf axils in large quantities throughout summer, although a few may appear during the rest of the year. The flowers are 10–15cm wide, and vary in colour. Red is the most usual colour, but they can be pink, yellow, apricot, white or orange, usually with prominent yellow stamens and red stigmas. There are also double forms, and some with cream leaf variegations. There is a vast range of named varieties grown, some with gigantic flowers up to 30cm wide. Grow the shrub in full sun in soil with good drainage. It needs

some water in summer to continue flowering. With age it can become a large, straggly shrub if left unpruned. To encourage the young growth that produces the flowers, shorten the old stems in spring. The shrub is also used as an attractive hedge, when it should be given plenty of summer water. As it will tolerate the root restriction of pot culture, it can make a spectacular pot or tub plant on terraces or balconies. Native to tropical Asia.

H. schizopetalus
JAPANESE LANTERN
An evergreen shrub, to 3m high and 1m wide, that is quite distinct as it has many slender drooping branches. The ovate, toothed leaves are up to 12cm long. The showy red or orange-red flowers hang along the stems on long stalks. They are 5–8cm across, with wonderful, deep-cut, recurving petals that are deeply and irregularly fringed and have long protruding stamens. The flowers are produced singly from the leaf axils throughout most of summer. As this shrub comes from the tropics, it requires a warm, sheltered location with a generous amount of summer water. Can be grown in full sun, but some light shade will help. Often trained as a wall shrub. Native to tropical east Africa, Mozambique, Tanzania and Kenya.

H

Hibiscus schizopetalus

Hibiscus syriacus

Hibiscus syriacus

H. syriacus ROSE OF SHARON ☽ or ☽☽

A hardy, deciduous shrub with upright growing branches 3–4m high, with a compact habit when young, but sometimes more open with age. The leaves are usually three-lobed and coarsely toothed; 5-8 cm long. The flowers, 7cm wide, open trumpet-shaped, and vary in colour from white, pink, red, blue to purple, blue being the usual colour. They are usually single, but occasionally double, appearing during summer and autumn. Grow the shrub in full sun or light shade. Once established it can take drought, but it grows better with some summer water. The only Hibiscus that is frost-hardy. For larger flowers, prune severely in winter. Native to China. The variety 'Blue Bird' has single, deep blue-mauve flowers with a crimson blotch at the base. 'Diana' has single white flowers.

'Woodbridge' has large, rosy-pink flowers with a maroon blotch at the base.

Hippeastrum 'AMARYLLIS'
Amaryllidaceae

A genus of about eighty species of bulbous perennials native to central and south America. Generally the spectacular large-flowered hybrids are grown. They are often wrongly referred to as Amaryllis, which is a separate genus.

H. aulicum (syn. *H. morelianum*)
LILY OF THE PALACE ☽☽

A bulbous perennial with four or more mid- to deep green, strap-shaped leaves, 30–50cm long and 5cm wide. In spring, two large funnel-shaped flowers are carried on strong hollow stems to 50cm high. Each flower is red with a green throat, and up to 15cm across. The bulb is normally grown in pots or containers, but can be grown outdoors in well drained soil in sun or partial shade. Once flowering has finished, remove the flower stem, but keep watering and feeding until the leaves turn yellow, which may be in late autumn. Only then withhold water, letting the bulbs dry out. A beautiful bulb that looks attractive when planted in groups in a border. Native to Brazil, Paraguay.

H. hybrids ☽☽☽

A bulbous perennial with four or more mid- to deep green, strap-shaped leaves up to 60cm long. Up to six large, funnel-shaped flowers are carried on strong hollow stems to 60cm high. Each flower can be 20–25cm wide, and they come in a range of colours from white, pink, salmon, orange to red, some with stripes, others with delicate shading. They are usually single, but there are some double forms. The flowers are usually produced in late spring but can be forced to flower much earlier. The bulb is normally grown in pots or containers, but can be grown outdoors in well drained soil in sun or partial shade. Once flowering has finished, remove the flower stem, and keep watering and feeding until the leaves turn yellow, which may be in late autumn. Only then withhold water, letting the bulbs dry out. Garden origin.

Hippophae
Elaeagnaceae

A genus of only two to three species of dioecious (male and female flowers on different plants), spiny shrubs or trees covered with silvery scales, native to Europe and Asia. Attractive orange berries are produced on the female plants.

Hippeastrum hybrid

H. rhamnoides SEA BUCKTHORN ☾

A tall, deciduous shrub or small tree, to 6m high and wide. The alternate, slender, willow-like leaves are silver or sage-green; up to 5cm long. The inconspicuous yellow flowers appear before the leaves. They are followed by deep orange berries (1cm) along the branches, freely borne on female plants; therefore grow the shrub in groups to contain both sexes. The berries contain an acrid juice, so birds avoid them. Particularly good on light sandy soils where they make excellent wind resisters in coastal areas; when established the plant withstands drought, but it grows better with some summer water. The silver leaves and stems make a good background to other plants. Hardy, as it is native to northern Europe across to northern China.

Homeria
Iridaceae

A genus of about forty species of cormous perennials native to South Africa. They are grown for their scented, showy flowers that are produced in succession.

H. collina (syn. H. breyniana, Moraea grandiflora) ☾

A cormous perennial that may have branched or unbranched stems to 45cm high. The one or two, narrowly sword-shaped leaves, 45cm long, appear on the lower part of the flowering stem during the late autumn or winter. The cup-shaped, scented flowers, 6–8cm wide, are golden yellow, peach or pink. They are borne in succession over several weeks during spring. The plant is summer dormant, so only needs water if winter rains are insufficient. It needs to grow in full sun. Good drainage is essential. Plant the corms during autumn.

Howea 'SENTRY PALM'
Arecaceae

A small genus of just two species of single-stemmed palms native to Lord Howe Island, Australia. They are the 'kentia palms' sold in florists, and make excellent pot or container plants indoors or on a shaded patio or terrace.

H. belmoreana Sentry Palm ☾☾☾

A handsome feather palm, to 8m high. The trunk is slim, dark green in young plants, becoming grey in older trees with rings of old leaf scars. The dark green, leathery, pinnate leaves, 2m or more long, have the leaflets forming a 'V' shape. They are borne on short, reddish stalks that are fairly upright and less drooping. The palm must have shade when young, but will later tolerate full sun. It needs generous summer water to grow well, but will take some watering neglect. When grown in a pot or container it is

Howea forsteriana

tolerant of low light and generally poor growing conditions. It is less well known than its famous cousin H. forsteriana.

H. forsteriana KENTIA PALM, THATCH LEAF PALM ☾☾☾

A popular, moderately slow-growing palm eventually reaching 15–18m high. The trunk is slim, dark green, with prominent rings in young plants, becoming grey in older trees. The long-stalked pinnate, leathery leaves, 2–3m long, are borne almost horizontally. The long, drooping leaflets are held in a flat plane, not rising upwards. The palm prefers a rich loamy soil and plenty of summer water. Shelter from

Hoya carnosa

strong drying winds. Frequently grown as a pot plant where it survives low light, dust, drought and general neglect. Slow-growing, it is the perfect palm for a low-lit spot in the home or terrace.

Hoya 'WAX FLOWER'
Asclepiadaceae

A genus of perhaps 200 species of evergreen climbing or shrubby perennials native to India, southern China and Australia. They are grown for their spectacular flowers, which often drip nectar.

H. carnosa WAX PLANT ☾☾☾

A vigorous climber up to 4m high, and spreading as wide. The young shoots and leaves are a rich wine red. The thick, fleshy, oval-oblong leaves, 5–10cm long, are shiny dark green. The tight, pendant clusters, to 6cm wide, of scented flowers are produced during summer. Each flower is 1–2cm wide and star-shaped, creamy-white with a five-pointed red centre. They have a wax-like appearance, giving it the common name. The flowers produce nectar in such profusion that it may drip. Do not prune out the old flower stumps, as each year new flower clusters appear from the old stumps. Grow the climber in a rich, light soil with some shade and ample summer water. Often grown in a pot on a terrace where it will flower better if potbound. Native to Australia, south China, India. There is also an attractive variegated form, 'Exotica', which has leaves marbled white and green with a pink tinge, but is more tender. 'Tricolor' has leaves tinged with pink and cream. Specialist growers list many forms.

Hydrangea macrophylla

Hydrangea
Hydrangeaceae

A genus of about eighty species of upright or climbing, deciduous and evergreen shrubs native to North and South America and east Asia. They are grown for their large flowerheads. Unfortunately few are suitable for the Mediterranean region.

H. macrophylla (syn. *H. hortensia*)
GARDEN HYDRANGEA ♪♪♪

An evergreen shrub that is deciduous in cold regions. It forms a rounded shrub, to 2m high and wide. The thick, shining leaves are coarsely toothed and dark green; up to 20cm long. There are two types, that differ according to the flowerhead: the 'hortensia' group form rounded flowerheads containing mainly sterile ray florets; the 'lacecaps' bear flattened heads of fertile flowers surrounded by a ring of coloured ray florets. The colour can be white, pink, red or blue. Flower colour is affected by the soil: thus acid soils with a pH of less than 5.5 produce blue flowers, while soils with a pH greater than this produce pink flowers. White flowers are not affected by the soil. Grow the shrub in a humus-rich, well mulched soil. It can grow in full sun, but is much happier with some shade. Needs generous summer water. Grows particularly well in pots or containers, and can look spectacular in a shady courtyard. Also looks good when planted under trees.

Hymenocallis (syn. Ismene)
'SPIDER LILY'
Amaryllidaceae

A genus of about twenty-five to thirty species of summer-flowering bulbs native to North and South America. They are grown for their spectacular fragrant flowers.

H. × festalis ♪♪

An evergreen, bulbous perennial with strap-shaped leaves to 90cm long and 5cm wide. In spring and summer the clusters of two to five, white, heavily fragrant flowers appear on long stems. The flower is a long, flared trumpet, 8–12cm across, surrounded at the base by six narrow petals. Plant the bulbs in a rich, well drained soil in sun or partial shade. Water during the growing and flowering period, then allow to dry out once the leaves have started to turn yellow. A good summer-flowering plant for borders. When grown in containers, move near the house to enjoy the scent. Garden origin.

H. narcissiflora (syn. *Ismene calathina*) PERUVIAN DAFFODIL ♪♪

A bulbous plant with strap-shaped leaves, to 60cm long and 5cm wide, which are joined together at the base to form a false stem. The clusters of two to five fragrant flowers appear on stems up to 60cm high in the early summer. They are white with a green stripe, 10cm long, funnel-shaped with fringed lobes and surrounded by six slender segments. Plant bulbs in a rich, well drained soil in autumn with the tips 3–4cm below the surface. Grow in sun or partial shade. Water during the growing and flowering period, then allow them to dry out once the leaves have started to turn yellow. A good summer flowering plant for borders or in containers. The variety 'Sulphurea' has pale yellow flowers. Native to Peru and Bolivia.

Hymenosporum
'AUSTRALIAN FRANGIPANI'
Pittosporaceae

A genus containing just one species of evergreen tree that is closely related to

Hymenocallis × festalis

Pittosporum. Native to eastern Australia and New Guinea. It is grown as an attractive tree with showy clusters of flowers.

H. flavum SWEETSHADE))

An evergreen tree or large shrub, up to 6m high with a spread of around 5m. The growth may be slow at first, but moderate once established. An attractive, shaped tree is formed, with well spaced slender, bushy branches. The shiny, dark green leaves are smooth and lance-shaped; up to 15cm long. The loose terminal panicles, to 20cm across, of yellow flowers, 3cm long, are deliciously fragrant. The flowers open creamy-yellow, ageing to orange-yellow, and often completely cover the crown of the tree from spring to summer. The tree grows well in full sun, but can take some shade. It requires an occasional deep watering during summer, rather than constant light watering, therefore it does not grow well in lawns. Grows best in well drained soil away from coastal winds.

Hymenosporum flavum

Hyophorbe 'BOTTLE PALM'
Arecaceae

A small genus of five species of single-stemmed, pinnate-leafed palms native to the Mascarene Islands east of Madagascar.

H. verschaffeltii SPINDLE PALM)))

A single-stemmed palm to 6m high, with a trunk that is narrow at the base,

Hyophorbe verschaffeltii

becoming wider in the middle, and then tapering again to the swollen crownshaft. This spindle shape gives it the common name. The trunk has rings left by the old leaves. The large leaves, up to 6m long, are quite stiff and fairly erect. The leaflets are fairly limp and hang gracefully, giving it an attractive appearance. The palm requires rich soil with plenty of summer water. As it is a tropical plant, grow in a warm, sheltered location in full sun. Ideal for coastal gardens as it withstands salt-laden sea breezes. A showy and unusual palm, with even large plants taking up little space.

Hyphaene
Arecaceae

A genus of about ten species of palmate-leafed palms native to Africa, Madagascar, the Arabian Peninsula and India. They are usually found in poor or exhausted soil in hot, dry areas. The genus has the only palms that branch naturally.

H. coriacea DOUM PALM)

A slow-growing palm that may have trunks up to about 9m high and 40cm in diameter; it occasionally branches, but may also occur as a short-stemmed cluster of plants. The trunks are scored horizontally and prominently with the scars from old leaf bases. Older and longer stems tend to recline. Suckering occurs from the base to allow clump development. The leaves are robust, thick and fan-shaped, up to 1.5m in diameter on a leaf stalk 1.5m long, armed with thick, black, recurved thorns along its margins. The foliage is an attractive grey-green with a whitish bloom on the leaf undersurfaces. Although relatively slow-growing, it is an ideal palm for a dramatic effect. Will do well in any sunny, well drained site in a frost-free garden. It needs little or no summer water but grows better with an occasional deep soaking. The somewhat limited garden use of this palm may be due to difficulties in germinating its seed. Native to South Africa, east Africa and Madagascar.

H. thebaica GINGERBREAD PALM)

A medium-sized palm that is one of the few truly branching palms. It grows 6–10m high, and spreads to 6m wide. Old trees have trunks that are blackish. Each branch ends in a tuft of deeply lobed, rounded, fan-shaped, greyish-green leaves up to 1m wide. These are borne on long, spiny stalks. With age the palm bears tiny, bowl-shaped flowers in large panicles in summer. The tree bears an irregularly oval fruit about the size of an apple. The fruit has a red outer skin and a thick, spongy, and rather sweet inner substance that tastes like gingerbread, giving it the common name. When established it withstands drought, but grows better with some summer water. Will do well in any sunny, well drained site in a frost-free garden. A dramatic and unusual palm. Native to north Africa.

H

Iberis 'CANDYTUFT'
Brassicaceae

A genus of thirty to forty species of small annuals, perennials and evergreen subshrubs native to central Europe and the Mediterranean region. They are grown for their showy flowers, often planted in rock gardens or in sunny borders.

I. saxatilis ⌣ or ⌣⌣

A small evergreen subshrub 10–15cm high, spreading to 30cm wide. The very narrow, fleshy, almost cylindrical leaves, to 2cm long, are carried on the upright stems. From spring to summer it bears flattened heads 3–4cm across of small white flowers often tinged pink with age. They are borne at the ends of short branches. A splendid plant for a sunny position in a rock garden, particularly if placed to drape over the rocks. Grow in poor to moderately fertile soil that is neutral to alkaline, but well drained. It is not drought-tolerant and prefers moist soil during summer. A bright, cheerful plant for the garden that is easily raised from seed. Native to southern Europe.

I. sempervirens
EVERGREEN CANDYTUFT ⌣

An evergreen, shrubby perennial, to 30cm high spreading to 60cm wide, forming neat, leafy mats of foliage. The leaves are narrow, shiny, dark green, slightly fleshy and 2–6cm long. They look good all the year. The white flowers rise above the foliage from winter to spring. The numerous clusters of fragrant white flowers, 5cm across, are borne on long stalks. These cover the plant, making a wonderful show. Grow in ordinary, well drained soil in a dry, sunny place. Ideal for the rockery, front of a border, or admirable for the top of a wall. When established it

withstands drought, but grows better with some summer water. It is easily raised from seed. Native to southern Europe. 'Little Gem' grows 10–15cm high, 'Snowflake' 10–30cm high with wider leaves and larger flowers.

I. umbellata GLOBE CANDYTUFT ⌣⌣

A mound-forming hardy annual 30–40cm high, spreading to 25cm wide. The lance-shaped leaves are up to 10cm long, with the lower leaves toothed. The brilliant, sweet-scented flowers are produced in abundance all summer. They appear in flat heads to 5cm across in colours of pink, rose, carmine, crimson, salmon, lilac and white. Sow the seeds *in situ* in early spring or autumn in a sunny position. Give a moderate amount of summer water. A beautiful plant for the border and splendid for cutting. They also make attractive pot plants. Native to the Mediterranean region.

Iboza
Lamiaceae

A small genus of about twelve species of perennials and shrubs from tropical and southern Africa, with stems that are normally square in cross-section.

I. riparia MISTY PLUME BUSH ⌣⌣

A small, evergreen, perennial shrub that grows 1–2m high, spreading to 1m wide. The whole plant is strongly aromatic. The broad, velvety, heart-shaped leaves, 10cm long, have toothed edges. The large, upright, terminal, branched inflorescence, 20cm or more long, consists of many tiny, creamy-white to purple fragrant flowers, produced in spring. They may well set seed. The shrub is rather tender, easily damaged by frost and cold wind. Grow in full sun or partial shade with a moderate amount of summer water. As it can become tall or untidy, cut back

Iboza riparia

after flowering. Native to South Africa.

Impatiens 'BALSAM, BUSY LIZZIE'
Balsaminaceae

A huge genus of 500–900 species of annuals and evergreen perennials or subshrubs widely distributed, particularly in the tropics and subtropics of Asia and Africa. All have lush, brittle stems and leaves, with brilliant flowers in a wide range of colours.

I. walleriana (syn. *I. holstii*, *I. sultani*)
BUSY LIZZIE ⌣⌣⌣

A variable, subshrubby perennial, sometimes grown as an annual. It grows vigorously to 30–60cm high, spreading as wide, usually with many branches from the base. The long-stalked, ovate leaves are deep green or bronze-green with finely serrated

Impatiens walleriana 'Variegata'

margins to 10cm long. The open, flat flowers, 2–5cm wide, each have a long – 5cm – slender spur. The varieties come in a wide range of vivid colours, in many shades of lilac, pink, red, orange, violet, purple or white, some striped with two colours. The bushy plants cover themselves with flowers for most of summer and autumn. There are numerous cultivars in a wide range of colours and forms, some dwarf to only 20cm high. Grow the plants in shade in a deep, rich soil with generous summer watering. Ideal for brightening up a shady courtyard or in the shade of trees. They also make attractive pot or container plants. The species is native to tropical east Africa, Tanzania and Mozambique. 'Variegata' has whitish margins to the leaf.

Iochroma
Solanaceae

A genus of about twenty species of evergreen or deciduous shrubs or small trees native to central and South America, often confused with Cestrum. They are grown for their attractive clusters of pendant, trumpet-shaped flowers.

I. coccineum ♪♪♪
A medium-sized, evergreen shrub up to 3m high and 2m wide; the young stems are covered in a soft down. The soft green, ovate leaves are 8–12cm long. The tips of the branches are covered in clusters of pendant carmine-red or orange flowers throughout summer. Each flower is narrowly tubular, 5cm long, with a flaring mouth. Grow the shrub in full sun or partial shade in a rich soil with a generous amount of water during summer. Give warmth and protection from drying winds. This attractive shrub can be pruned hard after flowering. Native to Central America.

I. cyaneum VIOLET BUSH ♪♪♪
A large, evergreen shrub that makes fast growth to 4m or more high and 2m wide, with downy shoots. The dark green, soft-hairy leaves are oval to lance-shaped, and 14cm long. The showy, elegant clusters of 4cm tubular violet-blue flowers hang in pendulous bunches from the tips of the stems. They are produced mainly from spring to late autumn, but can appear for most of the year. Grow the shrub in a rich soil with warmth and protection from the wind, and a generous amount of summer water. Grows best in full sun, but will grow in partial shade. Cut back hard after flowering to encourage new flowering growth. An unusual and desirable colour for the shrub border; a plant in flower is extraordinarily beautiful. Look out for red spider mite during summer. This is the most commonly grown Iochroma. Native to Colombia.

I. grandiflorum (syn. I. warscewiczii) ♪♪♪
A large, spreading, evergreen shrub that makes fast growth to 2m or more high. The dark green, soft-hairy leaves are oval to lance-shaped, 14cm long, with a depressed midrib. The showy clusters of rich, lavender-blue, 4cm tubular flowers hang in pendulous clusters from the tips of the stems. They are produced from spring to late autumn. Grow the shrub in a rich soil with warmth, protection from the

Iochroma cyaneum

wind, and a generous amount of summer water. It grows best in full sun but will take some shade. A beautiful and unusual shrub for the garden. Native to tropical America.

Ipheion
Alliaceae

A small genus of about ten species of bulbous perennials native to South America. They are grown for their scented, star-shaped spring flowers.

I. uniflorum (syn. Brodiaea uniflora, Milla uniflora, Triteleia uniflora)
SPRING STAR FLOWER ☽

A bulbous perennial that quickly multiplies to form a clump. During autumn the flattish, bluish-green, strap-shaped leaves, to 25cm long, appear. They smell like onions when crushed. In spring, solitary upward-facing flowers, 4cm across, appear on stems 15–20cm high. They are broadly star-shaped, sweetly scented, pale to deep blue, often with a deeper midvein. Grow the bulbs in full sun or light shade. Ideal for planting in drifts under deciduous trees or large shrubs. Summer dormant so they need no water, indeed they like to be baked during summer. Easy to grow in any soil, they will quickly multiply. They also make a bright, cheerful edging to a border or a groundcover in semi-wild areas. Native to Argentina. 'Album' has white flowers, 'Wisley Blue' lilac-blue flowers.

Ipomoea 'MORNING GLORY'
Convolvulaceae

A large genus containing about 500 species of twining or prostrate annuals or perennials. Some are shrub-like. Native to tropical and warm-temperate regions of the world. The flowers are all tubular, trumpet-shaped or bell-shaped, and usually brilliantly coloured.

I. alba (syn. Calonyction aculeatum)
MOONFLOWER ☽☽

A robust, perennial climber sometimes treated as an annual; fast-growing, it reaches 5–6m in a season. The heart-shaped leaves are 10–20cm long and nearly as wide. The large, flat white flowers, 12–15cm wide, are stunningly beautiful and powerfully fragrant,

Ipomoea alba

opening at night and dying in the morning, although they will stay open on dull days. Some people may find the scent too strong. The flowers are followed by pods containing large, hard black seeds: these need soaking or chipping before they will germinate. A good temporary climber for trellises or fences near the house where the scent can be enjoyed. To grow well it requires a moderate amount of summer water. Grow in full sun or partial shade. Native to tropical America.

I. indica (syn. I. acuminata, I. learii)
MORNING GLORY ☽

A vigorous evergreen perennial climber that can spread to 10m or more in all directions. The broad leaves are heart-shaped or often three-lobed, with fine, silky hairs underneath; up to 20cm long. The bright blue flowers, to 20cm across, come in clusters of three to five and are trumpet-shaped, often with a white tube. The plant will cover itself with flowers from spring to autumn. A rampant climber that needs little attention and little summer water once established. Often used to cover fences, banks or unsightly objects. Grows best in full sun. Native to tropical America, but widely cultivated in the tropics.

Iresine
Amaranthaceae

A genus of about seventy species of evergreen perennials and subshrubs, sometimes climbing, with ornamental leaves. Native to South America and Australia. They are grown for their colourful foliage, with a few species cultivated as house plants.

I. herbstii BEEFSTEAK PLANT ☽☽☽
A bushy, short-lived, tropical perennial

Ipomoea indica

up to 1m high, grown for its brilliant leaf coloration. The stems and branches are bright red. The waxy leaves are broadly ovate to round, up to 12cm long, and notched at the tip; in colour they are a glowing purplish-red, traced with light red or yellow veins. The small flowers are inconspicuous. For best colour grow the plant in partial shade and give plenty of summer water. Easily propagated, as the tip cuttings will root in water. Plants can become straggly with age, so replace them regularly. A good shady border plant. Looks most attractive when grown in a pot or

Iresine herbstii 'Brilliantissi

container. Native to southern Brazil. 'Aureoreticulata' has green or greenish-red leaves with yellow veins, red stems and leaf stalks; 'Brilliantissima' has rich crimson leaves.

I. lindenii BLOOD LEAF

A bushy, short-lived, tropical perennial, to 1m high. The stems and branches are bright red. The lance-shaped, pointed, glossy leaves, 5–10cm long, are deep blood-red with prominent red veins. The small flowers are inconspicuous. Cultivation is similar in most respects to I. herbstii. Native to Ecuador.

I. lindenii 'Formosa'
YELLOW BLOOD LEAF

Similar in most respects to I. lindenii

except that it has 5–8cm yellow leaves with crimson veins. An attractive, colourful form that grows well with some shade. A bright pot or container plant. Encourage leaf colour with a high potash fertilizer in summer. Garden origin.

Iris
Iridaceae

A large and remarkably diverse genus of 200-300 species of rhizomatous or bulbous perennials found in a wide range of habitats in the northern hemisphere. They vary in flower colour and form, cultural needs and flowering times. Most produce their colourful, even spectacular flowers during spring and summer. A few are evergreen but most are deciduous, some being summer dormant. The leaves are sword-like or grass-like, and the flowers are usually complex: the three inner petals are called 'standards' and may be upright, arching or horizontal. The three outer segments, the sepals, are like petals and are called the 'falls', and may be horizontal or drooping. Botanically, iris are divided into several subgenera and sections, but in horticulture they are divided into bulbous iris and rhizomatous iris.

The rhizomatous iris have sword-like leaves that overlap to form flat fans, and flowers that are bearded, beardless, or crested. The bearded are the most commonly grown. Many years of

hybridizing has produced a vast number of beautiful hybrids in a wide range of colours. They range in size from dwarf at 20cm high, to tall at 70cm or more high. All need excellent drainage and full sun.

I. germanica FLAG IRIS, FLEUR-DE-LIS
A very robust, rhizomatous, bearded iris, 60–120cm high, with branched stems bearing many flowers. The glaucous, grey-green leaves, up to 45cm long, overlap to form flat fans. In spring the tall, branched stems bear many fragrant flowers, 10cm across, and blue-violet in colour with yellow beards. An easily grown, drought-tolerant plant that needs no summer water. Grow in full sun in well drained soil. The rhizomes should be planted to lie on the surface of the soil. Clumps become overcrowded, reducing flowering after three to four years, so divide in late summer so that autumn rains settle them in. There are many cultivated varieties. Nativity unknown, probably the Mediterranean region, but they have escaped from cultivation and naturalized in various parts of the world.

I. histrio
A small, bulbous iris, to only 20cm high, with narrow, square-sectioned leaves, up to 10cm long, appearing shortly before flowering time. In late winter and early spring it bears

Iris germanica hybrids

beautiful, solitary blue flowers, 6–8cm across, with the falls deep blue at the margins, and creamy-white with blue blotches in the centre. The standards are also blue. Grow the bulbs in full sun in well drained soil. They are best planted in large drifts and left undisturbed for several years. As they are summer dormant they require no water. Native to Israel, southern Turkey, Syria and Lebanon.

I. xiphium hybrids
DUTCH IRIS, SPANISH IRIS ⌣

A vigorous, bulbous iris with a flowering stem 30–60cm high. The channelled, lance-shaped leaves are 20–70cm long. In late spring the bulb produces a slender stem with two flowers, 12cm across, on the top. The standards are narrow and upright. The oval to circular falls project downwards. In the species the colour is violet-purple, pale or deep blue, but the hybrids come in a wide range of colours, including white, mauve, brown, orange, yellow and bicolours. Plant the bulbs during autumn in well drained soil in full sun. They only need watering during any dry spell in winter while the plant is in growth. After flowering, allow the foliage to continue growing to replenish the bulb, then let them dry off during summer. The bulbs

Iris xiphium hybrid 'Dutch Iris'

Isoplexis canariensis

can be lifted once the foliage dies down. Excellent as cut flowers and good in containers. Native to southern Europe, north Africa.

Ismene

See *Hymenocallis*.

Isoplexis
Scrophulariaceae

A genus of just three species of evergreen shrubs or subshrubs native to Madeira and the Canary Islands. They are closely related to *Digitalis*. They are grown for their colourful tubular flowers.

I. canariensis ⌣⌣

A stiff, bushy, upright-growing shrub to 1.5m high, spreading to 1m wide. The thick, sharp-toothed, lance-shaped leaves are a glossy deep green, and up to 15cm long. They are softly hairy underneath and borne closely together on the stems. In summer it produces flowers in 30cm-long racemes. The flowers are tubular, strongly two-lipped, 3cm long, and a beautiful yellowish-brown to orange-yellow. Grow the shrub in full sun in well drained soil. When established it withstands some drought, but grows better with summer water. An easily grown and attractive shrub that is not often seen. Can be grown from seed sown in spring.

Ixia 'AFRICAN CORN LILY'
Iridaceae

A genus of about forty species of cormous perennials native to South Africa. They are grown for their star-shaped, brightly coloured flowers. There are many named varieties, with colours ranging from white, creamy-white with purple centres, to red and pink flowers.

I. maculata ⌣

A cormous perennial with flowering stems up to 60cm high. The upright, sword-shaped leaves, up to 35cm long, are strongly ribbed and usually twisted. In spring, the thin, wiry, flowering stalks bear a series of twelve to eighteen charming, cup-shaped flowers 3–6cm across. They are orange or yellow with dark purple or black centres. Plant the bulbs in drifts in full sun in well drained soil, and leave undisturbed for several years. As the bulbs are summer dormant they need no water. Ideal for floral arrangements, as the flowers are long lasting when cut.

I. viridiflora ⌣

A cormous perennial similar in most respects to *I. maculata*. The cup-shaped flowers are a beautiful metallic turquoise-green with a black-purple centre.

Jacaranda
Bignoniaceae

A genus of about forty species of deciduous and evergreen trees and shrubs that are native to tropical America. They are grown for their showy, often blue flowers. One species is widely planted as a specimen or street tree in most tropical and subtropical regions. The wood is durable and often used for carpentry work.

J. mimosifolia JACARANDA ⌣

A deciduous tree that will quickly reach up to 15m high, forming an open, broad head 7–10m wide. The finely divided, bipinnate leaves, 25–45cm long, are fern-like, and only deciduous in early spring. The magnificent, showy flowers appear during late spring, often entirely covering the bare trees. The loose, pyramidal panicles, 20–30cm long, contain many glowing, pure blue to lavender flowers. Each flower is 5cm long, trumpet-shaped, and white-throated with five lobes; the flowerheads cover the ground when flowering is finished. The tree may produce a few flowers during autumn in warm areas, although not so profusely. The large, flattened, red-brown fruits are attractive. The tree is not fussy about soil conditions, but grows best in sandy soils. Grow in full sun. When established, it withstands drought, but grows better with some summer water. The tree can be hard pruned in late winter if it becomes too big for the space. A popular and impressive specimen tree, often used as a street tree. Easily raised from seed, making an attractive pot plant in its early years. Native to Argentina and Bolivia.

Jacobinia carnea
See *Justicia carnea*.

Jacobinia suberecta
See *Dicliptera suberecta*.

Jacaranda mimosifolia

Jasminum azoricum

Jasminum
Oleaceae

A large genus containing about 300 species of deciduous and evergreen shrubs and climbers native to Europe, Asia and Africa. They are grown for their showy, often powerfully fragrant flowers.

J. azoricum MADEIRA JASMINE ⌣⌣

A large evergreen twining shrub that makes rapid growth to 5m high with a wide spread. The glossy, dark green leaves have three oval leaflets, each 5cm long. The white, very fragrant flowers, 2cm across, appear in terminal clusters in the late summer, and continue throughout autumn. Grow the climber in full sun in well drained soil, giving it some summer water. It will quickly cover a large area, and needs pruning occasionally to keep in shape. Ideal for covering large fences, walls, or a house where the scent and flowers can be appreciated. Native to Madeira.

J. humile ITALIAN JASMINE ⌣⌣

An evergreen or semi-evergreen shrub or climber with a spreading habit. The strong, angled branches can grow to 6m high and 3m wide; these usually arch over to form a mound. The alternate pinnate leaves have five to nine lance-shaped leaflets up to 5cm long. The fragrant, lemon-yellow

J

Jasminum mesnyi

1–2cm wide flowers appear in axillary and terminal clusters during summer. Grow the shrub in full sun, giving only occasional deep summer watering. Native to Asia. 'Revolutum': Similar to *J. humile* except that it has stout shoots and larger, deep green leaves with five to seven leaflets up to 2cm long. The larger, deep yellow flowers, to 3cm across, appear in clusters of up to twelve. This is more often grown than the species.

J. mesnyi PRIMROSE JASMINE

An evergreen, rambling shrub that can be treated as a climber, with square stems and long, arching branches 3–4m long. The opposite, glossy dark green leaves have three lance-shaped leaflets up to 7cm long. The unscented flowers are bright lemon yellow, 5cm across, semi-double or double, and are scattered singly throughout the plant from late autumn to spring. Grow in full sun, giving occasional summer water. A strong-growing shrub that needs space, but may need occasional severe pruning. Grows best when tied up at the desired height and allowed to spill down in a waterfall fashion. Use to cover pergolas or large walls. Native to south-west China.

J. officinale
COMMON WHITE JASMINE

A strong-growing, trailing or twining climber that can reach 10m high and wide. The semi-evergreen leaves are pinnate, with five to nine leaflets 6–7cm long. The white, star-shaped flowers, 2–3cm wide, are deliciously fragrant; they are borne in terminal clusters of up to five flowers during spring and summer. Grow the climber in full sun to flower well, and give regular summer watering. Good for twining around garden fences and climbing over walls or into trees, filling the air with its perfume, especially in the evening. Easily propagated, as the long trailing stems root into the ground as they go. Native to Iran to west China.

J. officinale affine (syn. *J. grandiflorum*) SPANISH JASMINE

Often sold as *J. grandiflorum* and similar to *J. officinale* in most respects. The spectacular flowers, 4cm wide, are produced for most of summer. They are also powerfully fragrant, with a pinkish outside to the buds. The flowers contain an essential oil used in perfumery, for which the variety 'De Grasse' is often used.

J. polyanthum

A beautiful, vigorous, deciduous or sometimes evergreen twining climber, up to 6m high and wide. The deep green, pinnate leaves have five to seven leathery, lance-shaped leaflets up to 9cm long. The intensely fragrant white flowers, up to 2cm wide, are flushed rose on the outside with long, pointed buds. They are borne in dense clusters, up to 10cm long, throughout summer and autumn. Grow the climber in full sun to flower well, and give regular summer watering. Use as a climber or groundcover. Also grows well in containers on sunny patios and terraces. Native to west China.

J. sambac ARABIAN JASMINE

An evergreen shrub rather than a climber, with angular stems and bushy growth to 2m high. The undivided leaves are a glossy green, up to 8cm long. The small clusters of fragrant white flowers, each up to 2cm wide, are produced in summer. One of the most powerfully fragrant jasmines, used to make perfumes. In Asia the flowers are used to flavour jasmine tea. The shrub grows best in full sun in a sheltered location where winter temperature does not drop below 10°C. Also protect from cold winds during winter. Grow in good rich soil, giving copious amounts of water, and feed during summer. Native to Asia.

J. sambac 'Grand Duke of Tuscany'
GARDENIA JASMINE

A slow-growing variety that is even more tender, but well worth trying, as

Jasminum polyanthum

it is the grandest of them all. The waxy, quilted, oval leaves grow in whorls on stiff, silky-hairy stems. The large white flowers, 3–4cm wide, are of a tightly double Gardenia type, with a penetrating sweet fragrance. When older this variety is even more fascinating, in providing flowers of different shapes and sizes on the same plant at the same time. Grows well in partial shade, in well drained, moist soil, with as much shelter as *J. sambac*. Garden origin.

J. sambac 'Maid of Orleans' ☽☽☽

A woody, evergreen shrub with open habit and slow growth. The broad, ovate leaves are deep green, 3–4cm wide. The waxy-white, round, five-petal, semi-double flowers, 2–3cm wide, are somewhat cup-shaped and intensely fragrant. The shrub grows well when given a full drenching of water after the soil is a little on the dry side. It needs as much shelter as *J. sambac*. Give fertilizer during the summer months for better flowers. Garden origin.

J. × *stephanense* ☽☽

A deciduous, vigorous, rambling climber growing to 6m high, with slender green shoots. The opposite pairs of olive-green, pinnate leaves, up to 5cm long, have three to five leaflets. The fragrant, pale pink flowers, 1–2cm long, appear in terminal clusters of five to six or more throughout summer. For best flowering, grow in a sunny position. Grow in a good, well drained soil with a moderate amount of water during summer. Prune from time to time to limit growth. It is a cross between *J. beeseanum* and *J. officinale*. Garden origin.

Jubaea
Arecaceae

A genus of just one species of single-stemmed palm native to Chile, where it is now endangered. In the past it has been over-exploited for the manufacture of 'palm wine'. A massive palm that makes a majestic specimen or avenue palm.

J. chilensis CHILEAN WINE PALM ☽

A slow-growing, single-stemmed palm, up to 25m high, with the leaves spreading to 9m wide. The trunk is extremely massive, large and heavy, and can grow to 1.8m in diameter. It is grey, often swollen in the middle, and smooth, as it sheds leaves cleanly. The long, finely divided, arching fronds, up to 5m long, form a dense, terminal, round head. The leaflets are in pairs, standing out in different directions, and split at the apex. On mature trees the flower stalk, 1–2m long, appears from among the leaves during summer. It bears many small, bowl-shaped, dull purple or maroon and yellow flowers. These are followed by edible, very large

Jubaea chilensis

seeds, resembling coconut in flavour. Grow the palm in full sun. When established it withstands drought, needing no summer water. It will tolerate severe cold and frost once established. A wonderful palm for all warm temperate regions, but extremely slow-growing.

Juglans
Juglandaceae

A genus of about twenty species of deciduous trees, with separate male and female flowers on the same plants, native to North and South America and from south-east Europe to south-east Asia.

J. regia COMMON WALNUT ☽

A hardy, deciduous, fast-growing tree, up to 30m high and wide, with a silvery-grey bark. The pinnate leaves, 30cm or more long, have five to nine widely spaced leaflets, 12–15cm long. In early summer the male, greenish-yellow flowers appear in drooping catkins, while the female flowers appear in clusters. They are followed by the round, green fruit, 5cm in diameter. They contain the edible nut, and should be left on the tree until late autumn to ripen. Trees produce fruit when about ten years old, but named varieties of grafted plants produce fruit

Jasminum sambac

J

Juglans regia

earlier. Established trees can exist without summer water, but for good fruit production, regular deep watering is needed. They are not particular about soil, but need to be grown in full sun. Walnuts make attractive, large ornamental specimen trees. The timber is highly prized and very valuable. Native to south-east Europe and Asia.

Juniperus 'JUNIPER'
Cupressaceae

A genus of about sixty species of evergreen, coniferous trees and shrubs, with a wealth of marvellous forms ranging from prostrate or creeping alpines, to dense bushy shrubs, and tall, conical or columnar trees. They are widely distributed throughout the northern hemisphere. The leaves of juvenile plants are usually needle-like or narrowly wedge-shaped, and usually pointed up to 1.5cm long. The adult leaves are usually scale-like, over-lapping and crowded, either lying flat along the shoots or spreading; 2–6mm long. In some cases they retain the juvenile form. Male and female cones are borne on the same or separate plants. The fruits are usually roundish, fleshy and berry-like, 4–10mm across, and persistent, often taking two to three years to ripen.

Junipers are a versatile genus containing plants that tolerate a wide range of soils and conditions, particularly suitable for chalky soils. They are ideal for hot, sunny sites with little or no summer water. The colour ranges from green to yellow, grey and steel-blue. The prostrate forms are excellent as groundcover, while the upright forms make attractive specimens. They look good near swimming pools. Nurseries offer a vast number of named varieties.

J. chinensis CHINESE JUNIPER
An extremely variable, dioecious, spreading shrub to conical tree, growing to 20m high, with brown bark that peels in long strips. The pungently scented foliage is normally dark green, and the narrow, wedge-shaped, pointed juvenile leaves and the scale-like adult leaves grow on the same plant. The rounded fruits, 5–7mm across, ripen in the second year. Ideal for coastal gardens, as it withstands salt-laden sea breezes. Native to China, Japan. A wide range of named cultivars are available, from prostrate shrubs to tall trees.

J. communis COMMON JUNIPER
A variable, dense, bushy, grey-green shrub or small rounded tree, 1–6m high. The leaves are needle pointed and glossy green, 10–15mm long, and marked with a broad, white, lengthways stripe. The yellow male and female cones are usually on separate plants: they are berry-like, 6mm in diameter, and turning to bluish-black when they ripen in the second year. Oil of Juniper is distilled from the green fruits and used to flavour gin. Native to North America, Europe, Asia. A wide range of named cultivars are available, from prostrate shrubs to small trees. 'Compressa': a dwarf, upright-growing shrub that grows very slowly to 80cm high. Ideal as a specimen for the rock garden.

J. horizontalis CREEPING JUNIPER
A dwarf or prostrate shrub, up to 30cm high, with long, often horizontal branches with an indefinite spread. The

Juniperus horizontalis

mainly juvenile leaves on cultivated plants are needle-like, with long, sharp points. The colour is glaucous green, grey-green or blue, but varies in intensity, often turning plum-purple in winter. Fruits are rarely produced in cultivation. This is one of the best species for groundcover. Native to North America. 'Blue Chip' has bright blue foliage throughout the year. 'Plumosa Youngstown' has glaucous leaves that become bronze-tinged in winter.

J. oxycedrus PRICKLY JUNIPER

A large shrub or small tree, usually 3–4m high, with an open, drooping habit. The leaves are awl-shaped and very sharp-pointed, 16mm long, and green above, marked with two white bands underneath. The roundish fruits, 9–13mm long, turn a shining red-brown when they ripen in the second year. The fragrant wood produces 'Oil of Cade', used medicinally. Native to the Mediterranean region.

J. phoenicea PHOENICEAN JUNIPER

A shrub or small tree, to 3m high, of dense, rounded or broadly conical habit with stout cord-like, upright twigs covered with closely pressed, scale-like leaves. The leaves are awl-shaped on juvenile plants, and scarcely 1mm long. The roundish fruits, 6–15mm in diameter, are formed on the ends of the branches. They ripen to a shining red in the second year. Native to the Mediterranean region.

J. sabina SAVIN

An extremely variable, usually spreading or occasionally upright shrub, with flaking reddish-brown bark. It can grow from 2–5m high, and spread to 6m or more wide. Typically it forms a spreading shrub 2–3m wide, with slender, ascending branchlets. The mainly adult leaves are green or grey-green and mostly

Justicia adhatoda

Justicia brandegeeana

scale-like, with a pungent, disagreeable smell when crushed. The roundish fruit, 5–7mm across, are bluish-black with a whitish bloom, and ripen over the first winter. Native to central Europe, west Asia. 'Broadmore' grows 40cm high with dense growth to 3m wide, and has soft, bright green foliage. 'Tamariscifolia' grows 1m high, spreading to 2m wide, with dense, mainly juvenile, blue-green foliage.

J. scopulorum
ROCKY MOUNTAIN JUNIPER

A small tree of conical habit to 9m high, often with several main stems. The bark is red-brown and shedding. The branches are stout and spreading, with slender branchlets. The leaves are scale-like, green, often glaucous, and scarcely or not overlapping, lying flat to the branches. The fruits are roundish, 6mm across, dark blue and covered in bloom. Native to USA (Rocky Mountains). It has given rise to many forms, notably 'Skyrocket', a spectacular form that is extremely narrow and columnar in habit, growing only 30cm wide and 6–7m high. With its blue-grey foliage it makes an attractive specimen.

Justicia (syn. Beloperone, Drejerella)
Acanthaceae

A large genus containing about 400 species of evergreen perennials and shrubs native to tropical and sub-

tropical regions worldwide. The often brilliant flowers are mostly in terminal spikes or clusters.

J. adhatoda (syn. Adhatoda vasica, Adhatoda duvernoia)

An evergreen shrub with upright growth to 2.5m or more, only spreading to about 1m wide. The long-ovate, mid- to deep-green, corrugated leaves, up to 20cm long, hang sharply downwards and are covered with fine hairs. The terminal and axillary flower spikes, 5cm or more long, are produced throughout summer and contain many tubular, two-lipped flowers 2cm long. They are white with a lower lip with reddish markings, while the upper lip is distinctly curved. The shrub can be grown in full sun or partial shade. It grows better in a rich soil with a generous amount of summer water. Easily propagated from cuttings. Native to India and Sri Lanka.

J. brandegeeana (syn. Beloperone guttata) SHRIMP PLANT

An evergreen shrub that makes a mound of soft stems to 1m high and 60cm wide, with soft, downy stems. The softly-hairy, ovate leaves are up to 8cm long. The true flowers are white, 3cm long, and are concealed underneath showy, overlapping reddish-brown bracts. They are formed in axillary and terminal branches where they droop down, reaching up to 10cm in length. And they do indeed resemble pink shrimps! They are produced

Justicia carnea

J

mainly in summer, but can appear on the plant for most of the year. The shrub is easily grown in sun or partial shade. It requires moderate summer water, but dislikes waterlogged soil. Pinch out the tips to keep it bushy, cutting back hard if it becomes too leggy. Makes a good pot or container plant, also attractive when grown alongside paths. Native to Mexico. The variety 'Chartreuse' has lime-green bracts that sunburn more easily that the brown bracts. 'Yellow Queen' has bright yellow bracts.

J. carnea (syn. *Jacobinia carnea*)
BRAZILIAN PLUME FLOWER ᕧᕧᕧ
An upright, soft wooded, evergreen shrub, to 2m high and 1m wide, with reddish stems. The oblong leaves, 25cm long, are deeply veined, mid-green and satiny. The flowers are produced in dense, short terminal and axillary spikes 10–15cm long. Each two-lipped flower is about 5cm long, flesh-pink to crimson, sometimes rosy-purple; they are produced throughout summer and autumn. The shrub needs shade, rich soil and ample summer water to grow well. Makes a spectacular display as a pot plant or when grown in a shady courtyard. Cut back in spring to encourage new shoots. Native to northern South America.

J. suberecta
See *Dicliptera suberecta*.

Kalanchoe
Crassulaceae

A genus of about 125 species of mainly annuals and succulents, with a few perennials, shrubs, climbers and trees, mostly native to Africa and Madagascar, as well as the Middle East, Asia and Australia. Some are grown as pot plants for their attractive leaves or flowers, while others will grow well in a dry garden.

K. beharensis FELT PLANT, VELVET ELEPHANT EAR ☽

An often tree-like perennial succulent up to 3m high and wide. The stems, which are covered in fine hairs, are usually unbranched, with the leaves crowded at their tips, generally in six to eight pairs at the tips. The thick, broadly triangular to lance-shaped, slightly toothed leaves, 10–20cm long and half as wide, are borne on long stalks. They are covered with a dense, felt-like coating of minute, fine silver or golden hairs. The leaves are also strikingly waved and crimped at the edges, giving a dramatic effect. In winter, older plants bear panicles of greenish-yellow bell-shaped flowers, 7mm long; these are not showy. This spectacular succulent prefers full sun,

Kalanchoe beharensis

Kalanchoe blossfeldiana

but can take considerable shade. Grow in well drained soil with little or no summer water. Ideal for the larger rock garden or raised bed. Native to Madagascar.

K. blossfeldiana CHRISTMAS KALANCHOE, FLAMING KATY ☽

A compact, branching succulent to 30cm high. The oval, dark glossy green leaves, 6cm long and 2–4cm wide, are fleshy, and often edged with red and scalloped. The small, tubular flowers, 1cm long, are borne in large branched clusters held well above the leaves. The colour is normally red, but may vary to white, yellow or pink. The plant is adaptable, as it will take sun, partial shade, or full shade. A common pot plant, valued for its winter flowers that remain fresh for almost a month. As it needs little summer water it makes an attractive addition to the dry garden. There are many hybrids and named

varieties that can be raised from seed. Native to Madagascar.

K. daigremontiana MATERNITY PLANT, MEXICAN HAT PLANT ☽

An upright, single-stemmed succulent, up to 1m high and 30cm wide. The fleshy, lance-shaped leaves, 15–20cm long and 3–4cm wide, are brownish-green, often spotted with red. Young plantlets form on the notches of the toothed leaf edges, often forming roots on the plant. In winter, clusters of pendant, tubular, greyish-purple flowers to 2cm long are produced. The succulent is easily grown, as it needs no summer water. Grows well in full sun or shade in any well drained soil. A useful pot or container plant. It can be grown in the dry garden, where it will quickly form a clump as the plantlets drop to the ground and root. Native to Madagascar.

K

Kalanchoe fedtschenkoi 'Marginata'

K. fedtschenkoi 'Marginata'
AURORA BOREALIS PLANT ☽

The shiny erect branches of this succulent grow to 60cm high, but any that touch the ground will root. The rather crowded leaves are oval, 5–8cm long, fleshy and softly toothed. The colour is a pale bluish-grey, margined creamy-white and flushed with pink. The clusters of purple or yellow flowers, 2cm long, are produced on stalks held well above the plant during winter or early spring. The plant is extremely easy to grow in full sun with little summer water. It makes an attractive pot or container plant or can be planted in beds or borders in the dry garden. Easily rooted from cuttings. Native to Madagascar.

Kennedia 'CORAL PEA'
Papilionaceae

A genus of about fifteen species of climbing shrubs and herbaceous plants native to Australia which are grown for their pea-like flowers.

K. rubicunda DUSKY CORAL PEA ☽
A vigorous evergreen twining shrub, 4–6m high, the young growth covered in silky brown hair. The alternate leaves, 10–15cm long, have three to five oval hairy leaflets. The dark red, pea-shaped flowers, 4cm long, appear in pairs in the leaf axils during spring

and summer; they are followed by seedpods, 10cm long. The shrub will endure dry conditions, needing no summer water once established. Grow in full sun or in partial shade. A vigorous climber that will quickly cover a large area, so restrictive pruning may be necessary. It can also be used as a groundcover. Native to eastern Australia.

Kleinia rowleyana
See *Senecio rowleyanus*.

Kniphofia
'RED HOT POKER, TORCH-LILY'
Asphodelaceae

A genus of about sixty to seventy species of evergreen or deciduous, grass-like perennials with cord-like roots and thick basal leaves. Native to Madagascar, tropical and southern Africa. Most are clump-forming and produce spikes of brilliant flowers in summer. They have been in cultivation long enough for a large number of hybrids to have been raised, and these come in a wide range of colours: red, orange, yellow, greenish to white; and some open red, then turn to yellow. They range in height from 50cm to 1.8m high.

K. uvaria RED HOT POKER, TORCH-LILY, POKER PLANT ☽
An evergreen perennial that forms a large, dense clump about 1.2m high, spreading to 60cm wide. The grass-like leaves are grey-green in colour, and 1m long. During spring and summer it sends up flower spikes that can be up to 2m high. They are topped with clusters, up to 30cm long, of drooping, bright orange-red or yellow tubular flowers, 5cm long. The plants can be grown in full sun, but will take some shade. They are good for the dry garden as they require little summer water once established. Cut old leaves to the ground in autumn. They are easily

Koelreuteria bipinata

propagated by division in winter. Native to South Africa. Nurseries offer many named varieties.

Koelreuteria
Sapindaceae

A genus of about four species of deciduous trees native to Japan, China and Korea. All are fine specimen trees with fragrant flowers that are attractive to bees. They grow best in areas with hot summers.

K. bipinata CHINESE FLAME TREE ꜱꜱ

A deciduous tree that makes moderate growth to 10m high and 8m wide. The leaves, 30–60cm long, are divided into nine to sixteen, narrowly ovate leaflets, to 10cm long. They hang on the tree until winter before turning yellow and dropping. The leaf stalk may stay until well into the following spring. The large, showy, pyramidal panicles of small, golden-yellow, star-like flowers, 1cm across, appear in late summer. They are followed by showy, dull red or orange pods, 5cm long; these are said to resemble 'Chinese Lanterns'. The tree is best grown in full sun. It grows in most well drained soils, but requires moderate summer watering. As the roots are deep and not invasive, it makes a good shade tree for the lawn or patio. Native to south-west China.

K. paniculata
GOLDEN RAIN TREE, PRIDE OF INDIA ꜱ

A broad-headed tree that grows to perhaps 10m high with an equal spread. The branches are rather open, giving light shade. The doubly pinnate leaves can be 45cm long, with nine to eighteen, ovate toothed or lobed leaflets, 3–8cm long. They open pinkish-red, become green, then turn a beautiful yellow in autumn before dropping. The large, pyramidal, showy panicles of small yellow flowers, 1cm wide, are 20–30cm long. They appear during summer and develop into conspicuous bladder-like seedpods. They resemble clusters of Chinese lanterns, and vary in colour from dull red to brown. The tree is easy to grow in all soils, and it will withstand the cold, heat, drought and wind once established, although it needs regular watering when young. This is the hardiest and most widely cultivated species. Native to China and Korea. The cultivar 'Fastigiata' has a narrow

Koelreuteria paniculata

Kolwitzia amabilis 'Pink Cloud'

columnar habit, growing 8m high and only 1m wide.

Kolkwitzia
Caprifoliaceae

A genus of just one species, a deciduous shrub native to central China. It is grown for its spectacular flowers that cover the plant.

K. amabilis BEAUTY BUSH ꜱꜱꜱ

A graceful, hardy, deciduous shrub with long, arching shoots that forms a dense, twiggy bush 3m high if grown in part shade, less in full sun. The simple opposite, ovate leaves are up to 8cm long. In late spring and early summer the arching branches are draped with masses of small, soft pink, yellow-throated, bell-shaped flowers 1–2cm across. The shrub grows best in partial shade, although it tolerates full sun. Regular summer water is needed. 'Pink Cloud' is a lovely seedling with bright, deep pink flowers, selected and raised at Wisley in 1946; a spectacular plant for the shrub border.

Lagerstroemia
Lythraceae

A genus of about fifty species of evergreen and deciduous trees and shrubs, often with exotic flowers. They are native to the warmer parts of Asia, the Pacific islands and Australia. They make showy ornamentals that are easily cultivated. Sometimes grown as attractive pot plants.

L. indica CREPE MYRTLE ◡ or ◡◡

A beautiful, deciduous shrub or small tree, rarely reaching 6m high with a wide spread. With age it develops a smooth trunk with mottled bark that flakes off to reveal a smooth grey or pink inner bark. In spring the new foliage is light green tinged with bronze. The mature, 3–6cm oblong leaves are dark glossy green and may be opposite, alternate or in whorls of three. In autumn they turn a lovely yellow or orange red. The terminal panicles (15–30cm long) of white, pink, red or mauve flowers, 2–3cm across, have crumpled petals. They are produced from late summer into autumn, and make a dazzling display. The flowers are even produced when young. The shrub should be grown in full sun. Give moderate summer water for the best flowering, although it will withstand some drought. Native to China. There are many named cultivars available, with pink, rose or white flowers. A dwarf strain that is easily grown from seed; it grows 30cm in the first year, eventually reaching 1m high. Flowers are produced in the first year if the seed is sown in spring.

Lagunaria
'NORFOLK ISLAND HIBISCUS'
Malvaceae

This genus contains only one species of evergreen tree, native to the Norfolk Islands.

Laguanria patersonii

L. patersonii
COW ITCH TREE, PRIMROSE TREE ◡

A handsome, easily grown tree that will quickly reach 15m or more high and 8m or more wide, forming a distinct pyramidal shape with dense foliage. The thick, leathery leaves are oval in shape and dark green in colour, whitish underneath; they are 5–10cm long. The flowers, 5cm wide, are rather like Hibiscus, with five rosy pink, recurved petals appearing singly in the upper leaf axils. They are produced during summer, and are followed by brown seed capsules that hang on the tree for a long time. Handle these with care as the seedpods contain short, stiff hairs that can easily cause skin irritation. Grow the tree in full sun with little summer water once established. It is not fussy about soil conditions. As it resists ocean winds and salt sprays it is good

Lagerstroemia indica

Lampranthus spectabilis

for coastal gardens. A fine accent, windbreak, or a showy specimen tree.

Lagurus
Gramineae

A genus of just one species of annual grass native to the Mediterranean coastal regions. It is grown for its attractive flowerheads.

L. ovatus HARE'S TAIL GRASS ⚘
An annual, tufted grass, growing 40cm high and 30cm wide. The linear, arching leaves are pale green, and up to 20cm long. In summer the dense, egg-shaped, silky flowering heads, to 6cm long, appear on long, thin stalks; they open pale green, and mature to creamy-buff. The flowerheads are useful in floral arrangements both fresh and dried. Sow the seeds *in situ* in spring in full sun. The plant prefers light, sandy soil. Only give water during dry periods in the spring growing season. An attractive and striking grass that is easily grown.

Lampranthus 'ICE PLANT'
Aizoaceae

A genus of about 160 species of upright or prostrate subshrubs or succulents native to coastal areas of South Africa. They are grown for their often brilliant, daisy-like flowerheads that are produced throughout summer.

L. aurantiacus GOLDEN ICE PLANT ⚘
A succulent shrub forming a dense bush of upright habit to 45cm high, spreading almost indefinitely. The three-sided leaves are olive-green or greyish, 3–5cm long. Flowers are produced profusely in spring and summer: they are large, 3–5cm, and glossy, an iridescent bright orange, opening in full sun. The plant will grow in poor, well drained soil. Splendid for hot, dry, sunny places: ideal for the desert garden as it requires no summer water. Looks most attractive when

grown in groups. Good for covering low banks. When buying plants, choose those with flowers the colour that you want, as nurseries often mix 'Ice Plants' together, including other genera.

L. purpureus ⚘
Similar to *L. aurantiacus*. The flowers are an iridescent bright pinkish-purple.

L. roseus PINK ICE PLANT ⚘
Similar to *L. aurantiacus*. The flowers are an iridescent, bright rose-pink.

L. spectabilis TRAILING ICE PLANT ⚘
Similar in most respects to *L. aurantiacus*. A more branching plant with long, prostrate, reddish-flowering stems. The flowers are an iridescent bright reddish-purple, red, white or pink, and 5–7cm across.

Lantana
Verbenaceae

A large genus of about 150 species of evergreen or deciduous shrubs native to tropical regions of America and South Africa. They are grown for their showy flowers, which are produced for most of summer.

L. camara cultivars ⚘ or ⚘⚘
A prickly stemmed, evergreen shrub that may reach 2-3m high and wide. The coarsely toothed leaves are dark green and aromatic, and 3–8cm long.

Lantana camara

L

Lantana camara yellow

The many small, rounded flowerheads, 2–5cm across, of pink or yellow flowers change colour with age to red or orange. Several colour combinations may be found on the same plant. There are many hybrid varieties, with white, cream, orange-red, light pink, magenta or combinations of these and other colours. The main flowering season is from early summer until late autumn, but some flowers may be produced during the rest of the year. The shrub is easily grown as it is not particular about soil conditions. Grows well in full sun with a moderate amount of water during summer. Makes an excellent and colourful hedge. It looks good near swimming pools. Ideal for coastal gardens as it withstands salt-laden sea breezes. The species is probably native to the West Indies, but is naturalized throughout the tropical regions.

L. montevidensis (syn. L. sellowiana)
WEEPING LANTANA 🌙 or 🌙🌙
A low, spreading shrub with trailing branches to 1m long that can form a dense mat. Usually covered with coarse, short hairs. The dark green leaves, 2–3cm long, with coarsely toothed edges, are sometimes tinged red or purplish in cold weather. During spring and summer it continuously produces small, rosy-lilac flowers in showy, rounded clusters, 2–4cm wide. Grow the shrub in full sun. Ideal for planting on dry banks, rock gardens, or tumbling over the tops of walls. May become dormant during periods of drought, but soon recovers when watered. Native to South America.

Latania 'LATAN PALM'
Arecaceae

A genus of just three species of robust, single-trunked palms native to the Mascarene Islands east of Madagascar. They make attractive bold specimen trees with large, stiff blue-green leaves. The three species are difficult to distinguish when older, but have different leaf colour when young.

L. loddigesii BLUE LATAN PALM 🌙🌙
A handsome fan palm, up to 15m high, with a rough, slender trunk, faintly ringed with old leaf scars, bearing a crown of numerous leaves. The rigid, blue-green leaf blades, up to 1.5m across, are deeply divided into many narrow lobes with much waxy scurf on the underneath. The leaves are partially folded into a trough shape from the centre of the leaf. Mature trees may bear panicles 1.5m long of greenish-white flowers in summer. Grow the palm in full sun or partial shade, in average, well drained soil. Give moderate but regular water throughout summer. It can be quite fast-growing.

Latania loddigesii

This beautiful palm is distinguished by having purplish-red leaves at the seedling stage.

L. lontaroides RED LATAN PALM 🌙🌙🌙
A robust, rapid-growing palm, to 16m high, with a grey trunk swollen at the base and about 20cm in diameter. In most respects it is similar to L. loddigesii. The young plants have a beautiful red coloration on the leaves and leaf stalks, which they retain longer than L. loddigesii. This palm loves warmth and moisture with good drainage.

L. verschaffeltii YELLOW LATAN PALM 🌙🌙
In most respects this palm is similar to L. loddigesii. The leaves are a striking light green, with yellow margins. They are a distinctive yellow-green when young. This is perhaps the most drought-tolerant of the species, but it still needs adequate water during dry weather.

Laurus
Lauraceae

A genus of only two species of aromatic, evergreen shrubs or medium-sized trees, one native to the Mediterranean region, and one to Madeira and the Canary Islands.

L. nobilis BAY LAUREL, SWEET BAY 🌙
A slow-growing tree that may eventually reach 12m high, forming a dense compact plant, often a pyramidal shape with suckers. The leathery, lance-shaped leaves, 10cm long, are dark glossy green. These are the traditional 'bay leaves' used in cooking. The clusters of tiny yellowish flowers appear in spring. They are followed, on female plants, by small black or dark purple berries. The tree thrives in full

Lantana montevidensis

Laurus nobilis

sun or partial shade. When established it withstands drought, but grows better with some summer water. It is not fussy about soil conditions and grows well in coastal regions. Takes clipping well, so can be used as hedging. Often grown in containers formally clipped into shapes. The variety 'Angustifolia' has long, wavy-edged leaves, and 'Aurea' has golden-yellow leaves; these may scorch in full sun. Native to the Mediterranean region.

Lavandula 'LAVENDER'
Lamiaceae

A genus of twenty to twenty-five species of aromatic, evergreen shrubs native to dry areas of the Mediterranean, north-east Africa to south-west Asia and India. The stems are mostly square in cross-section. Oil of lavender, used in perfumery, is distilled from *L. angustifolia* and *L. stoechas*. The dried flower-heads are often used in sachets and potpourri. Lavender has been in cultivation for centuries and tends to interbreed, with the result that many hybrids have arisen so names are difficult to establish. They look good when planted near swimming pools. Nurseries list a large number of varieties.

L. angustifolia ENGLISH LAVENDER
A dwarf, compact, aromatic, evergreen bushy shrub; up to 1m high and wide. The narrow oblong leaves, up to 6cm long, are grey-green, turning greener in summer. The long, unbranched flower stalks appear during summer: they are dense spikes up to 6cm long, of fragrant purple-blue flowers. Ideal for the dry garden as this shrub needs little summer water once established. It grows best in full sun in a well drained soil. Prune immediately after flowering to keep plants compact and neat. Native to western Mediterranean region. Many named varieties are available. 'Hidcote' is more compact with purple flowers. 'Jean Davis' has pink flowers. 'Nana Alba' is more compact, with white flowers.

L. dentata FRENCH LAVENDER
A bushy shrub up to 1m high and wide with a more spreading habit. The grey-green, narrow leaves are 3–4cm long with toothed edges. The long, un-branched flower stalks appear during the late summer, but may flower almost continuously. The lavender-purple flowers are in short, dense spikes up to 6cm long, each topped with a tuft of petal-like bracts. The shrub grows well in full sun in well drained soil. When established it withstands drought, but grows better with some summer water. Native to southern Spain and the Balearic Islands.

Lavandula angustifolia

Lavandula stoechas

L. stoechas SPANISH LAVENDER
A compact, bushy shrub, up to 60cm high and wide. The leaves are grey-green and narrow; up to 4cm long. The tiny, fragrant flowers are dark purple, in dense short spikes up to 4cm long, each topped with a conspicuous purple tuft of bracts. They appear from late spring to early summer, but another flush may appear in autumn. The dark purple flowers make this lavender conspicuous and unmistakable. The shrub grows well in full sun in well drained soil, and needs little summer water once established. Native to the Mediterranean region.

Lavatera 'MALLOW'
Malvaceae

A genus of twenty to twenty-five species of annuals, perennials, ever-green or deciduous shrubs native mostly to the Mediterranean region, but also to the Canary Islands, central Asia, Australia and California.

L. arborea TREE MALLOW
An almost tree-like, short-lived ever-green perennial with stout stems, woody at the base, up to 3m high, and spreading to 1.5m wide. The leaves are a rounded heart shape, hairy, up to 20cm in diameter, with five to seven

broad, toothed lobes and grey-woolly underneath. The large funnel-shaped rose-purple flowers are veined with deeper purple 3–5cm across in terminal clusters. They are produced profusely throughout summer. The plant is well suited to poor, dry, coastal gardens as it needs little summer water. Grow in full sun. Easily raised from seed, usually flowering the first year. Often used as a quick and easy screen or as a wind-break. Native from Spain to Greece and north Africa, but naturalized further east.

L. maritima (syn. L. bicolor) ☽

An upright, soft-wooded, fast-growing, evergreen shrub, up to 1.5m high and 1m wide. The grey-green leaves are almost rounded, with shallow lobes, or toothed; up to 6cm long. They are densely covered with soft whitish hairs. Throughout summer and autumn the shrub produces solitary, axillary flowers, 4–8cm across, pale pink with dark-rose veining and crimson-purple centres on long stalks. This attractive shrub is easily cultivated and is ideal for coastal gardens as it withstands salt-laden sea breezes. Grows well in full sun, needing little summer water. Native from Spain to Italy, Morocco and Algeria.

Lavatera maritima

Leonotis leonurus

L. timestris ANNUAL MALLOW ☽

A softly hairy, upright, branching annual, 1m or more high. The leaves are roundish, 3–6cm in diameter, with five to seven shallow lobes, or toothed. The axillary, solitary, saucer-like flowers are satiny and showy to look at; they are 6–10cm across. The colour is generally white, pink or rose, but many named varieties have been raised with more intense colours. The flowers are produced throughout summer. The plant is easily raised from seed sown in spring. Useful as a colourful summer hedge, also makes good cut flowers. Ideal for coastal gardens. Native to Portugal and the Mediterranean region.

Leonotis
Lamiaceae

A genus of about thirty to forty species of annuals, perennials and shrubs native to South Africa, with stems that are mostly square in cross-section.

L. leonurus LION'S TAIL, LION'S EAR ☽☽

A much branched shrub with many erect, grey woolly stems; 1–2m high and 1m wide. The 6–12cm, oblong leaves with coarsely toothed edges, are arranged in whorls along the stem. From the leaf axils appear dense clusters of tubular, two-lipped, bright orange flowers, 5cm long and coated with fine hairs. The shrub flowers almost continuously from spring until autumn, making a spectacular display. Grows best in a hot position in full sun in well drained soil. When established it withstands drought, but grows much better with some summer water. As the flowers are produced on the new growth the plant benefits from being cut back occasionally to prevent it becoming rather straggly or untidy.

Leptospermum 'TEA TREE'
Myrtaceae

A genus of about eighty species of evergreen shrubs and small trees, native mostly to Australia but also to south-east Asia and New Zealand. They are grown for their aromatic foliage and profusion of small, rose-like flowers. The common name 'tea tree' comes from the fact that Captain Cook had the leaves brewed into tea to prevent scurvy among his crew.

L. laevigatum AUSTRALIAN TEA TREE ☽

A large, sturdy, dense shrub or small tree 3–10m high and as wide. The young stems are often red, flushed with soft hairs. With age it often forms picturesquely twisted grey-brown trunks. The fine textured, leathery, aromatic leaves, up to 3cm long, are hairy and vary in colour from green to silvery-green, sometimes with recurved points. Solitary, single white flowers 2cm wide appear in great numbers from late spring to summer. The shrub grows well in a sandy, acid or neutral soil that is well drained. Grows best with some shade, but will take full sun. When established it withstands drought, but grows better with some summer water. When planted close together they make a good windbreak or screen, or can be clipped into a hedge. Native to south-east Australia and Tasmania.

L. scoparium
MANUKA, NEW ZEALAND TEA TREE ☙
A variable species of shrub, rarely tree-like; grows to 3m high and wide, with upright or arching branches. The young growth is silky and dense. The leaves are tiny, less than 2cm long, rigid and sharp pointed, and are dotted with fragrant oil glands; they are often silver-hairy when young. In late spring and early summer the plant is covered with tiny white or pink-tinged flowers, 1–2cm across. The true species is of little interest, but there are many varieties with larger, showier flowers in white, pink or red, with some double forms. Some varieties only grow to 30cm high, with sprawling, weeping branches that are suitable for the rock garden. They are best grown in a well drained, sandy, acid or neutral soil. Native to Australia and New Zealand.

Leptospermum scoparium

Leucanthemum
Astreaceae

A genus of twenty-six species of annuals and evergreen perennials native to Europe and temperate Asia. They are grown for their cheerful flowers with white petals and yellow centres.

L. × superbum (syn. *Chrysanthemum maximum*) SHASTA DAISY ☙
A strong-growing, clump-forming

Leptospermum scoparium 'Bullatium'

perennial to 90cm high, spreading to 60cm wide. The leaves are arranged alternately along the stems and in a rosette at the base of the plant. The basal, dark green, shiny leaves, up to 20cm long, are narrow with toothed edges. The stem leaves are shorter and stalkless. In early summer the plant bears solitary, single or double white flowers up to 10cm wide on erect stems. Grow the plant in full sun or partial shade in any well drained soil. When established it withstands drought, but grows better with some summer water. The flowers are long-lasting when cut. The plant may need dividing in early spring after two to three years. Garden origin. Nurseries offer a large number of single and double, named varieties.

L. vulgare MARGUERITE ☙
A hardy, extremely variable perennial, to 60cm high and 30cm wide. The dark green, basal leaves, up to 10cm long, are spoon-shaped on long stalks. The stem leaves are smaller and sometimes lobed. The solitary white flowers with bright yellow centres are 8cm wide on upright stems; they are produced in profusion during spring. Grow the plant in full sun or partial shade in any well drained soil. When established it withstands drought, but it flowers better with some summer water. Re-move fading flowers and cut old stems to ground level in autumn. Native to most of Europe and temperate Asia.

Leucojum 'SNOWFLAKE'
Amaryllidaceae

A small genus of nine species of bulbous perennials native from Spain to the Middle East and north Africa. They are generally spring or autumn flowering, and are similar to 'snowdrops' (*Galanthus*) to which they are related.

L. aestivum SUMMER SNOWFLAKE ☙
A hardy, bulbous perennial with strap-shaped upright leaves, to 45cm long. In late spring the bulb produces stems up to 45cm high that carry up to eight flowers. The dainty, waxy white flowers are bell-shaped and faintly scented, 2cm long, with green edges. The bulbs are best planted in large drifts under deciduous trees or shrubs where they can naturalise. They prefer partial shade in summer and sun during the flowering period. Give little or no water during summer to allow the bulbs to become dormant. They should remain undisturbed for many years. Native to central and southern Europe.

L. autumnale AUTUMN SNOWFLAKE ☙
A bulbous perennial with upright, narrow, grass-like leaves, to 16cm long, produced at flowering time. Each bulb produces up to four slender stems to 25cm high in autumn. These carry two to four white, bell-shaped flowers 1cm long, flushed with pink. The bulbs are ideal for planting in a rock garden or well drained border. A delicate-looking plant that prefers full sun. Give little water during summer to allow the bulbs to become dormant. They should remain undisturbed for many years.

Leucanthemum × superbum

L

Native to Spain, Italy and north Africa.

L. trichophyllum ☽
A bulbous perennial with three upright, narrow, grass-like leaves to 10cm long, that are well developed at flowering time. In winter the flower stem, 8–30cm high, appears with two to three narrow, bell-shaped white or pinkish hanging flowers, to 2cm long. A pretty plant to grow in any well drained soil in full sun. Give little water during summer to allow the bulbs to become dormant. Native to southern Portugal, south-west Spain and Morocco.

Ligularia tussilaginea
See *Farfugium japonicum*.

Ligustrum 'PRIVET'
Oleaceae

A genus of about fifty species of deciduous and evergreen shrubs or trees native mainly to Asia and Australia, and to Europe and North Africa. Often used as hedging plants, they also make fine evergreen specimen shrubs or small trees.

L. japonicum JAPANESE PRIVET ☽☽
A fast-growing, upright, dense evergreen shrub to 3m or more high with an equal spread, which can be kept lower by trimming. The glossy, leathery, deep green, oval leaves are up to 10cm long. The white flowers are produced in upright conical clusters to 15cm long in midsummer to early autumn. They are followed by oblong black fruit. Useful, tough shrubs that make good hedges, screens or background plants. Grow in any soil in full sun or shade. Suitable for formal containers clipped into globes, pyramids or other shapes. The leaves may sunburn in hot spells. Grows best if given regular summer water, but will quickly recover from periods of drought. Native to China, Korea and Japan.

L. lucidum GLOSSY PRIVET ☽☽
An evergreen shrub or round-headed tree to 12m high and 7m wide. The glossy, dark green, leathery, oval leaves are up to 15cm long. Produces small, white, fragrant upright panicles of flowers, up to 20cm long, from late spring, and which continue throughout summer. The flowers are followed by blue-black fruit. The disadvantage is that a large fruit crop will drop, making an untidy mess. Useful as a coastal windbreak or can be used for hedging. Makes an attractive small street tree due to its long flowering season. Grows best if given some summer water. Native to China, Korea and Japan. 'Excelsum Superbum' has bright green leaves with yellow margins.

L. ovalifolium CALIFORNIA PRIVET ☽☽☽
A densely branching semi-evergreen shrub with an upright habit to 4m high spreading as wide. The glossy, oval, mid-green leaves are up to 6cm long. The white flowers are produced in dense erect clusters to 10cm long in mid-summer. The flowers are said to be unpleasantly scented, and are followed by shiny black berries. A useful hedging plant that should be clipped regularly to keep in shape. To grow well it needs to be generously fed and watered during summer. The roots are greedy, so other plants nearby suffer. Grows well in full sun and tolerates heat. Native to Japan. 'Argentium' has leaves margined with creamy-white, while 'Aureum' has leaves with yellow margins. Both these varieties may be susceptible to sunburn in summer.

Ligustrum ovalifolium 'Argentium'

Lilium 'LILY'
Liliaceae

A genus of about 100 species of bulbous perennials native to Europe, the Mediterranean region, Asia and North America. They are grown for their showy, sometimes extremely fragrant flowers. Most lilies prefer an acid or neutral soil. There are also a great many hybrids and cultivars listed by specialist nurseries.

L. candidum MADONNA LILY ☽
A bulbous perennial, generally growing with a single stiffly erect stem up to 1m high. The broad, glossy, lance-shaped basal leaves, up to 20cm long, becoming progressively shorter up the stem. The clusters of five to ten trumpet-shaped flowers are pure waxy white, 5–8cm long, delicately fragrant, the upper ones erect, the lower ones

Ligustrum lucidum

Ligustrum ovalifolium

drooping. The flowers are produced in late spring. The plant starts growing with the first rain in autumn, and dies down soon after flowering. Grow it with the top in full sun, however the roots prefer some shade. It requires a neutral to alkaline soil. Summer dormant so no water is needed. Looks best when grown in groups near a path or house where the scent can be appreciated. Native to Turkey.

L. longiflorum EASTER LILY ◡

A bulbous perennial with a single, stiffly erect stem 30–80cm high. The lance-shaped leaves are up to 18cm long. In early summer it produces clusters of between one and six extremely fragrant, pure white, trumpet-shaped flowers up to 20cm long, with prominent yellow anthers. After flowering, the stems will ripen and die down. Grow the plant in sun or partial shade in soil with good drainage. As it is summer dormant it needs no summer water. The plant is lime-tolerant, which is unusual for lilies. The flowers, with their strong scent, are excellent for cutting. It also makes a good pot or container plant. Native to southern Japan and Taiwan.

Lilium candidum

Lilium sp

Limonium 'SEA LAVENDER, STATICE'
Plumbaginaceae

A genus of 150 species of annuals, biennials, perennials and subshrubs distributed worldwide. Most species are found near the coast or in salt marshes. Many produce flowers that are suitable for cutting and for drying.

L. perezii ◡

An evergreen perennial up to 60cm high with a woody base. The rich green leaves are up to 30cm long and 15cm wide: they sprout in tufts from the procumbent stem. The deep indigo blue, white-flecked flowers grow in clusters on long stems up to 1m high and nearly as wide. They appear throughout most of summer. The flowers are long-lasting and good for drying. The plant is ideal for coastal gardens, as it often naturalizes on the coast. Grows well in full sun, needing little summer water once established. Tolerates heat and most soils, but needs good drainage. Native to the Canary Islands.

L. platyphyllum (syn. *L. latifolium*)
SEA LAVENDER ◡

A rosette-forming evergreen perennial with a woody base, growing 60cm or more high and 45cm wide. The basal leaves are oblong to spoon-shaped, and smooth-edged up to 25cm long with a long leaf stalk. The much-branched, wiry flowering stems appear up to 30cm high in summer. The stems are covered with many tiny, tubular, lavender-blue flowers. The flowers are long-lasting and good for drying. Grow the plant in full sun. Ideal for dry coastal gardens as it needs little summer water once established. The lavender-blue flowers associate well with silver-leaved plants. Native to Bulgaria and Russia.

L. sinuatum STATICE ◡

A perennial usually grown as a summer annual, up to 40cm high, rough-hairy throughout. The basal rosettes of oblong to lance-shaped leaves, up to 10cm long, are deeply lobed with wavy edges. The upright, branched, bright green, winged flower stems also carry leaves. The stems carry clusters of tiny funnel-shaped flowers that are blue, pink, red, white or yellow, and are produced in summer and early autumn. The plants are grown for their bright flowers that can be cut fresh or used when dried. Grows well in full sun needing little summer water once established. Seed is available in single colours and in mixtures. Native to the Mediterranean region.

Lippia citrodora
See *Aloysia triphylla*.

Livistona
Arecaceae

A genus of about twenty-eight species of single-stemmed palms native mostly to Australia, but also found in the warmer parts of Asia. These fan palms resemble Washingtonia, and also make attractive specimen trees.

L. australis AUSTRALIAN FAN PALM,
CABBAGE PALM ◡◡ or ◡◡◡

A medium to tall palm that grows slowly at first, then once fully established grows fast up to 15m or more. The grey- or brown-ringed trunk can be up to 30cm in diameter. The attractive, dark green, almost circular leaves are 2m or more across, divided more than halfway to the base with many linear lobes, often arching at the tips. They are carried on long, thorny leaf stalks that hold the leaf upright at first, then droop with age. Young trees make good container plants. Grow in full sun or partial shade in well drained soil. It needs regular summer water for good growth, but can survive periods of drought. It is attractive as a specimen in a lawn or as bold groups in large gardens. Native to eastern Australia.

L. chinensis CHINESE FAN PALM,
FOUNTAIN PALM ◡◡ or ◡◡◡

A spectacular, slow-growing palm to 12m high with the leaves spreading to 8m wide. The upright, robust trunk is

L

swollen at the base, grey in colour, with barely distinguishable rings. The roundish, glossy, bright green or yellowish-green leaves are more broad than long, to 2m wide. They are cut halfway into many narrow segments that are split again, with the tips hanging down like a fringe. The leaf stalks are toothed along the edges. Grow in full sun or partial shade in well drained soil. It needs regular summer water for good growth, but can survive periods of drought. It is attractive as a specimen, or as bold groups in large gardens. Young trees make good container plants. It is the most widely planted of the genus, and was popular in Europe and America in parlours, hotels and winter gardens. It needs a large space. Native to the southern Japanese islands and Taiwan.

Livistona chinensis

Lonicera 'HONEYSUCKLE'
Caprifoliaceae

A genus of more than 150 species of usually deciduous, sometimes evergreen, erect or climbing shrubs widespread in the northern hemisphere. They are grown for their usually tubular flowers that are often fragrant.

L. etrusca ETRUSCAN HONEYSUCKLE
An evergreen, vigorous, twining climber up to 4m or more high, that spreads as wide. The pairs of oval leaves, up to 10cm long, are joined at the base and hairy underneath. The tubular, two-lipped, sweetly scented yellowish flowers are 5cm long, becoming flushed with red and darkening as they age. The flowers are produced in terminal and axillary whorls from summer to autumn and are usually followed by red berries. When established, the climber withstands drought, but grows better with

Lonicera japonica 'Purpurea'

some summer water. Thrives in full sun. It is good for covering large walls or fences. It may become untidy with a mess of dead wood, when it should be cut to the ground in early spring to start again. Native to the Mediterranean region.

L. hildebrandiana
GIANT BURMESE HONEYSUCKLE
An extremely vigorous, evergreen twining climber up to 10m or more high, that spreads as wide. The pairs of large, broadly oval, glossy dark green leaves are up to 15cm long. The tubular, two-lipped, strongly fragrant flowers, 10–15cm long, open white, then turn yellow to dull orange. The flowers are produced in pairs in terminal and axillary racemes from summer to autumn. The flowers are slow to drop, and may be followed by red berries. A big plant that needs a lot of room and sturdy supports. Grows well in sun or partial shade with moderate summer water. Native to China and south-east Asia.

L. japonica JAPANESE HONEYSUCKLE
A vigorous, twining climber up to 5m or more high, that spreads as wide. Normally evergreen, but can be deciduous in cold gardens. The pairs of broadly oval leaves are up to 8cm long. The strongly fragrant white flowers,

which age to yellow, are produced in pairs in the leaf axils from spring to autumn. They are 4cm long, tubular, and two-lipped. The climber is good for covering large walls or fences, but can become invasive. With age it can become untidy with a mess of dead wood, when it should be cut to the ground in early spring to start again. Grows best in full sun when given moderate summer water. Native to Japan. 'Aureoreticulata' has leaves with yellow and green veins. Grow in partial shade as the leaves burn in full sun. 'Purpurea' has leaves tinged with purple and purple veins. The young shoots are also purple. The bright red flower buds open cream, fading to white.

L. japonica 'Halliana'
HALL'S HONEYSUCKLE
A vigorous evergreen twining climber up to 10m or more high that spreads as wide. The 8cm long, young leaves are lightly hairy. The flowers are produced in profusion in spring, and continue through to autumn, with a few at other times. They come in pairs, creamy-white ageing to yellow, and very fragrant. A tough climber for difficult situations such as poor soil, hot winds and hot walls in full sun. Drought-

Lophospermum erubescens

Lotus berthelotii

tolerant once established, but grows and flowers better if given some summer water. It will quickly cover fences, pergolas or climb into trees, easily enveloping a small tree with its twining stems. Often used as a bank or groundcover, where it will soon cover a large area, smothering other plants. Prune severely once a year to restrict size. Garden origin.

Lophospermum (syn. Asarina)
Scrophulariaceae

A genus of about eight species of tender evergreen and deciduous perennials, most climbing by means of coiling the leaf stalk. Native to North and central America.

L. erubescens (syn. *Asarina erubescens*) CREEPING GLOXINIA ↵↵↵
A strongly climbing, evergreen perennial to 2m high with hairy stems and leaves. The alternate triangular greyish-green leaves are 4–8cm long, and toothed along the edge with twining leaf stalks. The large, beautiful, 8cm trumpet-shaped flowers with five lobes are rose-pink with a pale throat, spotted pink. They are produced throughout summer and autumn. An easy climber for a sunny position or partial shade. Grow in a well drained soil and give regular summer water. It looks attractive when grown through shrubs or into trees. Although a

perennial, it is normally treated as an annual as it sets seed readily. Native to Mexico.

Lotus
Papilionaceae

A large genus of more than 150 species of annuals, perennials, evergreen and deciduous subshrubs found throughout most of the world. They are grown for their attractive pea-like flowers that come in a range of colours.

L. berthelotii PARROT'S BEAK ↵↵
A much-branched subshrub, only growing to 20cm high, with trailing stems 1m or more long, and covered in silver hairs. The small, 1cm long, semi-evergreen leaves are silver-grey and narrow. The flowers are 2–3cm long, bright red or scarlet and beak-shaped, resembling lobster claws. These form a startling contrast to the grey foliage. They are produced abundantly in waves during spring and summer, at their best in spring. Grow the shrub in full sun or partial shade with free-draining soil. Looks good in pots or containers, on banks, or on the tops of walls where its striking silver-grey foliage can be seen at its best. To grow well it requires moderate summer water. Not a long-lived plant, as after four or five years it can become untidy or exhausted and should be replaced. Native to the Canary Islands.

L. maculatus ↵↵
A low-growing evergreen subshrub, up to 20cm high, with prostrate silver-hairy branches. The alternate tiny grey leaves are divided into needle-like segments. The flowers are winged, 4–5cm long, and bright yellow tipped with a slender brown beak, resembling lobster claws. They are produced singly or in groups of two to five in spring and early summer. The plant is similar in most respects to *L. berthelotii*, as are the cultural conditions. Native to the Canary Islands.

L

Lotus maculatus

Lycianthes rantonetii
See *Solanum rantonetii.*

Lycoris 'SPIDER LILY'
Amaryllidaceae

A genus of about twelve species of bulbous perennials native to China and Japan to Myanmar (Burma). They are grown for their spectacular umbels of tubular flowers with protruding stamens.

L. aurea (syn. *L. africana*)
GOLDEN SPIDER LILY ⌣

A bulbous perennial with strap-shaped leaves that appear in spring, ripen and die down before the flowers appear. The leaves, to 60cm long, are mid-green, shiny and held semi-erect. In autumn the bare flowering stem, to 60cm high, appears, bearing clusters up to 10cm across of five to six tubular, wavy-margined, golden-yellow flowers. They are 8cm long, with segments that are curved backwards at the tips, and

Lycoris radiata

long protruding stamens, giving the flower a spidery look. Grow in a border in full sun or partial shade, leaving the plants undivided until a thick clump forms after several years. Give water during the flowering and growing period, then give a rest by drying out when the leaves die down. Plant bulbs with the tip just below the surface. The bulbs can rot in waterlogged soil. They make attractive pot or container plants when in flower. Native to China, Japan.

L. radiata RED SPIDER LILY ⌣

A bulbous perennial, with strap-shaped leaves 30–60cm long, with a silver band along the middle. They appear in spring, and die down before the flowers appear. The flowers are similar to *L. aurea* except they are rose-red or deep red with gold sheen. They are also produced in autumn. Cultural requirements are the same as *L. aurea*. This is the best known and easiest to grow. Native to Japan.

L

Macfadyena
Bignoniaceae

A small genus of only three or four species of woody, evergreen, shrubby climbers native to the West Indies, Mexico, Brazil and Argentina. Only one species is generally grown for its attractive, tubular yellow flowers.

M. unguis-cati
(syn. *Doxantha unguis-cati*, *Bignonia tweediana*, *Bignonia unguis-cati*)
CAT'S CLAW VINE ☽

A vigorous, normally evergreen climber growing to 9m or more high and as wide. The roots form tubers. The dark green leaves are oval to lance-shaped, 5–10cm long, and divided into two leaflets with a terminal tendril. Each tendril has three sharply curved, claw-like points that will cling to any support. The bright yellow, 5cm-long, trumpet-shaped flowers are produced during spring, completely covering the plant. They are solitary or in clusters of two to three at the ends of the stems or in the leaf axils. They may be followed by slender bean-like seedpods 45cm long, which hang from the branches. As it flowers on the ends of new growth, cut some stems back hard after flowering in order to promote new growth, and also stop it becoming untidy. Often seen grown on fences and walls, it also looks effective when grown into trees. The climber flowers best if grown in full sun, though it can take partial shade. Once established it can withstand hot, dry summers, needing little water. It is also ideal for coastal gardens as it withstands salt-laden sea breezes. Native to Mexico and Argentina.

Macleaya 'PLUME POPPY'
Papaveraceae

A small genus of just two to three species of large perennials native to China and Japan, which have yellow sap. Only one species is generally grown for its attractive leaves and plumes of flowers.

Macleaya cordata

M. cordata (syn. *Bocconia cordata*)
☽☽☽

A stately, tall-growing perennial with silver-grey flower stems 2m or more high, with rhizomatous roots spreading 2m or more wide. The greyish-green rounded or heart-shaped leaves are up to 25cm wide, with rounded, toothed lobes and white down on the underneath. The plume-like terminal panicles, up to 60cm long, of creamy-white flowers appear in summer. The plant grows best in full sun, but will take some shade. To grow well it needs regular summer water. With the feathery flower plumes rising majestically above other plants, it makes a bold display at the back of a border. It can be invasive, and needs to be controlled, or it will crowd out smaller plants.

Macfadyena unguis-cati

Maclura
Moraceae

A genus of about fifty species of evergreen or deciduous, dioecious (male and female flowers on different plants) trees, shrubs, or climbers native from eastern Asia to Australia and from southern USA to South America. They are usually extremely thorny, with the branches sometimes reduced to spines. Only one species is generally grown, its orange-like inedible fruit making it a curiosity in the garden.

M. pomifera OSAGE ORANGE

A hardy, fast-growing deciduous tree, to 15m high and 12m wide, with a spreading, open habit. The russet-brown bark is fissured. The branches are thorny, particularly when young, becoming less so with age. The dark green, ovate, pointed leaves are up to 10cm long, and turn golden yellow in autumn. The insignificant yellow-green flowers in summer are followed by orange-yellow globe-like fruit, to 14cm across, consisting of numerous seeds in a rubbery pulp. Male and female trees need to be grown together to obtain fruit. Grow in full sun. When established it withstands drought, needing no summer water. A tough plant for adverse conditions, it can take heat, cold, wind and poor soil. It is excellent for chalky soils. Used as an impenetrable hedge in the USA. Native to Arkansas and Texas in the USA.

Magnolia
Magnoliaceae

A genus of about 120 or more species of evergreen and deciduous trees and shrubs. Native from the Himalayas to eastern and south-eastern Asia, and from North America to central America and Venezuela. They are grown for their large and often scented flowers. Only one species is commonly grown in the Mediterranean region.

M. grandiflora ☽ or ☽☽

A magnificent evergreen tree that may reach 20m high, but is more often seen as a massive, round-headed shrub that can spread to 12m wide. The oblong, 25cm-long, thick green leaves are shiny above and reddish-brown underneath, at least when young. The enormous, powerfully fragrant, creamy-white cup-shaped flowers can be up to 25cm wide. They are produced throughout summer and early autumn, making a beautiful sight. The flowers are followed by rust-brown, cone-like fruit capsules. The plant is fairly lime-tolerant if given a good, rich, well drained soil. Thrives in hot, dry conditions, needing little summer water once established, but grows and flowers better with ample summer water. It can take several years to flower, so buy named, grafted cultivars that usually flower younger. The tree tends to produce strong, shallow surface roots, so do not plant

Malope trifida

underneath it. Native to south-eastern United States.

Malope 'ANNUAL MALLOW'
Malvaceae

A small genus of three to four species of tall, bushy annuals or perennials native to the Mediterranean region. They are grown for their showy, trumpet-shaped flowers.

M. trifida ☽

A tall, bushy annual to 1m high with stout stems and upright, bushy branches. The stems and leaves are covered in hairs. The rounded, deep green leaves have three to five pointed lobes. In summer it is covered in broadly trumpet-shaped, white to rose or purple flowers, 5–8cm across, with five heavily veined petals. An easily grown and free-flowering annual that is attractive in a sunny border. The flowers are produced over a long period and are suitable for cutting. When established it withstands drought, but flowers better with some summer water. Native to Spain and north Africa. 'Alba' has white flowers; 'Grandiflora' has large, deep rose-red flowers. Seed of mixed colours is available with pink, red, purple and white flowers.

Magnolia grandiflora

Malva 'MALLOW'
Malvaceae

A genus of about thirty species of annuals, biennials and perennials native to dry areas of Europe, north Africa and temperate Asia. They are related to, and resemble 'hollyhock' (*Alcea*), but are smaller and bushier.

M. alcea CUT-LEAVED MALLOW ⚘⚘

A variable, bushy, woody-based perennial up to 1m high or more, spreading to 60cm wide. The stems and leaves are covered in hairs. The upper leaves, to 15cm long, are usually deeply five-lobed with further lobes or teeth, while the lower leaves, to 30cm long, are more heart-shaped. The saucer-shaped, bright pink flowers with notched petals are 2–5cm wide; they cover the plant from early spring through to autumn. Easily grown, as it needs average soil with good drainage and moderate summer water. Grows best in full sun. When raised from seed sown in early spring it will flower the first year. With long-lasting and showy flowers it is suitable for a border or wildflower garden. Native to Spain and France. 'Fastigiata' grows more narrow and upright to 80cm high, with pink flowers.

Malvastrum capensis
See *Anisodontea capensis*.

Malvaviscus 'SLEEPY MALLOW'
Malvaceae

A genus of just three species of evergreen shrubs from tropical America that are closely related to Hibiscus.

M. arboreus 'Mexicanus'
TURK'S CAP, WAX MALLOW ⚘⚘⚘

A soft-stemmed shrub 4m or more high, with open branches spreading to 3m wide. A variable shrub that may have velvety stems and leaves. The broadly ovate, long-tipped leaves are serrated and up to 15cm long. They are dark green and softly pubescent. The usually solitary, bright red flowers appear in the upper axils, and are tubular, up to 10cm long, with protruding stamens. They resemble a closed Hibiscus flower hanging down. The flowers are produced mainly during summer and autumn, but may

Malvaviscus arboreus 'Mexicanus'

continue throughout the year. The shrub can become leggy, so cut back hard in winter. It needs a warm, sheltered location in full sun with plenty of summer water. A white form is sometimes seen. An easily grown and spectacular plant. Native from Mexico to Peru and Brazil.

Mandevilla (syn. Dipladenia)
Apocynaceae

A large genus of more than 100 species of mostly tuberous rooted, woody-stemmed, twining climbers, some perennials and shrubs native to tropical America. Most have milky sap. They are grown for their showy flowers, some of which are fragrant.

M. × amoena 'Alice du Pont' (syn. M. × amabilis 'Alice du Pont', Dipladenia splendens, Dipladenia amoena)
PINK DIPLADENIA ⚘⚘⚘

This hybrid species is a beautiful, woody-stemmed, evergreen climber that may reach 10m high and wide with twining stems. The pairs of dark green, oblong-elliptic leaves are 8–20cm long and wrinkled. The spectacular, large, trumpet-shaped flowers flare open to 10cm wide. Each flower is a glowing pink, appearing in clusters amongst the leaves throughout summer. This is an extremely tender climber that will not survive where there is frost. In summer it

prefers some shade, ample water, and high humidity. Grows best in a soil rich in humus and well drained. Often grown in pots or tubs on a patio where it will not grow so large. Can be restricted to almost any height, as even a small plant will flower well. Garden origin.

M. boliviensis (syn. Dipladenia boliviensis) WHITE DIPLADENIA ⚘⚘⚘
An evergreen, woody, twining climber,

Mandevilla amoena 'Alice du Pont'

M

Mandevilla boliviensis

to 3m high and wide, with slender stems that branch freely. The shining green, oblong, slender, pointed leaves are 5–8cm long. The 5cm-long, funnel-shaped flowers are white with an orange-yellow throat. They are produced in axillary racemes of three to seven throughout summer and autumn. A few flowers may be produced at other times. The climber grows best in partial shade, as the leaves may burn in full sun. Give ample water during summer. Grow in a humus-rich soil that is well drained. Train over a frame or trellis. A choice and beautiful plant. Native to Ecuador, Bolivia.

M. laxa (syn. M. suaveolens) CHILEAN JASMINE ♪♪♪

A vigorous, woody, twining climber that can reach 5m high with an equal spread. The deciduous leaves are 5–10cm long, and oval with a slender point and heart-shaped bases. The clusters of five to fifteen, powerfully

fragrant, white or cream flowers are trumpet-shaped to 5cm across. They are produced at the leaf axils throughout summer and autumn. Often they are followed by pairs of long, 40cm pods. The climber grows best in a rich, well drained soil with ample summer water. Grows well in full sun or partial shade. Although preferring a warm position, it will survive short periods of frost. It can be cut to ground level in early spring to encourage bushiness. Native to Bolivia and Argentina.

M. splendens (syn. Dipladenia splendens) DIPLADENIA ♪♪♪

A woody, low-growing, evergreen twining climber, to 3m high, with stems that are finely hairy. The dark green, oval leaves are 10–20cm long, with heart-shaped bases and slender pointed tips. The spectacular, large, deep pink, tubular flowers flare open to 10cm wide, with a yellow and white throat. The flowers are produced throughout summer. The plant is tender and will not stand any frost, needing a warm, sheltered aspect. The climber does not like growing against a hot sunny wall, but is ideal for training on light trellises with some shade. Makes a good pot plant for a shady patio or terrace. Grows best in a deep, rich, well drained soil. As it needs humid conditions, spray with water whenever possible during summer. Flowering even when small, it produces masses of flowers

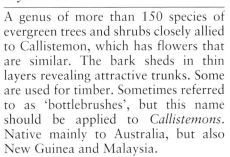

Mandevilla splendens

once established. Native to central and South America.

Melaleuca 'PAPERBARK' *Myrtaceae*

A genus of more than 150 species of evergreen trees and shrubs closely allied to Callistemon, which has flowers that are similar. The bark sheds in thin layers revealing attractive trunks. Some are used for timber. Sometimes referred to as 'bottlebrushes', but this name should be applied to *Callistemons*. Native mainly to Australia, but also New Guinea and Malaysia.

M. elliptica GRANITE BOTTLEBRUSH ♪

A shrub or small tree up to 3m high and wide, with brown, shedding bark. The growth is upright at first, then becoming spreading. The tiny, elliptic leaves, 1–2cm long, are deep green above and paler underneath. They are mostly at the ends of the branches. The large, showy, bright pink to crimson flowers, up to 8cm long with stamens the same colour, are produced on side branches in early spring. As the flowers are produced abundantly, the shrub is spectacular when in flower. When established it withstands drought, but it grows better with some summer water. Grows well in full sun. A useful shrub as it withstands heat, wind, poor soil and salt air. Native to Western Australia.

M. ericifolia HEATH MELALEUCA ♪

A shrub or small tree up to 8m high with bark that is light brown or grey, soft and fibrous, and tends to shed in strips. The 1–2cm, dark green, needle-like leaves are produced in pairs along the branches. The dense spikes of yellowish-white, bottlebrush-like flowers are 2–3cm long. They are produced along

Mandevilla laxa

Melaleuca elliptica

the stems of the shrub during spring and early summer. After flowering the woody seed capsules hang on the branches for several years. A useful shrub as it withstands heat, wind, poor soil, drought and salt air. Keep well pruned to encourage a good shape. With age it can make an attractive, multi-trunked tree. Native to New South Wales, Victoria, Tasmania.

Melaleuca ericifolia

M. hypericifolia DOTTED MELALEUCA
A large, graceful shrub or small tree up to 5m high spreading to 3m wide, with pendulous branches. The trunk has thin, peeling bark. The narrow, oblong evergreen leaves are 2–5cm long. The flowers appear from spring to summer in rich red, bottlebrush-like, dense spikes, 5–8cm long, but can be hidden by the leaves. When established the shrub withstands drought, but grows better with some summer water. Grows well in full sun. It will tolerate being clipped into a hedge, but this reduces its flowering. Useful for coastal gardens, as it withstands salt-laden sea breeze. Native to New South Wales.

M. nesophila PINK MELALEUCA
A tree or large shrub that makes fast growth to 3–7m, possibly up to 9m high, spreading to 3m wide. Grows naturally into a tree with freely branching stems and peeling, spongy bark. The greyish-green, obovate leaves

are 2–3cm long. From spring to summer it bears mauve, ball-shaped flowers, 3cm across or more, at the ends of the branches. They fade to white with yellow tips. A useful shrub as it withstands heat, sea breezes and poor soil. It is extremely drought-tolerant once established. Can be clipped into a hedge or trained into a tree with striking branch structures, or used as an informal screen. Native to western Australia.

Melia
Meliaceae

A genus containing fewer than ten species of deciduous trees or large shrubs that are native to Asia and Australia, some having scented wood. Only one species is generally cultivated for its attractive flowers and berries.

M. azedarach CHINABERRY, INDIAN BEAD TREE, PERSIAN LILAC
A deciduous, fast-growing tree 9–15m high, spreading to 5–8m wide. Forms a many-branched, round, open-headed tree with attractive rough bark. The beautiful, dark green, large, 30–90cm long, doubly pinnate leaves have many 2–5cm, oval-toothed leaflets. The clusters of small, star-shaped, fragrant lilac flowers, 2cm across, appear on the branches during spring. They are followed by clusters of pea-sized, yellow, bead-like fruit that hang from the bare branches long after the leaves have fallen, often until the following spring. They are plump when ripe, becoming wrinkled with age. The fruit is poisonous. The seed of the fruit can be used as beads for rosaries, thus giving it the common name. The tree grows easily from seed, and makes fast growth. Commonly grown as a street tree in many warm countries, and often grown as a patio shade tree. Grows

Melia azedarach (berries)

Melia azedarach

Melia azedarach

well in full sun. Resistant to drought, needing no summer water. An easily cultivated tree that needs little care. A good tree for difficult sites, as it tolerates poor alkaline soils as well as being wind-resistant. Native to northern India, central and western China.

Melianthus
Melianthaceae

A small genus containing about six species of tender evergreen shrubs native to southern Africa and India, with attractive foliage and unusual flowers. Only one species is generally grown.

M. major HONEY BUSH
A handsome, evergreen, semi-woody, spreading shrub. The upright, hollow grey or green stems have few branches and make fast growth up to 3m, with leaves in terminal clusters. Most of the stems appear from ground level. The deeply toothed, pinnate leaves are 30–45cm long, with nine to seventeen leaflets in pairs, a glaucous blue-green above, paler underneath. The boldly patterned leaves give it a striking subtropical effect. The leaves have a disagreeable smell when crushed. The deep reddish-brown flowers, 2–3cm long, appear in spring in terminal erect racemes 30–80cm long. The flowers are

M

Melianthus major

rich in nectar. It is chiefly grown as a foliage shrub. Adaptable to most soils. Grow in full sun or partial shade, with an average amount of summer water, though it will tolerate some drought. As the new growth is most attractive, the occasional removal of old straggly stems encourages new growth from the base. Makes a good silhouette plant for a raised bed or a striking accent plant. Good near swimming pools. Native to South Africa.

Mesembryanthemum cordifolium
See *Aptenia cordifolia*.

Metrosideros 'POHUTUKAWA' *Myrtaceae*

A genus of about sixty species of evergreen shrubs, trees and woody climbers native to South Africa, Malaysia, Australasia and the Pacific Islands. They are grown for their showy flowers that are sometimes similar to Callistemon 'Bottlebrush'.

M. excelsus NEW ZEALAND CHRISTMAS TREE ◡◡ *then* ◡
A handsome tree 10–20m high, with spreading branches to 10m wide. The oval-pointed, leathery, shiny green leaves are 5–10cm long, with dense white felt underneath. The flowers are in terminal, branched clusters up to 10cm across. They consist mainly of showy, brilliant scarlet stamens up to 4cm long, that extend beyond the small petals. The flowers are produced in summer, around Christmas in New Zealand, hence the common name. Grow the tree in humus-rich, well drained soil that is neutral to acid. Grows best near the coast, which is its native habitat, so is extremely wind-resistant. Will also take moderate frost. Moderate water is needed for the first two to three years to establish, then a little summer water. Makes a beautiful specimen tree. Sometimes used as a street tree. Native to New Zealand. 'Aureus' has rich yellow filaments.

M. kermadecensis ◡◡ *then* ◡
A bushy, spreading tree 15–20m or more tall in its native habitat, but usually seen as a bushy shrub 2–3m high in cultivation. The leaves are broadly ovate to 5cm long, dark green above and densely white-felted underneath. The spectacular flowers are in broad, branched, terminal clusters, to 10cm wide, with crimson filaments and yellow anthers. They are produced abundantly, mainly in spring and early summer. Cultivation is the same as for *M. excelsus* and is often confused with it. Native to New Zealand. 'Variegatus'

Metrosideros excelsus

Metrosideros kermadecensis 'Variegatus'

is extremely attractive and showy. The dark green leaves are edged with broad, irregular creamy-white to yellow margins. The flowers can cover a young plant only 50cm high. The shrub only grows to 60cm high and wide after five years. It needs a frost-free site.

Milla uniflora
See *Ipheion uniflorum*.

Mimulus (syn. Diplacus) 'MONKEY FLOWER' *Scrophulariaceae*

A genus of about 150 species of annuals, perennials and evergreen shrubs native to South Africa, Asia, Australia, North, central and South America; particularly abundant in California.

M. aurantiacus (syn. M. glutinosus, Diplacus glutinosus, Diplacus aurantiacus)
STICKY MONKEY FLOWER ◡◡
A much-branched evergreen shrub with a woody base up to 1m high, with sticky stems and leaves. The branches are upright or lax. The lance-shaped to oblong, rich green leaves, up to 7cm long, are glossy above and densely hairy underneath. The showy, open trumpet-shaped, soft orange flowers, 3–4cm long, have notched, widely spreading petal-lobes. They are borne in pairs from spring to late summer. The shrub grows best in partial shade, in humus-rich, well drained soil. Although drought-tolerant, it grows best with moderate summer water. A short-lived plant, so propagate regularly by taking cuttings, which root easily. The soft orange colour of the flowers makes a useful addition to the garden. Looks good when grown in the shade of trees. Native to California.

M

The variety 'Puniceus' has distinctly reddish-purple flowers.

Mirabilis
Nyctaginaceae

A genus of about sixty species of annuals and herbaceous perennials native to the southern USA and South America. The roots are usually thick and tuberous, used in former times as a purgative medicine.

M. *jalapa* MARVEL OF PERU, FOUR O'CLOCK PLANT ⌣

A deep-rooted, herbaceous perennial that is much branched, and grows to about 1m high, quickly forming large clumps. The roots form large tubers that, in ideal conditions, can weigh up to 20kg. The leaves are deep green, oval, 5–10cm long, and shiny above. The clusters of fragrant, trumpet-shaped flowers are red, pink, white or yellow, often striped or mottled, and 3–5cm wide. The flowers appear continuously from summer until late autumn. They tend to open in the late afternoon and die by morning, hence the common name of Four O'Clock Plant. The flowers are followed by small green fruit containing one seed, black when ripe. The plant grows best in full sun in any well drained soil. It is drought-tolerant, requiring no summer water once established. Often seen in beds or borders, as it is easily raised from seed. Native to Peru.

Monstera
Araceae

A genus of twenty-two species of climbing plants that are often epiphytic, most with cut or perforated leaves, native to tropical America. They cling by aerial roots arising from stout

Mirabilis jalapa

Monstera deliciosa

Monstera deliciosa (fruit)

stems. One species, M. *deliciosa*, is commonly used as a pot plant for the home, but may be grown outdoors in favourable locations.

M. *deliciosa* MEXICAN BREADFRUIT, SWISS CHEESE PLANT ⌣⌣⌣

A strong-growing, woody-stemmed climber, with thick, sparingly branched stems. The plant has two leaf forms: the juvenile leaves are relatively small, with few, if any, holes or perforations. Mature plants have large, glossy, leathery, heart-shaped leaves that can be 80cm or more long and as wide, with cuts or large perforations in them. They are carried on long leaf stalks. The plant will naturally climb up trees, supporting itself by means of aerial roots that hang down to the ground and root in the soil. The small, creamy flowers that form on mature plants give

way to a long, green fruit formed on a thick spike; this is surrounded by a white spath about 30cm long. The edible fruit remains on the plant for a year before ripening; it has a curious taste that is a cross between pineapple and banana. Only the pulp should be eaten, as there are small needle-like oxalic acid crystals between the segments, that are extremely unpleasant if they enter the mouth. The climber grows best in light shade. Give strong support such as a tree or wall, as it will eventually become large. Ideal for planting against a shady wall. Give it generous water during summer. Native to southern Mexico to Panama.

Montanoa
Asteraceae

A genus of between thirty to fifty species of pithy-stemmed shrubs or small trees, native from northern Mexico to Colombia and Venezuela. They are grown for their showy winter flowers.

M. *bipinnatifida* DAISY TREE ⌣⌣

An open-growing shrub up to 3m high, with grey woody stems. The large, opposite leaves, 40cm or more long, are deeply indented or lobed. They are dull green and roughly hairy on both sides. The large, terminal, branched flower clusters contain many white flowers with protruding yellow stamens up to 8cm across. The flowers are daisy-like, giving it the common name. They are produced from autumn, but are usually at their best in mid-winter. Prune hard after flowering to encourage new stems, which will grow quickly. The shrub grows well in full sun when given regular summer water. It is attractive, with large bold leaves and showy winter flowerheads. Tropical-looking as a background plant. Native to Mexico.

M

Montanoa bipinnatifida

M

Montbretia crocata
See *Tritonia crocata.*

Moraea grandiflora
See *Homeria collina.*

Morus 'MULBERRY'
Moraceae

A genus of about ten species of deciduous trees or large shrubs native to North and South America, Africa and Asia. Some are grown for their edible fruits, also attractive to birds, and some for their attractive foliage.

M. alba WHITE MULBERRY ☽ or ☽☽
A spreading deciduous tree to 10m or more high and wide. The ovate, corrugated leaves are 20cm or more long, coarsely toothed and glossy green above. They turn a beautiful yellow in autumn. Small, inconspicuous male and female flowers appear in drooping catkins in spring. The female flower develops into a white berry to 3cm long. The berry ripens to pink or red in late summer. The sweet but insipid fruit stains where it drops onto paths and clothing, so the fruitless forms may be better for the home garden. The tree withstands heat, full sun and alkaline soils. It will provide quick shade. Drought-tolerant once established, but grows better with some summer water. Useful for planting near the coast. As it produces shallow surface roots, do not cultivate the ground beneath the tree. The leaves were traditionally fed to silkworms in China. Native to central and eastern China. 'Chaparral' is a weeping, non-fruiting variety; 'Pendula' grows 3m high, spreading to 5m wide, with weeping shoots.

M. nigra BLACK MULBERRY ☽ or ☽☽
A deciduous tree up to 10m high, with dense, wide-spreading branches up to 15m wide. The tree is extremely long-lived, becoming gnarled and picturesque with age. The leaves are heart-shaped, often doubly toothed, up to 15cm wide, rough above and downy underneath. The flowers are borne in drooping catkins in spring. They are followed by abundant, rough green edible fruit up to 3cm long, that are somewhat hidden on the undersides of the branches. They ripen to a juicy dark red to black, and have a pleasant, slightly acidic taste. The fruit stains where it drops onto paths and clothing. The tree withstands heat, full sun and alkaline soils. It will provide quick shade. Drought-tolerant once established, but grows better with some summer water. Only prune in mid-winter as it will 'bleed' at other times. Native to west Asia.

Musa 'BANANA'
Musaceae

A genus of over thirty species of giant, palm-like, suckering, evergreen perennials native to tropical Africa, northeast India, and from south-east Asia to Japan and northern Australia. The leaf blades are often huge and paddle-shaped. The genus contains some ornamental plants and several different species and cultivars that produce the edible banana.

M. acuminata 'Dwarf Cavendish'
DWARF BANANA ☽☽☽
A variable, upright-growing, suckering perennial up to 3m high, with short, pseudo-stems formed by the sheathing leaf stalks. The glossy paddle-shaped leaf blades are 1.5m long. In summer the large, heavy, drooping flower clusters, with reddish bracts and yellow flowers, appear. They are followed by seedless, sweet fruit up to 15cm long, borne in long bunches. After fruiting the stem dies and is replaced by new suckers. Grow the plant in rich soil in full sun. Give generous water in any dry period, especially during summer. The plant is fast-growing and needs generous feeding. As the large leaves are easily tattered by the wind, grow in a well sheltered position. This is the most suitable cultivar for the home garden, as it should produce fruit annually. Ideally the minimum winter temperature should be around 15–18 degrees C, but it will withstand more cold than other bananas. Looks attractive near swimming pools; it also makes a good tub or container plant. Garden origin.

Muscari 'GRAPE HYACINTH'
Hyacinthaceae

A genus of about forty species of bulbous perennials native to the Mediterranean region and south-west Asia. They are grown for their dense spikes of fragrant, globular, usually blue flowers.

M. armeniacum ☽
A bulbous perennial that produces narrow, channelled basal leaves, to 30cm long, which are semi-erect, appearing in autumn. In spring, tubular, nodding, bright blue flowers with constricted white mouths are borne in tight unbranched tapering spikes. The spikes are up to 8cm long on stems to 20cm high. They are best

Musa acuminata 'Dwarf Cavendish'

Mutisia oligodon

grown in a sunny, well drained position. As they are summer dormant they require no summer water. The bulbs look best when planted in drifts under trees or shrubs or edging paths. Ideal for the rock garden. The bulbs are long-lived, usually becoming over-crowded, so lift and divide congested clumps when dormant in summer. Native to Turkey. 'Blue Spike' is a double form with large heads of dark blue flowers.

Mutisia
Asteraceae

A genus of about sixty species of upright or climbing shrubs native to South America. They are grown for their showy, daisy-like flowers that are produced throughout the summer and autumn.

M. decurrens JJJ
A much-branched, glabrous, suckering climber, to 3m high and wide. The oblong to lance-shaped dark green leaves, to 12cm long, are entire or toothed. Each leaf ends in a two-lobed tendril. The vivid orange flowers, 10–12cm across, are borne singly from the leaf axils throughout the summer. The climber grows best in partial shade, although it will take full sun. It needs generous watering during summer. It looks attractive when planted in

a small courtyard garden or grown into trees. Also useful for covering fences or trellis. Trim back untidy growth during spring. Easily propagated from suckers. Native to Chile and Argentina.

M. oligodon JJJ
A weak-stemmed climber, to 1m high and wide. The simple, oblong to elliptic, dark glossy green leaves, to 4cm long, are covered with white wool underneath. Each leaf ends in a long

tendril. The pink flowers with a yellow centre are 7cm across, and are borne on long stalks singly from the leaf axils throughout the summer and autumn. The climber grows best in partial shade, although it will take full sun. It needs generous watering during summer. A delicate plant that needs the support of a wall or trellis. Native to Chile and Argentina.

Myoporum
Myoporaceae

A genus of about thirty species of evergreen shrubs and trees, native mostly to Australia, and a few to New Zealand, Hawaii, China and Japan. They are tough, fast-growing plants often used for hedging.

M. laetum JJ
A vigorous evergreen shrub or tree of exceptionally fast growth to 10m high, spreading to 6m wide, which forms a dense, billowing mass of dark green. The older growth is stiff and woody, while the young growth is flexible. The fleshy, glossy, bright green leaves are lance-shaped up to 10cm long, with translucent oil glands. In summer, clusters of two to six bell-shaped, 1cm wide flowers appear. They are white with purple markings, and may be followed by deep reddish-purple berries. The shrub grows well in full

M

Myoporum laetum

Myrtus communis

sun when given moderate summer water. Good for coastal gardens as it withstands salt-laden sea breezes. Makes a good background shrub that will block sound, wind and sun. If left unpruned it will form an attractive multi-stemmed tree, or it can be clipped into an informal hedge. A greedy plant with invasive roots, so do not grow choice plants nearby. Native to New Zealand.

Myrsine
Myrsinaceae

A genus of about five species of dioecious (male and female flowers on different plants) evergreen dwarf shrubs to small trees native to Asia and Africa. They make attractive shrubs that are often used for hedging.

M. africana
AFRICAN BOXWOOD, CAPE MYRTLE
A slow-growing evergreen shrub up to 2m high, spreading to 75cm wide. The upright, downy red shoots are angled, and tend to be floppy when young, but gradually stiffen. The stems are closely set with roundish, aromatic, glossy, dark green leaves to 2cm long. The flowers produced in late spring are insignificant. Grow the shrub in full sun or partial shade in any humus-rich, well drained soil. It will not grow well in shallow, dry chalky soil. It needs little summer water once established. A tough plant that is tolerant of frost, drought and smog. It is ideal for low hedges, clipping into formal shapes, low backgrounds and small beds. Also good in pots and containers. Native to the Azores, east and southern Africa, Himalayas and China.

Myrtus 'MYRTLE'
Myrtaceae

A small genus that has been much changed by taxonomists. It is now recognized as having just two species native to the Mediterranean region, north Africa and South America. They are grown for their aromatic leaves.

M. communis COMMON MYRTLE
An evergreen, bushy shrub that normally grows to 3m high, though old plants can occasionally reach 5m high and 6m across. The pairs of glossy, bright green, oval, pointed leaves are 2–3cm long, and strongly scented when crushed. The white or pinkish flowers, 2–3cm wide, are sweetly scented and have many creamy-white protruding stamens. The flowers appear on the axils of the upper leaves in spring and summer. They are followed by bluish-black berries. The shrub is not fussy about soil conditions, but needs good drainage. Grows well in full sun, but will also take partial shade. Needs no summer water once established. May be grown as a free-standing specimen, or it makes a good low hedging plant. There are also a number of compact and variegated forms. Native to the Mediterranean region.

Nandina
Berberidaceae

A genus of just one species of frost-hardy, evergreen shrub native to India, China and Japan. It is grown for its attractive flowers, fruit and elegant foliage.

N. domestica HEAVENLY BAMBOO,
SACRED BAMBOO ى
An evergreen shrub that forms a clump of slender, upright, cane-like shoots to 2m high, spreading to 1.5m wide. The leaves, to 30cm long, are divided into two to three lance-shaped, pointed leaflets, 3–6cm long. The new leaves open pinkish to reddish-purple, turn a soft green as they mature, then become bronze in autumn. Often they are bright red in winter. In late spring or summer large, branched sprays, to 30cm long, of star-shaped, creamy-white flowers, each 1cm wide with large yellow anthers, appear at the tips

Nandina domestica

of the stems. They are followed by long-lasting, showy, bright red berries. The shrub is best grown in groups, as single plants seldom fruit heavily. Will grow in shade, but for best colour grow in full sun. Thrives in a rich soil with regular summer water, but can withstand some drought. Good as a hedge or screen, and as a pot or container plant. Somewhat similar to bamboo in appearance, it is dramatic with night lighting. 'Firepower' is a dwarf form with excellent autumn colour; 'Pygmaea' (syn. 'Nana') only grows to 30cm high so is ideal for pots; 'Richmond', a strong, vigorous, free-fruiting form, grows to 2m or more high.

Narcissus 'DAFFODIL'
Amaryllidaceae

A genus of over fifty species of bulbous perennials native to Europe and north Africa. Many thousands of cultivars

Narcissus papyraceus

have been developed. Most daffodils need a cold spell to initiate flower production, so are unsuitable for growing in warm areas.

N. papyraceus PAPER-WHITE NARCISSUS ى
A bulbous perennial with broad, upright leaves, to 1cm wide and 30cm long. The upright flower stems, to 30cm high, carry clusters of five to ten strongly fragrant, pure white flowers. They are small, cupped 1–2cm across, appearing in midwinter and early spring. When planted in drifts underneath deciduous trees or shrubs they make a wonderful sight with their snowy-white flowers. They will seed and naturalize well. As they are summer dormant they need no water. As with other bulbs, allow the leaves to grow until they turn yellow and die naturally. Native to southern Spain, southern Portugal and north Africa.

Neanthe bella
See *Chamaedorea elegans*.

Neodypsis decaryi
See *Dypsis decaryi*.

Nerine
Amaryllidaceae

A genus of more than twenty species of bulbous perennials native to southern

Nerium oleander 'Variegata'

Africa. The large, colourful flowers appear before the leaves in autumn. Many cultivars have been developed.

N. bowdenii ☽ or ☽☽

The bulb produces glossy green, strap-shaped leaves 3cm wide and 30–45cm long, which usually appear after the flowers have faded. In autumn the clusters of eight to twelve flowers appear on stems 45cm high. Each flower is up to 8cm across and deep rose pink with a darker line on each segment, and a wavy edge re-curving at the tips. The blooms last for several weeks. Grow the bulbs in a border in full sun or partial shade. For best flowering, leave the plants undisturbed until a thick clump forms after several years. Plant bulbs with the tip just below the surface. Give water during the growing and flowering period, then give a rest by drying out during summer. The bulbs can rot in water-logged soil. They are attractive when grown as pot or container plants. Native to South Africa.

N. sarniensis GUERNSEY LILY ☽ or ☽☽

The bulb produces slightly glossy, strap-shaped basal leaves, 30cm long and 2cm wide. The leaves appear after the flowers have faded. In autumn the flower stalk, up to 45cm high, appears with large clusters of ten to twenty trumpet-shaped, crimson flowers. They are 4cm long, with the segments slightly crisped and protruding bright red, nearly straight stamens. Many varieties have been bred with pink, orange, scarlet and white flowers. Culture is the same as *N. bowdenii*, but is more hardy. Native to the mountainous regions of the Cape in South Africa.

Nerium
Apocynaceae

A small genus of only one or two species of upright evergreen shrubs or small trees, native from the Mediterranean region to China but widely naturalized. They are grown for their wonderful show of flowers that are produced for most of summer. Numerous cultivars have been developed.

N. oleander OLEANDER ☽ or ☽☽

An evergreen shrub or small tree, generally growing 2–6m high, and nearly as wide. There is a vigorous, white-flowered variety that can reach 7m. The leathery leaves are usually in whorls of three around the stem. They are dark green, lance-shaped on short leaf stalks, and 10–30cm long. During summer and autumn, large terminal clusters of flowers are continually produced. Each flower is funnel-shaped, 5–8cm across, with some varieties having a distinct fragrance. The colours range from white, yellow, pink, salmon and crimson to purple. There are some double, as well as single forms. There is also an attractive form with golden variegated leaves, though it needs plenty of sun and air or it will not flower freely. Grows in any well drained soil. When established it withstands drought, but grows and flowers better with some summer water. This is one of the basic Mediterranean evergreen shrubs, as it is adaptable to a wide range of situations. Often used as roadside screens, as hedges, specimens or as pot plants. Ideal for coastal gardens as it with-

Nerium oleander

Nicotiana alata

Nicotiana glauca

parts of the plant are poisonous if eaten.

N. alata (syn. N. affinis)
FLOWERING TOBACCO ♪♪♪
A tender perennial that is often treated as an annual, which grows to 1m or more high. The coarse, ovate leaves are 10–15cm long. The branched stem is topped with a raceme of tubular flowers 5–10cm long, which flare at the mouth into five pointed lobes. They are strongly fragrant, normally opening towards evening. In the original species the colour is greenish-yellow. It has been much hybridized, and there is now a wide range of colours, from white to pink and red, including lime-green; they also stay open during the day. They are easily raised from seed, and will self-seed. A good plant for beds and borders near the house where the scent can be enjoyed. To grow well they need regular summer water. Grows and flowers best in full sun, but will take some shade. Native to southern Brazil.

N. glauca TREE TOBACCO ♪ or ♪♪
A mostly glabrous branched shrub or small tree that quickly grows 3–9m high and wide, with arching, glaucous shoots. The bluish-green, ovate to lance-shaped leaves are 15cm long. The stems are topped with large, loose panicles of yellow flowers, about 4cm long. They cover the entire shrub for most of summer. The flowers are followed by small seedpods containing many seeds that will readily germinate. A good plant for the dry garden, as it requires only occasional watering, but it looks better with regular watering. Grows best in full sun. The leaves are toxic to animals. Native to South America.

Nolina recurvata
See Beaucarnea recurvata.

stands salt-laden sea breezes. Caution is needed however, as all parts of this plant are poisonous!

Nicotiana 'TOBACCO PLANT'
Solanaceae

About seventy species of annuals, perennials or shrubs native to tropical and warm temperate North and South America, Australia and Polynesia. All

Odontonema
Acanthaceae

A genus of perhaps more than forty species of evergreen perennials and shrubs native to the tropical regions of America. They are bold and beautiful when in flower, with terminal spikes of white, yellow or red flowers. They are easily grown.

O. strictum CARDINAL FLOWER ꜩꜩꜩ

An evergreen shrub that grows up to 2m high, with upright green stems spreading to 1m wide. The oblong, shiny, rich green, slightly crumpled leaves are up to 18cm long with a slender point. The flowers are borne in an erect terminal spike, 45cm or more long. The waxy, bright orange-red to scarlet tubular flowers are 2–3cm long. These make a very attractive show when they cover the plant during summer. The shrub grows best in

Odontonema strictum

partial shade with a generous amount of summer water. It dislikes chalk soil as it can become chlorotic, therefore it is best grown in a humus-rich, well drained soil. Also makes an attractive pot or container plant for the shaded patio. Easily rooted from cuttings. Sometimes wrongly named as *Justicia coccinea*. Native to central America.

Odontospermum maritimum
See *Asteriscus maritimus*.

Oenothera
'EVENING PRIMROSE, SUNDROPS'
Onagraceae

A genus of over 100 species of annuals, biennials and perennials that are widely distributed throughout the world, many coming from North and South America. They include the evening primroses, which as their name suggests, are evening flowering.

O. macrocarpa (syn. O. missouriensis) Evening Primrose ꜩ

A prostrate, sprawling perennial, to 30cm high, with a woody base. The leaves are soft, hairy, lance-shaped, and up to 10cm long. The large, lemon-yellow, funnel-shaped flowers open from slightly red spotted buds: they flare to nearly 10cm wide, opening in the evening. They are produced almost continuously from late spring throughout summer. A useful perennial for the dry garden, making a glorious show, and needing little summer water. Grow in a well drained soil in sun or light shade. Easily propagated by seed. Native to southern central USA.

O. speciosa 'Rosea' (syn. O. berlandieri 'Childsii')
MEXICAN EVENING PRIMROSE ꜩ

A perennial to 30cm high that spreads by runners to 1m wide, with basal rosettes of leaves. Each mid-green,

Oenothera speciosa 'Rosea'

lance-shaped leaf, up to 5cm long, is lightly toothed. The long, arching stems bear slightly smaller leaves. During late spring and summer very fragrant, solitary, pale pink, cup-shaped flowers, 5cm wide, cover the plant. The flowers open during the day. Usually the stems will die back after flowering. The plant needs little summer water. Thrives with little or no care once established. It can become invasive unless controlled, but makes a good groundcover for dry slopes.

Olea 'OLIVE'
Oleaceae

A genus of about twenty species of evergreen trees and shrubs, with opposite leathery leaves. Native to the warm dry areas of the Mediterranean region, Africa, Asia and Australasia. Along with figs and almonds, the olive tree typifies a Mediterranean region.

O. europaea OLIVE TREE ꜩ

A slow-growing tree to 6m or more high, with an equal spread. Young trees grow fairly fast, then slow with maturity. The 8cm, lance-shaped leaves are grey-green above, with a silvery underside. The insignificant yellowish flowers are produced in axillary racemes in early summer. They are followed by 1–3cm long fruit, which are green turning shiny black when

Olea europaea

ripe. The olive oil of commerce is extracted from these fruit. They can also be eaten if treated by soaking in brine. The trees need to be grown in full sun in a well drained soil. They require no summer water once established. They can withstand hard pruning, indeed old trees can be reduced to stumps and will shoot out well, completely rejuvenating themselves. Old trees with gnarled trunks can, with care, be lifted and transplanted in large crates, adding maturity to a young garden. Native to the eastern Mediterranean region, but cultivated since time immemorial.

Olearia 'DAISY BUSH, TREE DAISIES'
Asteraceae

A genus of about 130 species of evergreen shrubs and small trees, native chiefly to New Zealand, Australia and Tasmania. Most species come from areas where the humidity is relatively high. They are attractive, easy to grow, and are covered in daisy-like flowerheads in summer. Most species are particularly suitable for coastal gardens, and grow well in chalky soils.

O. × haastii

A rounded, dense, much-branched shrub, to 2m high and wide. The alternate, oval leaves, to 3cm long, are white-felted underneath. They open glossy dark green, ageing to a dull grey-green. The fragrant, daisy-like white flowers appear in dense clusters, to 8cm across. In early summer they smother the shrub. Grow in full sun in any well drained soil. When established it withstands drought, but grows better with some summer water. An excellent, well proven hedging plant. Tolerates pollution, so useful for town gardens. Ideal as a windbreak in coastal gardens. A natural hybrid from New Zealand.

Olearia × haastii

O. 'Henry Travers'
(syn. O. semidentata)

A rounded, much-branched shrub, to 3m high and 2m wide, with slender shoots covered in white felt. The slightly toothed, lance-shaped, dark green leaves to 10cm long are silvery underneath. In early summer the shrub bears solitary, daisy-like flowerheads, 5cm across, lilac with purple centres. Cultivation is the same as O. × haastii. A natural hybrid from New Zealand.

O. traversii

A fast-growing evergreen shrub or small tree 6–10m high, spreading to 5m wide, with stout, four-angled shoots covered in white felt. The opposite leaves, to 6cm long, are broadly oval to oblong, leathery, glossy dark green above, with white felt underneath. The daisy-like, white flowerheads produced in summer are insignificant. An ideal evergreen windbreak for coastal gardens. Grows well even in poor sandy soils. Cultivation is the same as O. × haastii. Native to New Zealand.

Opuntia
Cactaceae

A vast genus containing perhaps 300 or more species of prostrate to tree-like cacti native to the dry regions of tropical America. They have become naturalized all over the world in arid or semi-arid regions. They generally fall into two groups: those with flat pads, and those with round joints. Some species have edible fruit.

O. ficus-indica

PRICKLY PEAR, INDIAN FIG

A large, flat-jointed cactus that makes a bush to 4m high and wide. The large, smooth green or glaucous, bluish segments are from 30–60cm long. Some

Opuntia ficus-indica (fruit)

O

Opuntia ficus-indica

forms are spineless, or nearly so, but with clusters of irritating yellow bristles. The luminous, yellow, cup-shaped flowers are 10cm across, appearing in spring or early summer. They are followed by pear-shaped, juicy, red or yellow fruit, 6–8cm long. They are edible but not delicious, and like the plant are covered in irritating hairs. Any segment of the plant that falls to the ground will root quickly, so that it has become a weed in warm countries. Can be used to make an impenetrable barrier requiring no attention and no summer water. Ideal for coastal gardens as it withstands salt-laden sea breezes. Origin unknown, probably Mexico. Widely cultivated, possibly the world's most widely grown cactus.

Ornithogalum 'STAR OF BETHLEHEM'
Hyacinthaceae

A genus of about 100 species of bulbous perennials native to Europe, the Mediterranean region, Asia and South Africa. They are grown for their showy spring flowers.

O. arabicum ⌣

A bulbous perennial with bluish-green, rather long, floppy leaves up to 60cm long and 1–2cm wide. In late spring, stems up to 60cm high are topped with clusters of up to twenty-five cup-shaped flowers. They are fragrant, waxy white, and 3–6cm across, with conspicuous black pistils in the centre. They make an excellent cut flower. Grow the bulbs in full sun in any free-draining soil. As the leaves are produced in the wet winter months, they need no summer water. Ideal for planting in drifts under trees where the bulblets will naturalize well. Native to the Mediterranean region.

O. narbonense ⌣

A bulbous perennial with semi-erect, grey-green leaves up to 60cm long, which remain green during flowering. In late spring, stems 30–60cm high are produced with a long, pyramidal, many-flowered spike of small white flowers. Each star-shaped flower, 2cm across, has petals with a narrow green band. Grow the bulbs in full sun in any free-draining soil. They need no summer water. Native to the Mediterranean region.

O. umbellatum STAR OF BETHLEHEM ⌣⌣

A bulbous perennial with grass-like leaves up to 30cm long with a broad white mid-vein. Clusters of flowers, 2–3cm wide, striped green on the outside, are produced on the top of a stem 30cm high in spring. The leaves gradually die as the flowers open. They make excellent cut flowers, but they close at night. Grow the bulbs in a shady situation where they do not dry out. If conditions are right it will naturalize, and may become weedy. Native to the Mediterranean region and north Africa.

× Osmarea

See *Osmanthus*.

Osmanthus (syn. × Osmarea)
Oleaceae

A genus of about fifty species of evergreen shrubs and trees native to the southern USA, Asia and the Pacific Islands. They are grown for their attractive foliage, and mostly fragrant white flowers.

O. × burkwoodii (syn. Osmarea burkwoodii) ⌣

A shrub that makes dense, slow growth to 2m high and wide. The dark, shiny, oval green leaves are leathery, 2–5cm long, with finely toothed edges. They form a dense cover on the plant. The small groups of tubular, strongly fragrant white flowers, about 1cm across, appear profusely in early spring. The shrub will grow in full sun or partial shade in most garden soils. Makes a useful, slow-growing hedge as it responds well to clipping. When established it withstands drought, but grows better with some summer water. Useful where the scent can be appreciated. Garden origin.

O. delavayi (syn. Siphonosmanthus delavayi) ⌣

A densely bushy, slow-growing shrub, 2–3m high, with arching branches. The dark green, leathery, oval leaves are 2–3cm long with finely toothed edges. The terminal clusters of four to eight tubular, jasmine-like, fragrant white flowers 1cm across, are produced in great quantity in early spring. A beautiful shrub that can be pruned to shape. Looks attractive throughout the year. Will grow in full sun, although prefers some shade. If grown in chalky soil it may become chlorotic. When established it withstands drought, but grows better with some summer water. Native to western China. It has been well described as one of China's gems.

O. heterophyllus
CHINESE HOLLY, FALSE HOLLY ⌣

An extremely attractive, dense evergreen shrub or small tree up to 6m high and wide. The opposite, holly-like leaves are highly variable: they are usually glossy green or bluish-green, leathery and toothed, 4–6cm long, usually with a few large, spine-tipped teeth. The fragrant flowers 5–6mm across, with a short tube and recurving lobes, are borne in small axillary clusters in late summer and autumn. They are followed by small black fruit. Grow the shrub in full sun or partial shade. Needs little summer water once established. Native to Japan and Taiwan. There are many variegated forms with yellow or creamy-white edges to the leaves, which may burn in summer sun. 'Aureomarginatus' has leaves with golden yellow margins; 'Goshiki' is an attractive form with leaves speckled with cream and pinkish young growth; 'Variegatus' is a compact variety to 3m high and wide, with leaves broadly edged with creamy-white. It makes an attractive hedge.

Osteospermum 'AFRICAN DAISY'
Asteraceae

A genus of about seventy species of annuals, perennials or evergreen subshrubs native to southern Africa. They are grown for their daisy-like flowers produced throughout most of the year. Osteospermums have been much hybridized, and numerous named cultivars have been raised.

Osteospermum jucundum

Osteospermum fruticosum

O. ecklonis (syn. *Dimorphotheca ecklonis*) ⏺⏺

A variable evergreen upright or pros-trate subshrub 60cm high and wide. The narrow-toothed leaves are up to 10cm long. The plant is covered from early autumn until late spring with daisy-like flowers, 6–8cm across, which close at night. The petals are white above and pale blue underneath, with a dark centre. The solitary flowers are borne on long stalks. The plant grows in any well drained soil in full sun. Will withstand neglect and drought once established, but for better flowering give moderate summer water. Ideal for planting in large groups on slopes or along the edges of paths. Native to South Africa.

O. fruticosum (syn. *Dimorphotheca fruticosum*) TRAILING AFRICAN DAISY ⏺⏺

A low, woody perennial spreading rapidly by trailing, rooting branches. Plants will cover 1m or more in a year, growing to 30cm high. The 10cm long, fleshy leaves have several points, and are hairy and almost sticky to touch. The daisy-like flowers are up to 6cm across, white above and violet, lilac or rosy-lilac underneath, with a dark purple centre and large ray florets. Flowers are produced from early autumn until late spring. The plant makes a good groundcover, or looks attractive when tumbling over rocks. Grow in full sun in a well drained soil. Grows well in coastal gardens as it withstands salt-laden sea breezes. Survives summer drought, but will grow and flower better if given moderate water. Cuttings will root easily in the ground if given water. Can become weedy and tired after a few years, when it should be replaced. Native to South Africa.

O. hybrids ⏺⏺

Osteospermums seed and hybridize easily, with many named hybrids raised. The range includes 'Buttermilk', with pale yellow flowers with a dark centre; 'Cannington John', with pink, spoon-shaped petals and a white centre; 'Port Wine' with dark purple flowers; and 'Weetwood', with white petals with deep mauve underneath and a yellow centre. Cultivation is the same as *O. ecklonis*.

O. jucundum (syn. *Dimorphotheca barberae*, *Osteospermum barberae*) ⏺⏺

A straggling, somewhat shrubby ever-green perennial, 60cm or more high and wide. The sparsely toothed, oblong leaves are up to 8cm long. The almost flat, daisy-like flowerheads are 5–8cm across on a stalk up to 20cm long. They are open only during the day. The flowers are normally magenta to lavender pink but it hybridizes easily and many colours have been raised. The flowers are produced from early autumn until late spring. Seedlings vary in height and colour. Cultivation is the same as *O. ecklonis*. Native to South Africa.

O

Paeonia 'PEONY'
Paeoniaceae

A genus of about thirty-three species of clump-forming herbaceous perennials or upright deciduous shrubs known as 'tree peonies'. Native from Europe across to eastern Asia, and western North America. The herbaceous kinds are rhizomatous, with thickened tuberous roots.

Peonies are among the most popular flowering garden plants, and specialist nurseries list a vast number of named hybrids. The beautiful, large, brightly coloured, showy flowers may be single, semi-double or fully double, and are borne in spring and early summer. The colours range from pure white through cream, pink to deep red, even chocolate tones and pure yellow. The flowers are usually upright and solitary, sometimes several to a stem. They make excellent cut flowers. Most of the cultivars are scented and tend to flower more profusely than the species. The large, deep green, divided leaves are attractive even when the plants are not in flower. They may take one to two years to become established, and may not reach their full size for about five years. As the plants resent disturbance they should be left where they are for many years. They grow well in any fertile soil with plenty of organic matter. They will grow in full sun, but the flowers will last longer with some shade. Give regular, generous summer water.

P. broteroi ꙮꙮ
An herbaceous perennial up to 50cm high and wide. The glossy pinnate leaves are divided into nine leaflets. The single, cup-shaped, pink flowers are 10–13cm across, with a boss of yellow stamens. Native to Portugal, southern and western Spain.

P. cambessedesii Majorcan Peony ꙮꙮ
An herbaceous perennial up to 55cm high and wide. The glossy, pinnate, purple-veined leaves are divided into nine leaflets. They are dark green above and have a reddish tint underneath. The beautiful, single, deep rose-pink flowers, 10cm across, have wavy-margined petals and yellow stamens. Native to the Balearic Islands.

P. humilis ꙮꙮ
An herbaceous perennial up to 80cm high and wide with hairy stems and leaf stalks. The pinnate leaves are divided into nine leaflets deeply cut into oblong lobes. The single, purple-red flowers are 10–13cm across, with yellow stamens. Native to south-west Europe.

P. mascula (syn. *P. corallina*) ꙮꙮ
An herbaceous perennial up to 1m high and wide. The pinnate leaves are divided into nine leaflets. The red, pink or occasionally white flowers are 12cm across with a central mass of yellow stamens. Native to southern Europe.

P. officinalis COMMON PEONY ꙮꙮ
An herbaceous perennial up to 70cm high and wide, with upright stems that are slightly hairy at first. The deep green, pinnate leaves are divided into nine leaflets. The fragrant, single, shiny flowers are crimson to rose pink, 15cm across, with yellow stamens. This is the parent of the traditional cottage-garden peonies. Native to Europe.

Pancratium
Amaryllidaceae

A genus of about sixteen species of bulbous perennials native to the Canary Islands, Africa, and the Mediterranean region to tropical Asia. They are grown for their showy, fragrant flowers.

P. maritimum SEA DAFFODIL ꙮ
A perennial, long-necked bulb with strap-shaped basal leaves to 50cm long. They are produced in autumn, and grow through the winter, dying in the heat of summer. In late summer terminal umbels of up to six showy white flowers on stalks to 30cm high are produced. Each strongly fragrant flower has six spreading outer petals and a central cup; up to 10cm across. Grow the bulbs in sandy soil with excellent drainage in full sun. Keep dry in summer when dormant. Ideal for sandy, coastal gardens. The plants can often be seen growing naturally in coastal sand dunes. Native to south-west Europe, the Mediterranean region.

Pandanus 'SCREW PINE'
Pandanaceae

A large genus of at least 600 species of dioecious (male and female flowers on

Pandanus utilis

different plants) evergreen, small to large trees native throughout tropical regions of Africa, India, Asia, Australasia and the Pacific islands. They are not trees in the generally accepted sense, but are monocotyledons distantly affiliated to palms, bananas and lilies.

P. utilis COMMON SCREW PINE

A tropical tree that rarely grows more than 9m high in cultivation, spreading to 4m wide. It has a smooth, cylindrical, trunk-like stem with many aerial roots. The whorls of spreading branches bear rosettes of stiff, dark green, linear, leathery leaves up to 1.8m long and 10cm wide. They bear small red teeth along the margins. As the plant grows older, leaves drop from the lower trunk, leaving foliage only at the top. The flowers are produced in summer, with each male flower spike being 20–30cm long. The female flower develops into a round fruit 15–25cm across, originally green and yellowing as it ripens, with a small amount of edible pulp. Grow the tree in full sun in a well sheltered location in average, well drained soil. When established it withstands drought, but grows better with some summer water. In its native habitat the tree is commonly found growing near the seashore and is therefore tolerant of saline soil and sea spray. A dramatically exotic plant for a tropical-looking, frost-free garden. Native to Madagascar, but widely planted throughout the tropics.

Pandorea
Bignoniaceae

A genus containing seven or eight species of ornamental, evergreen, woody twining climbers native to Malaysia and Australasia. They are related to Tecomaria and Tecoma and have been placed in the genus Bignonia and Tecoma in the past.

P. jasminoides (syn. Bignonia jasminoides) BOWER PLANT

An evergreen climber that can quickly reach 5m high and wide, with the slender stems clothed with leaves to the ground. The pinnate, dark glossy green leaves have five to nine slender, glossy, pointed leaflets, each one 3–5cm long. During summer and autumn the plant is covered with small clusters of attractive trumpet-shaped flowers. Each flower is white to light pink with a darker pink to red throat and spreading lobes 4–5cm across. Grow the climber in a deep rich soil in sun or partial shade, and give protection from wind. Give generous summer water and feeding to keep in flower. Suitable for growing on an arch or wall, or it looks effective when cascading from a tree. Native to northern Australia. There are many cultivars, such as 'Alba' with pure white flowers; 'Lady Di', with white trumpet-shaped blooms; while 'Rosea' has pink flowers with rose pink throats. Showy 'Variegata' has leaves vividly edged with cream; a prolonged period of frost will kill this tender plant.

P. lindleyana
See Clytostoma callistegioides.

P. pandorana (syn. Bignonia pandorana, Tecoma australis) WONGA WONGA VINE

A fast-growing climber to 6m or more high and wide, with slender branching stems. The attractive, glossy green pinnate leaves have three to nine lance-shaped leaflets up to 10cm long. They open a wonderful bronze to reddish-green. From spring until early summer the many-flowered panicles of yellow or pinkish-white flowers cover the plant. Each tubular flower, 2–3cm long, has a throat spotted violet or brown. The climber can take summer drought once established. Grows well in full sun or shade. When flowering is finished, remove the dead flower trusses and tie in the new growth, but give it plenty of room to grow. A delightful plant to trail over a wall or climb over a pergola. Even when not in flower it is worth growing for its foliage. Native to Malaysia, Indonesia, and northern Australia.

P. ricasoliana
See Podranea ricasoliana.

Paraserianthes lophantha
See Albizia lophantha.

Parkinsonia
Caesalpiniaceae

A small genus of about twelve species of deciduous and evergreen spiny shrubs or medium-sized trees, usually with green branches, native to the drier regions of Africa and tropical America. Only one species is commonly grown, for its attractive yellow flowers.

P. aculeata JERUSALEM THORN

A deciduous tree up to 10m high with a spread of up to 8m wide, with a short trunk and a rounded crown. The trunk

P

Pandorea jasminoides

Parkinsonia aculeata

and branches are light green, except in the older wood that becomes grey. Makes rapid growth at first, but slows down with age, making a charmingly translucent tree. The sparse pinnate leaves are 30cm long, with many tiny leaflets that filter the sun without blocking it. The numerous, yellow, five-petalled fragrant flowers are 2cm wide and hang loosely on racemes 8–15cm long; they appear in spring and summer. The flowers are often followed by seedpods, up to 15cm long, which look squashed on the stem. Grow in full sun in any well drained soil. The tree is drought-tolerant once established. It does not grow well with lawn watering, but thrives on alkaline soil and the saline soil near the coast. With its light, airy texture it is a perfect patio tree. Native to the drier regions of southern Mexico and central America.

Passiflora
'GRANADILLA, PASSION FLOWER'
Passifloraceae

A large genus of more than 400 species of evergreen climbers that climb by tendrils, and a few annuals, perennials, shrubs and trees. Most have exotic flowers, and some are important economically for their edible fruit. Native mainly to tropical North and South America, tropical Asia, Australia and New Zealand, but found in all tropical and subtropical parts of the world.

P. antioquiensis
BANANA PASSION FRUIT ⏝⏝
A vigorous climber with slender, branched, downy stems 5m or more high. The leaves are either simple and lance-shaped, the juvenile form, or deeply three-lobed, 10–15cm long and 8cm wide, the mature form, with the undersides covered in fine down. The brilliant red, pendulous flowers are 10cm across with a tube 2–4cm long. They appear singly at the leaf axils for most of the year, but principally at the end of spring and in summer. They may be followed by 10cm-long fruits that are edible and shaped like small bananas. Given average summer water this climber will make rampant growth. One of the easiest and most colourful flowers in the genus. Native to Colombia.

P. caerulea BLUE PASSION FLOWER ⏝⏝
A fast-growing, evergreen or semi-evergreen climber, with stems somewhat angled and grooved, up to 10m or more high. The beautiful, rich green leaves, up to 15cm across, are deeply lobed with three to nine lobes but usually having five. The mildly fragrant flowers, 7–10cm wide, are white tinged with pink or purple with coronas of blue, white and purple bands. They are produced throughout summer and early autumn. The flowers are followed by oval yellow or orange fruit 6cm long; these are edible with red seeds. One of the hardiest passion flowers. Grow in full sun and give moderate summer water. One of the easiest and most widely grown species, probably the most rampant and fastest growing. Native to southern Brazil and northern Argentina. There are several hybrids and cultivars. 'Constance Elliott' has distinctive fragrant white flowers with blue or white filaments; 'Grandiflora' has larger flowers up to 15cm wide.

Passiflora antioquiensis

Passiflora caerulea

P. edulis
PASSION FRUIT, GRANADILLA ♊

A vigorous, semi-evergreen climber with woody angular stems up to 6m high. The ovate, three-lobed leaves are up to 20cm long with wavy edges. The flowers are 6cm across with white petals, and a corona with curly filaments that are purple at the base and white at the tips. They are usually borne singly on long stalks throughout summer. The flowers are attractive, but not particularly showy. They are followed by 8cm round fruit that are deep purple when ripe. The edible pulp is delicious in drinks, fruit salads and ice cream. The climber grows and flowers best in full sun with average summer water. It can be trained over trellises or walls, but may grow into a tangled mess after a few years, when it can be cut back in the early spring or replaced. Easily propagated from seed. Native to southern Brazil, Paraguay and Argentina.

P. manicata ♊
A strong-growing climber with angled stems growing up to 3m high. The glossy, three-lobed leaves are 10cm long and densely hairy underneath. The saucer-shaped flowers, 10cm across, are produced from spring to autumn. They are bright red with short purple-blue and white coronas. They are followed by oval, green fruit, 5cm long.

The climber grows and flowers best in full sun with moderate summer water. Prune occasionally to keep tidy. Native to Venezuela to Peru.

P. quadrangularis GIANT GRANADILLA ♊
A sparsely branched, fast-growing climber that can grow to 15m or more with an equal spread. The stems are four-angled. The rich green leaves, 10–25cm long, are broadly ovate with

Passiflora edulis

abrupt, slender points. The 12cm-wide, nodding, bowl-shaped flowers are red, violet and white. The prominent coronas of wavy filaments, 6cm long, are banded with violet and white. The flowers are produced from summer to autumn and may be followed by edible fruit. The fruits of this species are the largest of the genus, and can be up to 30cm long. They are oblong in shape and become orange when ripe, containing sweetly acidic pulp. The plant is widely grown in the tropics for its fruit. Grows well in full sun in frost-free gardens. Give moderate summer water. Prune occasionally to keep it tidy. When in full flower this climber makes a wonderful sight, and the edible fruit is a bonus. Native to Central and South America, West Indies but grown throughout the tropics.

Passiflora quadrangularis

P. racemosa RED PASSION FLOWER ♊
A vigorous climber with woody, four-angled stems that climb by tendrils up to 5m high. The leathery, glossy, three-lobed leaves are up to 10cm long on mature plants. Juvenile plants have unlobed leaves. The 10cm-wide, bowl-shaped flowers are borne in pendulous clusters to 30cm long. The narrow petals are rosy-crimson and spreading, with a corona having outer filaments in purple with white tips, and short, bright red inner ones. The flowers are produced for most of the summer and autumn, and are followed by oblong green fruit, up to 8cm long, with a leathery skin. Grows well in full sun in frost-free gardens. Give moderate summer water and occasional pruning to keep it tidy. When in full flower this climber makes a wonderful sight. Native to eastern Brazil.

P

Paulownia
Scrophulariaceae

A small genus of six species of deciduous trees native to east Asia. They are usually fast-growing, with large leaves and attractive flowers.

P. tomentosa FOXGLOVE TREE ♪♪♪

A fast-growing tree with a rounded top 9–12m high, and silvery-grey smooth bark. Trees can vary greatly in size and leaf dimensions. The heart-shaped, light green leaves are sometimes shallowly lobed, 12–25cm long and wide. They are hairy above and below. Brown flower buds form in autumn, and open before the leaves appear in early spring. The fragrant, trumpet-shaped, mauve flowers, 5cm long, have purple and yellow markings inside. They are held in upright panicles to 30cm long at the ends of the stems. The trees make a beautiful sight when in flower. Grow the tree in full sun in a rich, damp, well drained soil. It flowers well in areas with long hot summers. Although it is quite frost hardy, it is unsuited to areas where late spring frosts are common, as this will cause the buds to drop off. The brittleness of the wood may cause the branches to break, and strong wind will damage the large leaves. Tolerant of atmospheric pollution. With its wide crown, dense shade and shallow surface roots, this is not a tree to garden under. Native to China.

Paurotis wrightii
See *Acoelorrhaphe wrightii.*

Pelargonium
Geraniaceae

A large genus of about 280 species of mainly evergreen perennials, some annuals, succulents, subshrubs and shrubs native mostly to South Africa. They are commonly but wrongly known as 'Geraniums'. Countless cultivars have been raised from about twenty species to give the popular garden plants we have today. Many authoritative books have been written about pelargoniums. They all have the ability to survive periods of drought and neglect, but flower better if given some summer water.

Pelargonium × domesticum 'Grand Slam'

P. × domesticum
REGAL PELARGONIUM ♪ or ♪♪

A bushy, evergreen perennial with erect or spreading short-jointed stems to 1m high. The crinkled, dark green, heart-shaped leaves are 5–10cm wide. The large, showy clusters of usually single, but sometimes double flowers are up to 5cm across. They come in single or combined shades of white, pink, red, orange, lavender or purple. The flowers usually only appear for about a month in spring, although some may appear throughout summer. Garden origin. 'Grand Slam' is one of the most widely grown. It has red, satiny flowers to 5cm across, with dark purple internal markings. It makes an excellent pot plant.

P. 'Graveolens'
LEMON GERANIUM ♪ or ♪♪

A vigorous evergreen perennial with strong stems to 45cm high, with an equal spread forming a dense bush. The rough, deeply cut and lobed leaves with a central bronze marking can be up to 10cm long, and have a strong lemon scent. These are the source of oil of geranium. The pink or mauve, star-like flowers are 2cm across in clusters throughout spring and summer.

P. × hortorum COMMON OR ZONAL
GERANIUM ♪ or ♪♪

An erect, shrubby, succulent-stemmed, evergreen perennial up to 1m or more, with older plants becoming woody. Leaves rounded, 8–14cm wide, velvety-hairy and soft to touch. They are deep green, but are often zoned with dark bronze-green, bi-coloured or multi-coloured. The flowers are 3–5cm across in showy clusters, usually on a long stalk. They come in many vivid colours, primarily scarlet, red, purple, pink, salmon, white or bi-colours, both single and double. There is a vast number of named varieties. As they flower throughout the summer months they are familiar as pot plants, in window-boxes and in garden beds. Named varieties are grown from cuttings, but many F1 hybrids are grown from seed. 'Frank Headley' has variegated leaves with salmon flowers, 'Caroline Schmidt' has variegated leaves with bright red flowers.

P. odoratissimum
APPLE GERANIUM ♪ or ♪♪

A bushy evergreen perennial up to 30cm high that can spread to 60cm

Pelargonium graveolens

Pelargonium × hortorum 'Frank Headley'

wide. The pale green leaves are rounded, 4–5cm across, with crinkled edges, and are apple-scented when crushed. From spring to summer the plant is covered in clusters of three to ten star-shaped, white flowers, 1–2cm across.

P. peltatum
IVY-LEAVED GERANIUM ☽ or ☽☽
A bushy evergreen perennial with trailing brittle stems to 1m or more long. The stiff, glossy leaves, 5–8cm wide, have pointed lobes. The round clusters of single or double flowers, 2–3cm wide, are produced throughout summer. They come in a wide range of colours from white, pink, rose, red to lavender, and many combinations. They can be used as groundcover or as climbers, but are mostly grown as hanging plants. They look their best when seen tumbling down over a wall

Pelargonium pelatatum

or hanging from pots or containers. 'L'Elegante' has bluish-green leaves with a white edging; these turn purple if kept very dry. It bears white or lilac single flowers in clusters to 8cm across.

Pennisetum
Poaceae

A genus of over eighty species of annual or perennial clump-forming grasses found in most parts of the world. The plants bear appealing bottle-brush flowers in summer and autumn. They are among the most graceful of ornamental grasses.

P. alopecuroides
CHINESE FOUNTAIN GRASS ☽☽
A clump-forming, densely tufted, perennial grass 90cm–1.2m high. The flat, linear, pointed, bright green leaves are 30–60cm long. They turn yellow in autumn and brown in winter. In summer it produces brown or pinkish, bristly, bottle-brush flower spikes 20cm long on stems 1.2m tall. The plant thrives in full sun or partial shade in most well drained soil. When established it withstands some drought, but grows much better with some summer water. An attractive grass that looks good in a mixed border or when covering a bank. The flowers are useful for both fresh and dried arrangements. Native to Asia and western Australia. 'Hameln' is a dwarf, early flowering form, with greyish-brown spikes to 12cm long.

P. villosum (syn. P. longistylum)
FEATHERTOP, ABYSSINIAN FOUNTAIN GRASS ☽☽
A perennial grass with clustered stems to 60cm high and wide. The upright or arching stems bear mid-green leaves 15cm long. In late summer the plant produces gracefully nodding, softly furry, cylindrical, plume-like flower spikes 5cm long. They start white and become golden when mature. The plant thrives in full sun or partial shade in most well drained soil. When established it withstands some drought, but grows much better with some summer water. Although a perennial it is often treated as an annual. Wonderful for flower arrangements. Native to north-east Africa. It has

become a weed in parts of Australia.

Penstemon
Scrophulariaceae

A large genus of about 250 species of deciduous and evergreen perennials or subshrubs, one species native to northeast Asia, the rest to North America. Specialist nurseries have produced numerous, bushy, free-flowering hybrids that come in a wide range of colours.

P. barbatus SCARLET BEARD-TONGUE ☽
A hardy, erect perennial with an open, rather sprawling habit to 1m high, with evergreen basal leaves and deciduous stems. The lance-shaped, bright green leaves are up to 15cm long. Loose spikes of pendant, tubular red flowers 2–4cm long appear throughout summer. Many colourful, named varieties have been raised from this species. The plant thrives in full sun or partial shade in most well drained soil. When established it withstands some drought, but grows and flowers much better with occasional summer water. Usually a fairly short-lived plant of between three to four years. Native to western USA to Mexico.

Penstemon hybrids

P. hybrids
BORDER OR GARDEN PENSTEMON ☽☽
A compact, herbaceous perennial with upright stems to 1m or more high. The dark green, lance-shaped leaves are up to 10cm long. Spectacular spikes of large, tubular flowers up to 5cm long appear throughout summer. They come in a wide range of colours, predominately blue, red or purple. Numerous named hybrids have been raised, all easy to grow. If cut back after the main flush of flowers fade, they will flower again. They thrive in full sun or partial

P

shade in most well drained soil. When established they withstand some drought, but grow much better with regular summer water. Garden origin. Some hybrids include 'Alice Hindley', with pale lilac-blue flowers with white inside; 'Firebird', with bell-shaped flowers 7cm long; 'Hewell Pink Bedder' with reddish-pink flowers with shiny leaves; and 'Snow Storm' with white flowers.

Perovskia 'RUSSIAN SAGE'
Lamiaceae

A small genus of seven species of deciduous subshrubs native from central Asia to the Himalayas. They are grown for their prominent grey stems, aromatic leaves and spikes of blue flowers. The stems are mostly square in cross-section.

Perovskia atriplicifolia 'Blue Spire'

P. atriplicifolia ⌡

A hardy, woody-based, multi-stemmed subshrub with stiff, upright-growing stems up to 1m high, spreading as wide. The stems are a greyish-white. The aromatic, deeply cut, grey-green, narrow leaves are up to 6cm long. The many-branched terminal panicles, to 30cm long, of small, tubular, violet-blue flowers appear from midsummer until autumn. These form a haze above the foliage. The plant grows well in full sun in very well drained soil. Give little summer water once established; indeed too much coddling in the form of rich soil or too much water means that when it starts flowering, the stems flop, topple over or lie down. An ideal plant for the Mediterranean garden as it is hardy, drought-resistant and likes summer heat. It is useful for coastal gardens as it withstands salt-laden sea breezes. Cut down to ground level in early spring before the new shoots appear. Native to Afghanistan. 'Blue Spire' has larger spikes of flowers up to 30cm long, and the richest-coloured flowers.

Persea
Lauraceae

A large genus of about 150 species of evergreen trees and shrubs widely distributed throughout tropical and warm temperate regions. Only one species, *P. americana*, is widely grown for fruit; others are grown in tropical regions for their ornamental foliage. Most of them have greenish, reddish or shiny young shoots.

P. americana AVOCADO ⌡⌡⌡

A much-branched, round-headed tree, 6–10m high, spreading as wide. The large, leathery, elliptic or oval leaves are 10–30cm long and glossy. The terminal clusters of many small, greenish flowers appear during spring. The large, fleshy apple- or pear-shaped edible fruit is about 10cm across, with green or purplish skin, and contains a single large seed. The flesh is greenish-yellow with a buttery consistency of high nutritional value, rich in vitamins containing 7–23 per cent fat. As male and female parts of the flower are open at different times on the tree it is best to grow more than one tree for good fruit production. Many people grow them from seed, but although they may make large trees, only grafted plants produce fruit of good quality. The tree grows fast in well drained soil that is rich in humus, and generous applications of organic feed help. The main requirement is good drainage: most roots are in the top 60cm of soil, so water lightly and frequently, enough to keep that layer moist but not waterlogged. Protection from wind is also very important. Trees should bear fruit when four to eight years old, but even a light frost will kill the flowers, although not harm the plant. Even if fruit is not produced, this makes an attractive, bold-leaved tree, ideal as a specimen. Originally native to central America, but widely cultivated. There are many varieties: 'Bacon' has medium-sized fruit of good quality, 'Hass' has large purple (almost black) fruit.

Pseudogynoxys chenopoides
See *Senecio confusus*.

Petrea
Verbenaceae

A genus of about thirty species of deciduous and semi-evergreen shrubs and twining creepers native to Mexico, the West Indies and to Brazil. These spectacular, frost-tender plants give an impressive show of flowers.

Persea americana

Petrea volubilis

P. volubilis QUEEN'S WREATH ♪♪♪

A tender, semi-evergreen climber with woody or wiry open stems which, under ideal conditions, will reach 12m high and wide. The almost evergreen leaves are rough-surfaced and elliptic; they are 10cm long. They are deep green to grey-green above, and paler underneath with a prominent midrib. The stunning violet-blue, tubular, star-like flowers appear profusely on 30cm-long racemes cascading from the new season's growth. The flowers appear in flushes several times a year during warm weather. This frost-tender plant has been described as being among the world's loveliest climbers, and is well worth seeking out. It will grow in sun, but may need some midday shade. Grow against a warm wall to give it support and protection from wind and shelter. Give it copious amounts of water and feeding during summer. Native to Mexico, central America and the West Indies.

Philadelphus 'MOCK ORANGE'
Hydrangeaceae

A genus of about sixty-five species of mainly deciduous shrubs. They are mostly erect, but with curving branches. Native to north and central America, east Asia and Europe. They are cultivated for their showy, usually fragrant flowers.

P. mexicanus
EVERGREEN MOCK ORANGE ♪♪♪

A spreading shrub to 3m high and wide, with long, supple branches. The evergreen, oval to lance-shaped leaves are up to 11cm long and sometimes sparsely toothed. The clusters of two to three, strongly rose-scented, creamy-white, cup-shaped flowers, 4cm across, are produced in spring and early summer. There are both double and single forms. Grow the shrub in full sun or partial shade. Use as a climber or groundcover. With support it can reach up to 6m high. Give it a moderate amount of summer water. If pruning is needed it should be done after flowering, as the flowers appear on the wood of the previous year. Native to Mexico and Guatemala. 'Rose Syringa' has fragrant white flowers with a purple blotch in the centre.

Philodendron
Araceae

A large genus of perhaps 500 species of tropical perennials that are often epiphytic, evergreen shrubs, or small trees and climbers with aerial roots. Native to Mexico, the West Indies and central and tropical South America.

P. bipinnatifidum
TREE PHILODENDRON ♪♪♪

A large, tree-like shrub with a single stout stem that may recline with age, up to 5m high and spreading to 5m wide. The huge, waxy green, stiff leaves are up to 1m long, with a stalk of the same length. They are heart-shaped, deeply bipinnate, with ten to twelve segments each side of a prominent midrib. The lobes are narrow, and divided again with a long lobe at the apex. Old plants may develop greenish inflorescence up to 30cm long. This shrub thrives best in sun with some midday shade, but will grow in considerable shade. Grows best as a large specimen, or excellent in a large container. Give it generous summer water. A truly exotic-looking plant; most effective when used for a tropical jungle look near a swimming pool. Grow in fertile, humus-rich, well drained soil. Native to southern Brazil and Paraguay.

Phlomis
Lamiaceae

A genus of about 100 species of mainly low-growing shrubs, subshrubs and sage-like herbaceous perennials native to Europe, north Africa and Asia. They have attractive silver-grey foliage, and showy, tubular flowers in dense clusters.

P. chrysophylla ♪

An evergreen shrub up to 1m high and wide, with stiff, spreading branches. The oval leaves, to 8cm long, are grey-green when young, taking on a golden tinge after midsummer. Golden-yellow, tubular flowers, up to 5cm long, appear in spikes or pairs along the stem in early summer. To grow and flower well the shrub requires full sun and soil with good drainage. It will even tolerate poor soil. Once established it needs little summer water. Effective when massed in a border, making good foliage plants even when not in flower. Native to south-west Asia.

P. fruticosa JERUSALEM SAGE ♪

A much-branched, evergreen shrub with grey-green stems that grows up to 1m or more high, spreading to 1.5m wide. The grey-green, ovate, lance-shaped leaves are 10cm or more long, and woolly underneath with wrinkled

Philodendron bipinnatifidum

edges. The bright yellow, tubular flowers, 3–4cm long, appear in whorls containing twenty to thirty flowers spaced along the upper half of the stems. These appear in spring and early summer. The shrub is drought-tolerant, but grows better with some summer water. Grows well in a variety of soil types in full sun, but it can tolerate light shade. The variety 'Compacta' has smaller leaves and is lower growing. Native to the Mediterranean.

P. italica ☽

A stiffly upright, soft-wooded shrub with white hairy stems up to 1m high and 60cm wide. The grey-woolly, dull green, lance-shaped leaves are up to 10cm long. The dull purple or pink tubular flowers are produced in whorls at the ends of the branches in summer. It is a rather untidy-looking plant. Like other phlomis, it requires full sun and good drainage. It will tolerate poor soil and needs little summer water once established. Native to Balearic Islands.

Phoenix
Arecaceae

A small genus of perhaps seventeen species of dioecious (male and female flowers on different plants) palms which can be single or cluster-stemmed. Native to tropical and subtropical Africa, Asia and the Canary Islands. Many species are widely planted as ornamentals, and one, the date palm, is of major commercial significance. Palms are used to give a tropical look to a garden, and are easy to move even when mature, giving immediate effect.

P. canariensis CANARY ISLAND PALM ☽

A solitary, stout, heavy-trunked palm 15m or more high, growing slowly until it forms a trunk, then speeding up. The trunk can become 1m wide with age. It is crowned with many arching leaf fronds which may reach 6m in length. The deep green leaflets, to 30cm long, grow off the central rib, almost meeting, with a sharp point at the tip. Each leaflet is folded lengthways to form a V shape. Older trees produce clusters of small, yellow, bowl-shaped flowers in large hanging bunches to 1m long in summer. They are followed by large clusters of small, round fruit that ripen to orange. The palm is easy to

Phoenix canariensis

grow, requiring a moist soil when young but needing little summer water once established. Grow in full sun. It is frost-hardy and will thrive in poor soils, but prefers good drainage. Ideal for coastal gardens. Bottom leaves need to be removed to keep this palm looking neat. One of the most popular palms in temperate, subtropical and tropical regions, used extensively for avenues or as street trees where it makes a truly impressive sight. Native to the Canary Islands.

P. dactylifera DATE PALM ☽

A tall, slender-trunked palm that with age may reach to 18m high. Young plants tend to produce suckers, though these are usually removed. The leaves are up to 3m long, with leaflets to 30cm long. They are grey-green to almost silvery or bluish, and the bases are armed with stout spines. Bowl-shaped cream or yellow flowers appear in panicles to 2m long in summer. The great pendant fruit clusters contain many cylindrical fruit, which ripen to brown. Not only are they edible, but delicious, too! The trees have been grown for their fruit for thousands of years. Although the tree is frost hardy, fruit is only produced in areas with a hot, dry climate. As it is indigenous to desert areas, it withstands drought once established, but grows better with some summer water. It is an excellent tree for coastal gardens, tolerating salt-laden winds. If fruit is required, both male

and female plants are needed. Probably native to north Africa and the Middle East, but as it has been cultivated for so long its origin is obscure.

P. reclinata SENEGAL DATE PALM ☽☽☽

A beautiful, clustering palm to 9m high. The clumps consist of many slender trunks curving away from each other; a well grown plant may have twenty or more trunks. Each one is ringed and usually carries twenty to thirty leaves. Each leaf – up to 2.5m long – has many bright green leaflets growing at several

Phoenix dactylifera

Phoenix reclinata

angles, and has orange-coloured bases to the leaf stems. Bowl-shaped cream or yellow flowers appear in panicles to 1.5m long in summer. These are followed by rather dry, orange-red to black fruit, to 2cm long, that are edible but rather astringent. It puts out both suckers and flowers while still very young, even before it has developed a trunk. Grow in full sun in a deep, rich soil with mulches and dressings of high nitrogen fertilizer. In its native habitat the tree grows along riverbanks, so give it generous summer water. Although it grows in tropical regions it is quite tolerant of cold and frost. The tree is a perfect candidate for planting near ponds or swimming pools; the gracefully reclining trunks give a wonderful tropical look. Native to tropical Africa.

Phoenix roebelenii

P. roebelenii PYGMY DATE PALM, MINIATURE DATE PALM

A beautiful, single-trunked palm that grows slowly to only 2m high. It has a relatively thin trunk with a rounded crown of fifty or more leaves. The dark green fronds, 1–1.2m long, are generally curved, or arch gracefully with many regularly spaced, deep green, glossy leaflets to 20cm long. The leaves are unusual in being lightweight and soft in texture. Mature trees produce bowl-shaped cream or yellow flowers in panicles to 45cm long in summer. Plants will grow in a sunny or shady position and are frost-hardy. In its native habitat the tree grows along riverbanks, so give it generous summer water. Grow in a humus-rich soil with dressings of high nitrogen fertilizer. When young it makes an excellent pot or container plant for the terrace. Native to Vietnam, Laos, Cambodia and Thailand.

Phormium 'FLAX LILY'
Agavaceae

A genus of probably two species of large evergreen perennials native to New Zealand and Norfolk Island. They are called 'New Zealand' flax, as the leaves – among the toughest in the world – produce a tough fibre that can be used for making twine and rope.

P. tenax NEW ZEALAND FLAX

A large, bold, clump-forming evergreen perennial up to 4m high and 2m or more wide. It is grown mainly for its attractive leaves, perhaps 3m long and up to 15cm wide, often with a V-shape. They are dark or brownish-green above, and bluish-green underneath with reddish margins, often splitting at the tip. The leaves grow stiffly upright from the base, giving a bold appearance. The flowers are carried in clusters on long-branched stems up to 3m high, appearing in early summer. Each tubular flower is dull red, 3–5cm long, and secretes much nectar. The plant is best grown in full sun, but will take some shade. It is not fussy about the soil type, and can grow in wet conditions just as well as dry. It is useful for coastal gardens, as it tolerates salt-laden sea breezes. The plants look good when grown in containers. They make good architectural plants that are attractive when grown near a swimming pool. Numerous cultivars have been raised, with bronze, purple-red, and dark purple to bronze leaves. Many are dwarf forms, only growing up to 1m high. 'Variegatum' has creamy-white or yellow markings along the leaf edges, making a bold and dramatic plant in the garden. The paler forms may burn in full summer sun, so these are best grown in partial shade and given more water.

Phormium tenax 'Variegatum'

Photinia
Rosaceae

A genus of about sixty species of large, mainly evergreen or deciduous shrubs and small trees native from the Himalayas to south and east Asia. The evergreen shrubs are grown for their brilliant new leaves and attractive flower clusters.

P. × fraseri

A variable hybrid, making an upright, vigorous, evergreen shrub or tree up to 4m high and as wide. The dark glossy green, leathery lance-shaped leaves are 10–20cm long. The new growth is bright bronze-red and very showy. In mid to late spring the small white flowers appear in clusters, up to 15cm wide. Grow the shrub in full sun with moderate summer water. As it is heat-resistant it is ideal for the hottest gardens. Makes an attractive hedge, as it withstands clipping. An attractive plant throughout the year, but especially in spring with its flush of new growth. Makes a useful screen or background. Garden origin. 'Red Robin', a spectacular clone raised in New Zealand, is more compact, and has sharply toothed leaves that are brilliant red when young.

Photinia x fraseri 'Red Robin'

P. glabra JAPANESE PHOTINIA ↴↴

A rounded evergreen shrub with dense growth to 3m high and wide. The oblong, dark green, leathery leaves are bronze-red when young and up to 9cm long. In early summer, small white flowers with a hawthorn fragrance appear in clusters to 10cm wide. They are followed by red to black berries. The shrub grows best in full sun, with moderate summer water. It can be clipped in summer in order to encourage the new bronze-red growth. Makes an attractive hedge. Native to Japan.

Phygelius 'CAPE FUCHSIA'
Scrophulariaceae

A small genus of two species of evergreen or semi-evergreen subshrubs native to South Africa. They are grown for their large clusters of fuchsia-like flowers.

P. aequalis ↴↴

An upright, suckering, bushy shrub to 1m high and wide, with four-angled stems. The ovate, dark green leaves are up to 10cm long. Throughout summer it produces upright pyramidal spikes, to 25cm long, of dusky pink-red tubular flowers with an attractive yellow throat. These short-lived shrubs will tolerate drought but prefer moist, fertile, free-draining soil. It will grow in full sun but prefers some shade. Remove the dead flowerheads to encourage further flowering. 'Yellow Trumpet' is a striking form, with pale creamy-yellow flowers and pale green leaves.

P. capensis CAPE FIGWORT ↴↴

An upright, suckering, bushy shrub to 1m high, with a more sprawling habit than *P. aequalis*. The young branches have a purple tint. The opposite, ovate, dark green leaves are up to 12cm long. Throughout summer it produces upright, pyramidal loose spikes of flowers to 60cm long. Each tubular flower is orange to deep red, and yellow-throated; up to 5cm long. The shrub will grow in sun but prefers partial shade. Although it will survive with little summer water, it grows and flowers better with moderate water. Grow in a fertile, free-draining soil.

P. × *rectus* ↴↴

A hybrid between the two above species, which has produced many interesting named varieties. 'African Queen' has pendant pale red flowers; 'Devil's Tears' has deep pink flowers with yellow throats; 'Moonraker' has pale creamy-yellow flowers; 'Salmon Leap' has orange flowers. All require similar conditions to the above.

Phyllostachys
Pohcehe

A genus of about eighty species of tall, graceful, medium to large, evergreen, hardy bamboos native to east Asia and the Himalayas. All have creeping rhizomes that send up new shoots some distance from the plant each year, in time forming large clumps that can be invasive.

P. aurea GOLDEN BAMBOO ↴ or ↴↴

A bamboo that forms clumps, with stiffly upright canes growing from 2–4m high, with wide-growing rhizomes so it has an indefinite spread. The hollow canes are flattened on one side, 3cm thick, and brilliant yellow with the internodes closely spaced. The canes are very hard when mature. The leaves are narrowly lance-shaped, 5–10cm long, and yellowish to golden green. This bamboo is characterized by the cup-shaped swelling underneath each node, and the crowding of the nodes at the base of each cane. The young shoots that are produced in spring are edible. The dense foliage makes it a good plant for a screen. Grow in full sun or partial shade. The plant can take much drought, but grows better if given water during the fast growing season in spring. Native to south-east China.

P. nigra BLACK BAMBOO ↴ or ↴↴

A clump-forming bamboo with arching slender canes 2.5–3.5m high. The canes are green at first, becoming speckled

Photinia glabra

Phyllostachys aurea

with dark brown or black, then becoming an even jet black in their second or third year. The slim branchlets carry many lance-shaped, dark green leaves about 8cm long. The young shoots that are produced in spring are edible. This attractive bamboo enjoys a sunny position, but grows best with some afternoon shade where summers are hot. Can withstand drought, but grows better if given water during spring. Native to east and central China.

Physalis 'GROUND CHERRY'
Solanaceae

A genus of about eighty species of bushy annuals or perennials that sometimes form rhizomes. They are found worldwide, but come mainly from North and South America.

P. peruviana CAPE GOOSEBERRY ☽☽
A tender perennial sometimes grown as an annual, which forms a much-branched bush, to 40cm high, with hairy soft stems. The hairy, triangular leaves are 5–10cm long and are slightly toothed. The 2cm-wide, bell-shaped yellowish flowers with purple markings are produced from the leaf axils in spring. They are followed by green spherical calyxes that enclose the fruit,

turning brown and papery as the fruit ripens. The small orange fruit is edible, rather sweet, and can be used fresh, in pies, or in preserves and pickles. The plant grows best in a warm position in full sun or partial shade. Productive in long hot summers if given moderate water. The fruits contain many seeds which germinate readily, so seedlings can appear anywhere in the garden. Native to tropical South America.

Phytolacca 'POKEWEED'
Phytolaccaceae

A small genus of about twenty-five perennials, shrubs and trees native to the tropical and subtropical regions of Africa, Asia and North to South America. They have large leaves and spikes of tiny flowers.

P. dioica
TREE POKE, UMBRA TREE ☽ or ☽☽
A large, vigorous, evergreen, soft-wooded tree, with male and female flowers produced on separate plants. It makes a heavy-limbed tree, 15–20m high, with a thick trunk and a huge swollen base. The leaves are shiny, soft and oblong, and up to 15cm long; they have a red midrib when young. The small flowers are white or greenish, in pendant terminal racemes 10cm long, and appear in early spring. They are followed by dark purple, berry-like fruit on female plants. Grow the tree in

full sun in a position where the base has room to develop, as with age this can be huge, up to 18m wide. It is formed by the extraordinary lower trunk and surface roots, which are massive. Drought-tolerant, but grows better if given some summer water. This outstanding plant makes a wonderful shade tree for the larger garden. The canopy is massive, open and graceful. Native to South America, but widely grown in the Mediterranean region.

Phytolacca dioica

Pinus 'PINE'
Pinaceae

A genus of about 120 often tall, evergreen coniferous trees widely distributed throughout the northern hemisphere. Pines are valuable timber trees, produce edible nuts, and include many ornamental and shade trees. They need to be grown in soil that has

Phytolacca dioica

P

very good drainage. Many grow naturally on rocky slopes or in pure sand. They are pioneer trees for difficult dry terrain, but are vulnerable to pollution. They should be grown in full sun.

P. halepensis ALEPPO PINE ☽

A conical tree 10–20m high, with silver-grey bark when young. With age it becomes more or less umbrella-shaped to 6m wide. The bright green, needle-shaped leaves are in pairs, very distant, sparse and slightly twisted, to 10cm long. The cones are pendulous or with downward-curved stalks, and 5–12cm long; they remain on the tree for three years before opening. An important and widespread tree, extremely drought-tolerant, and will grow on dry, shallow, chalky soils. Native to the Mediterranean region where it forms extensive forests.

P. pinaster MARITIME PINE ☽

A tall, pyramidal tree, 20–30m high, with spreading branches 6–8m wide. Distinguished by its reddish trunk and brown shoots. The leaves are in pairs, thick, stiff and slightly twisted, 10–20cm long. The large cones are 8–18cm long, in clusters, bright shining brown when ripe, and more or less sharp pointed. The cones remain on the trees for several years. The tree is extremely drought-tolerant and will

grow on sandy soil in coastal conditions. Often grown for reclaiming sand dunes. A valuable source of resin, turpentine and timber. Native to the western Mediterranean region.

P. pinea STONE PINE, UMBRELLA PINE ☽

A conical tree when young, but becoming a tall one, to 18m or more high. With age it develops a characteristic dense, flat-topped or umbrella-shaped head. The dark green needle leaves grow in pairs to 15cm long; they are well spaced, stiff, and slightly twisted, with sharp points. The shining, nut-brown female cones are up to 15cm long and contain large, edible seed kernels, the 'pignolia' or pine nuts of commerce. A tree particularly suitable to sandy soils in coastal areas, as it withstands heat and drought. Careful staking is needed when young. Also useful as a container plant when young. Native to southern Europe and Turkey.

Pistacia 'PISTACHIO'
Anarcardiaceae

A small genus of about ten species of dioecious (male and female flowers on different plants) evergreen and deciduous trees and shrubs native to dry habitats in the Mediterranean region, central Asia and south-west USA. They are grown for their attractive foliage, autumn berries or nuts.

Pinus pinea

Pistacia lentiscus

P. atlantica MOUNT ATLAS MASTIC ☽

A semi-evergreen or deciduous ornamental tree to 18m high, with slow to moderate growth. The glossy, medium green, odd pinnate leaves consist of seven to eleven leaflets; up to 7cm long. The small flowers are characterized by not having petals; these are followed by berry-like fruit, 1cm across, if male trees are nearby; they are red at first, turning purple when ripe. Established trees need no summer water, and can take great heat and strong winds. Grow in full sun. Trees only drop their leaves in cold winters. Native to north Africa and the Mediterranean region to Pakistan.

P. lentiscus LENTISC, MASTIC TREE ☽

An evergreen, dense shrub or small bushy tree to 3m high and wide. The leathery, pinnate leaves have six to eight ovate, glossy green leaflets to 10cm long, with winged stalks and midribs. Panicles of inconspicuous male and female flowers are produced in spring. These are followed by small red fruit that ripen to black. Grow in full sun. Established shrubs need no summer water and can take great heat. Useful as screening in hot, dry gardens. Thrives in poor soil. The sap yields mastic, an aromatic resin used in medicine and varnish. Native to the Mediterranean region.

P. terebinthus
TREBINTH, TURPENTINE TREE ☽

A deciduous, freely branching shrub or tree 2–5m high and wide. The pinnate leaves, 10–20cm long, are aromatic; they have three to six pairs of glossy dark green leaflets. They are oval or lance-shaped, with untoothed margins and a terminal leaflet. In spring, greenish-red flower clusters appear on the previous year's growth. These are

Pittosporum crassifolium

followed by small reddish fruits that turn purplish-brown. Grow in full sun. Established shrubs need no summer water and can take great heat. Thrives in poor soil. The sap yields a sweet-scented gum used in tanning and formerly in turpentine. Native to the Mediterranean region.

P. vera PISTACHIO ☙
A spreading deciduous tree to 10m high and wide. The pinnate leaves have one to five pairs of oval leaflets, that are large and downy when young. The dense panicles of inconspicuous, brownish-green, unisexual flowers are produced in spring. These are followed by clusters of oblong reddish fruit 2–3cm long. Inside the husk is the pistachio nut of commerce. The trees thrive under long hot summers with low humidity, but need moderately cold winters to satisfy their chilling requirements. Often seen where olives and almonds grow. Trees need no summer water once established. Grow in full sun. Native to western Asia, but long cultivated in the Mediterranean region.

Pittosporum
Pittosporaceae

A large genus of about 200 species of evergreen trees and shrubs native to Australasia, southern Africa and Asia. They make attractive ornamental garden plants, thriving especially well near the sea. Several have small fragrant flowers, but they are chiefly grown for their foliage.

P. crassifolium KARO ☙
An evergreen shrub or small tree 5–10m high spreading to 5m wide, which can be pruned annually to keep it smaller. The upright stems are covered in white felt when young. The bark is smooth dark grey. The oval leaves are 5–7cm long, thick, leathery, deep green above and covered in white felt underneath. The terminal clusters of small dark crimson or purple flowers 1cm wide appear in spring. Female plants produce pale green seedpods. An excellent, tough plant for dry or windy sites, making a dense screen. Good in coastal areas as it withstands salt-laden sea breezes. The shrub is fairly drought-resistant, but responds well to some summer water. Native to New Zealand. 'Compactum' is a smaller, denser shrub growing to 2m high.

P. tenuifolium KOHUHU ☙☙
An evergreen shrub or small tree rarely reaching 5m high, with an equal spread. The pale green, 7cm, oblong undulated leaves are attractively set on black twigs. The small, dark purple, bell-shaped, honey-scented flowers appear in spring. Grow the shrub in full sun or partial shade. A good foliage plant for cutting for floral arrangements. Good for coastal gardens as hedging, or can be trained to form a small tree. Fairly drought-tolerant, but grows better with some summer water. Native to New Zealand. There are many variegated and coloured-leaved forms with silver, yellow or bronze purple leaves. Many of these tend to burn in summer heat unless grown in shade.

Pittosporum tobira 'Variegatum'

P. tobira JAPANESE MOCK ORANGE ☙
A rather slow-growing, evergreen, broad, dense shrub or small tree up to 5m high and 3m wide. The dark grey, smooth trunk is rarely straight, giving it a picturesque look. The ovate, leathery, glossy, dark green leaves are 5–13cm long, with recurved margins and lighter-coloured midribs. They are clustered near the ends of the branches in whorls. The spectacular clusters of creamy-white, strongly scented flowers, 2–3cm wide, appear on the branch tips in spring. They age to deep yellow, filling the air with the fragrance of orange blossom. The shrub makes a good hedge or screen, and is especially useful for coastal gardens as it withstands salt-laden sea breezes. Grows well in full sun, but also grows in partial shade. Drought-resistant once established. Native to southern Japan, Korea and China. The variety 'Variegatum' is a beautiful plant, the grey-green leaves having an irregular creamy-white margin; it grows to only 1.5m high. Makes a most attractive hedge that will grow in partial shade.

Pittosporum tobira

P. undulatum VICTORIAN BOX, AUSTRALIAN MOCK ORANGE ☙
An evergreen tree that makes moderately fast growth up to 5m, then slow growth to around 8m high with an equal spread. The undulated leaves are dark shiny green, 7–15cm long. They are fairly thin, oblong-lance-shaped and paler underneath, with a paler coloured midrib. The terminal clusters of creamy-white, bell-shaped, sweetly scented flowers, 1–2cm wide, fill the air with their scent in the early spring. The scent is similar to orange blossom. They are followed by small yellow or orange fruit. Fairly drought-resistant once established, requiring little summer water. Makes a good specimen or background tree. Native to

P

Pittosporum undulatum

eastern Australia. The variety 'Varie-gata' is a beautiful silver-variegated form.

Platanus 'PLANE'
Platanaceae

A genus of six to seven species of large, deciduous trees native to North America, south-east Europe and south-east Asia. They are often grown as street or park trees.

P. × hispanica (syn. P. × acerifolia)
LONDON PLANE ☽

A large, deciduous, fast-growing tree to 30m or more, with a wide spread to 20m. The attractive bark flakes in patches revealing new bark underneath that is brown, grey and cream. The upper trunk and limbs can be smooth and cream-coloured. The bright green, three to five-lobed leaves are 10–25cm broad and long. The insignificant spring flowers develop into green, rounded flower clusters 2–3cm across, which hang in groups on long stalks. They ripen to brown persisting on the tree during autumn and winter. The tree tolerates most soils, even poor, compacted soil. Also tolerates drought, air pollution and pollarding, making it suitable for planting in streets. Widely grown in the Mediterranean region as a shade tree. Because of its large size it is unsuitable for small gardens. Garden origin.

P. orientalis ORIENTAL PLANE ☽

A large deciduous tree to 30m or more with a wide spread to 30m, with upright or weeping branches. The bark flakes similarly to P. × hispanica. The bright green, deeply five-lobed leaves are up to 25cm wide and long. The flower clusters are also similar to P. × hispanica. The tree tolerates most soils, even poor compacted soil. Also tolerant of drought, but prefers some summer water. A magnificent, large tree that lives to a great age. Only suitable for the largest gardens and parks. Native to south-east Europe.

Plecostachys
Asteraceae

A genus of just two species of shrubby perennials native to South Africa, formerly included in Helichrysum. They are grown for their attractive leaves.

Platanus orientalis

P. serpyllifolia (syn. Helichrysum microphyllum) ☽☽

An evergreen subshrub with white, woolly, trailing or climbing, branching stems to 1m or more. The tiny, alternate, woolly, oval leaves are 1cm across, greyish-green above, and silver underneath. The terminal clusters of creamy-white flowers are 2cm across and appear in late summer. Give the plant moderate summer water for best growth. As it is grown mainly for its silver foliage effect, it should be grown in full sun to be seen at its best. The trailing branches can hang down over the edges of beds and borders, be used as groundcover, or climb through trees and shrubs.

Plecostachys serpyllifolia

Plectranthus
Lamiaceae

A large genus of 350 species of annuals and evergreen perennials native to tropical and southern Africa and Australasia. Most species have square stems, many of which are trailing, with attractive leaves. Some are popular pot plants for the home.

P. forsteri 'Marginatus' (syn. P. coleoides) ☽☽☽

A trailing, dense, bushy, evergreen perennial up to 30cm high, spreading up to 1m wide. The plant is mainly grown for its 4–8cm oval leaves that are green with a bold cream edge and scalloped margins. The spikes of insignificant pale white to lilac flowers are produced during summer. The plant can be grown in full sun, but prefers partial shade, and will even grow in full shade. During summer it needs to be well watered. Grow as a most attractive groundcover, on the tops of walls where its trailing stems can hang down, or in pots or containers. Easily propagated from

P

Plectranthus forsteri 'Marginatus'

cuttings that will root in water. Can be cut back at the end of summer if it becomes too big or untidy, or treated as an annual. Native to Australasia.

Plumbago 'LEADWORT'
Plumbaginaceae

A genus of about twenty species of annuals, perennials or evergreen shrubs, some of which are climbers, native to warm-temperate to tropical regions worldwide. One species is extremely popular for its attractive blue summer flowers.

Plumbago auriculata

P. auriculata (syn. P. capensis)
CAPE PLUMBAGO ☽

A slender-stemmed, rambling evergreen shrub with brownish arching stems. If left unsupported it becomes a sprawling bush 2m high and 2–3m wide, but if given support it can reach 4m high. The leaves are light green, oblong and 2–5cm long. The large terminal racemes of slender-tubed flowers are 15cm wide. Each flower is usually sky blue, 4cm long, with five spreading lobes and sticky calyces; these cover the plant from summer to late autumn, making a brilliant show. The shrub is a great favourite for subtropical gardens, where it clambers over other plants, makes attractive hedges, sprawls down banks or becomes a good wall shrub. Grows well

even in poor soil. Once established it needs very little summer water. Thrives in full sun or in semi-shade. Native to South Africa. The cultivar 'Alba' has white flowers, and 'Royal Cape', a recent introduction from South Africa, has richer blue flowers.

Plumbago auriculata

Podranea
Bignoniaceae

A small genus of about two species of climbing shrubs that are native to tropical and southern Africa. They are grown for their showy, foxglove-like flowers.

P. ricasoliana (syn. Bignonia rosea, Pandorea ricasoliana, Tecoma ricasoliana)
PINK TRUMPET VINE ☽ or ☽☽

An evergreen climbing shrub that can grow up to 10m high, and spreading as wide, with long slender stems. The pinnate leaves, up to 25cm long, contain seven to eleven serrated leaflets, each one 2–5cm long, dark green above and pale green underneath. The trumpet-shaped flowers are 5cm long, light pink, usually striped with red, opening into five rounded lobes. They are produced in loose terminal panicles of about twelve on the ends of young shoots. The flowers appear from midsummer until autumn and into

Podranea ricasoliana

winter, making a spectacular show. The climber tolerates dry conditions, but with regular summer water it may become too vigorous. Grows best against large walls or pergolas, where it has room to spread. Good also as a groundcover, sprawling over rocks. It even tolerates coastal sea spray. For best flowering it should be grown in full sun, though it will also grow in partial shade. Can be pruned severely in spring to keep a reasonable size. Native to South Africa. The cultivar 'Rosa Superba' is an improved form. The name 'Podranea' is an anagram of the name for the closely related Australian plant *Pandorea*.

Podranea ricasoliana

Polygala 'MILKWORT'
Polygalaceae

A large genus of between 500-600 species of annuals, evergreen perennials, and shrubs and trees widely distributed around the world. They are grown for their colourful, pea-like flowers.

P. myrtifolia ☽☽☽

An erect, much-branched evergreen shrub up to 2.5m high, spreading with age to 2m wide. The leathery, obovate, mid- to deep green leaves are 3cm long. The greenish-white flowers, 2cm long, are veined with purple, the lower petal having a fringed crest. They appear from spring to autumn in short, terminal clusters. Grow the shrub in sun or light shade in humus-rich, well drained soil. It needs generous summer water. Makes a good temporary filler, as it is not a long-lived plant. Native to South Africa. 'Grandiflora' has larger, deep violet-purple flowers with a white crested lip.

P

Polygala myrtifolia

Polystichum
Dryopteridaceae

A large genus of about 200 usually evergreen, woodland ferns, native to most parts of the world.

P. munitum SWORD FERN ☽

An evergreen fern with leathery, dark green, upright fronds to 1m high, spreading to 1.2m wide. Each frond is narrowly lance-shaped and pinnate, with each leaflet 3–4cm long. Established plants may have up to 100 fronds. The fern tends to spread by overground runners, which makes it good for groundcover. A good plant for shady beds and borders, but it does not like the sun. When established it withstands drought, but grows better with some summer water. Fronds are useful for flower arranging as they are long lasting when cut. Native to USA.

Polystichum munitum

Populus 'ASPEN, POPLAR'
Salicaceae

A genus of about thirty to forty species of dioecious (male and female flowers on different plants), large or small deciduous trees with soft wood, distributed throughout northern temperate regions. All are known for their rapid growth. They have invasive roots and should not be grown next to lawns, roads, paths or underground service lines. They are generally unsuitable for small gardens.

Populus alba

P. alba WHITE POPLAR ☽ or ☽☽

A fast-growing tree up to 20m tall, with white young shoots and a white trunk. The tree suckers freely, which can be a problem. The 12cm long, oval, three- or five-lobed, maple-like leaves are green above and white woolly underneath. Even in a light breeze the tree flickers as the leaves turn white and green, giving a pleasing effect. The pendant red male catkins, 7cm long, or green females 5cm long, are borne in spring. Grows well in full sun. When established it withstands drought, but it grows better with some summer water. Resistant to salt-laden sea breezes and exposed sites, which makes it a good shelter tree. Native to central and south-east Europe and central Asia.

P. × *canadensis*
CAROLINA POPLAR ☽ OR ☽☽

A hybrid between *P. deltoides* and *P. nigra*. A vigorous, columnar, deciduous tree to 30m or more. The triangular, glossy bright green leaves, 10cm long, turn a brilliant yellow in autumn. In spring it bears red male or green female catkins, 10cm long. The tree grows best in full sun. When established it withstands drought, but grows better with some summer water. Makes an excellent screening tree for the larger garden, but is invasive. There are many named clones. Garden origin.

P. nigra 'Italica'
LOMBARDY POPLAR ☽ or ☽☽

A narrow, columnar, deciduous tree with upward-reaching branches, which grows fast to 20m or more. The bright green glossy triangular leaves, 10cm long, turn a golden yellow in autumn. In spring it bears red male or green female catkins 5cm long. The tree grows best in full sun with some summer water. Suckers are produced freely, which can be a problem. Its formal columnar habit makes it a striking tree for skyline effect, or as a windbreak. There are several forms including 'Lombardy Gold' with golden-yellow leaves, though these may burn in summer sun. Garden origin.

Populus nigra 'Italica'

Prostanthera 'MINT BUSH'
Lamiaceae

A genus of about fifty species of strongly aromatic, evergreen shrubs or subshrubs native to Australia. They are grown for their abundant flowers. The stems are mostly square in cross-section.

P. rotundifolia
ROUND-LEAVED MINT BUSH ♪♪♪
An upright, bushy shrub up to 2m high, spreading 1m wide, with slender pubescent stems. The small, roundish leaves are 1–2cm long, deep green above and pale green underneath, usually with notched edges. They have a fragrant minty scent. In late spring and early summer the plant is covered in a profusion of small, bell-shaped purple flowers 1cm across. Each flower has an upper lip with two lobes, and a lower lip with three lobes. Grow the shrub in fertile, acid or neutral, humus-rich, moist but well drained soil: excellent drainage is important. Grow in full sun. It tends to be short-lived, but grows quickly and flowers well. A showy plant for frost-free gardens. When pruning, avoid cutting into old wood. Native to south-east Australia, including Tasmania.

Prunus 'ORNAMENTAL CHERRY'
Rosaceae

A large genus of over 400 species of mainly deciduous, but some evergreen, trees and shrubs found mainly in northern temperate regions. It includes many beautiful flowering trees suitable for temperate regions, some of which are grown for their foliage, others for their fruit.

Prunus cerasifera 'Pissardii'

Prunus dulcis

P. cerasifera 'Pissardii' (syn. P. pissardii) PURPLE-LEAVED PLUM ♪
A small, deciduous, rounded tree to 10m high, with new shoots purple-red. The ovate leaves are 6–8cm long, dark red-purple and shiny above, becoming greenish-bronze in late summer. The solitary, bowl-shaped, white flowers, 2–3cm wide, appear in great profusion in early spring. They are followed by a heavy crop of small, edible red plums, 3cm across. A popular form plant that is easy to grow in most soils. Grow in full sun or partial shade. Survives with little water, but grows better if given some summer water. 'Nigra' has darker purple leaves that are red when young. Garden origin.

P. dulcis COMMON ALMOND ♪
An upright, deciduous tree to 6m high. The lance-shaped, long-pointed, finely toothed leaves, up to 12cm long, appear in spring and drop in late summer. The flowers, up to 5cm across, are solitary or in pairs, white or pale pink, and appear before the leaves in winter. They are followed by velvety-covered green fruit to 6cm long, which split open when ripe to reveal the edible nut. Grow the tree in full sun in any well drained soil. It needs no summer water once established. Widely grown in the Mediterranean region as the source of the important nut. Native to north Africa and Asia, but naturalized in the Mediterranean region.

P. lusitanica PORTUGAL LAUREL ♪
A large, dense, bushy evergreen shrub or small tree to 6m high with an equal spread. The dark green, lance-shaped leaves are up to 12cm long and glossy above. The small – to 2cm wide – cup-shaped, strongly fragrant white flowers appear in slender racemes in early summer. They may be followed by small red fruits that ripen to black. Makes a beautiful specimen tree if allowed to develop naturally, or a good hedging plant. Can be grown in full sun or partial shade. Needs little summer water once established. Grows in most soils, even shallow chalky soils. Native to Spain and Portugal. 'Variegata': an attractive form, its leaves conspicuously margined with white.

Pseudopanax
Araliaceae

A small genus of about ten species of dioecious (male and female flowers on different plants) evergreen shrubs or trees native to Australia, New Zealand and Chile. They are grown mainly for their attractive leaves, as the flowers are inconspicuous. They make attractive architectural or specimen plants.

P. lessonii HOUPARA ♪♪♪
A large shrub or small multi-stemmed tree that makes moderate growth to 6m high and 4m wide. The bright green, leathery leaves are divided into three to

five coarsely toothed leaflets 5–10cm long. The inconspicuous yellowish-green flowers appear in clusters in summer. They may be followed by small black fruit. Grow the shrub in full sun, partial shade or even deep shade. A well drained soil is important. Give it generous summer water. Good as a container shrub for a patio or terrace. Native to New Zealand. 'Gold Splash' has leaves variegated with gold, and is the variety more frequently grown. 'Purpurea' has bronze-purple foliage.

Pseudosasa
Poaceae

A small genus of about three species of tall, woody, evergreen, rhizomatous, clump-forming bamboos native to China, Japan and Taiwan. They are grown for their canes that are often used as screening. They can be vigorous and invasive.

P. japonica (syn. *Arundinaria japonica*) ARROW BAMBOO ربربرب

A rhizomatous, wide-creeping bamboo with stems to 4m high and an indefinite spread. The canes are 1–2cm in diameter, olive green when young, maturing to pale beige, with one branch at each joint. The lance-shaped leaves, up to 25cm long, have yellow midribs and long pointed tails. Grow in fertile, well drained soil in full sun or partial shade. This strong-growing bamboo needs generous summer water. It can form a rampant thick hedge, ideal for screening. Can also be used as an attractive specimen. It needs room to grow. Native to Japan.

Pseudosasa japonica

Psidium
Myrtaceae

A genus of about 100 species of ever-green trees and shrubs native to tropical America. Several species are grown for their edible fruit.

P. guajava GUAVA TREE ربرب

A shrub or small-branching tree that makes moderate growth to 4m high. The bark and trunk are scaly, greenish-brown to golden brown. The branchlets are four-angled. The light green, corrugated leaves, to 15cm long, are hairy underneath, with prominent veins and midrib. The new leaves in spring are an attractive salmon colour. The large, white, slightly fragrant flowers, composed mainly of stamens, appear singly or in groups in the leaf axils in early summer. They are followed by round to pear-shaped edible fruit, 10cm or more in diameter. When ripe it has yellow or pink flesh with a sweet, mildly acidic flavour and is considered a delicacy. Somewhat insipid when raw, it is canned, preserved, or made into jam or jelly. The juice is often used in drinks or punch. Grow the shrub in full sun in a rich, well drained soil. Give it occasional summer water. Although often grown for its fruit, it makes an attractive ornamental tree. There are many named cultivars. Native to West Indies, Mexico to Peru.

Punica granatum

Punica
Punicaceae

A small genus of just two species of deciduous shrubs or small trees that originate from south-east Europe, south and western Asia. The pome-granate is extensively grown through-out the Mediterranean region where it has become naturalized.

P. granatum POMEGRANATE ب

A shrubby tree growing 4–5m high and almost as wide, that is often seen as a dense, many-stemmed thicket. The stems are sometimes spiny. The narrow, oblong leaves, 8cm long, are glossy bright green, while the new growth is often bronze. The flowers are 4–5cm across, brilliant scarlet with crinkled petals and a red calyx. They appear singly, or clustered at the ends of the branches for most of summer. The fruit is up to 13cm in diameter, with a thick skin that is brownish-yellow to purplish-red. It contains many seeds, each enclosed in a juicy, edible red pulp with a refreshing taste. The tree has been cultivated for its fruit since ancient times. Pomegranates should be grown in full sun for the fruit to ripen. Will grow in highly alkaline soil that would kill most plants. Drought-tolerant, but the fruit is better

Pyracantha cocinea var.

if given regular watering during summer. Native to south-east Europe to the Himalayas. There are several double-flowered forms, including 'Flore Pleno' orange-red, 'Alba Plena' white, and a dwarf form 'Nana' which can be used as a pot plant.

Pyracantha 'Firethorn'
Rosaceae

A small genus of about seven species of evergreen, usually thorny, upright or spreading shrubs native to south Europe, and south-west Asia to China. They are grown for their leaves, flowers and showy clusters of fruit.

P. coccinea ⌣
A dense, bushy, rounded shrub up to 3m high, spreading as wide, which will grow much taller if trained against a wall. The new growth has greyish hairs. The oval to lance-shaped, finely toothed leaves are dark green and up to 4cm long. The small, creamy-white flowers are borne in clusters on spurs of last year's growth, and appear in early spring. They are followed by clusters of small, bright red berries. Although the berries are small, the shrub usually covers itself with fruit. An easily grown shrub that looks best in full sun. Can be trained against a wall, and used as a screen or hedge. Looks good alone among rocks where little else will grow.

It needs little summer water, but a soaking in late summer as the berries are forming will encourage them to swell, producing a better crop. Native to south Europe. Many cultivars have been raised, including 'Golden Charmer', with bright yellowish-orange berries; 'Mohave', that produces a heavy crop of orange-red fruit; 'Orange Charmer' with dark orange berries; while 'Soleil d'Or' has golden-yellow berries.

Pyrostegia
Bignoniaceae

A small genus of about four species of evergreen, tendril climbing shrubs that are native to South America. Only one species is widely grown.

P. venusta (syn. P. ignea, Bignonia venusta)
FLAME VINE, GOLDEN SHOWER ⌣⌣
An evergreen, woody climber that makes fast growth to 10m or more with numerous slender stems, attaching itself by tendrils. The compound leaves have two or three oval, 5–8cm long, opposite rich green leaflets and a coiling tendril. A profusion of flowers appears on dense, terminal racemes that hang with the weight making an impressive sight during winter and early spring. Each tubular, waxy, deep orange flower, 8cm long, flares open into five reflexed lobes. The climber grows quickly in rich soil and full sun, but will take some shade. A heat lover, which is ideal for a sunny wall. Can be trained into a tree, or is outstanding over a pergola or arch, or over a fence. Give it average watering during summer. Pruning should be carried out in spring when flowering has finished, which may be necessary quite often to keep the plant a manageable size. Native to Bolivia, southern Brazil, northern Argentina.

P

Pyrostegia venusta

Quercus 'OAK'
Fagaceae

A large genus of over 600 species of small to very large evergreen or deciduous trees and shrubs native to most of the northern hemisphere. They are grown as ornamentals or for timber. One species is an important source of cork.

Q. coccifera KERMES OAK ☽

Usually an extremely slow-growing, bushy, evergreen shrub, up to 2m high, that forms a dense thicket, but if left it may become a small tree. The variable, leathery, holly-like leaves are 3–5cm long and persist for two to three years. They may be spiny margined or flat and smooth, bright green and shiny, usually on both surfaces. Solitary acorns with prickly cups may be seen. An ideal backcloth for the dry rock garden.

Quercus coccifera

Grow the shrub in full sun with no summer water. An exceedingly tough plant that will resprout after fire, cutting to the ground or browsing by animals. Often seen growing in arid, stony ground. Native to Portugal and the Mediterranean region.

Q. ilex HOLM OAK, EVERGREEN OAK ☽

A large, slow-growing tree with a rounded shape, up to 20m high and an equal spread, having attractive, corrugated bark. The branches may become pendulous with age. The leathery leaves vary in size and shape, generally from 4–8cm long and 2–3cm wide, persisting for two to three years. They are dark glossy green above, and pale green to white underneath, entire or toothed. The shape and size of the leaves varies greatly with the age of the tree and the growing conditions. Bears acorns either singly or in groups of two to three. Although it can grow into a large tree, it is also often seen as a shrub that forms a thicket similar to *Q. coccifera*, with which it will happily grow. Thrives on poor, rocky soils with no summer water. Valuable for coastal

plantings. Native to Portugal and the Mediterranean region.

Q. suber CORK OAK ☽

A slow-growing, evergreen tree up to 20m high with a round top that can spread almost as wide. The heavy trunk and larger limbs are covered with a thick, deeply furrowed and spongy bark, which can be 15cm thick and is used for the cork of commerce. The bark is removed down to the cambium layer every seven to ten years, but it then grows again, with no serious harm to the tree. Cork trees support an important industry. The shining, dark green, leathery leaves, up to 8cm long, have toothed margins and greenish-grey felt underneath. Generally grows best in hot regions away from the coast, where established trees can take considerable drought. Tolerates most soils but needs good drainage. A mature specimen in the garden makes an impressive sight. It makes a good garden shade tree. Native to southern Europe and north Africa. An important tree of commerce in Portugal and Spain.

Quercus suber

R

Retama
Papilionaceae

A genus of just four species of deciduous shrubs native to the Mediterranean region and west Asia. They are closely related to, and often sold as, Genista. Only one species is generally cultivated for its fragrant white flowers.

R. monosperma (syn. *Genista monosperma*)
BRIDAL VEIL BROOM, SPANISH BROOM ☽
An upright growing, deciduous shrub to 6m tall and 3m wide, with slender, arching, silky grey-green, almost leafless stems. The small, linear leaves, to 2cm long, appear in winter and soon fall. In early spring the shrub is covered with small, very fragrant, pea-like milky-white flowers in dense axillary racemes to 4cm long. An ideal shrub for the dry garden, as it prefers full sun with no summer water once established. It grows best in a sandy soil, but will grow in any sharply drained soil. A useful shrub with its elegant arching habit. Native to Portugal, Spain, north Africa, Canary Islands.

Rhamnus
Rhamnaceae

A genus of about 150 species of deciduous and evergreen shrubs and small trees, widely distributed, chiefly in temperate regions of the northern hemisphere and a few in Brazil and South Africa. They are largely grown for their form and foliage effect.

R. alaternus ITALIAN BUCKTHORN ☽
A bushy, fast-growing shrub up to 6m high, spreading to 4m wide. The small alternate, ovate, dark glossy green leaves are up to 7cm long. The tiny, yellowish-green flowers appear in spring in short

Rhamnus alaternus 'Argenteovariegata'

racemes. They are followed by bluish-black fruits, 1cm long. The shrub is valuable as a fast-growing screen, or it can be clipped into a hedge. Grows well in full sun or partial shade. Takes great heat and will survive with little summer water once established. A tough plant that can stand coastal conditions and industrial pollution. In Spain, a small-leaved, creeping form can be found covering rocks. Native to the Mediterranean region, Portugal, Spain and Morocco.

R. alaternus 'Argenteovariegata' (syn. *R. a.* 'Variegata') ☽
A bushy, fast-growing shrub up to 6m high with an equal spread. The leaves are edged with a beautiful creamy-white margin. A striking plant that makes a brilliant splash against a dark background. One of the best variegated shrubs that will take great heat and survive with little summer water. Sometimes it sends out plain green shoots that must be removed. Garden origin.

Rhaphiolepis
Rosaceae

A small genus of about fifteen species of dense, glossy evergreen shrubs native to Asia. They are grown for their attractive dense foliage, compact growth, and their fragrant apple-like flowers.

R. indica INDIAN HAWTHORN ☽☽
A small, bushy shrub, growing about 1m high, although it may become taller in deep shade. The lance-shaped, glossy dark green, toothed leathery leaves are 4–6cm long. During winter and early spring the fragrant white flowers, tinged with pink and about 1–2cm across, are produced in terminal clusters 8–10cm across. The shrub usually produces the new leaves, sometimes bronze-red, at the same time as the flowers, which gives added interest. Grow in a sunny position in a well drained, fertile soil. Tolerates deep infrequent watering or regular watering. Ideal for large-scale groundcover or for low hedges. They make dense shrubs that are attractive throughout

Rhaphiolepis indica

the year, and they look good when planted near swimming pools. Native to southern China. They are very popular in California where a large number of named clones are available.

Rhapis 'LADY PALM'
Arecaceae

A genus of twelve species of small, clustering, fan-leaved palms native to southern China, Laos, Vietnam and Thailand. Two species are widely planted in warm climate regions.

R. excelsa
LADY PALM, MINIATURE FAN PALM ⌣⌣⌣
A small, slow-growing, clump-forming palm that eventually reaches 3m high and wide, with leaves to ground level. The multiple, slender, upright, bamboo-like stems are almost completely covered in tan-coloured fibres, which age to dark grey or even black. The leaves grow along the stems and are carried on long leaf stalks up to 45cm long. The dark green leaves have five to eight widely spread segments 20–30cm long that are stiff and held erect. They form an almost complete circle, with the ends of the leaflets squared off or jagged. The palm will grow in full sun, but the leaves may be burnt, so for best results grow in partial shade. Ideal for planting under trees. It is not drought-tolerant and needs a generous amount of summer water. Will even tolerate a degree or two of frost. As an indoor palm it is probably one of the best, tolerating low light levels. It can remain in the same container for many years without re-potting. The palm is popular in Japan where a large number of cultivars have been raised, some variegated or coloured-leaved, while others are dwarf. Its main drawback is its high price due to slow growth. Native to southern China.

Rhus 'SUMACH'
Anacardiaceae

A genus of about 200 species of usually dioecious (male and female flowers on different plants) deciduous or evergreen shrubs, trees and climbers supported by clinging roots, widely distributed in temperate and subtropical regions of North America, South Africa, Asia and Australia. They are mainly grown for

Rhus trichocarpa

their striking foliage, often with brilliant autumn colour.

R. cotinus
See *Cotinus coggygria*.

R. trichocarpa SUMACH ⌣
A deciduous tree up to 8m high and spreading as wide, with soft, hairy young shoots. The large, pinnate leaves, 50cm long, are divided into thirteen to seventeen downy, pointed leaflets, that start coppery-pink, turn dark green, and end up a bright orange or red in autumn. Male and female flowers are produced on separate plants. The small yellow flowers are produced in upright conical flower spikes to 10cm long during summer. The yellow, bristly fruits are borne on drooping clusters on female plants in autumn. The tree grows well in full sun with little or no summer water. Thrives even in poor soils. May produce suckers if the roots are disturbed. This tree, with its large leaves, will give a tropical look to a garden. Native to China, Japan and Korea.

Ricinus
Euphorbiaceae

This genus contains just one variable species of fast-growing tropical shrub, which probably originated in tropical Africa but has become naturalized in many warm regions of the world. Often grown as an annual in cooler climates for its large palmately lobed leaves and spikes of small flowers.

R. communis CASTOR OIL PLANT ⌣
A large shrub or small tree up to 6m high, although often grown as an annual in cooler climates. Given good conditions it can grow 2–3m in one season. The large, dark green, glossy,

palmate leaves have five to eleven lobes, and are toothed; 15–45cm across. They are borne on long leaf stalks. There is a rich purple-leaved form that is more often seen. The small, greenish-yellow, unimpressive flowers appear in terminal spikes to 15cm long from early spring until late autumn. They are followed by attractive, deep red or brown seed capsules, 3cm wide, and covered in soft spines. The seeds are poisonous if eaten, but yield an oil used for medical purposes and in the manufacture of paint, varnishes and formerly of soap. The shrub is easily grown, requiring little or no summer water once established, but like other plants, it grows more luxuriant with water. Grow in an open sunny position in any well drained soil. Makes a magnificent bold shrub quickly, and can be used effectively as a screen or hedge. Easily raised from seed, but the seed coats are hard and take a long time to break down, so soaking them in tepid water for 24 hours prior to sowing will aid germination. Numerous named cultivars have been raised.

Ricinus communis

Robinia
Papilionaceae

A small genus of about twenty fast-growing deciduous trees and shrubs that are native to the United States and northern Mexico. They have pea-shaped flowers. Their stems are often armed with hooked thorns.

R. hispida ROSE ACACIA ⌣
An often suckering, deciduous shrub 2m or more high and wide. The branches and leaf stalks are covered in red bristles. The dark green, pinnate leaves, up to 30cm long, are divided into six to ten pairs of oblong leaflets. The deep rose, pea-shaped flowers,

2–4cm long, are produced on pendant racemes to 12cm long during spring. They may be followed by bristly brown seedpods. Grow the shrub in full sun. Extremely drought-tolerant, needing no summer water, and tolerating even poor, dry soils. Looks effective when trained against a wall. Native to south-east United States.

R. pseudoacacia
BLACK LOCUST, FALSE ACACIA ✴

A deciduous tree that quickly grows to 20–24m high, spreading to 15m wide, with open branches and spiny shoots. With age the bark becomes deeply furrowed and grooved, so that an old tree can become gnarled, giving it an ancient, rather picturesque appearance. The pinnate leaves, up to 30cm long, have seven to nineteen soft green leaflets 2–5cm long. In spring the drooping racemes, 10–20cm long, of white, fragrant flowers, 1–2cm long, are produced; they are particularly attractive to bees. They are followed by 10cm-long pods that can remain on the tree until winter. Once established it tends to sucker freely, forming a dense thicket of thorny stems. Drought-tolerant, and especially useful for dry or sandy soils. Native to eastern USA. The cultivar 'Frisia' was raised in a Dutch nursery in 1935 and is now one of the most popular golden foliage trees; this is smaller growing, but in other respects similar to the type. The leaves are more delicate and may be scorched by the sun.

Robinia pseudoacacia

'Inermis', the 'Mop Head Acacia', becomes a small tree with a compact head. The branchlets are unarmed. 'Pyramidalis' is a narrow columnar tree with spineless branchlets. All cultivars are equally drought-tolerant, but may require some protection from strong winds.

Romneya
'MATILIJA POPPY, TREE POPPY'
Papaveraceae

A small genus containing just two species of erect, glaucous, subshrubby perennials with woody bases and colourless sap that are native to southern California. They are grown for their attractive foliage and large, showy white flowers.

R. coulteri CALIFORNIA TREE POPPY, FRIED EGG PLANT ✴

A subshrubby perennial with tall, glaucous, grey-green stems up to 2.5m high that will spread almost indefinitely by suckers. The grey-green, deeply cut leaves are 8–10cm long with five to nine lance-shaped lobes. The single white flowers are poppy-like and fragrant; up to 13cm across. The petals are like crepe paper and surround a central boss of bright golden stamens, which accentuate the whiteness. The flowers are produced throughout most of the summer. Grow the plant in full sun. Will tolerate drought once established, indeed this may restrict its

Romneya coulteri

rampant spread. Tolerates most soils, but prefers light, well drained soil. The shrub is sometimes difficult to establish, but once it settles down it can become invasive. Can be used on hillsides as a soil binder. The plant resents root disturbance and transplants with great difficulty. The variety 'Trichocalyx' is often sold as a separate species as it is quite similar but has more finely divided leaves; it grows to 1.5m high. 'White Cloud' is a stronger-growing, larger-flowering hybrid.

Romulea
Iridaceae

A genus of about eighty species of small, cormous perennials native to the Mediterranean region, north Africa and South Africa. They are grown for their charming spring flowers that usually open at midday and close in the evening.

R. bulbocodium (syn. R. grandiflora) ✴
A small cormous perennial with grooved, thread-like, linear basal leaves to 10cm long. In spring a short stem 2–3cm long bears one to five funnel-shaped flowers. Each flower, 2–3cm long, is deep lilac to purple with lines of purple or yellow, often fading to greenish on the outside and yellow within. The bulb is ideal for the dry rock garden in full sun, where it can be baked during summer. Grow in well drained or sandy soil as it is native to dunes and sandy places by the sea. Native to the Mediterranean region, Portugal, Spain and Bulgaria.

Rosa 'ROSE'
Rosaceae

A genus of more than 100 species of evergreen or deciduous shrubs and

R

climbers, some trailing, native to Asia, Europe, north Africa and North America. The rose has been in cultivation for centuries and is probably the best loved flower and most widely grown shrub in temperate regions. Many authoritative books have been written about roses. Plant breeders have developed many thousands of varieties of roses, with many new ones being added each year. While many will grow and flower spectacularly in hot dry gardens, others will have their delicate petals scorched by the hot sun. It is best to take local expert advice on the types and varieties to grow. Roses can be rested during the hot summer months by reducing the water and pruning where necessary, so that they will then grow and flower well during the next spring and early summer.

Rosmarinus officinalis

R. banksiae 'Lutea' BANKSIAN ROSE ن

A tall-growing evergreen climber to 6m or more high and spreading as wide. The slender green stems have no thorns. The glossy, pale green leaves have three to five lance-shaped leaflets, 3–6cm long. The large clusters of fully double yellow flowers are 2cm across. They appear in early spring and cover the climber, giving a wonderful show. Grows easily, and is good for covering large banks, walls or growing into trees. Drought-tolerant, needing no summer water, but like other plants it grows and flowers better with some

water. Flowers best in full sun, but will still flower well in partial shade. Needs little pruning other than removing old, weak or dead growth. Native to China.

Rosmarinus 'ROSEMARY'
Lamiaceae

A small genus of about three species of evergreen aromatic shrubs that are native to the Mediterranean region. The dried leaves are used in cooking, while oil from the fresh-flowering tops is distilled for use in perfumery.

R. officinalis COMMON ROSEMARY ن

A dense shrub up to 2m high and wide, with stems that are mostly square in section. They are clothed with leathery, glossy, linear leaves, 5cm long, green on top and silver-grey underneath. The tubular flowers are produced in axillary clusters towards the ends of the branches of the previous year's growth during spring. They are generally pale blue or white, and up to 1cm long. One of the best low-growing plants for dry climates, as it requires little or no summer water once established. It endures hot sun and poor soil so long as it has good drainage. The shrub makes an attractive, informal hedge. A large number of named varieties have been raised, including 'Lady in White' with white flowers; 'Miss Jessup's Upright', a fastigiate form; and 'Prostratus', which makes a large, dense, prostrate mat that will trail over a wall or raised bed.

Roystonia 'ROYAL PALMS'
Arecaceae

A small genus of about twelve species of tall, majestic, pinnate-leafed palms native to the Caribbean Islands and tropical America. Some of the world's tallest palm species are in this genus, and are much planted throughout the tropics.

R. regia CUBAN ROYAL PALM ننن

A tall palm up to 20m high with a smooth grey trunk somewhat swollen

Rosa banksiae 'Lutea'

Roystonia regia

above the middle, with a prominent green crownshaft. The terminal crown bears gracefully arching leaves 3–5m long. The many linear leaflets are 75cm long, bright green, prominently ribbed and arranged in several ranks. A tropical palm that requires a warm, sheltered, frost-free location in full sun. Grow in a rich, moist, well drained soil. In summer it needs generous water. As it is resistant to wind and salt spray it is good for coastal gardens. Often seen in avenues in the tropics, this tall palm can dominate the landscape. Considered by many people to be one of the most beautiful palms in the world.

Ruscus 'BROOM'
Ruscaceae

A small genus of about six species of usually dioecious (male and female flowers on different plants) evergreen subshrubs spreading by underground stems, native to the Azores and Madeira through western Europe and the Mediterranean region.

R. aculeatus BUTCHER'S BROOM ⌣
A small, evergreen shrub that forms thick clumps to 1m wide of stout, erect, green-branched stems, up to 75cm high. The flattened, leaf-like branches

(cladodes) do the work of leaves. They are spine-tipped, dark glossy green, 2–3cm long, and densely borne on the upper part of the stems. Tiny flowers on female plants are followed by an abundance of showy scarlet berries if male plants are present. They are at their showiest in midwinter. Tolerant of deep shade, where few other plants will grow, but will also take full sun. They will tolerate drought conditions, or regular summer water. Individual shoots are short-lived, but new ones are produced each year. Dead shoots should be removed at the base in spring. When dried, the shoots with their berries are good for floral arrangements. Native to southern Europe, north Africa.

Russelia
Scrophulariaceae

A genus of about fifty species of evergreen or deciduous shrubs and subshrubs that are native to tropical America. Only one species is commonly cultivated, for its showy red flowers.

R. equisetiformis
CORAL PLANT, FOUNTAIN PLANT ⌣⌣⌣
A much-branched, dwarf shrub with rush-like, green, nearly leafless stems that

Ruscus aculeatus

Russelia equisetiformis

can trail down to 1m or more. The drooping clusters of small tubular scarlet flowers to 3cm long are produced from spring to autumn, making a bold splash of colour. A tender shrub that will not survive a frost. The shrub grows best in full sun in a well drained soil, with ample summer water. Useful for planting on wall tops or on banks, where its bright flowers can be seen at their best. Looks good in large containers, but these must not be allowed to dry out. To encourage growth it should be given regular feeding. Easily propagated from cuttings. Native to Mexico.

Ruta 'RUE'
Rutaceae

A small genus of about eight species of aromatic deciduous and evergreen shrubs or herbaceous perennials native from the Mediterranean region to west Asia. They are sometimes used as medicinal or culinary herbs.

R. graveolens COMMON RUE ⌣
An evergreen shrub to 1m high and wide with blue-green stems. The glaucous, much-divided, blue-green leaves are fern-like, up to 15cm long, and with numerous obovate lobes. The terminal clusters of small, mustard-yellow flowers, to 2cm across, appear in midsummer. Grow the shrub in full sun. Drought-tolerant, it will grow in any well drained soil, even on dry slopes. Will grow happily on poor, chalky soils. An attractive shrub for the mixed border or for the herb garden. It has long been cultivated for its medicinal properties. Native to southern Europe. 'Jackman's Blue' is a striking form with intensely glaucous-blue foliage and a more compact habit. 'Variegata' has leaves variegated with creamy-white, but is a much more delicate shrub that needs some shade and some water during summer.

R

Sabal 'PALMETTO'
Arecaceae

A genus of about sixteen species of dwarf to mostly stout palms, with single trunk and palmate leaf, native to tropical and subtropical America. They are all slow-growing, to a greater or lesser degree, taking several years to form an above-ground trunk. All are frost-hardy.

S. causiarum
PUERTO RICAN HAT PALM ◡

Eventually a tall, single-stemmed palm, to 10m high, with a massive grey trunk that can be 50cm across. The trunk is slow-growing and except when young, is free of leaf bases. The palm has a dense, heavy, crown of up to fifty fan leaves. A dull green, each leaf is deeply divided, up to 2m long on a stalk as long. Grow in very well drained soil in full sun. When established it withstands drought, but grows better with some summer water and responds well to added fertilizer. An imposing and beautiful palm that is an excellent choice to line a driveway or as a single specimen. Native to Puerto Rico and the Caribbean.

S. mexicana (syn. *S. texana*, *S. exul*)
OAXACA PALMETTO ◡

A tall, single-stemmed palm to 15m high, with a grey trunk that can be 35cm across, bearing old leaf bases for several years. The fan-shaped, bright green or yellowish-green leaves, to 1m long, are divided halfway into many slender, pointed lobes. Grow in very well drained soil in full sun. The palm thrives in hot dry climates. When established it withstands drought, but grows better with some summer water, and responds well to added fertilizer. Attractive as a single specimen or in groups of different heights. Native to Mexico, Guatemala and southern USA.

S. minor BLUE PALMETTO PALM, DWARF PALMETTO PALM ◡◡◡

A dwarf palm with a subterranean stem, seldom forming a trunk, and then only growing 1–2m high, spreading to 3m wide. The leaves arise in a crown at the surface. The stiff, fan-shaped, blue-green leaves can be 1–2m wide, and are held on leaf stalks 1m long. Each leaf is deeply divided into many tapering segments. Old leaves fold at their base and hang down. Plants generally flower when quite young. The small, fragrant, cream flowers are borne in upright to arching panicles to 2m long in summer. Often followed by clusters of shiny black fruit. This palm is an excellent garden plant that can be grown in full sun or deep shade. It is one of the hardiest of all palms, but is rather slow-growing. It needs generous summer water and is adaptable to almost boggy conditions – some even grow in swamps. Grow in a good, rich soil. Native to south-eastern USA.

S. palmetto
CABBAGE PALM, PALMETTO PALM ◡◡◡

A tall, single-stemmed palm, to 20m high when mature, with a rough trunk to 30cm in diameter. The trunk is usually covered in a pattern from the old leaf bases. The green to yellow-green, fan-shaped leaves are borne in a large crown on leaf stalks to 2m long. Each leaf to 2m long is divided into numerous segments, with thread-like filaments hanging between them. In summer the cream flowers are borne in panicles just longer than the leaves. They are followed by round black fruits. The palm needs to be grown in moist soil and given generous summer water. Grows well in full sun or in partial shade. It is easy to grow and succeeds well in sandy soil. Tolerating sea spray it is good in coastal conditions. Well grown, mature plants are graceful, and look particularly good when planted in groups of different heights. Native to south-eastern USA, Bahamas and Cuba.

Sabal palmetto

Salix babylonica

Salix 'WILLOW'
Salicaceae

A genus of about 300 species of usually dioecious (male and female flowers on different plants) deciduous shrubs and trees that are found in most parts of the world except Australia. Many species hybridize readily, so names are often confused. Some make attractive ornamental shade trees.

S. babylonica WEEPING WILLOW ♫♫
A deciduous tree to 12m or more, with an equal or greater spread, having slender weeping branches and green or brown shoots. The pale green leaves are lance-shaped, 8–10cm long, and in spring as the leaves are appearing, slender greenish catkins, to 5cm long, are also produced. The tree grows surprisingly well in dry areas, as it is normally associated with river banks. If given regular summer water it will grow into a large tree, but with reduced water its size will also be reduced. Makes an interesting form tree for the larger garden. As it has invasive roots, plant well away from the house and drains as the roots will seek out water. Grows in any soil, especially poorly drained soil. Origin uncertain, but probably China. This species has largely been replaced in gardens by S. × sepulcralis 'Chrysocoma'.

S. × sepulcralis 'chrysocoma'
GOLDEN WEEPING WILLOW ♫♫
A vigorous, deciduous tree to 15m or more, with an equal or greater spread, having slender weeping branches with bright yellow shoots that often reach to the ground. The bright green or yellow-green leaves, paler underneath, are lance-shaped and up to 12cm long. In spring as the leaves are appearing, slender yellow male and green female catkins, to 5cm long, are also produced on the same tree. As with S. babylonica, it grows surprisingly well in dry areas. Cultivation notes are the same. Garden origin.

Salvia 'SAGE'
Lamiaceae   ✓ √ar.

A vast genus of more than 750 species of annuals, biennials, herbaceous perennials and shrubs. They are widely distributed throughout large parts of temperate and warmer regions of the world, usually growing in dry or stony sites. Included are many showy ornamentals, as well as some that are used for culinary or medical purposes. Most have stems that are square in cross-section.

S. argentea ♫
An herbaceous perennial or biennial up to 1m high that often dies after flowering. It forms a rosette of woolly, silver-green, toothed leaves, oval to oblong in shape, to 20cm long. The white or pinkish-white flowers, 1–2cm long, appear on many branched spikes on strong upright stems in midsummer. Grow in full sun in well drained soil. An attractive, short-lived perennial for the dry border. Drought-tolerant, therefore needs little summer water. Native to southern Europe, and east to Bulgaria.

S. cacaliifolia ♫♫
A bushy perennial that has upright, hairy stems to 1m high, spreading to 1m or more wide. The shiny, mid-green, almost triangular leaves to 8cm wide and long are covered in soft hairs. In early summer the branched stems bear branching, narrow clusters of flowers. Each pure blue, slightly hairy flower is 2cm long. Grow in full sun or partial shade. It needs regular summer water. For best flowering, cut old stems down to ground level each winter. A beautiful and striking plant for the border. Native to Mexico, Guatemala.

S. coccinea ♫
A small perennial or bushy annual growing 30–60cm high. The hairy, heart-shaped, toothed, dark green leaves are 3–5cm long. The small, bright red flowers, to 2cm long, are produced in long, open, terminal spikes, mostly during spring, but a few

Salvia cacaliifolia

S

Salvia coccinea

Salvia leucantha

during summer and autumn. The plant prefers to be grown in full sun. When established it withstands drought, but grows and flowers better with some summer water. For best flowering cut old stems down to ground level each winter. Native to Mexico, the West Indies and tropical Africa. 'Coral Nymph' has pink and white flowers; 'Snow Nymph' bears white flowers.

S. elegans 'Scarlet Pineapple'
PINEAPPLE SAGE ♪♪
An herbaceous perennial up to 1m high and 60cm wide, with soft, hairy, branching stems. The ovate, mid-green, toothed leaves, up to 10cm long, have a strong pineapple scent when crushed. The terminal spikes of attractive scarlet flowers, 3–4cm long, appear in autumn. The leaves are used in drinks or fruit salads. Grow in sun or partial shade. Although it will survive summer drought, it grows better with moderate water. Native to Mexico and Guatemala.

S. farinacea MEALY-CUP SAGE ♪♪
A bushy perennial that is often grown as an annual, with an upright habit to 60cm high. The stems have a white covering, giving it the common name. The narrow lance-shaped, glossy, wavy-edged leaves, up to 10cm long, are white and hairy underneath. Tiny violet-blue, lavender or purple flowers appear on tall, slender, dense spikes from summer to autumn. A showy plant that is easily raised from seed. Grow in full sun or partial shade. Grows best with moderate summer water. Native to the USA and Mexico. 'Alba' has white flowers; 'Victoria' is a bushier plant, growing to 50cm high, with deep purple-blue flowers.

S. greggii AUTUMN SAGE ♪ or ♪♪
An upright, evergreen subshrub up to

1m high and wide, branching freely from the base with hairy stems. The narrow, oblong leaves are softly hairy, deep green and 2–3cm long. They are aromatic when crushed. The pairs of red, purple, pink, yellow or violet flowers, 2cm long, appear in clusters on thin wiry stems in summer and autumn. Grow in full sun or partial shade in most soils. Grows and flowers better if given some water during the hottest months. Native to USA and Mexico.

S. leucantha
MEXICAN SAGE BUSH ♪ or ♪♪
A bushy, evergreen shrub or herbaceous perennial, 1–1.5m high, with graceful arching stems. The leaves, stems and flowers are covered in a dense white wool. The mid-green, lance-shaped leaves are up to 15cm long. White flowers 1–2cm long, with lavender-blue calyces, appear during autumn and winter on spikes up to 50cm long. The plant prefers sun, but will grow in light shade. Drought-tolerant, but grows better if given some summer water: given enough water it will continue flowering most of the summer. Remove old flowered stems to encourage new growth. Native to Mexico and central America.

S. officinalis COMMON SAGE ♪
An evergreen subshrub up to 80cm high, spreading to 1m wide. Grown mainly for its attractive, aromatic oval to oblong leaves, 3–8cm long and grey-green in colour. The terminal spikes of violet blue flowers, 1–2cm long, are produced in late summer; they are particularly attractive to bees. For best flowering, grow in full sun. Fairly drought-tolerant, needing little summer water once established. If grown in groups it makes a good groundcover. Long cultivated as a culinary herb, but also makes an attractive garden plant. Native to the Mediterranean region. 'Purpurascens' has purple leaves that darken through summer; 'Tricolor' has leaves edged with cream, with the young leaves tinged pink or purple.

S. splendens SCARLET SAGE ♪♪
A perennial, bushy subshrub, to 2m high, that is often grown as an annual. The oval, rich green, toothed leaves, to 10cm long, are slightly hairy. From summer to autumn, dense terminal flower spikes appear, bearing showy, bright red flowers with a fiery red

Salvia farinacea 'Victoria'

Salvia officinalis

calyx, to 5cm long. Grow in full sun or partial shade in most garden soils. Grows best with moderate summer water. A showy plant that is easily raised from seed and is used as a summer bedding plant in temperate regions. Modern seed selections are generally compact, only growing 30–40 cm high. Native to Brazil.

Salvia splendens

Sansevieria 'BOWSTRING HEMP'
Agavaceae

A genus of about sixty species of stiff, erect, evergreen perennials, with short, thick rhizomes native to dry, rocky regions of tropical and subtropical Africa, Madagascar and Asia. One species is popular as a house plant, but specialist nurseries list many other species and varieties.

S. trifasciata
MOTHER-IN-LAW'S TONGUE

An erect, evergreen perennial that forms a clump of leaves up to 1m high. The leathery, linear, lance-shaped, flat to concave leaves are marked with light green to grey-white cross-bands. The fleshy rhizomes bear an average of six to eight leaves. Tiny, greenish-white flowers that are fragrant at night are produced in loose racemes 30–75cm high at any time of the year. Ideal for pots or containers on the patio, or for planting in a courtyard garden. In completely frost-free areas it makes a novel edging to a pathway. Grows best when given some shelter from the hot midday sun. A tough plant that is tolerant of neglect. It only needs deep, infrequent watering, but good winter drainage is essential. Native to southern

Sansevieria trifasciata 'Laurentii'

Africa. 'Laurentii' is the leading commercial variety because of its elegant leaves, with yellow bands on either side of the deep green-banded centre.

Santolina
Asteraceae

A small genus of about eighteen species of greyish, aromatic shrubs or sub-shrubs that are native to dry, rocky areas of the Mediterranean region. They are grown for their foliage and button-like flowers. They are frost-hardy but short-lived.

S. chamaecyparissus COTTON LAVENDER
A low-growing, mound-forming, evergreen shrub up to 50cm high, spreading to 1m wide. The young branches are covered in white felt. The small, dense, grey or silver pinnate leaves are finely divided. The flowerheads are globular, 2cm across, and bright lemon yellow. They appear on the ends of slender, erect stalks throughout summer. To keep a compact shape, cut back hard during winter. Grows well in a dry, sunny position, but good winter drainage is important. Makes a good groundcover, also useful as a low, clipped hedge. Not a long-lived plant, but easily propagated from cuttings taken in autumn. Some of the low-growing stems may root themselves.

Santolina chamaecyparissus

Scadoxus 'BLOOD LILY'
Amaryllidaceae

A genus of nine species of tender evergreen or deciduous, bulbous plants that are native to tropical regions of Africa. They are closely related to Haemanthus, and some were formally included in that genus. They are grown for their spectacular round flower-heads.

S

S. multiflorus 'Katherinae' (syn. Haemanthus katherinae)
BLOOD LILY ♨♨

A tender, bulbous perennial with a large white bulb up to 10cm in diameter, stained with red, which gives it the common name. The broad, lance-shaped, basal leaves are wavy-edged, bright green and up to 30cm long. In summer, stout stems up to 60cm high are topped with round flowerheads 10–15cm across. They contain large numbers of narrow, bright salmon-red flowers with conspicuous, protruding red stamens. Plant bulbs during autumn. Grows best in light shade when given generous water during the growing period. Often grown in pots or containers on a shaded patio or terrace. They can also be planted out in a well drained soil in light shade. After flowering, gradually reduce watering; like most bulbs, they need a rest after flowering. Do not remove the leaves until they naturally turn yellow. Native to southern Africa.

Scaevola
Goodeniaceae

A genus of over eighty species of mainly evergreen perennials, but also climbers, shrubs and small trees that are native mostly to Australia. Generally only the perennials are grown, although they are short-lived. They are grown for their attractive flowers.

S. aemula FAIRY FAN FLOWER ♨♨

A tender evergreen perennial up to 50cm high, spreading as wide, with thick, short-jointed stems that sprawl across the ground. The dark green, spoon-shaped leaves, to 9cm long, are sharply toothed. The leafy racemes of blue, purple or white flowers, 2–3cm across, are borne mainly in spring and summer, but often appear almost continuously. Each flower has five lobes that radiate outwards on one side to form a fan shape. Grow in full sun or partial shade in rich, well drained soil. Give moderate summer water. A good plant for the front of a border, or attractive hanging down over a wall. Native to southern and eastern Australia. 'Blue Wonder' has lilac-blue flowers that are produced in great profusion almost continuously.

Schefflera (syn. Brassaia)
Araliaceae

A huge genus of about 900 species of evergreen tropical shrubs, climbers or small trees, native to south Asia to the Pacific region and central and South America. Some are popular foliage plants with their palmately compound leaves.

S. actinophylla (syn. Brassaia actinophylla) OCTOPUS TREE, QUEENSLAND UMBRELLA TREE ♨♨

An evergreen tree that makes rapid growth to 6m or more high. In its native habitat it can grow to 30m high. It forms a single-trunked or multi-trunked tree with few short side branches. With age it can form a spreading canopy. The horizontal tiers of spreading leaves are 60–120cm long. The leaves are divided into seven to sixteen oblong, dark glossy green, drooping leaflets up to 30cm long on stalks 8cm long. These radiate outwards like an umbrella, giving it the common name. During late summer the spectacular terminal flowering spikes appear on mature plants; these are narrow, horizontally spreading clusters, up to 1m long, which stick out well above the foliage. These spikes are set with small, honey-laden flowers with wine-red petals that form into purplish-

Schefflera actinophylla

red fruit. Makes a striking tropical effect. A good foliage plant near pools. Can be grown in full sun or partial shade. To grow well it needs a moderate amount of summer water and a fairly fertile soil. A tender tree that can be killed by frost. Cut out growing tips to encourage bushiness, and prune hard if it becomes leggy. When juvenile it makes a good pot or container plant. Native to Australasia.

Schefflera arboricola

S. arboricola 'Variegata' (syn. Heptapleurum arboricolum) ♨♨♨

An evergreen, freely branching shrub that in frost-free regions can grow to 5m or more high, with an equal spread. The glossy, palmate leaves are carried on stalks to 18cm long. Each of the leathery leaflets, 8–10cm long, radiates from, and forms a circle on the end of the stalk. In the variegated form that is normally grown, the leaflets are wonderfully splashed with yellow. The shrub tends to send out green shoots that should be removed. Flowers are rarely produced in cultivation. The shrub will grow in full sun, but prefers some shade. It needs regular summer water and a rich, friable soil to grow well. It gives a tropical look to a border, and colour to a shady situation. Can look dramatic when illuminated at night. It can also be trained as an espalier against a semi-shaded wall. Native to Taiwan.

S. pueckleri
See Tupidanthus calyptratus.

Schinus
Anacardiaceae

A genus of about thirty species of usually evergreen dioecious (male and female flowers on different plants) shrubs and trees that are native to southern America. They are often grown as street trees in the Medi-

S

Schinus molle

terranean and warm temperate areas, where they look spectacular when covered in berries.

S. molle PEPPER TREE ☽

An evergreen tree that makes rapid growth to 8–15m high, spreading to 5m or more wide. With age it develops a rough, gnarled trunk with knots that frequently sprout leaves or shoots. The gracefully drooping branches and weeping feathery foliage make it a highly decorative tree. The bright green, pinnate leaves, 10–30cm long, have many 4–5cm, narrow leaflets. The numerous small, yellowish-white flowers appear in short, drooping clusters 10–15cm long in spring. They are followed on female trees by small, rosy red berries that hang in pendant clusters in autumn. This is an easily grown tree, as it is drought-resistant once established, grows in any soil, and thrives in the heat. The roots are invasive, so do not plant near house foundations or drains. The surface roots are greedy so nothing can be grown underneath, but it makes a beautiful shade tree. Native to central and South America.

S. terebinthifolius
BRAZILIAN PEPPER TREE ☽☽
An evergreen tree that makes moderate growth to 5–7m, with upright or spreading branches 3–5m wide. The dark green, pinnate leaves, 10–17cm long, have only five to thirteen broad, leathery leaflets. In spring it produces panicles of small white flowers. The berries are bright red on female trees, making a good show in late summer and winter. This makes it a very ornamental tree. The roots are less invasive than other species. With training it can make a broad tree, which provides good shade for a patio. A tender tree that can be damaged by the cold. Grow in full sun in any well drained soil. Give it a moderate amount of summer water, which is best applied infrequently and deeply to prevent surface rooting. Native to Brazil.

Schotia
Caesalpiniaceae

A small genus of four to five species of deciduous and semi-evergreen shrubs and trees native to South Africa. They are grown for their showy summer flowers.

S. brachypetala
AFRICAN WALNUT, TREE FUCHSIA ☽
A large shrub or wide-spreading semi-evergreen tree to 10m high and up to 10m wide. The bark is reddish-brown and the young shoots are grey. The pinnate leaves emerge a rose-red turning to copper, then to bright green. The leaves are up to 18cm long, with four to five pairs of oblong leaflets 1–2cm long. Throughout summer and autumn the tree is covered with pendulous, crowded clusters to 13cm long, of glowing deep red flowers. The tree briefly drops its leaves during the spectacular flowering period. Each flower has a prominent red calyx to 1cm wide, minute petals and protruding red stamens. They are followed by long, bean-like pods to 18cm long, containing many seeds that are edible when roasted. A highly ornamental, slow-growing tree with flowers, attractive to bees. Grow in full sun. Drought-tolerant once established, needing little summer water. Useful as a windbreak near the coast. Easily propagated by seed.

Scilla
Hyacinthaceae

A genus of eighty to ninety species of bulbous perennials native to Africa, Europe and Asia. They are easily grown for their small, starry or bell-shaped flowers, usually in shades of blue.

S. peruviana PERUVIAN SCILLA ☽
A clump-forming, bulbous perennial with a basal cluster of almost upright leaves to 30cm long. They appear during autumn and die down during summer. During spring the large, dome-shaped clusters of bright blue flowers appear on 30cm stems. They may contain fifty to a hundred blue-violet, purple or white star-shaped flowers 2cm across. The strap-shaped leaves die down soon after flowering, and the bulb remains dormant during summer. An easy bulb to grow in full sun in any soil. As it grows during autumn and winter it needs no summer water. It looks wonderful when grown in large drifts between shrubs and deciduous trees. Also looks attractive when grown in pots. Despite its common name it is native to the Mediterranean region.

Sedum 'STONECROP'
Crassulaceae

A genus of perhaps 600 species of succulent annuals, biennials, evergreen and deciduous perennials, subshrubs and shrubs native to most parts of the northern hemisphere and South America.

Sedum morganianum

S

S. *morganianum* DONKEY TAIL

A lovely, succulent perennial with fleshy stems hanging to 1m long. The thick, fleshy, greenish-blue, nearly cylindrical leaves, to 2cm long with a silver-blue bloom, overlap each other along the stems to give a braided or rope-like effect. The pale pink to deep scarlet star-shaped flowers, to 1cm across, are produced in clusters in spring and summer. A beautiful succulent that should be grown in the shade. Give generous water and feed during summer. Fast-draining soil is essential. Grow in a hanging wall pot, in a container, or hanging over the top of a wall, or in a shady place in a rock garden. Native to Mexico.

S. × *rubrotinctum* PORK AND BEANS

A small evergreen succulent with sprawling, freely branching stems up to 20cm high that readily root in the ground. The alternate, thickly clustered leaves are fleshy and club-shaped; 2cm across, they are glossy green, turning coppery-red in sunshine. The yellow flowers are star-shaped to 1 cm across, and are produced in winter. A drought-tolerant plant that needs little summer water. Ideal for the rock garden where it will gradually form a dense mat. Also makes a good pot or container plant. The leaves or stems, which easily detach themselves, root readily. Native to Mexico.

S. *weinbergii*
See *Graptopelalum paraguayense*.

Sempervivum arboreum
See *Aeonium arboreum*.

Senecio
Asteraceae

A vast genus containing over 1,000 species. They are found in all parts of the world, and range from annuals, biennials, herbaceous perennials and shrubs, to climbers and succulents, while a few from east Africa are tree-like. All have daisy-like flowers.

S. *cineraria* DUSTY MILLER

An evergreen subshrub that forms a mound 60–70cm high, spreading as wide, with silver stems. Grown mainly for its attractive, woolly white leaves, 10–15cm long, which are cut into many blunt segments. These can become green

Senecio cineraria

on the upper surface. The clustered heads of yellow flowers, 2cm across, appear on beautiful, white-felted stalks in summer. An easily grown plant that is often used as striking groundcover, in which case it should be kept short and bushy by cutting back in spring. Needs only light watering in summer. Easily grown from seed, flowering the second year. Native to the Mediterranean region. Often listed in seed catalogues as *Cineraria maritima* 'Diamond'. Many cultivars are listed, including 'Cirrus', with broader, finely toothed silver-white leaves, and 'Silver Dust' with deeply divided grey-white leaves.

S. *confusus* (syn. *Pseudogynoxys chenopoides*) MEXICAN FLAME-VINE

An evergreen twining climber, up to 3m or more high. The dark green, lance-shaped leaves, up to 8cm long, are rather fleshy and coarsely toothed at the margins. The striking, daisy-like flowers are borne in large clusters at the ends of the branches for most of the year. Each fragrant flower is bright orange-red, up to 5cm wide, with golden centres. Grow in sun or light shade in fertile, well drained soil. Needs regular summer water as it is not drought-tolerant. Grow against a wall or fence or allow it to tumble over a bank. Native to Mexico to Honduras.

S. *greyi*
See *Brachyglottis greyi*.

S. *macroglossus* CAPE IVY, NATAL IVY

An evergreen twining climber up to 3m high, with purple-toned, semi-succulent stems that become woody with age. The triangular, succulent leaves, up to 8cm long, are ivy-like with three to five lobes. Single, pale yellow, daisy-like flowers with darker centres, to 6cm across, appear during summer and autumn. Can be grown in full sun, but prefers some shade. Ideal for planting against a shady wall, or can be used as a groundcover for a shady place. Drought-tolerant, needing little summer water. It needs a well drained soil, as waterlogged winter soil will kill it. Native to South Africa. 'Variegatus' has leaves that are green to milky green and glossy, with an irregular creamy-white to yellow margin, while other leaves are entirely cream. A tender climber that is more suited as a pot or container plant, where it can make an attractive creeper for the shady patio or terrace.

Senecio confusus

S. mikanioides (syn. *Delairea odorata*)
GERMAN IVY ◡

A tall climber reaching up to 6m high. The semi-succulent leaves are evergreen or nearly so, triangular with five to seven sharp lobes 8–10cm across, giving it an ivy-like appearance. In winter it produces clusters to 8cm across of small, yellow, daisy-like flowers. When established it withstands drought, so it requires little summer water. Grow in full sun or partial shade. A tough plant that is useful for growing up old trees or covering fences. Also useful as a groundcover, but it can become weedy. Native to South Africa.

S. petasitis CALIFORNIA GERANIUM ◡◡◡

An evergreen, shrub-like perennial that forms a mound up to 2m high, spreading almost as wide, with many branches from the base. The stems and leaves are covered in velvety hair. The ovate leaves are up to 20cm across, with nine to thirteen large lobes giving it a tropical look. During early spring it produces its large, terminal flowering heads that contain a mass of small, bright yellow, daisy-like flowers standing well above the foliage. A spectacular sight when in full flower. After the short blooming time, the white hairs of the seeds appear profusely. Grows best in a sheltered place when given plenty of summer water. Can be pruned hard after flowering to remove the seedheads and to keep tidy. Native to southern Mexico.

Senecio petasitis

S. rowleyanus (syn. *Kleinia rowleyana*) STRING OF BEADS ◡◡

An evergreen perennial succulent with thin creeping or pendant stems to 60cm long. The stems have adventitious roots, and the plant can form a dense mat. The globular-pointed, succulent, shiny leaves are dark green and up to 1cm in diameter. This gives it the common name. The flower heads, to 1cm long, produced during summer are cinnamon-scented, and the corolla is white with protruding brown stamens. This succulent can be grown in sun, but prefers some shade. Give moderate summer water. Makes an attractive wall pot or container plant. Looks good when hanging over the top of a wall. Native to south-west Africa.

Senna (syn. Cassia)
Caesalpiniaceae

A genus of over 200 species of evergreen or deciduous perennials, woody climbers, trees and shrubs. Native to the tropical and temperate regions of the world. Most have flowers of various shades of yellow. They are often included in the genus Cassia. They are all frost tender.

S. alata CANDLE BUSH ◡◡

A short-lived, large, deciduous shrub forming a mound 3m high and wide. The pinnate, bright green leaves are 20–60cm long, with twelve to twenty-eight oblong leaflets to 6cm long. The numerous, beautiful, golden-yellow flowers, 3cm long, are borne in tall, upright candle-like spikes. The flowers are protected by yellowish-green bracts when in bud. This makes an attractive winter-flowering plant. Grow in full sun. Give deep, infrequent watering during summer. Prune hard after flowering to encourage new growth. Native to the Tropics.

Senna *alata*

S. artemisoides FEATHERY CASSIA ◡

An evergreen shrub 2–3m high, spreading to 3m wide, with a light, airy appearance. The pinnate leaves, 3–6cm, long are divided into three to six pairs of narrow, grey-green, thickly downy leaflets, 2cm long. The leaves and stems are covered in a fine, grey, silky hair. The small, sulphur yellow, fragrant flowers are carried in 2cm wide, unbranched clusters of five to eight. They appear mainly in spring, but also intermittently throughout the year. When established it withstands drought, but grows better with some summer water. Grow in full sun. Can easily be raised from seed. Native to Australia.

S. corymbosa FLOWERING SENNA ◡

A lax evergreen shrub up to 3m high and wide, which needs the support of a wall or fence. The light yellowish-green pinnate leaves, to 60cm long, consist of six to eight, narrow, lance-shaped leaflets 3–5cm long. The showy clusters of small, golden-yellow, cup-shaped flowers, to 2cm across, are held in clusters up to 15cm long, and appear in summer or autumn. They are followed by green, bean-like pods that may be straight or curved, up to 12cm long, turning black when ripe. Grow in full sun. When established it withstands drought, but grows better with some summer water. To keep in shape it should be pruned after flowering. Native to Argentina.

S

Senna corymbosa

S. didymobotrya POPCORN-BUSH ⌣

An evergreen upright or spreading shrub up to 3m high and 2m wide. The young shoots and leaves are finely downy. The pinnate leaves, up to 35cm long, consist of eight to sixteen oblong leaflets. Yellow flowers, 3cm wide, grow in dense, upright clusters 20–30cm long. They are produced mainly in spring and summer, but also appear at almost any time of the year, making an impressive sight. Grow the shrub in full sun. Like other Sennas, it likes the heat and can withstand summer drought once established. Makes a large, bold, impressive shrub for the back of the border. Native to tropical Africa.

S. spectabilis ⌣

A deciduous, fast-growing, spreading tree, 4–5m high with young branchlets softly hairy. The long, pinnate, bright green leaves, 30cm or more long, have ten to fifteen pairs of ovate to lance-shaped leaflets 5–6cm long, which are softly hairy on the underneath. On the ends of the branches spectacular erect racemes 30–60cm long contain many beautiful, cup-shaped golden-yellow flowers 3–4cm in diameter, like shining lamps. They are followed by round seedpods 10–30cm long, which ripen to dark brown, each containing many seeds. Grow in full sun in a warm sheltered spot that is frost-free.

Drought-tolerant, requiring little summer water once established. Grows best in fertile, neutral to acid soil. Makes a spectacular specimen or street tree. Easily raised from seed. Native to tropical America.

Sesbania (syn. Daubentonia)
Papilionaceae

A genus of perhaps fifty species of evergreen perennials, shrubs and small trees that are usually short-lived.

Native to tropical and subtropical regions worldwide. They are grown for their showy, pea-like flowers.

S. punicea DWARF PONCIANE ⌣⌣⌣

A large shrub or small tree, to 2m or more high, spreading 1–2m wide. The deep green, pinnate leaves are up to 30cm long with six to twenty pairs of oblong leaflets to 3cm long. The flowers are borne in loose pendant clusters up to 10cm long in summer. Each flower is pea-like to 2cm across, and bright red to purplish-red. A choice shrub that needs a warm, sheltered spot in full sun. Grows well in a moist, well drained soil. Give it moderate to generous summer water. Generally a short-lived plant, but it flowers when small. The flowers are spectacular and it gives a quick effect in the shrub border. Easily raised from seed. Native to southern Brazil, Argentina and Uruguay.

S. tripetii SCARLET WISTERIA TREE ⌣⌣

A deciduous shrub or small tree that makes fast growth to 2–3m high, spreading up to 2m wide. The pinnate leaves, to 30cm long, are fern-like, with many pairs of narrow leaflets, 1–2 cm long. The showy, drooping clusters of flowers appear from late spring and continue through summer. The pea-like flowers, up to 2cm across, are a beautiful orange-red. They are followed by winged, four angled seedpods. As

Senna didymobotrya

S

Sesbania tripetii

the flowers are produced on new growth, prune severely in early spring. Grow in a warm, sheltered spot in full sun. Give it moderate summer water to grow and flower well. Generally short-lived, but is easily raised from seed. The drooping flower clusters look effective when the plant is trained into a standard tree with a 2m trunk. Native to northern Argentina and Brazil.

Setcreasea purpurea
See *Tradescantia pallida* 'Purpurea'.

Siphonosmanthus delavayi
See *Osmanthus delavayi*.

Solandra 'CHALICE VINE'
Solanaceae

A small genus containing about six species of tall, vigorous, evergreen climbing plants, native to tropical America. They are grown for their large, spectacular, night-scented flowers.

S. maxima CUP OF GOLD ♨♨
A strong-branching, climbing shrub that makes rampant growth up to 12m high, and can spread as wide. The bold, glossy, evergreen leaves are 10–15cm long. The large, solitary, trumpet-shaped flowers, 20cm long, flare back

to 15–20cm at the mouth. They are pale cream when first opening, but soon turn to orange-apricot, with five dark ribs on the inside; the scent of ripe apricots at night is distinctive. They appear on the tips of the new growth mainly from autumn to early spring, but intermittently at other times. Grow the climber in full sun near large walls, or by pergolas where there is plenty of room for it to grow. Particularly in the first few years, the young shoots should be cut back to encourage many side branches. Requires an average amount of water in summer, but will take some drought. If given too much water it will make strong growth at the expense of flower. Ideal for coastal gardens, as it withstands salt-laden sea breezes. Native to Mexico, Colombia and Venezuela.

Solanum
Solanaceae

A vast genus containing perhaps 1,400 species of annuals, biennials, herbaceous perennials, evergreen and deciduous shrubs, sometimes climbing, some very spiny, and rarely trees. They are present in most parts of the world. It includes many of the world's most important edible plants such as the potato, tomato and the aubergine or eggplant. Some are poisonous, such as the Nightshade.

Solandra maxima

S. aviculare KANGAROO APPLE ♨♨
An upright to spreading evergreen shrub that makes fast growth up to 3m high and 2m wide. The lance-shaped to ovate deep green leaves, up to 30cm long, are entire or irregularly lobed. In spring and summer it bears clusters of purple or white, shallowly lobed flowers, 2–3cm wide. They are followed by ovoid green fruit, 2–3cm, that ripen to yellowish. Grow in full sun or partial shade in a fertile, well drained, neutral to alkaline soil. Give moderate summer water. Native to New Zealand and Australia.

S. crispum CHILEAN POTATO TREE ♨♨
A vigorous deciduous or semi-evergreen shrub that annually produces scrambling, downy stems 2–5m long. The ovate, dark green leaves, up to 12cm long, are downy with crisped margins. During spring the slightly fragrant flowers are produced on loose clusters to 15cm across. Each star-shaped flower is a rich bluish-purple with a bright yellow centre, and 2–3cm across; they closely resemble those of the potato. The shrub grows well in full sun or partial shade, with moderate summer water. Ideal for growing against a wall, as it withstands hard pruning. This shrub is well suited for alkaline soils. It will withstand a few degrees of frost. Native to Chile and Peru. 'Glasnevin', an Irish cultivar, is an improved form with a longer flowering season and richer flower colour.

S. jasminoides POTATO VINE ♨♨
A vigorous evergreen shrub with twining stems that will often reach to 5m high. The glossy, dark green leaves are lance-shaped leaves and 4–8cm long. The older leaves are sometimes three- to five-lobed with a purplish tinge. The fragrant flowers are 2cm across, pale bluish-white, and star shaped with yellow anthers. They appear profusely in large, loose clusters mostly in spring, but there are some flowers on it throughout the year. Prefers growing in full sun, but will also grow in part shade. Give moderate summer water. Can be cut back severely at any time of the year to prevent becoming tangled. Ideal for covering walls or pergolas for light summer shade. Native to eastern Brazil. 'Album',

S

Solanum jasminoides 'Album'

a more beautiful, pure white variety, is the one more often seen growing in gardens. 'Aureovariegatum' is less strong-growing but with beautiful golden-yellow edges to the leaves.

S. mauritianum MAURITIUS NIGHTSHADE, TREE TOBACCO

A soft-stemmed tree or large shrub, up to 4m or more high and 2m wide, with open branches. The young branches are green and densely covered in felt. The large, softly hairy, dark green, lance-shaped leaves are up to 30cm long and silver-green on the underneath. During winter and spring, stiff terminal flower stems are produced, to 20cm long. They are topped with 15cm-wide clusters of star-like, white-striped violet

Solanum mauritianum

flowers to 2cm wide. These are followed by 1cm, round green or yellow ornamental fruit that are attractive to birds. Grow in full sun in any well drained garden soil. Grows best with moderate summer water, but will survive with little water. An interesting and attractive tree for the back of the border, with its shimmering silver-green leaves and violet flowers. Grows well as a pot or container plant that flowers when small. Easily raised from seed. Native to Argentina, but naturalized in many tropical countries.

S. muricatum PEPINO, MELON PEAR, MELON SHRUB

A sprawling perennial or subshrub to 60cm high, spreading to 1m or more wide, with young growth grey to white and hairy. The bright green, oblong to lance-shaped leaves are up to 20cm long and finely hairy. Often with a purplish tint on the underneath of young leaves, the leaf stalk and midvein. Bright blue flowers up to 2cm wide that appear throughout the year are followed by edible egg-shaped fruit to 10cm long. The fruit is yellowish, splashed with purple. The flesh is firm and yellow, with a taste like a cross between melon and cucumber, and is eaten fresh. Grow in full sun or partial shade. Give moderate summer water. An interesting and unusual fruit that can be grown from seed, but named varieties must be grown from cuttings. Native to the Andes.

Solanum muricatum

S. rantonetii (syn. Lycianthes rantonetii) BLUE POTATO BUSH

An evergreen spreading shrub with arching branches. When grown in the open it will grow to 2m high, but if trained against a wall it may reach 3m or more high. The bright green, oval to

Solanum rantonnetii

lance-shaped leaves are 6–10cm long, often wavy margined. Although ever-green, it may drop its leaves in severe cold. The trumpet-shaped flowers, 2–3cm across, are violet blue or pale blue with a yellow centre. They appear in loose axillary clusters to 6cm across from early spring until autumn, and often throughout the year. For best flowering, grow in full sun. Grows better with moderate summer water, although it tolerates some drought. An easily grown, attractive shrub, which may need severe pruning to keep in shape. Often seen in nurseries as a short-stemmed standard grown in a container, which looks most attractive on a terrace, patio or by a swimming pool. Native to Argentina and Paraguay. 'Royal Robe' is more compact, with a longer flowering season and fragrant, deep violet-blue flowers with yellow centres.

S. wendlandii
COSTA RICAN NIGHTSHADE

A beautiful, deciduous shrubby climber with stout woody stems to 5m or more high, with hooked spines on the stems and leaves. The bright green leaves, 10–25cm long, on the upper parts of the stems are three-lobed, while they are pinnate on the lower parts. The big, showy, branched clusters of lilac-blue flowers are 15cm across, containing many trumpet-shaped flowers, 4–6cm

Solanum wendlandii

wide; these weigh the branches down in late summer. Useful to clamber into trees or to cover pergolas. This is a beautiful plant, but very tender, and should only be grown in sheltered locations in full sun with a fairly rich soil. Given copious amounts of water in summer, and rich balanced feeding. Native to Costa Rica.

Sollya
Pittosporaceae

A small genus of about three species of evergreen climbing shrubs native to Australia. They are grown for their bell-shaped, usually blue flowers.

S. heterophylla BLUEBELL CREEPER ◡◡◡
A slender twining, loose spreading climber up to 2m, or more if given support. The light and delicate leaves are variable, usually oblong to lance-shaped, 2–5cm long, and glossy deep green. The clusters of brilliant blue, bell-shaped flowers, 1cm long, appear throughout most of summer. The small cylindrical fruits have many seeds. Grow in humus-rich, moist but well drained soil with regular summer watering. Grows well in full sun, but prefers some shade. Cut back frequently to keep it in shape. Can be used as a groundcover, or grow against a low wall which it can scramble over. Also makes a good container plant. There is a white-flowered form, 'Alba'.

Sophora japonica

Sophora
Papilionaceae

A genus of about fifty species of herbaceous perennials, deciduous and evergreen trees or shrubs which thrive in the sun. Native to tropical and temperate regions worldwide. They are cultivated for their panicles of pea-shaped flowers, but need long hot summers to flower well.

S. japonica JAPANESE PAGODA TREE ◡
A large, deciduous tree growing up to 30m high, with wide-spreading branches to 20m. With age the trunk takes on the appearance of an oak. The dark green leaves, 30cm long, have up to seventeen leaflets, each 1–5cm long. The loose, 30cm-long panicles of small, creamy-white, pea-shaped flowers appear in late summer. They are followed by pods 5–9cm long. This tree thrives in warm dry conditions. It flowers well in full sun, but will take partial shade. Needs moderate summer

water until it becomes established, then little or no water. Not fussy about soil. With age can make a refreshing shade tree. Native to China, Korea.

Sparaxis
Iridaceae

A small genus of about six species of cormous perennials native to South Africa. They are grown for their brightly coloured spring and summer flowers.

S. tricolor HARLEQUIN FLOWER ◡
A cormous perennial with a basal fan of upright, sword-shaped leaves, 30–40cm long. They are produced in autumn and die down during summer. Over a long period in spring wiry stems carry loose heads of two to five, wide funnel-shaped multicoloured flowers, 5–8cm across. The colours range from red, orange and yellow to purple, usually with a striking black or dark red throat. Grow in full sun in any well drained soil. Summer dormant, so needs no water. In frost-free areas grow in large drifts around deciduous trees and shrubs. Can be left in the ground for several seasons; when crowded, lift in summer and replant in autumn. They also look attractive when grown in pots. Easily propagated by seed.

Sparrmannia
Tiliaceae

A small genus containing three to seven species of evergreen, frost-tender shrubs and trees that are native to south-east Asia, South Africa and Madagascar. They are grown for their showy flowers and bold leaves that give a tropical look.

Sophora japonica

Sparaxis tricolor

Sparrmannia africana

S. africana AFRICAN HEMP))))

A many-stemmed, soft woody shrub, that will grow quickly up to 6m high, spreading to 3m wide, with hairy stems. The soft evergreen, broad leaves are roughly triangular, up to 20cm long, and nearly as wide with shallow lobes. They are light green, heavily veined and velvety, with soft hairs on both sides. The clusters of up to twenty pretty white flowers, 4cm across, with a brush of yellow stamens in the centre, stand above the foliage. The flowering period is mainly in winter and spring, but flowers may be produced at any time. The shrub needs generous amounts of water in summer. Grows best in full sun, but can take partial shade. A most attractive shrub with bold leaves that gives a tropical look to the garden, and good near pools. Native to South Africa.

Spartium
Papilionaceae

A genus comprising just a single species of deciduous shrub native to the Mediterranean region, including Portugal.

S. junceum SPANISH BROOM)

A hardy ornamental shrub with many green, upright, cylindrical, almost leafless stems up to 3m high and wide. The inconspicuous, dark green narrow leaves are up to 3cm long and silky hairy underneath. A profusion of bright yellow, fragrant flowers, 2–3cm long, appear in clusters at the ends of the branches in spring and early summer. They are followed by flattened hairy seedpods to 8cm long. Grow the shrub in full sun. Ideal for the dry garden as it needs no summer water. Thrives in coastal conditions, as it withstands salt-laden sea breezes. Makes a showy bank cover. Tolerates chalky soils, but needs good drainage. Easily raised from seed. All parts of the plant are poisonous.

Spathodea 'AFRICAN TULIP TREE'
Bignoniaceae

A genus of just a single species of handsome evergreen tree native to tropical central Africa. Often grown as a street or specimen tree in warm areas, with showy flowers and bold leaves.

S. campanulata))

A fast-growing, spectacularly showy evergreen tree 18–20m high, spreading to 10m wide, usually forming a broad-topped crown on a high-branched trunk. The leaves are usually densely set on the top part of the smooth branches, giving a dense canopy. The large, glossy, pinnate leaves are 45cm or more long. They are divided into nine to twenty-one oblong, leathery, deep green leaflets, 6–12cm long, each with a prominent midrib. The flowers are borne in dense, terminal, upward-facing clusters. Each spectacular cup-shaped, flame-red flower, 7–13cm wide, is edged with yellow and contains abundant nectar. The brown buds curve to a point, and are inflated with water. The flowers are produced mainly in spring and summer, but may appear at any time. Grow the tree in full sun in a warm, sheltered position in soil with good drainage. Give moderate to generous summer water. Grows rapidly, and flowers when young. The flower buds are easily damaged by frost. A spectacular specimen or shade

Spartium junceum

Spathodea campanulata

tree. Native to tropical east Africa. There is a pure yellow form that is equally spectacular, and comes true from seed.

Spiraea
Rosaceae

A genus of eighty to a hundred species of evergreen or deciduous shrubs widely distributed in Europe, Asia and North America. They are mainly sun-

Spiraea cantoniensis

loving plants with showy flower clusters.

S. cantoniensis BRIDAL WREATH ☽
An upright to spreading semi-evergreen shrub to 2m high and wide with arching branches. The lance-shaped, 4cm-long, dark green leaves are toothed. In spring the shrub covers itself with rounded clusters, 5–6cm wide, of small white flowers. They are borne on short, lateral shoots along the branches, which makes a spectacular sight. Grows best in full sun, but will take partial shade. When established it withstands drought, but flowers better with some summer water. Easy to grow in most well drained soils. Prune after flowering by removing old weak growth that has flowered. Native to China. 'Flore Pleno' has double white flowers.

Sprekelia
Amaryllidaceae

A genus of just a single species of frost-tender, bulbous perennial, native to Mexico and Guatemala. It is grown for its beautiful, large red flowers. Often sold as *Amaryllis formosisima*.

S. formosissima AZTEC LILY, JACOBEAN LILY, ST JAMES LILY ☽☽☽
A bulbous perennial with strap-shaped basal leaves to 50cm long. In spring the stems, to 30cm tall, bear dark crimson flowers 12cm across, with one erect

upper segment, two lower horizontal segments, and three narrow pendant segments rolled together into a tube at the base, then separating into pendant segments. The flower has long, prominent stamens. Grow in well drained soil in full sun. The bulb is briefly dormant in autumn, so give generous water while in growth. The plant is most effective in groups, but as the roots resent disturbance do not lift the bulbs until necessary. Looks good in a sunny border or especially in pots.

Stachys
Lamiaceae

A genus of 300 species of annuals, perennials and subshrubs widely distributed throughout the northern temperate regions. The stems are usually square in cross-section. They are grown for their leaves or flowers.

S. byzantina LAMBS' EARS ☽
A mat-forming perennial up to 45cm high, spreading to 60cm wide, with white-woolly stems and rosettes of leaves. The soft, thick, white-woolly leaves are lance-shaped and up to 10cm long. The upright woolly flower stalks bear many whorls of small purplish flowers in summer and autumn. The perennial is grown for its attractive silver leaves rather than the flowers. Grow in full sun or partial shade in well drained soil. Only needs occasional summer water. Ideal as an edging or for ground cover. Divide plants in early spring before growth starts. Native from the Caucasus to Iran. 'Silver Carpet' has intensely silvered white leaves.

Stenolobium stans
See *Tecoma stans*.

S

Stachys byzantina

Stephanotis
Asclepiadaceae

A genus of about fifteen species of climbing evergreen, woody-stemmed shrubs native from Malaysia to Madagascar. They are grown for their strongly scented, waxy, tubular, usually white flowers. One species is popular as a house plant and as a florist's flower because of its strong scent.

S. floribunda BRIDAL WREATH, MADAGASCAR JASMINE ❀❀❀

An evergreen, wiry, sparsely branched, twining climber that makes moderate growth up to 3m or more high. The opposite glossy, thick leathery, dark green leaves are 6–10cm long. In summer it produces axillary circular clusters of exquisite, waxy white flowers 4–5cm wide, with five intensely fragrant petals flaring from a tubular base. The flowers are long-lasting even when cut. If the conditions are favourable it will produce huge seedpods up to 15cm long, which can take up to two years to ripen. The shrub prefers its roots in shade, with filtered sun on the leaves. For best growth and flowering, grow in a rich soil that is high in humus material. Give generous water and feeding during spring and summer. Keep it drier during winter. Ideal for growing in a pot or container in a warm shady terrace by the house where the strong scent can be appreciated. Native to Madagascar.

Sterculia acerifolia
See *Brachychiton acerifolius*.

Stephanotis floribunda

Sterculia diversifolia
See *Brachychiton populneus*.

Sternbergia 'AUTUMN DAFFODIL'
Amaryllidaceae

A small genus of about eight species of frost-hardy bulbous perennials native to the Mediterranean region. They are grown for their crocus-like flowers that are usually yellow and produced in autumn.

S. lutea ❀

A bulbous perennial with narrow, lance-shaped leaves to 30cm long, deep green in colour. These are produced in autumn and remain green for several months, then die down with summer heat. The beautiful, golden-yellow, funnel-shaped flowers, 5cm long, appear during autumn on stems 15–20cm long. The leaves and flowers usually appear at the same time. Easily grown in full sun in most soils. The bulbs are intolerant of winter wet, so they need soil with excellent drainage. Summer dormant so no water is needed. Good for growing in sunny borders, rock gardens or near pools. Good cut flowers. When bulbs become crowded, lift, divide and replant in summer. Native from Spain to the eastern Mediterranean.

Stipa 'FEATHER GRASS, NEEDLE GRASS'
Poaceae

A large genus of about 300 species of frost-hardy evergreen or deciduous feather or needle grasses. Native to temperate and warm temperate areas worldwide. They are grown for their form, or for their large, open inflorescences.

S. calamagrostis (syn. S. lasiagrostis) ❀

A densely tufted perennial that forms rounded mounds to 1m high and 1.2m wide. The rush-like, cylindrical, blue-green leaves are up to 30cm long. In summer the arching, silvery or purple-tinted feathery plumes, 80cm long, ripen to buff. Easy to grow in full sun in any well drained soil. When established it withstands drought, but grows better with some summer water. An attractive grass for borders in a dry garden. Native to southern Europe.

S. gigantea GIANT FEATHER GRASS, SPANISH OATS, GOLDEN OATS ❀

A densely tufted evergreen perennial to

Stipa gigantea

2m high and 1.2m wide. Clumps of narrow, linear arching leaves grow 60–90cm high. The large, golden oat-like plumes, to 50cm long, appear in early summer on stems to 2m high. These shimmer in an attractive broad cloud. Easy to grow in full sun in any well drained, even poor soil. After flowering and during the heat of summer the plant becomes dormant, so it needs no water once established. The plumes are ideal for dry arrangements. Native to Portugal, southern and central Spain.

S. tenuissima MEXICAN FEATHER GRASS ❀

A densely tufted, evergreen perennial, to 60cm high and 30cm wide. The bright green, narrowly linear leaves, to 30cm or more long, form erect clumps that arch outwards at the top. Throughout summer this plant bears numerous thin flowering stems, to 30cm long. They divide and re-divide into almost hair-like fineness, green at first, ripening to golden. The whole plant billows in the slightest breeze. Grow in full sun in any well drained soil. When established it withstands drought, but grows better with some summer water. When planted among groundcover or boulders, single or scattered clumps can look most effective. Can self-sow in irrigated gardens. Native to southern USA, Mexico, Argentina.

Strelitzia 'BIRD OF PARADISE'
Strelitziaceae

A small genus of about five species of tender, clump-forming, evergreen perennials native to South Africa; two of them are large and form trunks. They are grown for their exotic flowers and large leaves that give a tropical look.

S

Strelitzia juncea

S. juncea (syn. *S. reginae* var. *juncea*) ❀❀❀

A compact, clump-forming, slow-growing, evergreen perennial up to 2m high, spreading to 1m wide. The blue-green or grey-green leaves, to 50cm long, have no leaf blade, only leaf stalks that are very erect and stiff, giving the plant a rush-like appearance. The flowers are almost identical to *S. reginae*, but are not held above the foliage. Because of the reduced chlorophyll-making areas, it needs to be grown in full sun. Grows well in a rich soil with generous summer water and feeding. Also makes a useful container plant. An excellent tropical-looking plant for growing near a pool where the strange foliage makes a perfect foil for the display of the flowers.

S. nicolai GIANT BIRD OF PARADISE ❀❀

A clump-forming evergreen perennial with many tree-like pseudostems, up to 10m high, spreading to 5m wide. The grey-green, banana-like, leathery leaves can be 60–120cm long and 30–60cm wide. They are carried on long, stout leaf stalks that are usually grooved or channelled. The leaves are arranged like a fan on the trunk, growing in a single plane from its top part. The boat-like, purplish spathes, 25–40cm long, enclose the projecting white flowers, up to 20cm long, with blue corollas. They are produced in summer and into autumn. The plant is often grown for its large leaves that make a dramatic display even when not in flower. Needs a moderate amount of summer water. Feed young plants generously until they become established. Grow preferably in full sun, though it will tolerate partial shade. Protect from the wind as the leaves can easily be damaged. Makes a dramatic effect when grown near a swimming pool. Withstands a light frost.

Strelitzia nicolai

S. reginae BIRD OF PARADISE ❀❀❀

A compact, clump-forming, slow-growing, evergreen perennial up to 2m high, spreading to 1m wide. The stiff, leathery oblong to lance-shaped bluish-grey leaf-blade is up to 50cm long and 10–15cm wide on a leaf stalk up to 1m long with a pale or red midrib. The flowers are produced on stems up to 1m high. Each inflorescence has a horizontal green boat-like spathe containing several flowers with gigantic brilliant orange sepals and brilliant blue petals. They are produced mainly in winter and spring, but also intermittently throughout the year. The common name comes from the striking resemblance of the flower to a tropical bird's head. This, the commonest species in cultivation, is extremely popular with florists and flower arrangers. Makes excellent cut flowers as they last a long time in water. Prefers to be grown in full sun, although it can take light shade. Grows well in a rich

Strelitzia reginae

soil with generous summer water and feeding. Also makes a useful container plant. An excellent tropical-looking plant for growing near a pool. Do not attempt to grow where frost is likely.

Streptosolen
Solanaceae

This genus contains just a single species of evergreen shrub native to Colombia and Ecuador which is grown for the brilliant display of flowers lasting most of the year.

Streptosolen jamesonii 'Ginger Meggs'

S. jamesonii MARMALADE BUSH ❀❀

A slender-stemmed shrub up to 2m high and 1–2m wide. If trained against a wall or trellis it may reach 3m high. The stems are clothed in rough, hairy, oval leaves 3–5cm long. The rounded terminal clusters contain many tubular flowers, 3–5cm long. They are funnel-shaped, with five corolla lobes opening to 2cm wide. The flowers open a brilliant orange, fading to a clear yellow, giving a bicoloured effect. Makes a striking display from early spring until late autumn, though a few flowers may be seen throughout the year. The shrub grows best in full sun, but will take partial shade. Grows much better if given regular summer water, but it will tolerate some

S

Streptosolen jamesonii

drought. These shrubs can become leggy with age, and can be severely pruned to regenerate them. When planted in a rock garden with the stems tumbling down, the effect is stunning. There is also a yellow-flowered form, 'Ginger Meggs', that makes a spectacular display of brilliant, pure yellow flowers.

Syagrus
Arecaceae

A complex genus of thirty-two species of pinnate-leaved palms native to South

Syagrus romanzoffiana

America. Most are single trunked, but a few have clustering trunks. Many are relatively cold-tolerant, and will grow in warm temperate and subtropical regions.

S. romanzoffiana (syn. *Arecastrum romanzoffianum, Cocos plumosa*)
QUEEN PALM

A solitary-trunked palm to 18m high and 6–10m wide. It is one of the world's fastest-growing palms, as under ideal conditions it can grow 30–60cm a year. The light grey trunk is ringed with old leaf bases. The arching, plumose, deep green leaves can be up to 6m long, with 1m long pendulous leaflets. The inflorescence, to 1m long, contains a large number of small white flowers and usually appears in summer. Grow in full sun in free-draining soil. When established it withstands drought, but grows better with some summer water. It grows best in a rich soil that is on the acidic side, as chalky soils cause the leaves to become yellow. The palm responds well to nitrogen fertilizer. Grows well in coastal gardens as it withstands salt-laden sea breezes. A mature palm is relatively frost-hardy. It makes a beautiful specimen tree. Native to southern Brazil, Paraguay, Uruguay, and north-eastern Argentina.

Syzygium
Myrtaceae

A large genus of about 500 species of aromatic evergreen shrubs and trees native throughout the tropics. One tropical species, S. *aromaticum*, yeilds the 'clove' of commerce, while others are grown for their attractive leaves and fruit. The flowers are conspicuous for tufts of stamens that look like small brushes.

Syzygium paniculatum

S. paniculatum (syn. *Eugnia australis, E. myrtifolia, E. paniculata*)
AUSTRALIAN BRUSH CHERRY, BRUSH CHERRY

A small evergreen tree which, if left unclipped, will grow to 10m or more tall. As a shrub it lends itself to shearing into a pyramid, formal shape or hedge. The slender branches are dense, with nearly stalkless leaves 8–10cm long. They are elliptic to lance-shaped, reddish-bronze when young, becoming dark glossy green. In summer it bears white flowers 2–3cm wide, with many yellow stamens in small axillary and terminal clusters. The fruit is pink to rose-purple, showy, 1–2cm long, edible but insipid. The shrub grows well in full sun, but will tolerate shade. Thrives in well drained garden soil with generous summer water. Hedges need frequent clipping to stay neat. As a tree it is beautiful, but formal in appearance. With its new red foliage and showy fruit it makes a most useful plant in the garden. Native to eastern Australia.

Syzygium paniculatum (fruit)

T

Tamarix 'TAMARISK'
Tamaricaceae

A genus of about fifty species of frost-hardy shrubs and small trees that are native to Europe, Africa and Asia. The naming of 'Tamarix' is much confused in the nursery trade and among botanists as the plants are difficult to distinguish with the naked eye.

T. parviflora

A spreading shrub 2–5m high, with graceful brown or purple arching branches and pale green scale-like foliage. The flowers are rose-pink, appearing towards the ends of the branches in plumes to 5cm long in spring on last year's growth. Prune after flowering to encourage strong new shoots. Grow in full sun. The shrub tolerates long periods of drought, and saline soils that would be toxic to other

Tamarix parviflora

plants. As it is resistant to salt-laden sea breezes and wind, it is ideal for planting in coastal gardens. Ideal for planting in light sandy soils. Often used as a windbreak or hedge in exposed areas. Native to south-east Europe.

Tecoma (syn. Tecomaria)
Bignoniaceae

A genus of about twelve species of frost-tender evergreen climbers, shrubs or small trees that are native to southern Africa, central and tropical America, and the West Indies. They are grown for their showy clusters of flowers.

Tecoma capensis 'Aurea'

T. australis
See *Pandorea pandorana*.

T. capensis (syn. *Bignonia capensis, Tecomaria capensis*)
CAPE HONEYSUCKLE or

A half climbing evergreen shrub with nearly upright slender branches, up to 5m or more high if given support, but more often seen as a lower-growing shrub. The dark green pinnate leaves, up to 15cm long, contain five to nine diamond-shaped, toothed leaflets. The orange-scarlet tubular flowers, 5cm long, with long, protruding, yellow-orange stamens, are produced in erect terminal racemes to 15cm long. They appear from late summer until winter,

Tecoma capensis

and some flowers can be seen for most of the year. The flowers may be followed by 15cm-long seedpods. Grow the shrub in full sun or partial shade. Also withstands hot, dry conditions. Not particular about the soil providing it is well drained, but can become chlorotic if the soil is too alkaline. To keep compact it requires regular severe pruning, which induces new growth where the flowers are produced. Can be used to make a low hedge, to cover banks, or it may be trained as a wall shrub. Makes a most striking shrub when in flower. Native to southern Africa. The cultivar 'Aurea' has yellow flowers with paler green leaves. This is much smaller-growing and is more tender, requiring a warm, sheltered position to grow well.

T. ricasoliana
See *Podranea ricasoliana*.

T. stans (syn. *Bignonia stans, Stenolobium stans*) YELLOW BELLS,
TRUMPET BUSH, YELLOW ELDER

An evergreen shrub or small tree that quickly reaches 5m or more high, spreading to 3m or more wide, with open, upright branches. The pale green, pinnate leaves, up to 35cm long, are divided into five to thirteen oblong-ovate to lance-shaped, toothed leaflets 5–10cm long. The dense, many-flowered, pendulous clusters, up to

Tecoma stans

15cm long, contain showy, bright yellow, funnel-shaped flowers 3–5cm wide; these are produced in great profusion during summer and autumn. They are followed by seedpods 15cm or more long that are narrow, thin, and hang on the shrub. For best results grow in full sun in a good deep soil where it makes a showy mass in a large garden. When established it withstands drought, but grows better with summer water. Requires heat to grow well. Makes an excellent windbreak for coastal gardens. Native to tropical America.

Tecomaria
See *Tecoma*.

Tetrapanax
Araliaceae

A genus containing just a single species of stoloniferous evergreen shrub or small tree native to southern China and Taiwan. It is grown for its tropical-looking, large, palmately lobed leaves and giant white flower clusters.

T. papyrifer (syn. *Aralia papyrifera, Fatsia papyrifera, T. papyriferus*)
RICE PAPER PLANT
A fast-growing, often multi-trunked, thicket-forming, evergreen shrub 5m high and wide. The light grey or brown trunks are ringed with many narrow fissures, they are never straight, always

leaning or curved, giving a picturesque look. The soft pith inside the stem is used for making the finest quality rice paper in Asia. The big, bold, long-stalked leaves are 30–60cm wide with five to eleven deep lobes. They are grey-green above and white-felted under-neath, and carried in clusters at the ends of the stems. In autumn, large, branched clusters, to 1m long, of creamy-white, sweetly fragrant flowers, 1cm across, appear on furry tan stems. The fruit are small, round berries,

Tetrapanax papyrifer

greenish in colour that ripen to black. As the leaves sunburn easily it is best to grow the shrub in shade, and to grow well it needs regular, generous water during summer. Suckering can be a problem, with shoots sometimes arising 6m from the parent; furthermore, digging around shoots stimulates sucker formation. A basically carefree and tropical-looking shrub that is damaged, but not killed by frost.

Teucrium 'GERMANDER'
Lamiaceae

A genus of about 300 species of evergreen and deciduous shrubs, subshrubs and herbaceous perennials of wide distribution, especially in the Mediterranean region. They are noted for their aromatic foliage.

Teucrium fruticans

T. fruticans BUSH GERMANDER
A bushy, evergreen shrub with loosely growing, silver stems up to 2m high and 2m wide. The aromatic, grey-green, lance-shaped leaves, up to 3cm long, are white-woolly underneath. In summer the loose, terminal spikes appear: these are 10cm long, with pale blue tubular to bell-shaped flowers, each 3cm long and usually with two to three lips. The shrub grows best in full sun. It needs well drained soil and is easily damaged by wet, poorly drained soil. When established it withstands drought, but grows better with some summer water. Good for informal hedging, as it tolerates shearing. Makes a tough, grey-leaved plant as a specimen, or in mass for the dry garden. Also grows well in coastal gardens. Native to the western Mediterranean. 'Azureum' has dark blue flowers; 'Compactum' grows to only 45cm high with a spread of 30cm.

Thamnocalamus spathaceus
See *Fargesia murieliae*.

Thevetia
Apocynaceae

A small genus of eight species of shrubs and small trees with milky sap native to tropical America and the West Indies. They are cultivated for their showy, funnel-shaped flowers with twisted petals. All parts of the plants are poisonous. Only one species is widely grown.

T. peruviana YELLOW OLEANDER ☘☘☘

A fast-growing, erect, open-growing shrub or small tree up to 6m high, usually clothed to the ground with branches. The shining green, narrow leaves, 10–15cm long, are lance-shaped with their edges rolled under. The terminal clusters contain a few large funnel-shaped flowers, 5–8cm wide. They are lemon-yellow to orange-apricot, and sweetly scented like tea roses, appearing at any time but mostly during spring to late summer. The plant can look attractive when trained into a 3m-high tree. Grows best in soil with ample summer water and good drainage, as it is shallow-rooted. Needs to grow in full sun, and thrives in heat, but dislikes wind. The form of this shrub with its attractive leaves and yellow flowers makes it an ideal pot plant for a sunny patio. All parts of the plant are poisonous. 'Alba' has white flowers. Native to the West Indies and Mexico.

Thrinax 'THATCH PALM'
Arecaceae

A small genus of seven species of slender-trunked, palmate-leafed palms native to tropical America. These frost-tender palms are ideal for the smaller garden.

T. radiata (syn. T. floridana) FLORIDA THATCH PALM, SILVER THATCH PALM ☘

A slow-growing palm that in time will reach 6m or more high, only spreading 2–3m wide. The smooth, slender, straight trunk is grey to light brown with leaves in a rounded crown at the top. The leaves, up to 1m wide, are fan-shaped, sometimes forming almost a complete circle. The bright green to yellowish-green leaf segments are cut to about half the depth of the leaf. On mature plants the inflorescences are long, erect panicles of whitish flowers, followed by white berries. Grow the palm in full sun. When established it withstands drought, but grows better with some summer water. It is quite tolerant of salt spray, so is ideal for exposed coastal gardens. Grows well in calcareous and alkaline soils but will also succeed in a wide range of soils. It makes a very attractive and long-lived container plant. Native to southern

Thrinax radiata

Florida, the West Indies, south-eastern Mexico and Belize.

Thuja
Cupressaceae

A small genus of six species of hardy, narrowly to broadly conical, evergreen coniferous trees widely distributed in northern temperate regions. They are normally clothed to the ground with slender branches, making attractive specimen plants. The foliage is aromatic when crushed.

T. occidentalis
AMERICAN ARBOR-VITAE, WHITE CEDAR ☘

An extremely hardy, medium-sized, columnar tree 10–20m high, spreading to 5m wide, with reddish-brown, peeling bark. The spreading branches, that tend to turn up at the ends are covered with flattened sprays of small, scale-like foliage. The leaves have conspicuous resin glands and are dark green above and paler green beneath, with an apple scent. The upright, egg-shaped female cones, 1cm long, consist of eight to ten pairs of overlapping scales joined at the base. Grow the tree in full sun in any soil, provided it is well drained. When established it withstands drought, but it also grows well with generous summer water. One of

Thevetia peruviana

T

the best conifers for its resistance to heat. It is invaluable for hedges and screens. Native to eastern North America. The species itself is seldom seen, but many garden varieties are common. 'Dancia' forms a dwarf, round bush only 50cm high; 'Rheingold' is a slow-growing conical bush with golden-yellow leaves 1–2m high.

Thuja occidentalis

Thunbergia
Acanthaceae

A genus of perhaps 100 species of annuals, evergreen perennials, shrubs and climbers native to the tropical parts of central and southern Africa, Madagascar and Asia. They are noted for their showy flowers and often fast growth.

T. alata BLACK-EYED SUSAN ⌣⌣
A twining evergreen perennial, often grown as an annual. As a perennial it may reach up to 3m high with an equal spread. The dark green leaves are triangular in shape, toothed, and up to 8cm long. They are carried on long, narrowly winged stalks. From summer to autumn the solitary funnel-shaped, creamy-yellow or orange flowers, 3–4cm wide, are produced. They often have a dark purple-brown centre, and cover the plant when it is in flower. Excellent for hot areas in full sun, but it

Thunbergia alata

does need regular summer water. This light, bright and easily grown creeper has many uses, for covering banks, trailing over terraces, or climbing trellis. Easily grown from seed. Native to southern east Africa, but naturalized in the Tropics.

T. erecta KING'S MANTLE ⌣⌣⌣
An evergreen perennial or bushy spreading shrub, up to 2m high and wide, with thin branches; often creeping or mat forming. The almost glossy, dark green leaves, ovate to elliptic in shape, are 3–6cm long, with long, tapering ends, and sometimes with a few broad teeth. The trumpet-shaped, blue to violet flowers are 6–8cm long, with deep purple-blue lobes and a yellow inside tube. They are produced in the leaf axils throughout summer. The plant grows best in rich, well drained soil in partial shade with

Thunbergia erecta

generous watering during summer. Native to tropical West Africa to South Africa.

T. grandiflora BLUE TRUMPET VINE, BENGAL CLOCK VINE ⌣⌣⌣
A rampant, strong-growing climber that will quickly cover 6–10m or more high and wide. The rough ovate to heart-shaped leaves are 10–20cm long, with long tapering ends and scalloped margins. The beautiful, sky blue, tubular flowers have a yellow or white inside tube and are produced in pendant racemes 10cm or more long. Each flower opens out to 12cm wide, with five distinct lobes or petals. The flowers completely cover the plant throughout summer. A spectacular climber to cover a pergola, fence or house wall, but it does need room to grow. Needs a strong support as it makes a dense mass of foliage. Can be grown in full sun or partial shade in a rich soil. Requires generous summer water and feeding to be seen at its best. 'Alba' has pure white flowers. Native to northern India.

Thunbergia grandiflora

T. gregorii ORANGE CLOCK VINE ⌣⌣⌣
A perennial, evergreen, twining climber or creeper often grown as an annual. It twines up to 2m high or spreads over

Thunbergia gregorii

the ground to 2m across. The slender, bristly stems have triangular, toothed leaves that are soft and hairy, 6–8cm long. The solitary flowers are tubular, flaring and bright orange, 4cm across. They are produced for most of the year. A showy, easily grown plant that can cover a fence or be used as groundcover. Also looks good when grown on the top of a wall, cascading down in a mass of flower and foliage. Grows well in full sun or partial shade. For best flower and growth, give generous summer water. Native to tropical Africa.

Thymus 'THYME'
Lamicaeae

A genus of over 300 species of aromatic small shrubs or evergreen perennials, native to Europe and Asia. They are usually found in chalky soils. They have long been grown for their culinary use, often in a herb garden.

T. vulgaris GARDEN THYME ☽
A cushion-forming, bushy subshrub, 20–30cm high, spreading to 40cm or more wide. A highly aromatic plant with densely branched, woody stems, the young branches covered in velvety white hairs. The tiny, narrow to oval leaves are finely hairy, and dark grey-green in colour; up to 1.5cm long. In late spring and early summer, tiny pink, white or lilac flowers are borne in oblong clusters. They are particularly attractive to bees. Grow the plant in full sun, though it will take partial shade. Prefers light, well drained soils. Drought-tolerant once established, needing little summer water. Makes a good edging plant or looks attractive in a rock garden, or in a container. Cut back occasionally to keep compact. Use the leaves in cooking, fresh or dried. Native to the western Mediterranean region and southern Italy.

Tibouchina
Melastomataceae

A large genus of over 350 species of shrubs, subshrubs and climbers native to tropical America, and particularly Brazil. They are grown for their attractive velvety leaves and their spectacular violet or purple flowers. They mostly have stems that are square in cross-section.

T. urvilleana (syn. T. semidecandra)
PURPLE GLORY BUSH ☽☽☽
A tender, branching shrub that in perfect conditions grows from 3–6m high, but normally only reaches 1–2m, with open, spreading, hairy branches. The stems are almost square. The branch tips, flower buds and new growth are covered in fine red hairs. The ovate to elliptic velvety-hairy leaves, up to 15cm long, are deeply veined. Older leaves may take on a reddish tint, particularly if the roots are dry. The five-petalled flowers are violet to reddish-purple, with long, curling, purple stamens. They are velvety-textured, saucer-shaped and up to 10cm across. These appear solitarily or in clusters of three or more on the ends of the branches intermittently during summer. This fast-growing shrub needs

Tibouchina urvilleana

rich growing conditions with some shade in summer and protection from the wind. Give ample water and feed during summer. Can become leggy with age so cut back hard in spring when it will quickly regrow. Also excellent for growing in pots. Native to Brazil.

Tilia 'LIME, LINDEN'
Tiliaceae

A genus of over thirty species of frost-hardy deciduous trees native to Europe, Asia and North America. They are grown for their attractive shape, foliage and flowers. They are often used as street trees.

Tilia tomentosa

T. tomentosa SILVER LINDEN ☽
A broadly pyramidal tree, to 20m high spreading to 9m wide, with slow to moderate growth. The upright-growing branches form a dense, compact crown. The rounded, sometimes lobed or toothed leaves, to 10cm long, are dark green above and silvery underneath, and shimmer and ripple in the slightest breeze. In summer the tree bears clusters of fragrant white flowers, 1.5cm across. The flowers are attractive to bees. Grow the tree in full sun in deep, rich soil. When established it withstands drought, but grows better with some summer water. With its shimmering leaves it makes an attractive specimen or avenue tree. Often seen as a street tree. Native to south-east Europe.

Tipuana 'TIPU TREE'
Papilionaceae

A genus containing just a single species of frost-tender, fast-growing tree that is native to southern Brazil to Bolivia. Grown for its beautiful, showy, pea-like flowers and attractive foliage. Often seen as a street or shade tree.

T

T. tipu PRIDE OF BOLIVIA ☽

A deciduous or semi-evergreen tree that makes rapid growth to 10m high, eventually making a gracefully spreading tree with a flattened crown 8m wide. Old trees can become picturesque with their massive low branches, which may be horizontal or contorted. The light green pinnate leaves, up to 45cm long, are divided into nine to twenty-five leaflets, 4cm long, with notched tips. The clusters of pea-shaped flowers, 2–3cm across, emerge in spring and summer and may be up to 30cm long; they are golden yellow or apricot, with crumpled petals and red veins, and appear in great profusion like small butterflies. The flowers are followed by woody pods, 6cm long. Grow in full sun. The tree grows well in poor soil, but may become chlorotic in strongly alkaline soil. When established it withstands drought, but grows better with some summer water. When grown in a lawn or near a patio or terrace it can provide a useful shade canopy. An avenue planted with these trees in full flower is a spectacular sight. The tree does not grow well in coastal conditions. The timber is the source of rosewood.

Tipuana tipu

Tithonia 'MEXICAN SUNFLOWER'
Asteraceae

A small genus of about ten species of stout annuals, perennials and shrubs native to Mexico and central America. They are sometimes grown as a summer annual.

T. rotundifolia MEXICAN SUNFLOWER ☽

A shrubby, fast-growing, upright annual that forms a bush 1–3m high and 30–40cm wide, with dark green hairy stems. The mid-green simple or three-lobed leaves, up to 30cm long, are hairy underneath and carried on hairy, stout, blackish stalks. The spectacular, mostly solitary flower heads, 8–10cm wide, have orange-scarlet petals and tufted yellow centres. They are borne from late summer to autumn on long hollow stems. The plant is easily raised from seed. Grows well in full sun. A bright, colourful annual for the dry garden, as it is drought-tolerant. Will grow in poor soils and naturalize if happy. It needs shelter from strong winds, as it may blow over. Provides long-lasting cut flowers. Native to Mexico and central America. Seed companies offer many varieties, including 'Goldfinger', which is more compact, growing to 75cm high. 'Torch' has vivid orange-red flower heads.

Toona
Meliaceae

A genus of about twenty species of frost-hardy deciduous and semi-evergreen trees with light-coloured wood, native to tropical America, east Asia and Australasia.

T. sinensis (syn. *Cedrela sinensis*) ☽☽☽

A broadly columnar deciduous tree that makes slow growth up to 15m high, with shaggy pealing bark. The pinnate leaves are up to 60cm long, with ten to twenty lance-shaped leaflets, hairy underneath. The new leaves are tinted in shades of cream, bronze-red to pink, and rose; the latter are most attractive. In summer, 30cm-long pendulous clusters of small, fragrant, white or greenish-white flowers appear. The tree grows well in full sun. For best growth give generous summer water. Makes an ideal specimen tree or shade tree when grown in a lawn. Unfortunately it suckers freely. Grows best in areas with hot summers. Native to China. 'Flamingo' has vivid pink young leaves.

Trachelospermum
Apocynaceae

A genus of about twenty species of frost-hardy, clambering, evergreen climbers, shrubby, with a twining habit and milky sap; native to India across to Japan. They are grown for their attractive leaves and showy, fragrant flowers.

T. asiaticum ☽☽☽

A twining, evergreen, hardy climber, up to 5m high and wide, which can also be grown as a groundcover. The dark green, glossy leaves are oval, and 2–5cm long. The fragrant, creamy-white flowers, which age to buff yellow, have five spreading lobes, and are 2cm across; they are produced in terminal clusters from mid- to late summer. The shrub can be grown in full sun or partial shade. Grows and flowers best with regular summer water. Normally grown against a sunny wall or near the house where the fragrance of the flowers can be appreciated. Native to Korea and Japan.

Trachelospermum jasminoides

T. jasminoides STAR JASMINE ☽☽☽

A rather slow-growing climber, 7m high or more, and as much across. The narrowly oval leaves are dark green, and 5–8cm long. The new foliage is a glossy light green, and the leaves turn bronze-red in winter. The flowers are 2–3cm across, and very strongly scented; white, becoming cream with age. They are produced profusely in small clusters on short side branches during summer and autumn. Flowers best in full sun with ample summer water. Can be grown as a climber, a wall shrub, or makes an excellent groundcover. Native to southern China, Taiwan, Korea and Japan. The cultivar 'Variegatum' has leaves margined and splashed creamy-white, often tinged red; but it is rare.

Trachycarpus
Arecaceae

A genus of about six species of small or moderate, dioecious (male and female flowers on different plants), palmate-leaved palms, usually with a single stem but sometimes forming a clump. Native to the Himalayan region.

T. fortunei
CHUSAN PALM, WINDMILL PALM ꙮ
An unbranched, evergreen palm that makes a solitary, straight trunk up to 15m, but usually only 8m high in dry climates. The trunk is covered with a mat of long, dark brown fibres from old leaf sheaths. The fan-shaped, dark green leaves, 45–75cm long, are almost circular in outline. They are divided into numerous pointed, stiffish segments, and are carried on toothed stalks, 45cm long. The leaves are crowned on the top of the trunk. On older palms, panicles of yellow flowers appear in early summer. Only female plants bear small black fruit. The palm grows well in sun or partial shade in any well drained soil. When established it withstands drought, but grows better with some summer water. In the garden this slow-growing palm is best seen in groups, or it can make a wonderful specimen for patios and terraces when young. It will even grow indoors. An ideal palm for a small area such as a courtyard. Can be damaged by strong wind. Native to southern China.

Tradescantia
Commelinaceae

A genus of over sixty species of creeping, trailing or tuft-forming

Trachycarpus fortunei

evergreen perennials native to North and South America. Some make easy and fast-growing houseplants, while others make useful groundcover plants.

T. pallida 'Purpurea' (syn. Setcreasea purpurea, Tradescantia pallida)
PURPLE HEART ꙮ
A robust, trailing perennial that produces purple, fleshy stems up to 30cm long, that are first upright then tend to creep. The red-purple, broadly lance-shaped leaves are 8–15cm long. These are V-shaped in section. In summer the terminal clusters of small bright pink, or lavender-pink to rose-purple flowers are produced. For best leaf colour grow in full sun, restrict the root zone, and keep on the dry side during summer. Attractive when tumbling over the top of a wall. If the top growth is killed by frost it will soon spring from below ground level. Native to the arid regions of Mexico.

Triteleia uniflora
See Ipheion uniflorum.

Tritonia
Iridaceae

A genus of up to fifty species of cormous perennials native to South Africa. They are closely related to Crocosmia. They are grown for their showy summer flowers.

Tradescantia pallida 'Purpurea'

T. crocata (syn. Montbretia crocata) ꙮ
A cormous perennial with a basal fan of upright, sword-shaped leaves 30–40cm long. They are produced in autumn and die down during summer. Over a long period in spring, wiry stems carry spikes of up to ten cup-shaped orange flowers, 3–4cm long. Grow in full sun in any well drained soil. Summer dormant, so needs no water. In frost-free areas grow in large drifts around deciduous trees and shrubs. Can be left in the ground for several seasons. When crowded, lift in summer and replant in autumn. They also look attractive when grown in pots. 'Princess Beatrix' has deep orange flowers with dark markings.

Tropaeolum 'NASTURTIUM'
Tropaeolaceae

A genus of eighty to ninety species of climbing, trailing or bushy annuals and herbaceous perennials native to central and South America. The easily grown annuals are popular for their brilliant showy flowers.

T. majus
GARDEN NASTURTIUM INDIAN CRESS ꙮꙮꙮ
A fast-growing, somewhat succulent annual climbing 1–3m high, spreading to 3m wide, which climbs by coiling leafstalks. The bright green leaves are up to 8cm across, circular with a wavy edge, and carried on long stalks. The fragrant, yellow, orange or red flowers

Tropaeolum majus

are sometimes striped or spotted, up to 5–6cm across, with a distinctive long spur. They appear from spring to summer. The young leaves, flowers, and unripe seedpods are edible, with a peppery flavour, and may be used in salads. Easily grown from seed. Grow in full sun or partial shade, with regular summer water. Makes a spectacular, quick temporary cover for fences, banks or over rocks. Native to South America. Much hybridization has been carried out, with seed companies listing many named varieties with a wider range of flower colours, from creamy-yellow to orange and deep red, and some with variegated leaves. Particularly popular are the dwarf, bushy kinds that only grow to 40cm high and wide, covering themselves with showy flowers in spring. The dwarf varieties are suitable for growing in pots or containers.

Tulbaghia
Alliaceae

A genus of about twenty-four species of tuberous or cormous perennials native to tropical and southern Africa. They are grown for their many-flowered umbels of purple or white, star-like flowers.

T. violacea SOCIETY GARLIC ꙮꙮ

A clump-forming bulb with narrow, bluish-green leaves to 30cm long, that grow from a central point. They are evergreen in mild climates. The terminal umbels of eight to twenty lilac-pink to purplish pink, six-petalled flowers are up to 3cm across. They are produced during midsummer to early autumn. They rise above the leaves on stalks 30cm or more long. Grow the bulbs in full sun or partial shade, in free-draining soil. Give regular water during summer. Ideal for planting in drifts, where they will soon naturalize to form groundcover. The leaves and flower stems have an onion or garlic odour when crushed, so they are unsatisfactory as cut flowers. Native to South Africa. 'Silver Lace' has leaves edged in white, and larger flowers.

Tupidanthus
Araliaceae

A genus of just a single species of tropical evergreen tree native to India and south-east Asia. It is grown for its beautiful large leaves that are similar to Schefflera.

T. calyptratus (syn. Schefflera pueckleri) MALLET TREE ꙮꙮꙮ

A tropical evergreen, multi-trunked tree up to 6m high and wide. The low-branched trunk can be massive in older specimens. The large, palmate leaves, up to 60cm wide, have ten deep green,

Tupidanthus calyptratus

glossy leaflets that form a circle on the end of the petiole. Both the main and secondary petioles are red. Each drooping, often wavy-edged leaflet, to 30cm long, has a prominent pale or red midvein. The inflorescence, which is rarely produced in cultivation, consists of a spreading panicle of greenish, cup-shaped flowers 2–3cm wide. The tree will take full sun, but does best in half shade. It requires a rich, well drained soil and a sheltered location with generous summer watering. Good as an interior plant, for patios, or outdoors near a water feature or pool area where it creates a tropical look.

Urginea
Hyacinthaceae

A genus of about 100 species of bulbous perennials native to Africa, Europe, the Mediterranean region and India.

U. maritima SEA ONION, SQUILLS ☽

A bulbous perennial that forms a huge, reddish-brown bulb 10–15cm thick, which is partially above ground. In the late autumn the strap-shaped leaves appear, remaining until spring, and then the plant is summer dormant. The leaves are shiny, rather fleshy, and 30–40cm long. Before they appear the plant sends up a stout, erect stem 30–90cm long; at the top of this is a spike up to 60cm long, containing many tiny, star-shaped, white flowers, that open in succession. Grow in full sun in sandy or stony, free-draining soil, with the neck of the bulb exposed. Ideal for autumn colour in hot, dry gardens, as the bulb needs no summer water. A clump will make a striking effect. Ideal for coastal gardens as it withstands salt-laden sea breezes. Native to the Mediterranean region.

Urginea maritima

Vallota speciosa
See Cyrtanthus elatus.

Veltheimia
Hyacinthaceae

A small genus of only two species of frost-tender, bulbous perennials native to South Africa. They are grown for their terminal spikes of pendant flowers.

V. bracteata (syn. *V. capensis,*
V. viridifolia) FOREST LILY ☽ or ☽☽
A bulbous plant with broad, lance-shaped, bright green leaves up to 30cm long and 10cm wide, with distinct wavy edges. They form a rosette from the top of the scaly brown bulb. In winter or early spring a long reddish or purple flower stalk appears from the centre of the rosette. This bears a

densely packed flower spike up to 10cm long. The tubular, pink, nodding flowers, 4cm long, are tipped cream or green. The flower spikes can last for several weeks. The bold leaves make it attractive even when not in flower. Plant bulbs with the upper third out of the ground in partial shade. Keep the bulb moist while in leaf and flower, allowing it to rest by drying out in summer. Looks most attractive when grown in a pot or container.

Venidium
See Arctotis.

Venidoarctotis
See Arctotis.

Verbascum 'MULLEIN'
Scrophulariaceae

A genus of about 300 species of hardy biennials with a few annuals, perennials and subshrubs, native to Asia and Europe, chiefly the Mediterranean region. Most produce tall, upright flower spikes in summer.

V. dombyciferum ☽
A tall, upright, biennial or short-lived evergreen perennial, up to 2m high, with silky white hairs covering the stems. The oval, silvery leaves are up to 50cm long; they are mostly formed into a basal rosette to 30cm high. The upright, sparsely branched spikes, 60–120cm long, bear a succession of saucer-shaped lemon flowers, 4cm across, during summer. The plant is easily grown in any soil in full sun. Needs no summer water once established. Grow in a sunny border where its columnar habit and grey-green leaves will give a pleasing effect. Native to Turkey.

V. olympicum (syn. *V. longifolium*) ☽
A tall, upright, evergreen, short-lived perennial up to 2m high, with dense grey-white hairs covering the stems and leaves. The lance-shaped, soft, silvery-felted leaves are 15–20cm long. The flowers are clustered in long, branching spikes 75cm or more long. The saucer-shaped, bright yellow flowers, 3cm across, with yellowish-white and woolly filaments, appear in the second or third year. The plant generally dies after flowering. Grow in full sun. Ideal for the dry garden as it requires no summer water. Spectacular and easily grown from seed. Native to Greece.

Verbena
Verbenaceae

A genus of over 200 species of mostly annuals or perennials, many prostrate. They are widely distributed throughout North, Central and South America with a few from southern Europe. They are grown for their brightly coloured flowers. All need heat to thrive.

V. bonariensis (syn. *V. patagonica*) ☽
A rough, hairy annual or perennial with airy, branching stems up to 1.2m high. The leaves are mostly basal, dark green and elliptic, up to 10cm long, and often toothed. The stems carry many branched clusters, to 5cm across, of

Veltheimia bracteata

Verbena bonariensis

tiny lavender-blue to purple flowers. They appear from summer to autumn. When established it withstands drought, but it grows better with some summer water. Prefers to be in full sun, but will take some shade. The light, airy effect of the plant gives it a quality that is useful for the front of the border. Native to southern USA and Mexico.

V. × hybrida (syn. V. hortensis)
GARDEN VERBENA ⌣⌣
A much-branched, short-lived herbaceous perennial that is normally treated as an annual, growing 15–45cm high, spreading to 60cm wide. The spreading stems often root near the base. The leaves are oblong, 5–10cm long, conspicuously veined and toothed. The flowers are borne in flat, compact clusters, 5–8cm wide, in a range of colours and colour combinations that include white, salmon, pink, bright red or purple-blue, often with a white eye. An ideal plant to give a splash of summer colour to beds or borders. It thrives in the sun, but requires a moderate amount of summer water. Easily raised from seed. Garden origin.

V. rigida (syn. V. venosa) ⌣
An evergreen perennial with stiff stems, growing 30–45cm high. The rough, oblong leaves are 5–10cm long and strongly toothed. The lilac or bright purple flowers, to 1cm across, are carried in round clusters to 5cm across.

Verbena rigida

They are borne on the tops of the stems, gradually becoming spike-like with age. An ideal plant for low-maintenance gardens as it requires little summer water once established. The plant makes underground stems that, if given generous water, can become invasive. Easily raised from seed. Native to S. Brazil, Argentina.

V. tenera ⌣⌣
A shrubby, creeping perennial that roots into the ground at the nodes, spreading to 1m wide. The 2–4cm long, dark green leaves are much dissected. The rose-violet or pink flowers are borne in flat clusters that appear

continuously throughout summer. An ideal plant for groundcover in a sunny position if given some summer water. Native to Brazil, Argentina. Buy named varieties to obtain the best-coloured flowers. 'Albiflora' has white flowers, 'Maonettii' deep lilac with a white stripe.

Viburnum
Caprifoliaceae

A large genus of around 200 species of frost-hardy evergreen and deciduous shrubs, or occasionally small trees native to America, Europe and Asia. Most of the species have clusters of white flowers, some very fragrant, which are often followed by brightly coloured fruits.

V. × carlcephalum
FRAGRANT SNOWBALL ⌣⌣
A splendid medium-sized, deciduous, bushy shrub up to 3m high and wide. The dull greyish-green, heart-shaped, toothed leaves are 9–12cm long, and downy underneath. The leaves often turn a rich red colour in autumn. Large, dense, showy clusters 10–13cm across, of intensely fragrant waxy-white, trumpet-shaped flowers open from pink buds in spring and early summer. Fruit is seldom produced. Grow the shrub in full sun or partial shade. Tolerates most soils including alkaline or acid soils, as well as heavy soils. Needs regular summer water. Grow in a border where the scent from the flowers can be appreciated. Garden origin.

V. odoratissimum SWEET VIBURNUM ⌣⌣
A large evergreen shrub or small tree up to 6m high and wide, which makes a rather grand plant. Its striking glossy-green, leathery, oval leaves are 8–20cm long. The small tubular, fragrant, pure white flowers are carried in 8–10cm conical panicles in spring. Young plants tend not to flower. The small fruit is red at first, ripening to black. Grow the shrub in full sun or partial shade. Needs regular summer water. Tolerates most soils. A magnificent plant for the garden, making a good screening shrub with its large foliage. Magnificent when in full flower. Grow in a border where the scent from the flowers can be appreciated. Native to Asia.

Verbena × hybrida

V

V. suspensum (syn. V. sandankwa)
SANDANKWA VIBURNUM ♩

An evergreen shrub up to 3m high and as wide. The leathery, ovate, glossy, deep green, toothed leaves are up to 13cm long, with a paler underneath. The flat, loose, pendulous clusters of fragrant, white, rose-tinted flowers are up to 10cm across. They are produced in winter and early spring and are followed by bright red berries that turn black with age. The shrub grows well in full sun but will take considerable shade. Only needs occasional summer water once established. Easily grown as it tolerates most soils. Native to southern Japan.

Viburnum tinus

V. tinus LAURESTINUS ♩♩

A dense, compact, evergreen, bushy shrub up to 3m high and spreading 2m wide. The masses of dark glossy green, oval leaves are leathery, slightly folded under at the edges, and 5–8cm long. The terminal flat heads, 8–10cm across, of tiny fragrant white flowers, open from pink buds. The flowers appear continuously throughout winter. They are followed by bright metallic blue berries that often last throughout summer. The shrub tolerates deep shade, but flowers best if grown in full sun. Grows better with regular summer water. Easy to grow, as it tolerates most soils. With its dense foliage to the ground, it makes an attractive hedge or screening shrub. Native to the Mediterranean region. There are many cultivars, including 'Eve Price', a dwarf, compact form with smaller leaves and pink-tinged flowers; 'Lucidum', a vigorous form with much larger, glossier green leaves, and each flower 1cm long; and 'Variegatum', a beautiful, more compact form with boldly variegated, creamy-yellow leaves.

Viburnum tinus 'Variegatum'

Vinca 'PERIWINKLE'
Apocynaceae

A genus of about twelve species of trailing, slender-stemmed, evergreen subshrubs native to Europe, north Africa and central Asia. They form extensive carpets, so they are ideal as groundcover, both in the shade or in full sun, and have attractive flowers.

V. major GREATER PERIWINKLE ♩

A rampant evergreen subshrub up to 40cm high, with soft stems 3m or more long that trail along the ground, rooting at the tips as they go. The opposite ovate to lance-shaped leaves are 7cm long and dark glossy green. Erect shoots 30–50cm high bear the solitary flowers in the axils of the leaves during winter. The corolla is funnel-shaped with broad, spreading lobes 5cm across, bright blue with a white centre. The plant will grow in full sun or shade. It will survive with little or no summer water, but grows and flowers much better with some water. A tough plant that is easy to grow. It is excellent for covering unsightly banks, or it will help to prevent erosion on waste ground. Cut back to ground level in early spring if the growth becomes too tangled, in order to promote strong young growth. Native to the western Mediterranean region. The best form is 'Variegata', as

vigorous as the type, with leaves blotched and margined creamy-white and which rarely revert to green.

V. minor LESSER PERIWINKLE ♩

An evergreen subshrub up to 20cm high, with soft stems 1–2m or more long, that trail along the ground rooting at the tips as they go, usually forming a thick, dense mat. The

Vinca major 'Variegata'

Vitis vinifera

broad, spreading habit 3–6m high and wide, with grey downy young shoots. The leaves are dark green above, and grey underneath. They are divided into five to seven narrow oval to lance-shaped leaflets 12cm long, arranged fan-wise. The slender racemes of fragrant, tubular lavender-blue or violet flowers are up to 30cm long, covering the plant in late summer and autumn. The shrub grows well in full sun in any good garden soil. It requires high summer heat and little water for best flowering. If given a rich soil and ample summer water it will produce strong growth at the expense of flower. Can be trained to make a small shade tree. Native to southern Europe. 'Alba' has white flowers, 'Rosea' has pink flowers.

Vitis 'GRAPE VINE'
Vitaceae

A genus of about sixty-five species of woody, deciduous climbers native to northern temperate regions. Grape vines have been in cultivation since ancient times for the production of wine. While they are normally grown as a commercial crop, they can also make attractive plants in the garden.

V. vinifera
WINE GRAPE, EUROPEAN GRAPE
A woody deciduous climber to 7m high, with a wide spread. The young growth is glabrous, with intermittent tendrils. The leaves are rounded, 10–20cm wide, with three to five toothed lobes, smooth above and sometimes hairy underneath. They are borne on a leaf stalk 10cm or more long. In autumn the leaves turn a beautiful red. The fruit clusters that appear in late summer are large, and variable in size, form and colour. The best fruit is produced in areas with a long season of high heat. For cultivation as a fruit crop, refer to specialist books. Grows well in full sun in most well drained garden soils. Drought-tolerant once established, needing little summer water. Looks attractive growing over an arch or walkway. Particularly useful for giving summer shade to a terrace, and letting in light in winter, with interest in its branch pattern and dominant trunk.

opposite, glossy dark green, lance-shaped leaves are up to 5cm long. The star-like flowers with five petal lobes are bluish-purple, with white throats 2–3cm across. They are borne singly in leaf axils during spring and summer. The plant grows well in sun or shade. Survives with little summer water, but looks much better with regular watering. Cut back to ground level in early spring in order to promote strong young growth, especially if it has become tangled. Makes a good groundcover for shady spots. Native to southern Europe to Asia. There are many named cultivars: 'Alba' with white flowers, 'Argenteovariegata' with variegated leaves, and 'Multiplex' with double plum-purple flowers.

V. rosea
See *Catharanthus roseus*.

Viola 'PANSY, VIOLET'
Violaceae

A large genus of about 500 species of hardy annuals, biennials, or perennials including pansies and violets that are distributed throughout temperate regions worldwide.

V. odorata ENGLISH VIOLET
A stemless, tufted perennial that grows to 20cm high, spreading to 30cm wide, with long runners that root at the joints. The dark green, heart-shaped to rounded leaves, up to 6cm long, are toothed on the margins. The sweetly scented flowers are 2cm across, with a short spur, usually deep violet, but may be pink or white. They are produced in late winter and early spring. The plant grows best in shade, but will tolerate sun. When established it withstands drought, but grows and flowers better with some summer water. Ideal for planting at the base of a shady wall or terrace. It will make an excellent groundcover. Seed is produced freely, so will naturalize in a shady spot in the wild garden. Many different colours and larger-flowered forms, including doubles, have been bred. The violet has long been important as the source of perfume and in the florist trade. Native to west and southern Europe, but widely naturalized.

Vitex
Verbenaceae

A genus of about 270 species of deciduous and evergreen trees and shrubs native to tropical and subtropical regions. They are grown for their attractive foliage and autumn flowers.

V. agnus-castus CHASTE TREE
A deciduous, aromatic shrub or small tree, usually multi-trunked, with a

Washingtonia
Arecaceae

A genus of only two species of massive, usually single-stemmed palms. Both have bisexual flowers and are native to the arid regions of California, Arizona and northern Mexico. The two species hybridize freely when grown together. They are difficult to distinguish from each other when young, as the trunks and leaves look almost identical.

W. filifera
CALIFORNIA FAN PALM, PETTICOAT PALM

A medium to tall palm that grows slowly at first then, once fully established, fast up to 15m or more. The massive, greyish trunk can be up to 60cm in diameter. In nature it is usually covered in a dense thatch of old leaves that hang down giving it the common name of 'petticoat palm'. Wind or fire often removes these leaves, unless they are pruned off, to reveal the attractive trunk. The showy, palmate, greyish-green fronds are 1m or more across, and divided more than halfway to the base, with many long threads attached to the segments. The fronds are carried on long, thorny leaf stalks that hold the leaf upright at first, then droop with age. They stand well separated so that the crown is open and broad. Young trees make good container plants. They are popular with landscape designers, as street trees and as bold groups in large gardens. This palm needs regular summer water when young, then becomes drought-tolerant once established.

W. robusta MEXICAN FAN PALM

A tall, fast-growing palm to perhaps 30m high, spreading to 5m wide, with a slender trunk, usually about 30cm in diameter, that gradually tapers from ground level. The trunk is usually covered in a dense thatch of old leaves that hang down forming a shaggy skirt. The bright green leaf blade, to 1m long, is stiff, and lightly cut with slender points and no filaments. The leaf stalk is short, with a reddish streak on the underside, and is sharply toothed along the entire length. Older palms have a compact crown on a tall trunk. In summer it produces panicles up to 3m long, of tubular, creamy-pink flowers, followed by dark brown fruit. A spectacular palm that will grow in poorer soil conditions but grows fast in good soil. When established it withstands drought, but grows better with some summer water. Ideal for coastal gardens as it withstands salt-laden sea breezes. Often grown in avenues in warm-dry climates, to give a tropical effect. Less hardy than *W. filifera*. Native to northern Mexico.

Washingtonia robusta

Watsonia
Iridaceae

A genus of about sixty species of deciduous and evergreen cormous perennials, native to South Africa. They are grown for their showy spikes of tubular flowers.

W. borbonica (syn. W. pyramidata)
A cormous perennial 1–1.5m high that forms a clump with nearly linear, upright, basal leaves to 75cm long. The plant produces its leaves in autumn. In late spring and early summer it bears a branched flower spike carrying up to twenty showy, rose-pink, funnel-shaped flowers 3cm long, with a curved tube and lobes spreading out to a star shape. They make good cut flowers. Grow the plant in full sun in a well drained soil. Drought-tolerant, but grows best with occasional summer water. The clumps are best left undisturbed for several years. They make good pot or container plants. There are many excellent hybrids in a range of colours from scarlet, pink, to white and lavender.

Westringia
Lamiaceae

A small genus of around twenty-five species of tender evergreen shrubs native to dry areas of Australia. They are grown for their attractive foliage and flowers.

W. fruticosa (syn. W. rosmariniformis) or
A delicate, rather loose shrub up to 2m high and 1m wide. The whorls of deep green to grey-green narrow leaves, 1–2cm long, are densely white-felted underneath. This gives it a similar appearance to rosemary, but with a finer texture. The white, pale blue or

Westringia fruticosa

lilac flowers, 1cm across, are borne in axillary clusters throughout most of the summer. Grow the shrub in a sunny position in well drained soil. Grows well near the coast as it is wind-tolerant. When established it with-stands drought, but grows better with some summer water. Looks attractive when grown as an informal hedge. 'Variegata' is more compact, with cream edging to the leaves, softer growth and white flowers.

Wigandia
Hydrophyllaceae

A small genus containing around five species of frost-tender, large evergreen perennials, shrubs or small trees that are native to tropical America. Only one species is generally grown, for its beautiful large heads of blue flowers; nevertheless it is often grown as a foliage plant in subtropical gardens.

W. caracasana (syn. W. macrophylla)
⌣⌣ or ⌣

A large, robust, evergreen shrub up to 5m or more high and as wide, with open, soft stems. The stems and leaves are covered in fine silky hairs that can be irritating to the skin. The large, deep green, ovate leaves, up to 40cm long, have coarse teeth along the margins. The violet or blue flowers, 2cm wide, with a white tube are borne in large terminal panicles, to 30cm or more across. They are produced in great profusion during spring and early

summer. When in full flower the shrub makes an impressive sight. Grow it in full sun. When established it withstands drought, but grows better with some summer water. Useful as a background plant where the bold foliage will provide contrast for other plants. Can be severely pruned after flowering. Suckers readily and can become invasive, but is good for a large garden. Native to Mexico, Venezuela and Colombia.

Wigandia caracasana

Wisteria
Papilionaceae

A genus of about ten species of woody climbers with twining stems, native to temperate eastern Asia and USA. The beautiful climbers are grown for their showy, pea-like, often fragrant flowers. Their violet-blue, purple, pink or white flowers hang in long elegant racemes. Most are frost-hardy, but thrive in heat.

W. floribunda
JAPANESE WISTERIA ⌣ or ⌣⌣

A vigorous, twining, woody, deciduous climber to 10m or more high, spreading almost as wide. The stems twine in a clockwise direction. The pinnate leaves 30cm or more long, are composed of eleven to nineteen ovate, dark green leaflets. In spring the fragrant violet-blue, pea-like flowers appear in hanging, slender racemes 25–30cm or more long. The flowers begin to open at the base of the cluster, gradually opening towards the tip, which prolongs the flowering season. They are followed by bean-like, velvety

seedpods to 15cm long. For best flowering grow the climber in full sun, but it will take partial shade. Water young plants well, gradually reducing the water as the plants become older and established, which may take several years. Not fussy about soil, but needs good drainage. In alkaline soil plants may become chlorotic and need iron chelates. Excellent for covering walls, over an arch and pergolas, or for growing into old trees. An established plant will need an annual hard pruning in winter and a second pruning consisting of shortening leafy stems in summer after flowering. Native to Japan. Many varieties are obtainable in white, pink, and shades of blue, purple and lavender.

W. sinensis (syn. W. chinensis)
CHINESE WISTERIA ⌣ or ⌣⌣

A vigorous, twining, woody, deciduous climber to 30m or more high, spreading almost as wide. The stems twine in an anticlockwise direction. The pinnate leaves, 30cm or more long, are com-posed of seven to thirteen ovate, dark green leaflets. In spring the fragrant blue or white pea-like flowers appear in hanging slender racemes to 30cm long. The flowers open nearly the full length of the cluster at one time, and appear before the leaves unfurl. They may be followed by bean-like, velvety seedpods to 15cm long. Cultivation is the same as W. floribunda. A large specimen in full flower makes a wonderful sight. Native to China. 'Alba' is a white-flowered form. 'Caroline' is a more free-flowering form with deep, purple-blue flowers.

Wisteria floribunda

Xanthoceras
Sapindaceae

A genus comprising just two species of frost-hardy, deciduous shrubs or small trees native to north China. They are related to Koelruteria but very different in appearance. Only one species is generally grown, for its upright spikes of fragrant flowers.

sorbifolim ꜱ ꜱ

A beautiful, large shrub, or more commonly a small tree, to 4m high and 3m wide, with a rounded habit. The pinnate leaves, to 30cm long, have nine to seventeen lance-shaped, glossy, toothed leaflets. The white flowers with a carmine centre are up to 3cm across. They are borne in terminal upright panicles to 20cm long in spring, on shoots of the previous year; these combine beautifully with the young, fresh green leaves. The tree thrives in full sun with moderate summer water in most well drained soils. This is an excellent plant for chalky soils. It grows best in areas with hot summers that will ripen the wood and encourage abundant flowering. Although the tree is frost-hardy the buds are easily damaged by frost. Native to northern China.

Xanthorrhoea 'GRASS TREE'
Xanthorrhoeaceae

A genus of about twelve species of slow-growing, long-lived, woody perennials native to Australia. These strange grass trees are ideal for the desert or dry garden. They have the appearance of dense clumps of grass borne on tree trunks.

X. preisii BALGA, BLACKBOY ꜱ

A slow-growing woody perennial that will eventually form a trunk to 3m high. With great age the massive black trunks can become 60cm or more thick. At the top of the trunk is a tuft of hard, leathery, reed-like leaves to 1m long and less than 1cm wide, which radiate in all directions. The old leaf bases may be glued together by a black resinous gum. The magnificent inflorescence that arises from among the leaves can be 1m long on a stem of 1m. The dense spike contains many small white flowers that tend to open on the sunny side first. The spikes can be produced at almost any time of the year, but mostly in summer or autumn. Grow the plant in full sun. Ideal for the dry garden as it needs no summer water once established. It needs well drained soil – a sandy soil is ideal.

Xanthorrhoea preisii

These unusual and spectacular plants look good when associated with Yuccas, Agaves or Daisylirion.

Y

Yucca
Agavaceae

A genus of about forty species of evergreen perennials, shrubs or small trees, native to the southern United States, Mexico and the West Indies. They have bayonet leaves in bold tufts rising directly from the ground or on short woody stems. The showy flowers emit a scent at night that attracts insects that act as pollinators. All are lush, tropical-looking plants. Some are good near pools.

Y. aloifolia SPANISH BAYONET 🌙🌙
A slow-growing, evergreen shrub or small tree that forms a stiff rosette of leaves eventually up to 8m high, spreading to 4m wide. Usually it has a single trunk, but it may branch and sprawl along the ground. The thick, fleshy, sharp-pointed, dagger-like deep

Yucca elephantipes

green leaves are up to 75cm long and 6cm wide, and are set close together spirally around the stem. The cup-shaped flowers, up to 10cm wide, are creamy-white tinged with purple. They appear in dense erect clusters up to 60cm high, held well above the foliage during summer. The shrub grows best in full sun. When established it withstands drought, but grows better with an occasional deep soaking during summer. With age it can take on a picturesque appearance, especially if grown in groups. Remove old dead leaves with care, as the edges can easily cut the hand. Sharp points are a hazard if grown close to paths. Ideal as an accent plant for the dry garden. Tolerant of salt-laden sea breezes, so is good for coastal gardens, even by the beach. Native to south-east United States. 'Marginata' has glaucous green

Yucca aloifolia

leaves with creamy-yellow margins; 'Tricolor' has a central yellow stripe on the leaves.

Y. elephantipes (syn. *Y. guatemalensis*)
SPINELESS YUCCA 🌙🌙
A fast-growing upright shrub or small tree, usually with several trunks, that forms a magnificent, many-branched clump up to 10m high, spreading to 8m wide. The corky-textured trunk that rises from a swollen base is usually free of thatch and dead leaves. The plant tends to sucker, producing many sparsely branched trunks, creating a mound of foliage. The bright green, spineless leaves, with a slightly glaucous tinge, are up to 1.2m long and 10cm wide, and are held semi-erect. On mature shrubs large, stout flower spikes, up to 1m long, appear in spring. They are densely packed with large, pendant, creamy-white flowers 3–4cm

Yucca elephantipes 'Jewel'

long, shaded almost indiscernibly with green. Although this plant will take some drought, it grows best in a good, well drained soil with ample summer water. As yuccas go, it is remarkably shade-tolerant, but grows best in full sun. Tolerates salt-laden sea breezes, so is good for coastal gardens. A very decorative and durable pot or container plant. Native to southern Mexico and Guatemala. 'Jewel' is a beautiful form, with leaves striped with shades of green and cream; 'Variegata' has glaucous green leaves with creamy-white margins.

Yucca gloriosa

Y. filamentosa ADAM'S NEEDLE

A nearly stemless shrub forming bold rosettes of narrow, mid-green leaves up to 75cm high. The stiff, upright, lance-shaped leaves are bluish-glaucous, 75cm long, with curly threads on the margins. The pendulous, bell-shaped, creamy-white flowers, 5–8cm long, tinged with green or cream, appear in tall, dense panicles up to 2m high in summer. Easily grown, it makes a good accent plant. Grows best in full sun. When established it withstands drought, but grows better with an occasional deep soaking during summer. Native to south-east United States. The variety 'Variegata' has bluish-green leaves with a contrasting creamy-white margin.

Y. gloriosa SPANISH DAGGER

An upright shrub with stout, semi-woody stems, often seen as a many-stemmed rosette plant growing up to 3m high and wide. The stem is usually branched, covered in dead leaves, and topped with a rosette of young leaves. The spine-tipped leaves, 60–80cm long, are flat, sword-shaped and glaucous grey-green. During the late summer an erect flower panicle, up to 2m high, arises from the centre of the rosette. The pendulous, bell-shaped creamy-white flowers are sometimes purple-tinged and open 8–10cm wide. Easily grown, it looks best in full sun. Drought-tolerant once established,

although an occasional deep soaking during summer helps. Blends well with other tropical-looking plants. Occurs naturally along the coast, so is ideal for coastal gardens. Native to southern USA and northern Mexico. The variety 'Variegata' has leaves margined and striped creamy-yellow.

Y. recurvifolia LORD'S CANDLE

A stem-forming, tree-like shrub, usually with a single, unbranching trunk up to 3m high, that can lightly branch with age. The 5cm wide, thick leathery leaves are 60–90cm long, a soft blue-grey green and all but the central crown gracefully arching. They are lance-shaped, entire to slightly toothed, with a pliable but sharp point. The pendant, bell-shaped, creamy flowers, 6–8cm long, are borne in dense, erect panicles, up to 1m or more high, in midsummer. Easily grown in full sun or some shade. Once established it needs no summer water, although a deep soaking during summer helps. Grows fast by spreading suckers to make a large clump in time. Grow in any well drained soil. As with other yuccas, it is ideal for coastal gardens. This is the least dangerous of the yuccas, as the leaves are softer and bend to touch. Native to northern Mexico and south-east USA. There are variegated forms: 'Marginata' with yellow margins, and 'Variegata' with a central yellow stripe to the leaves.

Zamia
Zamiaceae

A genus of forty to sixty species of somewhat palm-like, low-growing, dioecious (male and female flowers on different plants) cycads native to tropical and subtropical America. They are grown for their unusual form, pinnate leaves and cone-like flower spikes. They are all frost tender.

Z. furfuracea CARDBOARD PALM ☽☽☽
A small cycad up to 1m high, spreading to 2m wide. The cylindrical stem is more or less tuberous, simple or rarely branched. It bears a tangled profusion of semi-upright or spreading pinnate leaves to 1m long on prickly stalks. Each leaf has up to thirteen pairs of thick, stiff, oval leaflets with in-rolled edges, to 20cm long. The leaves are medium green above and densely scurfy brownish underneath, or on both sides when young. On mature plants in summer felted, red-brown female cones 10–13cm long, or slightly larger male cones are produced. The plant will grow in sun, but does better in partial shade. Grow in fertile, well drained soil. Give regular summer water, enough to keep the plant moist. It makes a slow-growing, choice container plant ideal for the shady patio. Tolerant of sea spray and slightly saline

Zamia furfuracea

Zantedeschia aethiopica

soil, so is good for coastal gardens. Native to southern Mexico.

Zantedeschia 'ARUM LILY'
Araceae

A genus of only six species of evergreen, rhizomatous, clump-forming perennials native to southern Africa. They are grown for their large, arrow-shaped, glossy green leaves and trumpet-like flowers. There has been much hybridizing of the species, which has resulted in many beautiful forms.

Z. aethiopica CALLA LILY, ARUM LILY ☽☽☽
A robust, rhizomatous, marsh-loving perennial that forms a clump up to 1m high. The glossy, evergreen, arrow-shaped leaves, up to 45cm high and 25cm wide, are borne on long, fleshy stalks. Appearing from the base, the fragrant, pure waxy white, funnel-shaped, flaring flower bract (spathe) is up to 25cm long on stems up to 60cm. This covers the golden-yellow spadix, which are the true tiny flowers. The

spathes appear from late winter until late spring, and are frequently used as cut flowers. When established it withstands drought, but grows better with some summer water, and can grow happily in the edges of streams and ditches. With summer drought it becomes dormant. Can take full sun, but grows best in partial shade. Looks good when grown in large pots or containers. Native to South Africa.

Z. elliotiana GOLDEN CALLA ☽☽☽
A rhizomatous, marsh-loving perennial that forms a clump 20–30cm wide, and 60–90cm high. The evergreen basal leaves are fleshy, glossy and heart-shaped, and up to 45cm long. They are bright green and covered with translucent white spots. The flower spathe is 15cm long, green at the base turning to bright gold with the appearance of the yellow spadices during summer. The plant will take full sun, and thrives best with plenty of summer water. Native to South Africa.

Other species worthy of note are *Z. pentlandii*, with a lemon-chrome spathe; and *Z. rehmannii*, with a red or pink spathe. There are many hybrids that have pink, orange or green spathes. All of these require similar conditions to *Z. aethiopica*.

Zauschneria
Onagraceae

A genus of only four species of evergreen perennial, sometimes woody at the base, native to California and Mexico. They are grown for their masses of tubular, usually bright red summer flowers. They provide spectacular colour in the border.

Z. californica (syn. *Epilobium californicum*) CALIFORNIA FUCHSIA

An evergreen, woody-based perennial with upright or arching slender stems 30–60cm high, spreading to 50cm wide. The spreading underground stems may become invasive. The lance-shaped leaves are grey-green and hairy, up to 4cm long. The beautiful, rich scarlet, trumpet-shaped flowers with protruding stamens are 4–5cm long. The clusters of flowers on the ends of the stems make an attractive show from summer to autumn. Grow the plant in full sun in free-draining soil with little or no summer water once established. The plant can be killed by waterlogged winter soil. It thrives in hot, dry summers. Looks particularly good when grown at the front of a border, when scrambling over banks, or in a rock garden. Cut back during winter. Native to California. There is also a pure white and a pink form.

Ziziphus
Rhamnaceae

A genus of more than forty species of deciduous and evergreen shrubs and trees native to tropical and warmer regions of both hemispheres. They are grown as attractive specimen trees, or for the fruit.

Z. jujuba CHINESE JUJUBA

A deciduous tree with slow to moderate growth, 5–8m high, with angular, spiny, rather pendulous branches. Often seen with suckers from the base, which form a thicket. The glossy bright green leaves are oblong to lance-shaped, 2–5cm long, with three prominent veins that turn yellow in autumn. The clusters of small, insignificant, yellowish flowers are borne in late spring and early summer. They are followed by shiny, reddish-brown edible fruit that has a sweet apple-like flavour. When dried or candied the fruit resembles dates. Fruits best in hot summer areas. The tree is deep rooted and tolerates drought, heat and cold. Summer watering encourages the production of abundant larger fruit. Grows well in saline soils near the coast or alkaline soils, but prefers good garden soil. Grow in full sun. Makes an attractive specimen or shade tree that will thrive in a lawn. Native from the Mediterranean region to China.

Z

Plants for a Purpose

Climbers and Wall Shrubs

These plants are generally fast growing with long stems that can be guided to where you want them. They climb up the surface in several different ways: some have tendrils that wrap themselves around the support, while others twine their stems around another plant or support. Some do not attach themselves to the support at all, but only lean against it and need to be tied. Many of these climbers also make good groundcovers.

Actinidia
Akebia
Allamanda
Aloe (some)
Anredera
Antigonon
Aristolochia
Asparagus (some)
Beaumontia
Bignonia
Billardiera
Bougainvillea
Buddleja asiatica
Campsis
Cestrum aurantiacum
Clematis
Clerodendrum (some)
Clianthus
Clytostoma
Cobaea
Distictis
Eccremocarpus
Euonymus (some)
Ficus pumila
Hardenbergia
Hedera
Hibbertia
Hoya
Ipomoea
Jasminum
Kennedia
Lonicera
Lophospermom
Macfadyena
Mandevilla
Monstera
Mutisia
Pandorea
Passiflora
Petrea
Plumbago
Podranea
Pyrostegia
Rosa (some)
Senecio (some)
Solandra
Solanum (some)
Sollya
Stephanotis
Tecoma
Thunbergia
Trachelospermum
Tropaeolum
Wisteria

Coastal Garden Plants

When planting a garden close to the sea, consideration should be given to the salt-laden sea breeze that can damage many plants. The soil may also be saline, giving an added difficulty to the plants. Salinity is not only restricted to coastal regions, but can affect many areas in desert regions. Many salt-tolerant plants are drought-tolerant as well.

Agave
Aloe (some)
Araucaria heterophylla
Arbutus
Arctotis
Argyranthemum
Armeria
Artemisia
Arundo
Atriplex (some)
Aucuba
Bougainvillea
Brachyglottis
Canna
Carissa
Caryopteris
Colutea
Cordyline
Corokia cotoneaster
Correa alba
Corynocarpus
Crocosmia
Cupressus
Cytisus × praecox
Dodonaea
Dracaena draco
Elaeagnus (some)
Eriocephalus
Eryngium maritimum
Escallonia
Euonymus (some)
Euphorbia milii
Euryops
× Fatshedera
Foeniculum
Genista
Griselinia
Halimium
Helianthemum
Hippophae
Hyophorbe
Juniperus
Lagunaria
Lagurus
Lampranthus
Lantana camara
Laurus
Lavandula
Lavatera (some)
Ligustrum (some)
Limonium
Macfadyena
Melaleuca (some)
Myoporum
Narcissus
Nerium
Olearia
Opuntia
Osteospermum
Pancratium
Pandanus
Parkinsonia
Perovskia
Phlomis
Phoenix
Phormium
Pinus
Pittosporum
Podranea
Populus alba
Quercus ilex
Rhamnus
Rosmarinus
Roystonea regia
Sabal palmetto
Santolina
Solandra
Spartium
Spiraea
Syagrus
Tamarix
Tecoma stans
Teucrium
Thrinax
Tipuana
Trachycarpus
Urginea
Washingtonia
Yucca
Zamia

Container Plants

Gardeners love to put plants into pots or containers to add another dimension to the garden. A plant in a pot can transform a patio or terrace, while those with scented flowers are ideal near the house. Most plants resent conditions where their roots are restricted and confined; however, the ones listed below will tolerate such conditions. Trees and large shrubs should only be used while young.

Agapanthus
Agave
Aloe (some)
Aloysia
Araucaria heterophylla
Arbutus unedo
Argyranthemum
Armeria
Asparagus
Aucuba
Beaucarnea
Bolusanthus
Bougainvillea (some)
Buxus
Canna
Citrus
Clivia
Convolvulus sabatius
Cordyline
Correa alba
Corynocarpus
Cotyledon
Crassula
Cyperus
Cyrtanthus
Datura
Dicliptera

227

Echeveria
× Fatshedera
Fatsia
Felicia
Ficus elastica
Freesia
Gardenia
Gerbera
Graptopelalum
Halimium atriplicifolium
Hedychium
Helianthemum
Hibbertia
Hippeastrum
Hydrangea
Hymenocallis
Impatiens
Iresine
Iris xiphium hybrids
Jasminum polyanthum
Justicia brandegeeana
Kalanchoe (some)
Laurus
Ligustrum japonicum
Lilium
Lotus
Lycoris
Musa
Myrsine
Nandina
Nerine
Odontonema
Palms and Cycads (most when young)
Pelargonium
Philodendron
Phormium
Pinus (when young)
Plectranthus
Plumbago
Pseudopanax
Russelia
Sansevieria
Scadoxus
Schefflera
Sedum
Senecio (some)
Solanum (some)
Sollya
Stephanotis
Strelitzia (some)
Thymus
Tropaeolum
Veltheimia
Watsonia
Yucca
Zantedeschia

Easy Plants To Start With

These are tough plants that, given the right conditions, will generally grow easily. If you are new to gardening or new to the area, these plants will help you get started.

Abelia
Acacia
Albizia
Aptenia
Arbutus
Artemisia
Bougainvillea
Buddleja
Callistemon
Campsis
Celtis
Centranthus
Ceratostigma
Cercis
Cortaderia
Cotoneaster
Diospyros
Elaeagnus

Eucalyptus
Ficus carica
Gazania
Hedera
Hibiscus
Jasminum
Lantana
Lavandula
Ligustrum
Melia
Myoporum
Nerium
Olea
Osteospermum
Passiflora
Pelargonium
Phoenix
Pittosporum tobira
Platanus
Plumbago
Podranea
Populus
Prunus (some)
Quercus
Rosa
Santolinia
Schinus
Tamarix
Tecomaria
Teucrium
Thymus
Trachelospermum
Viburnum tinus
Washingtonia

Hedging and Screening Plants

In general, evergreen trees and shrubs that are slower growing and produce plenty of side shoots when clipped are used for hedges. They can be clipped into strict geometrical outlines for formal areas, or more relaxed shapes for informal areas. Hedges are garden features that can provide privacy, and/or shelter from wind and noise, or they can define boundaries.

Plants that have leaves to the ground and are fairly fast growing are good candidates for providing a screen. They are often used for more practical reasons such as hiding an unsightly object or providing shelter; however, this does not mean that they cannot be attractive as well.

Acacia
Acalypha
Acca
Albizia lophantha
Anredera
Asparagus setaceus
Atriplex (some)
Bignonia
Buxus
Campsis
Caragana
Carissa
Casuarina
Choisya
Cobaea
Cocculus
Corynocarpus
Cotoneaster
Cupressus
Cytisus
Dodonaea
Duranta
Elaeagnus
Escallonia
Euonymus (some)
Euphorbia (some)
Grevillea (some)
Griselinia
Hibiscus rosa-sinensis
Lantana camara

Lavatera (some)
Leptospermum
Ligustrum
Maclura
Melaleuca (some)
Myoporum
Myrsine
Myrtus
Nandina
Nerium
Osmanthus
Photinia
Phyllostachys
Pittosporum (some)
Plumbago
Populus (some)
Pseudosasa
Pyracantha
Rhamnus
Rhaphiolepis
Ricinus
Rosmarinus
Santolina
Syzygium
Tamarix
Tecoma
Thuja
Viburnum (some)
Westringia

Palms

These evergreen trees or shrubs all belong to one plant family that contains more than 200 genus. Although they come from tropical or subtropical regions, many are frost-hardy. Some can grow to large, tall trees, while others remain dwarf. They add a tropical feel to the garden, while others are used as houseplants.

Acoelorrhaphe wrightii
Archontophoenix cunninghamiana
Bismarckia nobilis
Brahea armata
Brahea edulis
Butia capitata
Butia yatay
Caryota mitis
Chamaedorea elegans
Chamaedorea microspadix
Chamaerops humilis
Copernicia alba
Copernicia macroglossa
Dypsis decaryi
Dypsis lutescens
Howea belmoreana
Howea forsteriana
Hyophorbe verschaffeltii
Hyphaene coriacea
Hyphaene thebaica
Jubaea chilensis
Latania loddigesii
Latania lontaroides
Latania verschaffeltii
Livistona australis
Livistona chinensis
Phoenix canariensis
Phoenix dactylifera
Phoenix reclinata
Phoenix roebelenii
Rhapis excelsa
Sabal causiarum
Sabal mexicana
Sabal minor
Sabal palmetto
Syagrus romanzoffiana
Thrinax floridana
Trachycarpus fortunei
Washingtonia filifera
Washingtonia robusta

Cycads

Cycads comprise a unique group of primitive seed plants, which is much older than flowering plants. They are distant relatives of conifers as they bear cones and do not form flowers. Most have short, sometimes branched, trunks. They are often included with palms as they are similar in general appearance, and are usually used in similar circumstances. Also, like palms, they add a tropical feel to the garden, giving attractive form to shady places.

Cycas circinalis
Cycas revoluta
Dioon edule
Encephalartos altensteinii
Encephalartos horridus
Encephalartos lehmanii
Zamia furfuracea

Plants for Fruit and Berries

The plants listed below are chosen for their usually colourful fruit or berries. Some are pleasant for us to eat, while birds and other animals enjoy many more.

Acca
Actinidia
Aesculus
Akebia
Annona
Arbutus
Atriplex (some)
Aucuba
Billardiera
Bismarckia
Brahea edulis
Broussonetia
Butia
Carica
Carissa
Carpobrotus
Casimiroa
Castanea
Catalpa
Celtis
Ceratonia
Cestrum (some)
Citrus
Clivia
Coprosma
Corkia (some)
Corynocarpus
Cotoneaster
Cydonia
Cyphomandra
Diospyros
Duranta
Elaeagnus
Eriobotrya
Eugenia
Ficus
Fortunella
Hedera helix
Hippophae
Hyphaene thebaica
Juglans
Koelreuteria
Ligustrum (some)
Lonicera (some)
Maclura
Melia
Monstera
Morus
Musa
Myoporum
Myrtus
Nandina
Olea
Opuntia
Pandanus

Passiflora
Persea
Phoenix (some)
Physalis
Phytolacca
Pistacia
Prunus (some)
Psidium
Punica
Pyracantha
Rhamnus
Rhus
Ruscus
Schinus
Solanum (some)
Syzygium
Viburnum (some)
Ziziphus

Plants for Dry Shade

A shady spot can be considered a problem, especially where it is on the dry side. There are some plants that, once established, will take these conditions, but their success will depend upon the degree of shade and the amount of water available. No plant will grow in total darkness, but these will thrive in part or full shade.

Abutilon × hybridum
Abutilon megapotamicum
Acanthus mollis
Arum italicum
Asparagus
Aspidistra
Aucuba japonica
Bergenia
Brunfelsia
Carpenteria
Chlorophytum
Clivia
Coprosma
Cordyline
Crassula
Cyclamen hederifolium
Echeveria
Echium pininana
Euonymus fortunei
× Fatshedera
Fatsia
Ficus pumila
Geranium maderense
Griselinia
Hedera helix
Helichrysum petiolare
Iris germanica
Laurus
Mimulus
Myrtus
Nandina
Osmanthus delavayi
Ruscus
Scilla
Sparrmannia africana
Strelitzia nicolai
Vinca
Viola
Zantedeschia

Plants for Scent (Leaves and Flowers)

It is a great joy to go into a garden and enjoy the fragrance of scented flowers. Fragrance adds another dimension to a garden and can be as memorable as its appearance. Flowers are often most profoundly fragrant on warm, still, humid days, many most powerfully scented in the evening or at night. Included are those plants whose foliage is scented when bruised or crushed. Many can be used in containers on a patio or planted near the house so the fragrance can be enjoyed.

Abelia
Acacia (some)
Actinidia
Aesculus californica
Agonis
Ailanthus altissima
Akebia
Aloysia
Alpinia
Amaryllis belladonna
Annona
Anredera
Artemisia abrotanum
Bauhinia variegata
Beaumontia
Brugmansia
Brunfelsia
Buddleja
Calodendrum
Caragana
Carissa
Carpenteria
Catalpa
Ceanothus (some)
Centranthus
Cestrum nocturnum
Cestrum parqui
Choisya
Cinnamomum
Cistus (some)
Citrus
Clematis
Clerodendrum (some)
Cordyline australis
Corokia buddlejoides
Crinum
Cupressus macrocarpa
Cyclamen
Cytisus
Datura
Dendromecon
Dombeya × cayeuxii
Elaeagnus
Epiphyllum (some)
Erica (some)
Eriobotrya
Eucalyptus (some)
Eucharis
Eugenia
Eupatorium sordidum
Fortunella
Freesia
Gardenia
Gelsemium
Genista aetnensis
Hedychium (some)
Heliotropium
Homeria
Hoya
Hymenocallis
Hymenosporum
Iberis
Iboxa
Ipheion
Ipomoea alba
Iris (some)
Jasminum
Juniperus (some)
Koelreuteria
Lavandula
Ligustrum (some)
Lilium
Lonicera
Magnolia
Mandevilla (some)
Melia
Mirabilis
Muscari
Myrtus
Narcissus (some)
Nerium oleander
Nicotiana

Oenothera (some)
Olearia × haastii
Ornithogalum arabicum
Osmanthus
Paeonia officinalis
Pancratium
Parkinsonia
Paulownia
Pelargonium (some)
Philadelphus
Pittosporum (some)
Prostanthera
Prunus lusitanica
Retama
Rhaphiolepis
Robinia pseudoacacia
Romneya
Rosa
Salvia (some)
Sansevieria
Senecio confusus
Senna artemisoides
Solandra
Solanum (some)
Spartium
Stephanotis
Tetrapanax
Thevetia
Thuja
Tilia

Toona
Trachelospermum
Tropaeolum
Viburnum
Viola
Vitex
Wisteria
Xanthoceras

Plants Good Near Swimming Pools

When planting near a swimming pool, consideration should be given to the plant used: it should all be as soft as possible, not sharp or prickly, and no thorns that could injure people. The volume of dead leaves and flowers that a plant produces should also be considered, as these can block the pool's filtration system.

Abelia
Agapanthus
Agave attenuata
Aloe
Alstroemeria
Anigozanthos
Armeria
Artemisia
Canna
Clivia
Copernicia alba

Cordyline
Cyperus
Elaeagnus × ebbingei
× Fatshedera
Fatsia
Gazania
Juniperus
Kalanchoe
Kniphofia
Lantana
Lavandula
Ligustrum
Melianthus
Musa
Philodendron
Phlomis
Phoenix reclinata
Phormium
Pittosporum
Rhaphiolepis
Santolina
Schefflera
Solandra
Solanum rantonetii
Sparrmannia
Sternbergia
Strelitzia
Tupidanthus

The Meaning of Plant Names

Why do gardeners use the difficult-to-understand Latin or botanical names for plants? The reason is that each country, region, nursery or even individuals can have their own names for plants, and this can be confusing or misleading. On the other hand there is only one botanical name for each plant, and this is recognized world-wide.

The botanical name tells you something about the plant. The genus name is usually a Greek or Roman classical name, or named after a person. The species name is usually a descriptive name. It may tell you about the place that the plant comes from, the colour of the flower or leaves, or the form of the leaf. It may tell you the shape of the plant, or about any peculiarities that the plant has, such as heart-shaped leaves, edible fruit, or if it grows tall, when fully grown. The same descriptive words are used often, so whenever you see 'africanus' you know that it comes from Africa, or 'grandiflora' that it is large-flowered. Once you know the meanings of these words they become easy to understand and help you to identify a plant.

Often the ending of the name provides the meaning. For example, the following endings are often used:

-ensis means 'from a place', as '*chinensis*', 'from China'.

-folia means 'leaves like another plant', as '*acerifolia*', 'leaves like an acer'.

-iana, -i or *-ii* means that it is named after a person, as '*bowdenii*', 'named after Bowden'.

-oides means 'like another plant', as '*jasminoides*', 'like jasmine'.

Grammatical note: Every Latin noun (including each genus) has a gender, either masculine, feminine or neuter, which has nothing to do with the sex of a plant. Any adjective attached to the noun, such as the species name, must 'agree' by having the same gender. You can often tell the gender by the ending, which follows these rules, although there are numerous exceptions:

Masculine *-us -is*
Feminine *-a -is*
Neuter *-um -e*

Below is a selection of the plant epithets (species names) that appear in this book. The feminine form is usually given, as this is the most common. A change of ending does not affect the meaning.

acerifolius – leaves like a maple
acetabulosa – saucer
actinophylla – radiating leaves
aculeata – prickly
acuminata – sharp-tipped
adenophorum – gland bearing
adhatoda – not touched by goats
aequalis – equal
aestivum – summer
aethiopica – from Ethiopia
affine – like, similar
africanus – from Africa
agnus-castus – chaste
alata – winged
alaternus – Latin name of uncertain shrub

alba – white
albidus – nearly white
albomarginatus – white-margined
alcea – a sort of mallow (Greek)
alexandrae – from Alexandra
aloifolia – aloe-like foliage
alternifolia – alternating leaves
altissima – very high
amabilis – deserves to be loved
amelloides – like Aster amellus
americana – from America
amoena – lovely, pleasing
angustifolia – narrow-leaved
antioquiensis – from Antioch
arabicum – from Arabia
arborea – treelike
arborescens – treelike
arboricola – tree dweller
arenaria – growing on sand
argentata – silvered
argentea – silvery-white
argyrata – silver
arizonica – from Arizona, USA
armata – armed, with thorns
armeniacum – from Armenia
artemisoides – like artemisia
asiatica – from Asia
atlantica – from the Atlas mountains
atripicifolia – leaves like atriplex
atropurpureum – dark purple
attenuata – weak
augusta – majestic
aurantiacum – golden or orange-coloured
aurea – golden
aureoreticulata – golden-veined
aureovariegatum – golden-variegated
auriculata – like an ear
australis – southern
autumnale – autumn
aviculare – small birds
azoricum – from the Azores
babylonica – from Babylon
baileyana – after Bailey
banksiae – after Lady Banks
barbatus – barbed or bearded
belladonna – beautiful lady
benjamina – small
betacea – beet-like or esculent
bifida – split in two
bignonioides – bignonia-like
bipinata – bipinnate
boliviensis – from Bolivia
bonariensis – from Bonaria, Buenos Aires
brachypetala – short-petalled
bracteata – with bracts
buccinatoria – shaped like a curved horn
buddlejoides – buddleja-like
byzantina – from Turkey
caerulea – sky-blue
caffra – from South Africa
californica – from California
campanulata – bell- or cup-shaped
canadensis – from Canada
canariensis – from the Canary Islands
candicans – becoming white
candida – pure white, shiny
canescens – grey or hoary
cantoniensis – from Canton
capensis – from the Cape of Good Hope area
capreolata – having tendrils

carnea – flesh-coloured
carnosa – fleshy
cathartica – purgative
caudatus – with tail
cerasifera – cherry-bearing
chilensis – from Chile
chinensis – from China
chlorantha – green-flowered
chrysophylla – golden-leaved
ciliaris – fringed
cineraria – ashen grey
cirrhosa – tendrilled
citrinus – yellow
citrodora – lemon-scented
cneorum – Greek name for Daphne gnidium
coccifera – berry-bearing
coccinea – scarlet
coerulea – sky-blue
coggygria – smoke tree
colchica – from Colchis, West Georgia
communis – common or social
comosum – many-leaved
compactus – compact, dense
confusus – confused
cordata – heart-shaped
cordifolia – heart-shaped leaves
cornuta – horned
coronarium – crown- or wreath-like
corymbosa – full of corymbs
cotoneaster – cotoneaster-like
crassifolium – thick-leaved
crinata – long-haired
crispum – curled
crista-gallii – a cock's comb
cyanaea – dark blue
dactylifera – date-bearing
dealbata – whitened
decipiens – deceiving
deliciosa – delicious
densiflorus – dense-flowered
dentata – toothed
didymobotrya – divided into two racemes
dioica – male and female on diferent plants
domesticum – cultivated
draco – dragon
dulcis – sweet
edulus – edible
elastica – elastic
elatior – taller
elatus – tall
elegans – elegant, slender, willowy
elliptica – ellipse-shaped
erecta – upright
ericifolia – erica-leaved
erubescens – blushing
etrusca – from Tuscany, Italy
europea – European
excelsa – tall, when fully grown
exotica – foreign
farinacea – starchy
festalis – festive
ficifolia – ficus or fig-leaved
ficus-indica – Indian fig
filamentosa – many filaments
filifera – bearing filaments
flavidus – pale yellow
flavum – pale yellow
flexuosa – bending, curvy
floribunda – abundant or free-flowering
foetida – bad-smelling

231

fruticans – becoming shrubby
fruticosa – shrubby
furfuracea – covered with scurf
generalis – general
germanica – from Germany
giganteum – of large size
glabra – without hairs
glauca – covered with bluish-grey bloom
globulus – like a small globe
gloriosa – glorious
grandiflora – large-flowered
graveolens – strong-smelling
halepensis – from Aleppo
halimus – of the sea
hederifolium – ivy (Hedera)-leaved
helix – spiral or twisted
heterophylla – leaves of varied shape
hirsuta – hairy
hispanica – from Spain
hispida – bristly
hortensis – of gardens
hortorum – of gardens
humile – low-growing
humilis – dwarf, or on the ground
ignea – glowing, on fire
indica – from India
indivisa – not divided
ingens – huge
insignis – remarkable
italica – from Italy
japonicus – from Japan
jucundum – pleasing
juncea – a rush, the form of the twigs
laetum – bright
landifer – ladanum-bearing
laurifolius – laurel-leaved
lavigatum – smooth
laxa – loose, slack
leonurus – lion's tail, the flower
leptocheilos – narrow-lipped
leptopus – slender-stalked
leucantha – white-flowered
leucocephala – white-headed
leucoxylon – white-wooded
limon – lemon
linearis – linear
littoralis – from the seashore
lobatus – lobed
longiflora – long-flowered
lophantha – crested flowered
lucidum – shining, clear
lusitanica – from Lusitania (Portugal)
lutescens – yellowish
luteus – deep yellow
macrantha – large-flowered
macrocarpa – long-fruited
macroglossus – large-tongued
macrophylla – large-leaved
macrorrhiza – long-rooted
maculatus – spotted
madagascariensis – from Madagascar
maderense – from Madeira
major – greater
majus – great
manicata – long-sleeved
margarita – pearly
marginata – margined with another colour
maritima – from the sea coast
mauritianum – from Mauretania (Morocco)
maxima – greatest
media – intermediate
mediopicta – medium-coloured
megapotamicum – belonging to a big river
metallica – metallic
mexicanus – from Mexico
microcarpa – small-fruited
microphylla – small-leaved
mimosifolia – mimosa-leaved

minata – vermilion-coloured
minor – smaller
mollis – soft or tender, usually means velvety
multiflorus – many-flowered
munitum – armed
muricatum – rough, with short hard points
mutabilis – variable in form or colour
myrtifolia – leaves like the genus Myrtus (myrtle)
nanus – dwarf
narbonense – from Narbonne
narcissiflora – narcissus-flowered
nesophila – island-loving
nigra – black
nobilis – notable, famous
nocturnum – of the night
nucifera – nut-bearing
nummularium – coin-shaped
nutans – drooping or nodding
oblonga – oblong-shaped
occidentalis – western
odorata – scented
odoratissimum – most scented
officinalis – from the shop, kept by herbalists
oligodon – few toothed
olympicum – from Greece
orbiculata – circular
orientalis – eastern, oriental
ovalifolium – oval-leaved
ovata – egg-shaped
pallida – pale
paniculata – in a panicle
papyraceus – paper-like
papyrus – paper
paradoxa – not of the expected
paraguayense – from Paraguay
parviflora – small-flowered
pauciflora – few-flowered
peltatum – shield-shaped
persicum – from Persia
peruviana – from Peru
petasitis – hat-like
petiolare – long petioles (leaf stalks)
pictum – coloured
platyphyllum – broad-leaved
plenus – double, full
plumbaginoides – plumbago-like
plumosus – plumed or feathery
polyanthum – many-flowered
populifolius – leaves like the genus Populus
  (poplar)
praecox – early ripening
procumbens – trailing
prostratus – prostrate
pseudoacacia – false acacia
pulcherrima – most beautiful
pumilla – dwarf, small
pungens – spiny, pungent
punicea – reddish-purple
purpurea – purple
quadrangularis – square
quinata – five-lobed
racemosa – flowers and fruits in racemes
radiata – bearing rays
radicalis – rising from rootstock
radicans – rooting freely
rectus – straight, upright
recurvata – curved back
recurvifolia – recurved leaves
regia – royal
reginae – of the Queen
repandum – curved up
repens – creeping
reptans – rooting
reticulata – net-veined
revoluta – rolled back
rigens – rigid or stiff
rigida – rigid, stiff
riparia – from riverbanks

rivularis – from brooklets
robusta – robust
rosea – red or rosy
roseus – rosy-coloured
rosmarinifolia – rosemary-leaved
rotundifolia – round-leaved
rubicunda – ruddy
rubiginosa – rust-red
rubra – red, ruddy
rugosus – wrinkled, rough
salicifolius – willow-leaved
saligna – willowy
salvifolia – sage-leaved
sanguinea – blood-red
saponaria – soapy
sarniensis – from Guernsey
sativa – cultivated
saxatilis – inhabiting rocks
scaber – rough feeling
scandens – climbing
schizopetalus – deeply cut petals
schizophylla – split leaves
scoparius – broom-like
sempervirens – always green
sepulcralis – of tombs
setaceus – bristle-like
siliquastrum – siliqua (pod)-like
sinensis – from China
sordidum – dirty-looking
speciosa – showy, spectacular
spectabilis – notable, spectacle
spinosa – spiny
splendens – shining, splendid
stans – sturdy, upright
striata – streaked
strictum – upright
suaveolens – sweet-smelling
suber – cork
suberecta – somewhat upright
suspensum – suspended
syriacus – from Syria
tenax – holding fast, tenacious
tenuifolium – slender leaves
ternata – in threes
ternera – tender, or soft to the touch
tinus – obscure
tobira – native Japanese name
tomentosa – felted, hairy
torquata – with a collar
triacanthos – three-spined
trichocarpa – hairy-fruited
trichophyllum – hairy-leaved
tricolor – three-coloured
trifasciata – with three stripes
trifida – three divisions
trifoliata – three-leaved
triphylla – three-leaved
ugandense – from Uganda
umbellatum – flowers in umbels
undulatum – wavy-edged
unedo – obscure
unguis-cati – clawed
uniflora – single-flowered
utilis – useful
uvaria – like a bunch of grapes
valentina – from Valencia, Spain
variegata – variegated leaves
ventricosum – swollen on one side
venusta – charming
vera – red
viminalis – long, slender shoots
violacea – violet-coloured
virgata – twiggy, wand-like, made of twigs
viscosa – treacle-like, viscid
vitifolium – leaves like the genus Vitis (grape vine)
volubilis – twining, twisting around
vulgaris – common

English Common Names

Many people only know the common name for a plant. Below are listed the generally accepted English common names for the plants in this book, although there are many other names in use.

Abyssinian Fountain Grass – *Pennisetum villosum*
Adam's Needle – *Yucca filamentosa*
African Blue Lily – *Agapanthus*
African Boxwood – *Myrsine africana*
African Corn Flag – *Chasmanthe aethiopica*
African Daisy – *Arctotis* × *hybrida*
African Daisy – *Osteospermum*
African Hemp – *Sparrmannia africana*
African Tulip Tree – *Spathodea*
African Walnut – *Schotia brachypetala*
Amaryllis – *Hippeastrum*
Amazon Lily – *Eucharis* × *grandiflora*
American Arbor-Vitae – *Thuja occidentalis*
Angels' Hair – *Artemisia schmidtiana*
Angels' Trumpet – *Datura inoxia* subsp. *inoxia*
Angels' Trumpets – *Brugmansia*
Annual Mallow – *Malope*
Apple Geranium – *Pelargonium odoratissimum*
Areca Palm – *Dypsis lutescens*
Argentine Trumpet Vine – *Clytostoma callistegioides*
Arrow Bamboo – *Pseudosasa japonica*
Arum Lily – *Zantedeschia*
Aspen – *Populus*
Aurora Borealis Plant – *Kalanchoe fedtschenkoi* 'Marginata'
Australian Banyan – *Ficus macrophylla*
Australian Brush Cherry – *Syzygium paniculatum*
Australian Fan Palm – *Livistona australis*
Australian Frangipani – *Hymenosporum*
Australian Mock Orange – *Pittosporum undulatum*
Australian Pine – *Casuarina*
Australian Willow Myrtle – *Agonis flexuosa*
Autumn Crocus – *Colchicum*
Autumn Daffodil – *Sternbergia*
Avocado – *Persea americana*
Aztec Lily – *Sprekelia formosissima*
Balga – *Xanthorrhoea preisii*
Balsam – *Impatiens*
Banana – *Musa*
Bay Laurel – *Laurus nobilis*
Bear Grass – *Dasylirion wheeleri*
Bear's Breeches – *Acanthus*
Beauty Bush – *Kolkwitzia amabilis*
Beefsteak Plant – *Iresine herbstii*
Belladonna Lily – *Amaryllis belladonna*
Bengal Clock Vine – *Thunbergia grandiflora*
Bindweed – *Convolvulus*
Bird of Paradise – *Strelitzia*
Bird of Paradise Bush – *Caesalpinia gilliesii*
Black Bamboo – *Phyllostachys nigra*
Black Calla – *Arum pictum*
Black Locust – *Robinia pseudoacacia*
Blackboy – *Xanthorrhoea preisii*
Black-Eyed Susan – *Thunbergia alata*
Bladder Senna – *Colutea arborescens*
Blanket Flower – *Gaillardia*
Blood Flower – *Asclepias curassavica*
Blood Leaf – *Iresine lindenii*
Blood Lily – *Haemanthus*
Blood Lily – *Scadoxus*
Blood Red Trumpet Vine – *Distictis buccinatoria*
Blue Daisy – *Felicia*
Blue Fan Palm – *Brahea armata*

Blue Leafed Cycad – *Encephalartos lehmannii*
Blue Marguerite – *Felicia amelloides*
Blue Mist – *Caryopteris* × *clandonensis*
Blue Potato Bush – *Solanum rantonetii*
Blue Trumpet Vine – *Thunbergia grandiflora*
Bluebell Creeper – *Sollya heterophylla*
Blueblossom – *Ceanothus thyrsiflorus*
Borage – *Borago officinalis*
Bottle Brush – *Callistemon*
Bottle Palm – *Beaucarnea recurvata*
Bottle Palm – *Hyophorbe*
Bottle Tree – *Brachychiton*
Bower Plant – *Pandorea jasminoides*
Bowstring Hemp – *Sansevieria*
Box – *Buxus*
Box Elder – *Acer negundo*
Boxwood – *Buxus*
Brazil Cherry – *Eugenia uniflora*
Brazilian Pepper Tree – *Schinus terebinthifolius*
Brazilian Plume Flower – *Justicia carnea*
Bread Tree – *Encephalartos altensteinii*
Bridal Veil Broom – *Retama monosperma*
Bridal Wreath – *Spiraea cantoniensis*
Bridal Wreath – *Stephanotis floribunda*
Broom – *Cytisus*
Broom – *Genista*
Broom – *Ruscus*
Brush Cherry – *Syzygium paniculatum*
Buckeye – *Aesculus*
Bugle – *Ajuga*
Bungalow Palm – *Archontophoenix cunninghamiana*
Bunya-Bunya – *Araucaria bidwillii*
Busy Lizzie – *Impatiens*
Butterfly Bush – *Buddleja davidii*
Butterfly Palm – *Dypsis lutescens*
Cabbage Palm – *Cordyline*
Cabbage Palm – *Livistona australis*
Cabbage Palm – *Sabal palmetto*
Cabbage Tree – *Cordyline*
Calico Flower – *Aristolochia littoralis*
California Fan Palm – *Washingtonia filifera*
California Fuchsia – *Zauschneria californica*
California Geranium – *Senecio petasitis*
California Lilac – *Ceanothus*
California Poppy – *Eschscholzia californica*
Calla Lily – *Zantedeschia aethiopica*
Camphor Tree – *Cinnamomum camphora*
Canary Island Palm – *Phoenix canariensis*
Candelabra Tree – *Euphorbia ingens*
Candle Bush – *Senna alata*
Candytuft – *Iberis*
Cape Chestnut – *Calodendrum capense*
Cape Figwort – *Phygelius capensis*
Cape Fuchsia – *Phygelius*
Cape Gooseberry – *Physalis peruviana*
Cape Honeysuckle – *Tecoma capensis*
Cape Ivy – *Senecio macroglossus*
Cape Jasmine – *Gardenia augusta*
Cape Mallow – *Anisodontea*
Cape Myrtle – *Myrsine africana*
Caper Bush – *Capparis spinosa*
Carandy Palm – *Copernicia alba*
Cardboard Palm – *Zamia furfuracea*
Cardinal Flower – *Odontonema strictum*
Carob – *Ceratonia siliqua*
Carolina Jasmine – *Gelsemium sempervirens*
Cast-Iron Plant – *Apidistra elatior*
Castor Oil Plant – *Ricinus communis*
Cat's Claw Vine – *Macfadyena unguis-cati*

Cedar – *Cedrus*
Century Plant – *Agave americana*
Chalice Vine – *Solandra*
Chaste Tree – *Vitex agnus-castus*
Cherimoya – *Annona cherimola*
Cherry Pie – *Heliotropium arborescens*
Chestnut – *Castanea*
Chestnut Dioon – *Dioon edule*
Chilean Jasmine – *Mandevilla laxa*
Chilean Potato Tree – *Solanum crispum*
Chilean Wine Palm – *Jubaea chilensis*
Chilean Glory Flower – *Eccremocarpus scaber*
Chinaberry – *Melia azedarach*
Chinese Fan Palm – *Livistona chinensis*
Chinese Flame Tree – *Koelreuteria bipinata*
Chinese Fountain Grass – *Pennisetum alopecuroides*
Chinese Gooseberry – *Actinidia deliciosa*
Chinese Holly – *Osmanthus heterophyllus*
Chinese Jade Tree – *Crassula arborescens*
Chinese Jujuba – *Ziziphus jujuba*
Chocolate Vine – *Akebia quinata*
Christmas Kalanchoe – *Kalanchoe blossfeldiana*
Chusan Palm – *Trachycarpus fortunei*
Cigar Flower – *Cuphea ignea*
Climbing Blueberry – *Billardiera longiflora*
Cockscomb – *Erythrina crista-galli*
Common Almond – *Prunus dulcis*
Common or Zonal Geranium – *Pelargonium* × *hortorum*
Common Walnut – *Juglans regia*
Confederate Rose – *Hibiscus mutabilis*
Copperleaf – *Acalypha wilkesiana*
Coral Pea – *Hardenbergia*
Coral Pea – *Kennedia*
Coral Plant – *Russelia equisetiformis*
Coral Tree – *Erythrina*
Coral Vine – *Antigonon leptopus*
Corn Flag – *Gladiolus communis* subsp. *byzantinus*
Corn Lily – *Ixia African*
Costa Rican Nightshade – *Solanum wendlandii*
Cotton Lavender – *Santolina chamaecyparissus*
Cow Itch Tree – *Lagunaria patersonii*
Cranesbill – *Geranium*
Crape Myrtle – *Lagerstroemia indica*
Creeping Gloxinia – *Lophospermum erubescens*
Creeping Rubber Plant – *Ficus pumila*
Cross Vine – *Bignonia capreolata*
Crown of Thorns – *Euphorbia millii*
Cuban Petticot Palm – *Copernecia macroglossa*
Cuban Royal Palm – *Roystonea regia*
Cup and Saucer Plant – *Cobaea scandens*
Cup of Gold – *Solandra maxima*
Curry Plant – *Helichrysum italicum*
Custard Apple – *Annona cherimola*
Cypress – *Cupressus*
Daffodil – *Narcissus*
Daisy Bush – *Olearia*
Daisy Tree – *Montanoa bipinnatifida*
Date Palm – *Phoenix dactylifera*
Day Lily – *Hemerocallis*
Dew Flower – *Drosanthemum floribundum*
Dew Plant – *Aptenia cordifolia*
Dipladenia – *Mandevilla*
Donkey Tail – *Sedum morganianum*
Doum Palm – *Hyphaene coriacea*
Dragon Tree – *Dracaena draco*
Dusty Miller – *Centaurea cineraria*
Dusty Miller – *Senecio cineraria*

Dutch Iris – *Iris xiphium* hybrids
Dutchman's Pipe – *Aristolochia macrophylla*
Dwarf Ponciana – *Sesbania punicea*
Elephant's Ear – *Alocasia macrorrhiza*
Elephant's Ears – *Bergenia*
Eucalypt – *Eucalyptus*
European Grape – *Vitis vinifera*
Evening Primrose – *Oenothera*
Evening Trumpet Flower – *Gelsemium sempervirens*
Everglades Palm – *Acoelorrhaphe wrightii*
Fairy Fan Flower – *Scaevola aemula*
False Acacia – *Robinia pseudoacacia*
False Heather – *Cuphea hyssopifolia*
False Holly – *Osmanthus heterophyllus*
Feather Grass – *Stipa*
Feathertop – *Pennisetum villosum*
Feathery Cassia – *Senna artemisoides*
Felt Plant – *Kalanchoe beharensis*
Fennel – *Foeniculum*
Fern Palm – *Cycas circinalis*
Ferocious Aloe – *Aloe ferox*
Ferocious Blue Cycad – *Encephalartos horridus*
Fescue – *Festuca*
Fig – *Ficus*
Fire Lily – *Cyrtanthus*
Firethorn – *Pyracantha*
Fish Tail-Palm – *Caryota*
Flag Iris – *Iris germanica*
Flame Tree – *Brachychiton acerifolius*
Flame Vine – *Pyrostegia venusta*
Flaming Katy – *Kalanchoe blossfeldiana*
Flannel Bush – *Fremontodendron*
Flax Lily – *Phormium*
Fleur-de-lis – *Iris germanica*
Flowering Quince – *Chaenomeles*
Flowering Maple – *Abutilon*
Forest Lily – *Veltheimia bracteata*
Fountain Butterfly Bush – *Buddleja alternifolia*
Fountain Palm – *Livistona chinensis*
Fountain Plant – *Russelia equisetiformis*
Four o'clock Plant – *Mirabilis jalapa*
Foxglove Tree – *Paulownia tomentosa*
Fragrant Snowball – *Viburnum x carlcephalum*
Fried Egg Plant – *Romneya coulteri*
Friendship Plant – *Billbergia nutans*
Fuchsia – *Correa Australian*
Garden Canna – *Canna × generalis*
Garland Lily – *Hedychium*
German Ivy – *Senecio mikanioides*
Germander – *Teucrium*
Ghost Plant – *Graptopelalum paraguayense*
Giant False Agave – *Furcraea foetida*
Giant Fennel – *Ferula communis*
Giant Reed – *Arundo donax*
Ginger Lily – *Alpina*
Ginger Lily – *Hedychium*
Gingerbread Palm – *Hyphaene thebaica*
Glory Flower – *Clerodendrum bungei*
Glorybower – *Clerodendrum*
Golden Bamboo – *Phyllostachys aurea*
Golden Calla – *Zantedeschia elliotiana*
Golden Cane Palm – *Dypsis lutescens*
Golden Garlic – *Allium moly*
Golden Oats – *Stipa gigantea*
Golden Rain Tree – *Koelreuteria paniculata*
Golden Shower – *Pyrostegia venusta*
Golden Swan Tritonia – *Crocosmia masoniorum*
Golden Trumpet Vine – *Allamanda cathartica*
Granadilla – *Passiflora*
Granite Bottlebrush – *Melaleuca elliptica*
Grape Hyacinth – *Muscari*
Grapefruit – *Citrus × paradisi*
Grape Vine – *Vitis*
Grass Tree – *Xanthorrhoea*
Ground Cherry – *Physalis*
Ground Morning Glory – *Convolvulus sabatius*
Guadeloupe Fan Palm – *Brahea edulis*
Guava Tree – *Psidium guajava*
Guernsey Lily – *Nerine sarniensis*
Guinea Gold Flower – *Hibbertia scandens*
Gum – *Eucalyptus*

Hackberry – *Celtis*
Hare's Tail Grass – *Lagurus ovatus*
Harlequin Flower – *Sparaxis tricolor*
Hazel – *Corylus*
Heath – *Erica*
Heavenly Bamboo – *Nandina domestica*
Heliotrope – *Heliotropium*
Hens and Chickens – *Echeveria elegans*
Herald's Trumpet – *Beaumontia grandiflora*
Hesper Palm – *Brahea*
Hollyhock – *Alcea*
Honey Bush – *Melianthus major*
Honey Locust – *Gleditsia triacanthos*
Honeysuckle – *Lonicera*
Hoop Pine – *Araucaria cunninghamii*
Horse Chestnut – *Aesculus*
Horsetail Tree – *Casuarina equisetifolia*
Hottentot Fig – *Carpobrotus edulis*
Houpara – *Pseudopanax lessoni*
Ice Plant – *Lampranthus*
Indian Bead Tree – *Melia azedarach*
Indian Bean Tree – *Catalpa bignonioides*
Indian Cress – *Tropaeolum majus*
Indian Fig – *Opuntia ficus-indica*
Indian Hawthorn – *Rhaphiolepis indica*
Indian Shot Plant – *Canna*
Ironbark – *Eucalyptus*
Italian Arum – *Arum italicum*
Italian Buckthorn – *Rhamnus alaternus*
Ivy – *Hedera*
Ivy Leaved Geranium – *Pelargonium peltatum*
Jacobean Lily – *Sprekelia formosissima*
Jade Plant – *Crassula ovata*
Japanese Aralia – *Fatsia japonica*
Japanese Lantern – *Hibiscus schizopetalus*
Japanese Laurel – *Aucuba japonica*
Japanese Mock Orange – *Pittosporum tobira*
Japanese Pagoda Tree – *Sophora japonica*
Japanese Sago Palm – *Cycas revoluta*
Japonica – *Chaenomeles*
Jelly Palm – *Butia capitata*
Jerusalem Sage – *Phlomis fruticosa*
Jerusalem Thorn – *Parkinsonia aculeata*
Joseph's Coat – *Amaranthus tricolor*
Judas Tree – *Cercis siliquastrum*
Juniper – *Juniperus*
Kangaroo Apple – *Solanum aviculare*
Kangaroo Paw – *Anigozanthus flavidus*
Kangaroo Thorn – *Acacia paradoxa*
Kapok Tree – *Chorisia speciosa*
Karaka – *Corynocarpus laevigata*
Karo – *Pittosporum crassifolium*
Kentia Palm – *Howea forsteriana*
King Palm – *Archontophoenix*
King's Mantle – *Thunbergia erecta*
Kiwi – *Actinidia deliciosa*
Kohuhu – *Pittosporum tenuifolium*
Kumquat – *Fortunella*
Kurrajong – *Brachychiton populneus*
Lad's Love – *Atemisia abrotanum*
Lady Palm – *Rhapis*
Lambs' Ears – *Stachys byzantina*
Latan Palm – *Latania*
Laurel-Leaved Snailseed – *Cocculus laurifolius*
Laurestinus – *Viburnum tinus*
Lavender – *Lavandula*
Leadwort – *Plumbago*
Lemon – *Citrus limon*
Lemon Geranium – *Pelargonium 'Graveolens'*
Lemon Verbena – *Aloysia triphylla*
Lentisc – *Pistacia lentiscus*
Lilac Vine – *Hardenbergia comptoniana*
Lily – *Lilium*
Lily of the Nile – *Agapanthus praecox* subsp. *orientalis*
Lily of the Palace – *Hippeastrum aulicum*
Lime – *Citrus aurantiifolia*
Lime – *Tilia*
Linden – *Tilia*
Lion's Ear – *Leonotis leonurus*
Lion's Tail – *Leonotis leonurus*
Lobster Claw – *Clianthus puniceus*

Loquat – *Eriobotrya japonica*
Lord's Candle – *Yucca recurvifolia*
Lords and Ladies – *Arum*
Love-Lies-Bleeding – *Amaranthus caudatus*
Lucky Bean Tree – *Erythrina caffra*
Madagascar Jasmine – *Stephanotis floribunda*
Madagascar Periwinkle – *Catharanthus*
Madeira Stork's Bill – *Geranium maderense*
Madeira Vine – *Anredera cordifolia*
Madrono – *Arbutus menziesii*
Mallet Tree – *Tupidanthus calyptratus*
Mallow – *Lavateria*
Mallow – *Malva*
Manuka – *Leptospermum scoparium*
Maples – *Acer*
Marguerite – *Argyranthemum*
Marguerite – *Leucanthemum vulgare*
Marmalade Bush – *Streptosolen jamesonii*
Marvel of Peru – *Mirabilis jalapa*
Mastic Tree – *Pistacia lentiscus*
Maternity Plant – *Kalanchoe daigremontiana*
Matilija Poppy – *Romneya*
Mauritius Nightshade – *Solanum mauritianum*
Meadow Saffron – *Colchicum autumnale*
Mediterranean Fan Palm – *Chamaerops humilis*
Mediterranean Field Gladiolus – *Gladiolus italicus*
Melon Pear – *Solanum muricatum*
Melon Shrub – *Solanum muricatum*
Mexican Blue Palm – *Brahea armata*
Mexican Breadfruit – *Monstera deliciosa*
Mexican Fan Palm – *Washingtonia robusta*
Mexican Feather Grass – *Stipa tenuissima*
Mexican Flame-Vine – *Senecio confusus*
Mexican Hat Plant – *Kalanchoe daigremontiana*
Mexican Orange Blossom – *Choisya ternata*
Mexican Sunflower – *Tithonia*
Milk Bush – *Gomphocarpus fruticosus*
Milkweed – *Asclepias*
Milkweed – *Euphorbia*
Milkwort – *Polygala*
Mimosa – *Acacia*
Miniature Fan Palm – *Rhapis excelsa*
Miniature Date Palm – *Phoenix roebelenii*
Mint Bush – *Prostanthera*
Mirror Plant – *Coprosma repens*
Misty Plume Bush – *Iboza riparia*
Mock Orange – *Philadelphus*
Monkey Flower – *Mimulus*
Monkey Puzzle Tree – *Araucaria araucana*
Montbretia – *Crocosmia*
Moonflower – *Ipomoea alba*
Moreton Bay Pine – *Araucaria cunninghamii*
Morning Glory – *Ipomoea*
Mother of Pearl Plant – *Graptopetalum paraguayense*
Mother-in-Law's Tongue – *Sansevieria trifasciata*
Mount Atlas Mastic – *Pistacia atlantica*
Mulberry – *Morus*
Mullein – *Verbascum*
Myrtle – *Myrtus*
Naked Ladies – *Colchicum*
Nasturtium – *Tropaeolum*
Natal Ivy – *Senecio macroglossus*
Natal Plum – *Carissa macrocarpa*
Needle Grass – *Stipa*
New Zealand Christmas Tree – *Metrosideros excelsus*
New Zealand Flax – *Phormium tenax*
New Zealand Laurel – *Corynocarpus laevigatus*
Night Jessamine – *Cestrum nocturnum*
Norfolk Island Hibiscus – *Lagunaria*
Norfolk Island Pine – *Araucaria heterophylla*
Oak – *Quercus*
Octopus Tree – *Schefflera actinophylla*
Oleander – *Nerium oleander*
Oleaster – *Elaeagnus angustifolia*
Olive – *Olea*
Onion – *Allium*
Orange Clock Vine – *Thunbergia gregorii*
Orchid Cactus – *Epiphyllum*
Ornamental Cherry – *Prunus*
Osage Orange – *Maclura pomifera*

Palmetto – *Sabal*
Pampas Grass – *Cortaderia selloana*
Pansy – *Viola*
Paper Flower – *Bougainvillea*
Paper Mulberry – *Broussonetia papyrifera*
Paper White Narcissus – *Narcissus papyraceus*
Paperbark – *Melaleuca*
Papyrus – *Cyperus papyrus*
Paris Daisy – *Argyranthemum frutescens*
Parlour Palm – *Chamaedorea elegans*
Parrot's Beak – *Clianthus puniceus*
Parrot's Beak – *Lotus berthelotii*
Passion Flower – *Passiflora*
Pawpaw – *Carica papaya*
Pea Tree – *Caragana*
Peony – *Paeonia*
Pepino – *Solanum muricatum*
Pepper Tree – *Schinus molle*
Peppermint Tree – *Agonis flexuosa*
Periwinkle – *Vinca*
Persian Lilac – *Melia azedarach*
Persimmon – *Diospyros kaki*
Peruvian Daffodil – *Hymenocallis narcissiflora*
Peruvian Lily – *Alstroemeria aurea*
Petticoat Palm – *Washingtonia filifera*
Pigeon Berry – *Duranta erecta*
Pig's Ear – *Cotyledon orbiculata*
Pincushion Tree – *Hakea laurina*
Pine – *Pinus*
Pineapple Guava – *Acca sellowiana*
Pink Ball – *Dombeya x cayeuxii*
Pink Trumpet Vine – *Podranea ricasoliana*
Pistachio – *Pistacia*
Plane – *Platanus*
Platter-Leaf – *Cocculus laurifolius*
Plumbago – *Ceratostigma*
Plume Poppy – *Macleaya*
Pohutukawa – *Metrosideros*
Poinsettia – *Euphorbia pulcherrima*
Pokeweed – *Phytolacca*
Pomegranate – *Punica granatum*
Ponytail Palm – *Beaucarnea recurvata*
Popcorn-Bush – *Senna didymobotrya*
Poplar – *Populus*
Pork and Beans – *Sedum rubrotinctum*
Portugal Laurel – *Prunus lusitanica*
Potato Vine – *Solanum jasminoides*
Powell's Swamp Lily – *Crinum × powellii*
Prickly Cycad – *Encephalartos altensteinii*
Prickly Pear – *Opuntia ficus-indica*
Pride of Bolivia – *Tipuana tipu*
Pride of India – *Koelreuteria paniculata*
Pride of Madeira – *Echium candicans*
Pride of the Cape – *Bauhinia galpinii*
Primrose Tree – *Lagunaria patersonii*
Privet – *Ligustrum*
Puerto Rican Hat Palm – *Sabal causiarum*
Purple Glory Bush – *Tibouchina urvilleana*
Purple Heart – *Tradescantia pallida* 'Purpurea'
Purple Hopseed Bush – *Dodonaea viscosa*
    'Purpurea'
Purple Orchid Tree – *Bauhinia variegata*
Purple-Leaved Plum – *Prunus cerasifera* 'Pissardii'
Pygmy Date Palm – *Phoenix roebelenii*
Queen of the Night – *Cestrum nocturnum*
Queen Palm – *Syagrus romanzoffiana*
Queen Sago Palm – *Cycas circinalis*
Queen's Wreath – *Petrea volubilis*
Queen's Wreath – *Antigonon leptopus*
Queensland Umbrella Tree – *Schefflera*
    actinophylla
Quince – *Cydonia*
Red Bauhinia – *Bauhinia galpinii*
Red Hot Poker – *Kniphofia*
Red Mountain Spinach – *Atriplex hortensis* var.
    rubra
Red Orache – *Atriplex hortensis* var. *rubra*
Reed Palm – *Chamaedorea microspadix*
Rice Paper Plant – *Tetrapanax papyrifer*

Rock Rose – *Cistus*
Rock Rose – *Helianthemum*
Rose – *Rosa*
Rose Acacia – *Robinia hispida*
Rose of China – *Hibiscus rosa-sinensis*
Rose of Sharon – *Hibiscus syriacus*
Rosemary – *Rosmarinus*
Royal Palms – *Roystonea*
Rubber Plant – *Ficus elastica*
Rue – *Ruta*
Russian Olive – *Elaeagnus angustifolia*
Russian Sage – *Perovskia*
Sacred Bamboo – *Nandina domestica*
Sage – *Salvia*
Sago Palm – *Cycas circinalis*
Saltbush – *Atriplex*
Saw Cabbage Palm – *Acoelorrhaphe wrightii*
Scarborough Lily – *Cyrtanthus elatus*
Scarlet Beard-Tongue – *Penstemon barbatus*
Scarlet Sage – *Salvia splendens*
Scarlet Wisteria Tree – *Sesbania tripetii*
Screw Pine – *Pandanus*
Sea Buckthorn – *Hippophae rhamnoides*
Sea Daffodil – *Pancratium maritimum*
Sea Holly – *Eryngium maritimum*
Sea Lavender – *Limonium*
Sea Onion – *Urginea maritima*
Sea Pink – *Armeria*
Senegal Date Palm – *Phoenix reclinata*
Sentry Palm – *Howea*
Shasta Daisy – *Leucanthemum × superbum*
Shaving Brush Plant – *Haemanthus coccineus*
She Oak – *Casuarina*
Shell Flower – *Alpinia zerumbet*
Shell Ginger – *Alpinia zerumbet*
Shrimp Plant – *Justicia brandegeeana*
Shrubby Goosefoot – *Atriplex halimus*
Shumach – *Rhus*
Siberian Pea Shrub – *Caragana arborescens*
Silk Tree – *Albizia julibrissin*
Silkweed – *Asclepias*
Silky Oak – *Grevillea robusta*
Silver Jade Plant – *Crassula arborescens*
Silver Saw Palmetto – *Acoelorrhaphe wrightii*
Silverbush – *Convolvulus cneorum*
Sky Flower – *Duranta erecta*
Sleepy Mallow – *Malvaviscus*
Smoke Bush – *Cotinus coggygria*
Snow on the Mountain – *Euphorbia marginata*
Snowflake – *Leucojum*
Snow-in-Summer – *Cerastium tomentosum*
Society Garlic – *Tulbaghia violaceae*
Sour or Seville Orange – *Citrus aurantium*
South African Sage Wood – *Buddleja salvifolia*
Southernwood – *Atemisia abrotanum*
Spanish Bayonet – *Yucca aloifolia*
Spanish Broom – *Spartium junceum*
Spanish Dagger – *Yucca gloriosa*
Spanish Iris – *Iris xiphium hybrids*
Spanish Oats – *Stipa gigantea*
Spider Lily – *Hymenocallis*
Spider Lily – *Lycoris*
Spider Plant – *Chlorophytum comosum*
Spindle Palm – *Hyophorbe verschaffeltii*
Spindle Tree – *Euonymus*
Spoon Flower – *Dasylirion wheeleri*
Spotted Laurel – *Aucuba japonica*
Sprengeri Fern – *Asparagus densiflorus* 'Sprengeri'
Spring Star Flower – *Ipheion uniflorum*
Spurge – *Euphorbia*
Squills – *Urginea maritima*
St James Lily – *Sprekelia formosissima*
Star Jasmine – *Trachelospermum jasminoides*
Star of Bethlehem – *Ornithogalum*
Statice – *Limonium*
Stonecrop – *Sedum*
Strawberry Tree – *Arbutus*
String of Beads – *Senecio rowleyanus*
Sugarberry – *Celtis occidentalis*

Sun Rose – *Cistus*
Sun Rose – *Helianthemum*
Sundrops – *Oenothera*
Surinam Cherry – *Eugenia uniflora*
Swan's Neck Agave – *Agave attenuata*
Sweet Bay – *Laurus nobilis*
Sweet Chestnut – *Castanea*
Sweet Orange – *Citrus sinensis*
Sweetshade – *Hymenosporum flavum*
Swiss Cheese Plant – *Monstera deliciosa*
Sword Fern – *Polystichum munitum*
Tamarisk – *Tamarix*
Tapa-Cloth Tree – *Broussonetia papyrifera*
Tea Tree – *Leptospermum*
Thatch Leaf Palm – *Howea forsteriana*
Thatch Palm – *Thrinax*
Thrift – *Armeria*
Thyme – *Thymus*
Tipu Tree – *Tipuana*
Tobacco Plant – *Nicotiana*
Torch-Lily – *Kniphofia*
Transvaal Daisy – *Gerbera jamesonii*
Treasure Flower – *Gazania × hybrida*
Trebinth – *Pistacia trebinthus*
Tree Anemone – *Carpenteria californica*
Tree Daisies – *Olearia*
Tree Fuchsia – *Schotia brachypetala*
Tree Houseleek – *Aeonium arboreum*
Tree Ivy – *Fatshedera lizei*
Tree of Heaven – *Ailanthus altissima*
Tree Philodendron – *Philodendron bipinnatifidum*
Tree Poke – *Phytolacca dioica*
Tree Poppy – *Dendromecon*
Tree Poppy – *Romneya*
Tree Tobacco – *Solanum mauritianum*
Tree Tomato – *Cyphomandra betacea*
Tree Wisteria – *Bolusanthus speciosus*
Triangle Palm – *Dypsis decaryi*
Trumpet Bush – *Tecoma stans*
Trumpet Creeper – *Campsis*
Trumpet Vine – *Campsis*
Turk's Cap – *Malvaviscus arboreus* 'Mexicanus'
Turpentine Tree – *Pistacia trebinthus*
Umbra Tree – *Phytolacca dioica*
Umbrella Plant – *Cyperus alternifolius*
Valerian – *Centranthus*
Variegated False Agave – *Furcraea selloa*
    'Marginata'
Vase Plant – *Billbergia*
Velvet Elephant Ear – *Kalanchoe beharensis*
Velvet Rose – *Aeonium canariense*
Venetian Shumach – *Cotinus coggygria*
Victorian Box – *Pittosporum undulatum*
Violet – *Viola*
Violet Bush – *Iochroma cyaneum*
Virgin's Bower – *Clematis cirrhosa*
Virgin's Palm – *Dioon edule*
Wattle – *Acacia*
Wax Flower – *Hoya*
Wax Palm – *Copernecia*
Weeping Chinese Lantern – *Abutilon*
    megapotamicum
White Cedar – *Thuja occidentalis*
White Sapote – *Casimiroa edulis*
Wild Cotton – *Gomphocarpus fruticosus*
Wild Rosemary – *Eriocephalus africanus*
Willow – *Salix*
Willow-Leaved Jessamine – *Cestrum parqui*
Windmill Palm – *Trachycarpus fortunei*
Wine Grape – *Vitis vinifera*
Winter Begonia – *Bergenia cordifolia*
Wire Netting Bush – *Corokia cotoneaster*
Wonga Wonga Vine – *Pandorea pandorana*
Yatay Palm – *Butia yatay*
Yellow Bells – *Tecoma stans*
Yellow Elder – *Tecoma stans*
Yellow Oleander – *Thevetia peruviana*
Yesterday-Today-Tomorrow – *Brunfelsia*
    pauciflora

Glossary of Terms

This glossary gives definitions of terms used in this book as well as a number used generally in gardening.

A

Accent Plant – Plant used in a formal bed or border to emphasize contrasts of height, colour or texture.

Acid (soils) – Which have a pH value of below 7.

Acuminate – The leaf tapers gradually to a point.

Acute – Ending in a short sharp point.

Adventitious – A plant organ that occurs other than the usual place.

Alternate - Arranged along a stem at different levels.

Aerial root - A root formed on the stem or trunk of a plant.

Alkaline (soils) - With a pH value above 7.

Alternate - Leaf arrangement, borne singly at each node, at differing heights along a stem in two vertical rows on either side of an axis. The term applies to all leaves whether they are simple or compound.

Anther - Pollen-bearing top of stamen.

Annual - A plant that grows to maturity, flowers, and fruits in one growing season and then dies.

Anther - Part of the stamen that releases the pollen; usually borne on a filament.

Apex - The tip or growing point of an organ (as a leaf).

Arborescent - Tree-like, resembling a tree in size and form.

Arrow-shaped - With a narrow, pointed tip widening at the base with two downward-pointing lobes.

Axil - The upper angle at which a leaf or other organ joins its stem.

Axillary - Originating from the leaf axil.

B

Bark - The outermost layer of a woody stem.

Basal - At the base of an organ.

Basal leaf - A leaf that grows from the lowest part of the stem.

Bell shaped - A flower with a broad tube ending in flared lobes.

Bicoloured - With two distinct colours.

Biennial - A plant that completes its life cycle in two years, usually growing in the first year, then flowering and fruiting in the second; it then dies.

Bipinnate leaves - Have pinnately divided leaves, with or without a terminal leaflet.

Bisexual (Hermaphrodite) - Flowers having both stamens and pistils.

Blade - The expanded portion of a leaf.

Botanical name - The Latin scientific name of a plant.

Bract - Modified leaves below a flower or an inflorescence, intermediate between flower and the normal leaves, frequently coloured.

Branch - A division of a stem or trunk; the axis of an inflorescence.

Broad-leafed - Broad, flat, usually deciduous.

Bud - Immature organ or shoot enclosing the embryonic branch, leaf or flower.

Bulb - A modified subterranean growth bud, with fleshy scales serving as a storage organ and consisting of overlapping leaf and often flower buds.

Bulbil - A small, bulb-like organ produced above ground on stems or in inflorescence and serving the same function as subterranean bulbs.

Bulbous - Having a bulb or stem that is swollen at the base resembling the shape of a bulb.

Bulbous Plants - Have underground storage organs.

C

Calcareous - Soil with a high chalk content.

Calyx - A collective term for a flower's sepals that form the outer circle or cup of floral parts (usually green).

Campanulate - Bell-shaped flower with broad base.

Capsule - A non-fleshy fruit that opens naturally to disperse the ripe seed.

Carpel - Female parts of a flower consisting of a style, stigma and an ovary.

Chlorophyll - The green pigment of plant cells which absorbs light energy in photosynthesis.

Chlorosis - The loss of green colour in a leaf (chlorophyll), usually due to a nutrient deficiency, usually of iron, to disease, or to insect attack.

Climber - A plant that climbs or clings by means of modified stems, leaves or leafstalks.

Clone - A plant that is derived by vegetative propagation from one individual plant and has the identical genetic material.

Cluster - An arrangement of several leaves, stems, roots or flowers that arise from a single point.

Compound leaf - A leaf of two or more leaflets.

Concave - Hollowed out.

Convex - Umbrella-like.

Cordate - Heart-shaped.

Corm - Thickened underground stem, bulb-like but solid, with food stored in the centre from which it produces a whole plant each year.

Corolla - A collective term for the complete circle of petals of a flower.

Corona - A crown or cup-shaped appendage inside a flower consisting of united stamens or other flower parts.

Corymb - A flat-topped, open flower cluster with the individual flowers opening from the outside inward.

Costapalmate - The leaf stalk extends well into the leaf. Usually in palm leaves.

Cotyledon - The first leaves to appear when a seed germinates.

Crenate - A term used to describe leaf margins that are scalloped with shallow, rounded teeth.

Creeper - A trailing shoot rooting at intervals.

Crown - 1. The growing point of a plant, usually at soil level, from which roots and shoots grow; 2. The crown of a tree or shrub is its entire branch structure including the leaves.

Culm - The peculiar hollow stem or stalk of grasses and bamboo.

Cultivar (cv.) - A variety or form of a species that originates in cultivation and is not found naturally, and retains its distinct uniform characteristics when propagated.

Cyme - A broad, usually flat-topped, branched flower cluster with centre flowers opening first.

D

Deadheading - The act of removing spent flowers from a plant to prevent seeding, and to encourage new flowers.

236

Deciduous - The shedding of leaves annually at the end of the growing season.

Decumbent - Growing close to the ground, reclining, but tip upward-growing.

Dentate - Describes a leaf margin with coarse teeth, usually directed outwards.

Dicotyledon - A seedling that produces two seed leaves (cotyledons), normally has woody tissues, and has floral parts in fours or fives.

Dioecious - The male and female flowers are on different plants.

Diurnal - A term used to describe flowers that open only during the day.

Divide - To propagate a plant by splitting it into separate parts each with its own roots and shoots.

Divided - Separated to, or very nearly to the base or the midrib.

Double flower - A flower that has, or seems to have, more petals than in the wild state, and with few if any stamens.

Downy - Clothed with soft, short hairs.

Drainage - Refers to the movement of excess water through the soil in the plant's root area.

Drought - A period of time when a region gets less than what is considered to be the normal amount of rain.

Drought-tolerant, drought-resistant - Plants that can withstand long periods with little or no water, or plants that have low water requirements.

Drupe - A fruit whose hard seed or seeds is surrounded by a fleshy area.

Dwarf - A small or low-growing form of a species.

E

Elliptic An elongated oval with the middle part the widest, and both ends tapering.

Elongate - Drawn out in length.

Endemic - Native to, or confined naturally to, a restricted region or area.

Entire - The margin of a leaf that is smooth and unlobed, and lacks any sort of indentation.

Epiphyte - A plant that grows upon another plant without taking food from its host.

Etiolated - Growth that has become long, thin and pallid because of lack of light.

Even-pinnate - An even number of leaflets in a pinnate leaf: the leaf usually ends in a pair of leaflets rather than in a terminal (final) leaflet.

Evaporation - The loss of water from the soil.

Evergreen - Retaining leaves for more than one growing season. An evergreen plant never loses all of its leaves at one time.

Eye - 1. Immature growth bud often on a tuber. 2. The differently coloured centre of a flower.

F

F1 hybrid - First generation hybrid derived by artificial cross-pollination between two distinct pure-bred lines, usually giving greater vigour and uniformity.

Family - The primary category in plant classification.

Fan-shaped - Wedge-shaped or semicircular, often with a pleated or boldly veined surface.

Fastigiate - Erect habit of growth, often narrow or columnar.

Filament - Threadlike stalk of a stamen attached to an anther.

Frond - Leaf of a fern. Also used to describe large leaves, such as palm leaves.

Funnelform - A tubular flower gradually widening upwards and spreading outwards, often lobed, like a funnel.

G

Garden origin - A plant that has been bred or selected and does not occur in the wild.

Genus - The primary grouping of different closely related species. (plural genera; adj. generic)

Glabrous - Smooth and not hairy.

Glaucous - Covered with a blue-green, blue-grey, grey, whitish or bluish bloom, or a waxy and powdery substance that is easily rubbed away.

Globose - Round or almost round, spherical.

Glutinous - Sticky.

Groundcover - Usually low-growing plants that are selected to grow over and cover an area of soil, and create a uniform appearance.

Growing point - Tip of a shoot from which the new growth appears.

H

Habit - The characteristic appearance of a mature plant.

Habitat - The kind of locality in which a plant grows in the wild.

Head - A short dense cluster of flowers.

Herbaceous - Any plant that does not form a persistent woody stem dies back to the ground each year.

Hermaphrodite - Stamens and pistils in same flower.

Humus - Dark brown, decomposing organic matter in the soil; may also refer to rotted garden compost. It is extremely water-retentive, and an ideal medium for soil life.

Hybrid - The result of crossing two distinct species, subspecies, varieties, cultivars or from two different genera.

I

Incised - The margins of a leaf, stipule or bract that is deeply, irregularly and sharply cut or slashed.

Incurved - Bending inwards.

Inferior ovary - One that is below the calyx leaves.

Inflorescence - The arrangement of flowers originating from a single point on the stem, branch or trunk, often referred to as a flower head.

Internode - The area on a stem between one leaf node and the next.

Involucre - A ring of leaf-like bracts surrounding the base of a flower head or an inflorescence.

K

Keel - The two lowermost petals of a pea-like flower.

L

Lance-shaped (lanceolate) - A leaf shape that is longer than wide, with the widest part of the blade near the point of attachment, tapering towards the tip.

Lateral - A stem or shoot that branches off from a bud in the leaf axil of a larger stem.

Latex - Milky-white sap or fluid that bleeds from some plants when the stem is cut.

Layering - A method of propagation where a branch will make roots while placed in close contact with the soil surface.

Lax - Loose, widely spaced, not compact.

Leader - The main, usually central stem of a tree or shrub.

Leaf axil - The angle formed between a leaf or leaf stalk and the stem of the plant.

Leaf blade - The part of the leaf that excludes the leaf stalk.

Leaflet - Single distinct division (blade) of a compound leaf.

Leaf node - The point where a leaf arises from a stem.

Leaf stalk - The stalk of a leaf.

Leathery - Tough, hard, like leather.

Lenticels - Raised pores on bark, providing access for air to the inner tissues.

Limb - Larger branch of a tree.

Lip - A petal or modified stamen that is usually larger than the other petals.

Linear - Long, narrow and flat margins, more or less parallel; usually used to describe a leaf.

Lobe - Any projection of a leaf, rounded or pointed.

Lobed - Leaf cut less than halfway to the base.

M

Micro climate - The climate of a small area or locality, as opposed to that of a larger area.

Midrib (Midvein) - The central main vein of a leaf or leaflet; usually the largest and most visually prominent vein in the leaf.

Monocarpic - A plant that flowers only once, sets fruit and then dies.

Monocotyledon - Produces seedlings with only one seed leaf (cotyledon), parallel-veined leaves, no cambium layer; the flowers usually have their parts in threes or multiples of three.

Monoecious - The stamens and pistils in separate flowers but borne on the same plant.

Monotypic - A genus or family of plants that consists of only one species.

Mulch - A layer of organic matter spread on the soil around plants.

N

Native - A species that naturally grows wild in a particular area.

Naturalized - A species that apparently grows wild in a particular area, but is introduced and not native.

Needle-shaped - Long, slender and rigid.

Nocturnal - A term used to describe flowers that open at night and close during the day.

Node - The place on a stem, sometimes swollen, from which a leaf or single group of leaves and side-shoots emerges.

O

Oblique - Slanting of unequal sides.

Oblong - Longer than wide, with sides more or less parallel for most of their length.

Obovate - A reversed, ovate shape, the narrower part being near the point of attachment.

Obtuse - Blunt or rounded at the end.

Odd-pinnate - An uneven number of leaflets in a pinnate leaf.

Offset - A young plant that arises naturally on the parent or on short lateral stems.

Opposite - Opposite each other, usually leaves borne in pairs at each node.

Organic matter - Derives from the decay of once living organisms, such as garden compost.

Ovary - The basal ovule bearing part of the pistil that contains the future seed.

Ovate - Egg-shaped, with the broadest part being near the middle and more or less rounded at both ends.

Ovule - The body that after fertilization becomes the seed.

P

Palmate - A compound or segmented leaf with three or more lobes or leaflets radiating fan-shaped from a common basal point of attachment.

Palmately lobed - Palmately divided leaf, not cut to base.

Panicle - A branched and elongated flower cluster.

Pedicel - The stalk of an individual flower.

Peduncle - The stalk of an inflorescence.

Peltate - Leaf-blade attached to stalk inside its margin, the stalk is usually attached to the centre of the leafs underside. The leaf is usually rounded in outline.

Pendant - Hanging down from its support.

Perennial - A plant that lives for at least two years. The term is usually used to denote an herbaceous plant or an herbaceous shrubby plant.

Perianth - A collective term for the calyx and corolla.

Petal - Modified leaf of the corolla, usually coloured and showy.

Petiole - The primary stalk of a leaf.

pH - Measure of acidity or alkalinity.

Photosynthesis - A complex series of chemical reactions in green plants with the conversion of carbon dioxide and water into carbohydrates, taking the energy from light, helped by chlorophyll.

Pinnae - Primary division of a pinnate leaf, its leaflets.

Pinnate leaf - A compound leaf whose leaflets are arranged alternately or in pairs on opposite sides of a central axis, and consist of more than three leaflets, with or without a terminal leaflet.

Pistil - The female reproductive organ of a flower consisting of the ovary, style and the stigma.

Plumose - With the leaflets radiating at different angles.

Pollen - The grains in the anther containing the male element necessary for fertilization.

Pollination - The transfer of pollen from an anther to a receptive stigma.

Procumbent (Prostrate) - Lying flat along the ground but not rooting, leaning.

Pseudobulb - Thickened and bulb-like portion of stem in epiphytic orchids.

Pubescent - Covered with soft, short, fine hairs, downy.

R

Raceme - An unbranched, elongated simple inflorescence with stalked flowers, the youngest flowers near the tip.

Radicle - The basal leaves that grow from or near the ground.

Recurved - Curved backwards or downwards.

Redonant - Flowering at intervals throughout the growing season.

Reflexed - Abruptly recurved or bent sharply back upon itself.

Rhizome - An underground, horizontal, creeping modified stem that acts as a storage organ and gives rise to roots, stems and leaves at its nodes or growing tips.

Rhizomatous - Provided with rhizomes.

Rosette - 1. A cluster of leaves radiating in a circle from a central point or crown of a plant, usually near the ground. 2. A cluster of leaves on a trunk or branch. 3. Whorled arrangement of petals.

Runner - A slender prostrate shoot, rooting at the end or at joints where plantlets are produced.

S

Salverform - A flower with a corolla that is tubular, long and slim, that ends in a more or less flat disk.

Scandent - Climbing, in whatever manner.

Sepal - Each segment of a calyx, or outer floral envelopes.

Serrate - A leaf whose margin is finely toothed, the points curved towards the leaf's apex, like a saw blade.

Serrulate - Minutely serrate.

Sessile - Without a stalk.

Sheath - A leaf whose base is constricted into an almost tubular shape clasping and surrounding a part of a plant, such as the basal part of a palm leaf that surrounds the stem.

Shoot - Main upright growth of a seedling. Also applied to side growths or branches.

Shrub - A branched perennial plant with persistent woody growth.

Sideshoot - A lateral shoot that develops from the side of the main shoot.

Silky - Having a covering of soft fine hairs.

Simple - Not compound, a leaf that has a single blade and is not divided into separate leaflets; it may, however, be deeply lobed or partially segmented.

Single - A flower with one set of petals.

Solitary - Flowers that are borne singly, alone, and not in clusters.

Spadix (Spadices pl.) - A usually thick and fleshy cylindrical flower spike of tiny, densely set flowers usually surrounded by a spathe.

Spathe - A relatively large and often coloured bract surrounding or found at the base of an inflorescence.

Species (sp.) - Individuals with the same character, and which can be bred with each other.

Spike - Elongated flower stem, with flowers not stalked.

Spine - Sharp, woody outgrowth from the stem.

Sport - A plant that is significantly different from its parents due to mutation such as a variegated shoot.

Spray - Cluster of flowers arranged on a single branched stem.

Spur - Tubular projection from the base of a petal or sepal.

Stamen - The pollen-bearing or 'male' organ of a seed plant, consisting of the filament and the anther.

Standard - A shrub that has been trained and pruned to form a rounded head of branches with a single clear stem.

Stem - The main leaf bearing and flower bearing axis of a plant.

Sterile - Any flower that is incapable of producing seed.

Stigma - The terminal part of the pistil or style that receives the pollen to fertilize the ovules.

Stipule - Leaf-like appendage at the base of a petiole.

Stolon - Shoot that creeps along the surface of the soil and roots at specific nodes, creating new plants.

Stoloniferous - Sending out, or propagating itself by stolons.

Stress - Any situation that goes against a plant's growing needs.

Style - The connecting stalk between the ovary and stigma.

Subshrub - Low-growing shrub, or one with soft stems and a woody base.

Subspecies (subsp) - Subdivision of a species.

Succulent - Plants with thick, fleshy leaves or stems adapted to life under arid conditions.

Sucker - Arises from the plant's roots, sometimes distant from the mother plant, and with time will develop into an identical plant.

Synonym (syn.) - A name rejected in favour of another.

T

Tap root - Goes straight down into the ground from the embryonic root.

Tender - Sensitive to frost, as opposed to hardy.

Tendril - Thread-shaped shoot used for climbing.

Tepal - Sepal or petal that is intermediate in form and not readily distinguished from either.

Terrestrial - Plants growing in the ground or soil, rather than epiphytically.

Throat - The opening part of the tubular part of a flower.

Tomentose - Covered in dense, short hairs.

Transpiration - Loss of water vapour from leaves and stems through their pores (stomata).

Trifoliate - Term used to describe a leaf with three leaflets.

Trumpet-shaped - Flower with a long narrow tube, flaring at the throat into lobes, often arching backwards.

Tuber - A thickened fleshy root, or an underground stem which stores food.

Tubular - Having form of a hollow cylinder.

Turgid - Inflated; swollen with fluid contents.

U

Umbel - Flat or round-topped inflorescence in which flower stalks or cluster arise from same point.

Unarmed - Without spines, prickles or other sharp points.

Underplant - To surround and interplant larger plants with smaller ones.

Undulate - Leaf, sepal or petals are wavy-margined or crimpled.

Unifoliate - Having compound leaves that are reduced to one leaflet.

V

Variegated - Leaves that are striped, edged or otherwise marked with a colour different from the primary colour of the leaf.

Variety (var.) - A naturally occurring variant of a species whose distinct character does not justify classification as a separate species.

Vegetative - Propagation by cuttings, division, layering or grafting, as distinct from seeds.

W

Weeping - Tree or shrub of pendulous habit.

Whorl - Circular arrangement of leaves, flowers or bracts around a single point or node.

Woolly - Clothed with long, soft and entangled hairs.

X

Xerophyte - Plant adapted to an arid environment.